URBAN AMERICA AND PUBLIC POLICIES

Urban America and Public Policies

SECOND EDITION

Marian Lief Palley   UNIVERSITY OF DELAWARE

Howard A. Palley   UNIVERSITY OF MARYLAND

D. C. HEATH AND COMPANY   Lexington, Massachusetts   Toronto

Cover photograph by Bruce Davidson/Magnum Photos, Inc.

Published simultaneously in Canada.

Printed in the United States of America.

International Standard Book Number: 0-669-04004-5

Library of Congress Catalog Card Number: 80-82491

For Elizabeth and Stephen

Preface

In the 1970s it was clear to most observers of American urban politics that the plight of many of the central cities and older suburbs was one of economic and social decline. Since the urban crisis was actually a national crisis, a national solution—expansion of federal-urban policy linkages—seemed both rational and just.

It seemed at first that urban problems were being solved by increased federal and state aid and by rising state tax revenues. However, by 1980 it was clear that the problems of a considerable proportion of urban America had not been solved and that federal aid had not been sufficient. In fact, by 1980 the real value of this aid began to diminish as a result of inflation and a national politics of budgetary restraint.

Given the conditions just noted, we believe that the concerns raised by the first edition of this volume are still very real. In the first edition we wrote:

> It has become increasingly apparent to many observers of the American political scene that the problems of urban areas cannot be disassociated from the broader context of American society. The "urban crisis" currently afflicting many of the nation's central cities and "urban suburbs" is America's crisis. Inasmuch as current urban problems affect the entire fabric of society, national policy solutions are required. Also, urban jurisdictions often cannot afford to provide the services required by their populations. To date the political support urban areas need to deal effectively with their problems has not been forthcoming. We hope that it is evolving. We believe that government jurisdictions are linked in such a manner that only federal legislative and administrative action, supported by willing public and cooperating state and local units, can provide the administrative oversight and financing [necessary] to alleviate current urban problems.

In this volume, seven urban policy problems will be considered. In each discussion, attention will be focused on the linkages, or lack of linkages, that have grown to provide the means for human and physical resource development. Our political system is built upon a tradition of federalism and is steeped in the values of individualism, localism, and private enterprise. The question we pose in this book is: Can this political system evolve and facilitate changes such that necessary linkages will be recognized and appropriate policies will be formulated to allow all Americans—wherever they live—to benefit from our affluent and advanced technological society? In this edition we have traced relevant policy developments up to 1980.

In the preparation of the two editions of this book, many people provided invaluable assistance. Margaret Andersen, George Hale, Frank Kalinowski, Jeffrey Raffel, and Karl Klockars each provided us with useful insights on portions of the manuscript. Kenneth Dolbeare, Dall W. Forsythe, and Douglas T. Yates, Jr., read the entire first-draft manuscript. Each of these individuals provided many useful suggestions for strengthening sections of the book. In addition, students in our classes in the Political Science Department at the University of Delaware and the School of Social Work and Community Planning of the University of Maryland continue to provide us with useful feedback; we used them as the "target groups" for the materials presented in this volume. Several of our students provided invaluable research assistance as we prepared the materials for this edition. In particular we would like to thank Riaz Ahmad, Douglas Hiland, and Christine Facciolo for their aid. The manuscript in its various drafts was typed by Jeanne Grill, who also typed copy for the first edition.

Marian Lief Palley

Howard A. Palley

Contents

The Economic and Fiscal Conditions of Urban America
57

Introduction / Intergovernmental Fiscal Relationships / Alternative Methods of Fiscal Allocation / The Role of States in Fiscal Allocation / The Federal Role in Fiscal Allocation / Conclusion

PART TWO   87

Education and the Local Tradition
89

Introduction / History of Education in the United States: A General Background / Distribution of Resources / Current Legislative Linkages / Some Current Problems / Conclusion

Public Welfare and Individualism
117

Introduction / The History of the Development of the Public Welfare System / Outline of the Current Problem / Public Welfare Today / Conclusion

Police Services in a Democratic Society
147

Introduction / A Historical Perspective on Local Police Jurisdictions / The Delivery of Police Services: Organization and Functions / Profile of the Policeman / The Role of Discretion in Police Activity / Some Contemporary Police Problems / The Changing Federal Police Role / Conclusion

10

Environmental Interdependence and National-Urban Policy Linkages
271

Introduction / The Historical Perspective / The Extent of the Contemporary Problem / The Development of a National-Urban Environmental Protection Policy / Conclusion

11

The New York City Fiscal Crisis: Its Implications for National-Urban Policy
299

Introduction / The Social and Economic Background / The Nature of the Municipal Borrowing Problem / The Crisis / The Apparent Interdependencies

Index
309

PART ONE

The first three chapters of this volume will provide a perspective on national urban policy linkages. More specifically, the historical, political, and economic forces that have influenced the development of *urban America* will be considered. Also, the scope of the "crisis of urban America" must be defined before solutions to the problem can be addressed.

The first chapter includes an overview of the conditions that have affected American urban development and a discussion of the historical evolution of the contemporary urban scene. The next two chapters discuss the interplay of political and economic forces in urban America.

In Chapter 2 some of the political implications of contemporary urban growth will be discussed. Once these political problems of urban areas—central city and suburban—have been outlined, the participatory styles and the often contradictory demands of the various class groups that comprise the urban electorate will be presented. Chapter 3 focuses on the economic and fiscal implications of current urban development patterns, especially the economic impact of the flight of the middle class and industry from the cities to the suburbs. The interplay, as well as the consequences, of the taxing system and proliferation of governments is also discussed.

1

A General Perspective

INTRODUCTION

In an integrative system, the problems of one unit are inextricably connected with other units. In urban America, the separate units are local,
state, and national governments. The local units can be further divided
into urban—both cities and suburbs—and rural. Solutions affecting one
unit will, in one way or another, affect all units. Thus, to understand
urban problems, we must understand the relationships between the urban areas and other units. Given the nature of public fund raising and
allocation of resources in the United States, recognizing the linkage between urban areas and the national government is especially important.
To improve our understanding of urban problems, then, we must

identify and analyze those recurrent sequences of behavior that originate on one side of the boundary between the two types of systems and that become linked to phenomena on the other side in the process of unfolding.[1]

This perspective was put into a more operative framework by Mayor William McNichols of Denver, Colorado, when he testified before the Joint Economic Committee of the U.S. Congress regarding New York City's fiscal crisis:

> Every city in the nation is like a tenant in the same building. If somebody says the third floor is going to collapse, you can't say that's not going to bother me because I'm on the second floor.[2]

In this chapter we will discuss the changing conditions that affect the way we think about urban America. The role of federalism and early urban development patterns will be considered, as well as the changing demographic characteristics of urban areas and shifts in industrial employment within urban areas. All these factors will be discussed to outline the scope of America's *urban crisis*. The *crisis* will be defined throughout this volume as the inability of many urban jurisdictions to maintain viable economic and social bases for the well-being of their citizens. The urban crisis is inextricably connected to the urban fiscal crisis, which is characterized by an inability of many urban jurisdictions to generate sufficient revenues in economically and socially decaying cities to provide adequate services for their populations. Part of the problem confronting economically ailing central cities (and some older suburbs) is the underlying assumption of American politics that local jurisdictions are responsible for their own populations. This assumption is an obvious extension of the notion of individual self-reliance and of the local basis of welfare stemming from the Elizabethan Poor Laws. Whereas urban "self-reliance" and local responsibility may be justified assumptions when the cities have populations balanced in terms of social class mix and industrial development, it does not seem to be a plausible policy assumption for decaying cities. Furthermore, when a city decays, other segments of the nation feel the negative side effects of this development. Throughout this volume, whenever decaying or declining cities are discussed, it should be recognized that this reference applies to certain urbanized suburbs as well as central cities. Also, we would note that some cities are prosperous and are undergoing economic growth and development.

More specifically, we will first consider the interplay of federalism with urban governments as well as the political constraints that have impeded a strong national response. Then we will discuss the development of urban America within the context of our federal system with special attention to growth patterns and changing demographic characteristics. Some of the issues and problems introduced in this chapter will be dealt with more fully in later chapters.

The Federal System

The Constitution establishes two levels of power and authority in the United States. In a manner emphasizing national power, the Preamble states that:

> We the People of the United States, in Order to form a more perfect Union, establish Justice, insure domestic tranquility, provide for the common defence, promote the general Welfare, and secure the Blessings of Liberty to ourselves and our posterity, do ordain and establish this Constitution for the United States of America.

More specifically, powers are delegated to Congress by the Constitution in Article I, Section 8. Seventeen specific grants of power are provided, as well as the power

> to make all laws that shall be necessary and proper for carrying into execution the foregoing powers, and all other powers vested by this constitution in the government of the United States or in any department or officers thereof.

This is known as the Necessary and Proper Clause. In addition, Article VI of the Constitution—the National Supremacy Clause—provides that:

> This constitution, and the laws of the United States which shall be made in pursuance thereof; and all treaties made or which shall be made under the authority of the United States shall be the supreme law of the land; and the judges in every state shall be bound thereby, anything in the constitution or laws of any state to the contrary notwithstanding.

Balancing these statements of federal power, "reserved" powers for the states were included in the Tenth Amendment to the Constitution:

> The powers not delegated to the United States by the Constitution, nor prohibited by it to the States, are reserved to the States respectively, or to the people.

Inasmuch as separateness of jurisdictions has been built into the federal system, programs have often originated and been implemented at the state and local levels. Also, many problems have been seen as subnational problems, and many of the logical connections between levels of government have been ignored in the development of solutions to these problems. Thus, some of the problems presently confronting urban areas are seen as solely the problems of the specific urban areas and are not being responded to on a regional or national level. Although national programs have aided urban populations with their problems, these programs have often, by design, been limited in scope. Also, the federal structure has provided a framework whereby even nationally funded programs have often, by design, been administered by the states. Consequently, when federal programs have been initiated to assist urban areas, the quality of their administration and impact has varied. This was made apparent by the results of a study of 591 program administrators in 8 separate states. According to the study, program administrators in agencies that receive federal grants-in-aid perceive considerable independence from their federal benefactors (as well as from their state funding sources). The study concluded that the intergovernmental grants system and regulatory politics resemble each other in two very significant ways:

> The manifest goals of government regulations over the private sector are to reduce domination of markets, alter behavior, curb abuses of public welfare, and establish a national economy. Similarly, grants-in-aid are ostensibly designed to reduce fiscal disparities among subnational jurisdictions, alter the behavior of subnational governments, and to establish national policies. Yet federal control is imperfect in each area. In addition, most observers agree that regardless of the original purpose of regulatory agencies, they tend to become the protectors or promoters of the regulated industry. Similarly, federal agencies often turn to subnational officials for political support and frequently delegate much of the day-to-day administration to these governments. In each case, then, the federal government influences but it is also influenced by those it regulates.[3]

Program fragmentation and variation have been fostered not only by federalism, but also by the proliferation of local governments. In the American system of government, local governments are creatures of the states. The exact nature of the powers and limitations of local governments is determined by state constitutions, state laws, and state administrative rules. Responsibility for determining the size and structure of local units, for controlling finances, and for regulating areas such as pollution abatement or restaurant sanitation rests with the states. In the late eighteenth or early nineteenth century, states laid out systems of local government through constitutional and legislative acts. Initially, states set up counties, municipalities, and school districts. The counties were established to aid judges of the state judicial system to conduct elections, to record legal documents, to maintain order, and to provide rural services.[4] Municipalities were organized to supply urban areas with local services, including fire protection, police protection, public welfare, and sanitation services, as well as public works. Special school districts were formed with geographical constraints so that students could travel to school by horse or on foot.

With the spread of urbanization, there has been some attempt to adjust patterns of government to changing needs.[5] These attempts have not always been successful. John Bollens and Henry Schmandt note that metropolitan reform has sometimes "resulted in plugs of adjustment being inserted in the metropolitan wall to avoid successive waves of disasters."[6]

None of this discussion is intended to suggest that a unitary system of program development and implementation would necessarily be superior or even preferable to the federalized structure that has operated since

1789. Quite to the contrary, the diversification of program development and implementation that has resulted from federalism is often beneficial. But, as the problems of society become more complex and their solutions more costly, local responses have become less and less adequate. As we approach the twenty-first century, localism in urban problem solving, with its associated localism in fund raising, is becoming increasingly insufficient for urban America. National solutions with national funding are becoming the last recourse for solving many of our urban problems, even though idiosyncratic conditions in communities sometimes require some degree of community control, or at least involvement in the actual implementation of programs.

At the outset, however, the massive urban problems relating to the delivery of health services, education, welfare, and housing, as well as to physical services and environmental controls, require a major national commitment. Anything short of this kind of commitment will lead to a continuation of economic decay and its resultant social disorganization for the cities, and to increasingly inadequate public services for the thousands of communities surrounding our central cities.

Some Additional Political Constraints[7]

Before the 1960s, no significant group of Americans expected the national government to maintain a predominant role in providing major urban services such as education, housing, or public assistance. Perhaps this lack of expectation was due in part to the tradition of federalism and in part to the fact that the urban population—until 1970 more central city than suburban—was not making strong demands for such intervention. Also, because the full fiscal and political impact of middle-class and industrial migration from many cities was not felt until the 1960s and 1970s, the need for federal involvement was not as apparent before 1960 as it was in the past two decades.

Since 1960, a variety of political forces have constrained both national solutions and local responses to urban problems. In addition to the tradition of program fragmentation institutionalized by the federalism of the Constitution, other forces have limited, though not totally inhibited, federal responses to urban problems. For example, there is a widespread belief among Americans that the cities are to blame for their own problems. In his book *Blaming the Victim*, William Ryan has suggested that Americans hold the poor responsible for their own poverty. This assumption of personal fault is consistent with our market economy and its market-oriented values. If the poor cause their own condition, why reorient our system to help them out of their poverty? This belief leads one to assume that people will not change even if we tamper with the system. If one were to replace "the poor" with "the city" in the previous discussion, the values of many Americans and their elected representatives might become clearer. It was this perspective on cities that led Ron Nessen, President Ford's press secretary, to describe New York City as a "wayward daughter hooked on heroin."

There are other constraints on political action to consider. The majority of Americans do not live in cities undergoing social and economic decline. Thus, representatives in both state legislatures and in Congress are predominantly *not* from decaying urban areas. Also, the most influential interest groups in the United States often do not support programs that would help cities in financial and economic distress solve their problems. For example, private industry often does not want to assume the costs of cleaning its processes so that the air we breathe and the water we drink will be purer. Similarly, the medical societies and the insurance companies are not anxious to nationalize health care so that all Americans could afford, and would have available, such services; and major automobile manufacturers do not support federal funding for mass transit and fewer superhighways. Other examples of such private pressures can be found in all the policy areas affecting urban areas. Perhaps one particular political constraint ought not be overlooked. Influential private interest groups have been successful in maintaining substantial tax loopholes for industry as well as for the individual rich. Thus, in both the state and the nation, revenue is too often *not* available to fund adequately or to administer properly programs that might improve the "quality of life" in many American central cities and increasingly in the older suburbs. American industry and commerce as well as wealthy individuals have generally opposed large-scale federal spending for social programs and the closing of tax loopholes to increase the revenue of the federal government. To summarize, some problems are not being solved adequately because strong interest groups successfully pressure both Congress and the bureaucracy. (Successful interest groups are often able to maintain a client relationship with the federal agencies or departments that make decisions affecting their operations.) These same pressures are reflected to some extent in state and local politics, too. (There are times when the private goals of interest groups are thwarted by public interest groups. These groups are sometimes quite successful in influencing decision makers to alter policies. It was such citizen protest that first brought the environmental concerns of the 1970s to the forefront of American political consciousness.)

Powerful and influential interest groups themselves are, however, sometimes instrumental in the policy change process. For example, in the months prior to their 1976 contract negotiations with the United Auto Workers (UAW), the big three automobile producers—General Motors, Ford, and Chrysler Corporation—voiced their criticism of the present health care delivery system and in particular the high prices they pay Blue Cross–Blue Shield for their unionized workers. It appeared that these industrial giants might add their managerial voices to the Congressional debate over changes in the federal role in the delivery of health care.[8] Of course political elites sometimes propose changes in existing policies because they fear that policies will be changed despite their protests. The American Medical Association developed its own publicly subsidized health insurance plan in the early 1970s when it became increasingly apparent that Congress would some day pass national health insurance legislation.

Certainly policy has been changed, and clearly, the laws and regulations of today are often substantially different from the laws and regulations of twenty-five years ago. But the changes tend to be made slowly, especially when they benefit the central cities and "urban" suburbs and their constituents—an increasingly poor population. When changes are made, they are often only reactions to specific problems. Change is fragmented because in the United States there is a strong nonplanning predisposition prevalent in domestic politics. There is no central plan in American politics, and thus we react to specific problems only as we are able to raise the necessary consciousness among the policy makers to pressure for particular programs.

One final constraint on policy-making ought to be noted at this point. Elected officials respond to voters. Political response to segments of the citizenry who do not participate in the electoral process will not be as strong as the response to groups that choose to exercise their franchise. As income declines, voting participation declines, too. As many cities become the home of primarily the poor, the cities' relative proportion of the vote also declines. As a result, elected state and national officials may reflect disproportionately the attitudes of those who "blame the victim," whether the victim is the individual in need or the community undergoing economic and social decline.

The Expansion of Urban America from Small City to Megalopolis

Modern urbanization is a product of industrialization. The great cities of antiquity—Alexandria, Thebes, Athens, and Syracuse—had populations under 500,000; even Rome and Constantinople had populations of less than 1,000,000.[9] Lewis Mumford observed the more recent urban phenomenon in Manchester, England. He noted:

> In 1685, Manchester had about 6,000 people; in 1760, between 30,000 and 45,000. Birmingham had 4,000 at the first date and almost 30,000 in 1760. By 1801 Manchester's population was 72,275, and by 1851 it was 303,382. ... [O]nce the concentration of factories abetted the growth of towns, the increase in the numbers became overwhelming.[10]

America's first urban centers were such East Coast trading ports as Boston, New York, Philadelphia, Baltimore, and Charleston. The raw materials of the hinterland were shipped to Europe from these centers and manufactured products were shipped inland from these ports. With the early westward movement of population, cities such as Cincinnati, St. Louis, and New Orleans developed because they were located along inland waterways that permitted transshipment and trading. The coming of the railroads further contributed to the development of these centers and created new centers such as Chicago. As the nation expanded, ease of transportation eventually resulted in New England's conversion from a center of trade to a center of industrialization. Simultaneously, other centers of industrialization grew throughout the nation, in such cities as Los Angeles, San Francisco, Milwaukee, St. Louis, and Dallas–Fort Worth. These trends have been reinforced by the expansion of air transportation.

With industrialization and commercial expansion, metropolitan growth —that is, urbanization beyond the central cities—developed in the United States. In 1886, a U.S. Census Bureau document first took note of this development. In 1900, the metropolitan population of the United States constituted under a third of the total population. By 1940, over 50 percent of the population lived within metropolitan configurations. By 1978, 67 percent of the national population, or 143,046,000 persons, lived in Standard Metropolitan Statistical Areas (SMSAs). A metropolitan area is defined as that area existing within a Standard Metropolitan Statistical Area (SMSA). A Standard Metropolitan Statistical Area is defined as an area with at least:

(a) One central city of 50,000 inhabitants or more, or (b) two cities having contiguous boundaries and constituting, for general economic and social purposes, a single community with a combined population of at least 50,000, the smaller of which must have a population of at least 15,000. The SMSA includes the county in which the central city is located, and adjacent counties that are found to be metropolitan in character and economically and socially integrated with the county of the central city. In New England, the requirement with regard to a central city as a nucleus still holds ... [however] the units comprising the area are towns rather than counties. The county (or town in New England) is the basic statistical unit. An SMSA may contain more than one city of 50,000 inhabitants. The largest city is always included in the title of the area; however, the title may include the names of one or two additional cities. The SMSA may cross state lines.[11]

American land has been settled in three stages. In the first stage, the rural frontier was settled. This stage began in colonial times and lasted until the end of World War I. In the second stage, the urban-industrial frontier was settled, and the city was the primary form of land use. This second stage started on the East Coast after the War of 1812 and began to decline in the 1920s. In the third stage, the metropolitan industrial frontier was developed; growth beyond the central cities—that is, the growth of suburbs—has characterized the third stage. This pattern began to unfold after World War II and continues today.[12] A variant of this third stage began to unfold after 1950 when intensified industrialization and land settlement led to the development of interconnected urban complexes termed "megalopolis." The initial megalopolis described by Jean Gottman in 1961 was

[A] continuous stretch of urban and suburban areas from southern New Hampshire to northern Virginia and from the Atlantic shore to the Appalachian foothills.... No other section of the United States has such a high concentration of population, with such a high average density, spread over such a large area. And no other section has a comparable role within the nation or a comparable importance in the world. Here has been developed a kind of supremacy, in politics, in economics and possibly even in cultural activities, seldom before attained by an area of this size.[13]

The growth of the megalopolis represents an achievement, or perhaps more precisely an effect, of modern technology, transportation, and communication forms. The Advisory Commission on Intergovernmental Relations predicts that between 1970 and the year 2000, four major urban centers will contain about 187 million persons and that this figure will constitute 60 percent of the nation's population. These four areas are (1) a 500-mile strip along the Atlantic seaboard from Boston to Washington, D.C., containing 67.9 million people; (2) a series of cities extending from the old Erie Canal in New York State along the Great Lakes for about 1,000 miles including Utica, New York; Cleveland, Ohio; Chicago, Illinois; and Green Bay, Wisconsin. It is estimated that this link will include 60.8 million people; (3) a 500-mile urban corridor on the Pacific Coast from San Francisco in the north, through Los Angeles to San Diego in the south containing about 44.5 million people; (4) a 350-mile corridor on the Atlantic Coast from Jacksonville and Miami, Florida, extending along the Gulf of Mexico to the Tampa–St. Petersburg metropolitan area containing about 13.8 million persons.[14]

It is evident that contemporary urban American society is the product of numerous demographic, social, and technological factors. Historically, the political ideology and governmental structure underlying American institutions were developed when this nation was thinly settled and primarily rural. In 1790, the population of the United States was approximately 3.9 million. By 1860 and the onset of heavy industrial development in the United States, it had reached 31.5 million. By 1967, the population of the United States had reached 200 million, and in 1978 the population stood at 217,700,000.[15] This rapid population growth has been due to both improved health conditions and liberal immigration policies. In 1800, the United States had both a very high fertility rate and a very high mortality rate. At that time, the rate of natural increase was about 2.5 percent per year.[16] By 1978, the rate of natural increase had declined to 0.006 percent.[17] Even though the rate of natural increase has declined sharply, the increase is based on an ever-increasing base population. For example, from 1970 to 1976 the rate of increase in population was 5.3 percent.[18]

In 1800, 94 percent of the population lived in rural areas, either on farms or in places having fewer than 2,500 persons. Only three cities had populations over 25,000. By 1920, over half of the population lived in urban places of over 2,500; more than 10 million persons lived in places of 1,000,000 or more.[19] The growth of cities often represented movement from centers of limited and declining economic opportunity to centers of greater opportunity. In other words, people moved to cities because jobs were available or because they believed that there would be jobs for them. Between 1900 and 1960, the urban population increase absorbed 92 percent of the nation's total population growth.[20] This trend continued during the 1960s. During this period, urban population increased by 24 million (or by 19.2 percent). In absolute terms, the urban population had increased from just over 125 million in 1960 to almost 150 million in 1970. In the same period of time, the rural population declined from approximately 54 million in 1960 to 53.8 million in 1970, a decline of 0.3 percent.[21] There is, however, some evidence of a more recent shift in this trend. Between 1970 and 1976, nonmetropolitan counties—that is, counties with no population center of at least 50,000 people—experienced a population growth of 8 percent. About 84 percent of this growth was the result of net in-migration. Metropolitan counties grew at a rate of only 5 percent during this same period.[22] The Census Bureau further reported a 3.4 percent decline in central city population between 1970 and 1976.[23]

Urban growth in the United States was due not only to the influx of rural people, but also to the second wave of immigration that took place during the late nineteenth and early twentieth century. These immigrants were characterized by the poet Emma Lazarus, a descendant of immigrants who stemmed from an earlier wave of immigration, in sympathetic yet unflattering terms:

> Give me your tired, your poor,
> Your huddled masses yearning to breathe free,
> The *wretched refuse* of your teeming shore,
> Send these, the homeless, tempest-tossed to me:
> I lift my lamp beside the golden door.[24]

The early and middle nineteenth-century immigrants were northern and western Europeans—mainly Irish, Germans, and Scandinavians. In the late nineteenth century, most of the immigrants were eastern and southern Europeans—Poles, Russians, Czechs, Jews, Greeks, and Italians. The jobs available to the most recent immigrants were often poorly paid and menial, and their initial dwellings were crowded and desolate. Moreover, the urban experience provided for a crude, sometimes cruel process of adjustment and "Americanization." Of the late nineteenth-century American immigrant experience of eastern European Jews, the Hebrew poet Menachem M. Dolitsky was to mourn:

Let us deal wisely and become drawers of water,
Load the peddlers pack and knock on the door,
Sit bent on the workbench,
Bore with the awl or sew breeches—
But of what avail is the wisdom of Israel? [25]

Unskilled and semiskilled jobs available in cities ranged from building subways, trolley tracks, and bridges to sewing garments and peddling fruit and other wares. Through dint of hard work, luck, and politics, the poor immigrant could provide for himself and his family and gradually advance to better housing, better working conditions, and better education for his children.

Although the literature on immigration often refers to "immigration waves," such references are not entirely accurate. While immigration from the United Kingdom, Ireland, and Germany occurred primarily during the early and mid-nineteenth century, this immigration never ceased. However, during the late nineteenth and early twentieth century, a higher proportion of the white population of foreign origin or mixed parentage stemmed from Russia, Poland, and other Slavic nations, and from Italy.[26]

Changing Social and Economic Character of City Populations

The Nonwhite and Hispanic Population

Today's in-migrants and immigrants to the central cities of metropolitan areas are more likely to be nonwhite (black or Oriental) or Hispanic than were earlier immigrants. (It is important to note that most Hispanics are classified as white by the U.S. Census Bureau. However, when for specific purposes the government disaggregates data for Hispanics to provide analysis parallel to that for blacks, Hispanics are defined largely on the basis of mother tongue, Spanish surname, or country of origin. Also, in New York, New Jersey, and Pennsylvania, persons of Puerto Rican ancestry are defined as Hispanic.) This is the case despite the occasional article on movement of affluent members of the white middle class back into the central cities and the revitalizing of older and decaying sections of these cities.[27] (This migration, referred to as "gentrification," will be considered more fully in Chapter 7.) American blacks— who until recently were primarily a rural group—are increasingly an urban population. By 1970, 60 percent of blacks lived in cities. This figure continued to increase in the decade of the 1970s. In fact, between 1970 and 1976, the black population of central cities rose 11.9 percent to 15.5 million persons; the black suburban population increased more dramatically, however, as more suburban communities opened their doors to nonwhite populations. Blacks living in suburbs increased by 36.3 percent during these same years.[28] In the nonmetropolitan areas the black population increased 1.5 percent (to 6.5 million). During this same time frame, the white population of metropolitan areas had increased 2.1 percent (to 121.4 million). Within the central cities, the white population had declined 7.6 percent (to 45.2 million); in non-metropolitan areas, the white population had increased 8.7 percent (to 61.2 million).[29] Since 1970, the Hispanic population, which is an 85 percent metropolitan cohort, increased by one-third to over 12 million.[30] The black population tends to be a young population (although the Hispanic population is even younger). Thus in 1976, the median age of the black population was 23.8 years and the Hispanic population, 22 years, while the comparable figure for the white population was 29.8 years.[31]

On the West Coast, there have been large urban in-migrations of Chinese, Filipinos, and Mexicans.[32] In addition to a large black population, some East Coast cities have large Korean and Puerto Rican and other Latin American populations. Southwestern cities and West Coast cities often have substantial Mexican-American populations.

The Hispanic population of the United States is largely urban; only 8 percent of Hispanic men are farm workers.[33] Thus, several large cities in Texas, California, and New York, the three states with the largest concentrations of Hispanics, have either majority or substantial minority Hispanic populations. San Antonio, Texas, has a majority Hispanic population. In Los Angeles, 27 percent of the population is of Hispanic origin; their children have, however, overtaken whites as the majority group in the schools. New York City's Hispanic population of between 1 and 2 million represents a significant proportion of that city's total people.[34]

Cities in other sections of the nation also are home to large Hispanic groups. For example, many Latin Americans (particularly Cubans) regard Dade County, Florida, as a haven from the ravages of the poverty of their countries of birth. Of Dade County's 1.6 million people, between 600,000 and 700,000 are thought to be of Latin origin.[35] In addition, 700,000 people, or 20 percent of Chicago's population, are Hispanic; 15 percent of Newark, New Jersey's 400,000 people are Hispanic; 25 percent of Elizabeth, New Jersey's population and 80 percent of Union City, New Jersey's population is Hispanic. In Hartford, Connecticut, the proportion of Hispanic children in the schools is 34 percent, and school officials expect that to increase to 40 or 45 percent by 1985.[36] Though there is some disagreement among demographers, Hispanics are expected to overtake blacks as the nation's predominant minority by 1985. This forecast is based in large measure on the fact that the Hispanic population, with an average age of 22, is younger on the average than the rest of the population of the United States. In addition, the Hispanic population has tended to have both cultural and religious resistance to birth control.[37]

For the most part, urban immigrants and in-migrants have not been among the best trained and educated groups found in urban areas. But while the early immigrants found unskilled and low-skilled jobs waiting for them, today's groups find few such opportunities. Around the turn of the century, the movement to the cities was, in fact, accompanied by a high demand for people to fill unskilled and semiskilled jobs. Since World War II, however, blacks, other nonwhite groups, and Hispanic-Americans have been moving into the cities at a time when industry and jobs have been moving out. For example, in just the three years between 1973 and 1976, central cities of metropolitan areas lost 2.5 percent of their total employment and a much higher percentage of their manufacturing jobs. During this same period, suburbs in the metropolitan areas experienced a gain of 7.9 percent in employment.[38] Therefore, some of the nation's cities have very serious unemployment problems. In 1979, it was reported that Newark, New Jersey, had double the national unemployment average; in Buffalo, unemployment was 81 percent higher than the national average; and in Chicago and New York City, the comparable figures were 66 percent and 56 percent, respectively.[39] Some cities with large service sectors have not experienced this phenomenon. For example, the employment gains in Baltimore and San Francisco in the first half of the 1970s were due to increases in the service sector.[40] However, service sector jobs are often geared not to the nonskilled and low-skilled urban in-migrants, but to trained and skilled middle class or working class individuals. The demand for low-skilled workers has declined in general, in part because our technological society demands high-skilled service personnel and trained technicians. These conditions have led to high unemployment rates and poverty for many low-skilled urban residents, who are disproportionately nonwhite and Hispanic.

In describing other effects of urbanization on the black, previously rural, population in the 1930s and 1940s, E. Franklin Frazier noted:

[I]f these families have managed to preserve their integrity until they reach the northern city, poverty, ignorance, and color force them to seek homes in deteriorated slum areas from which practically all institutional life has disappeared. Hence, at the same time that these simple rural families are losing their internal cohesion, they are being freed from the controlling force of public opinion and communal institutions. Family desertion among Negroes in cities appears, then, to be one of the inevitable consequences of the impact of urban life on the simple family organization and folk culture which the Negro has evolved in the rural south.[41]

The continuing process of family breakdown among lower-class blacks from 1940 to 1963 was described in *The Negro Family,* a 1965 Department of Labor report (also known as the Moynihan Report). This report cited that among nonwhites there were 235.9 illegitimate births per thousand live births in 1963 compared to 30.7 illegitimate births per thousand live births for whites. Furthermore, this rate among blacks represented more than a 70 percent increase in black illegitimacy since 1940.[42] Concurrently, however, the black middle class has grown stronger, both socially and economically.[43] This latter phenomenon can be seen in a variety of indicators of economic and social mobility and status. For example, in 1974 a total of 1,000 black students received bachelor's degrees from the Ivy League colleges and MIT. This figure is more than the total number of blacks graduated from these schools in all previous years combined.[44]

The problem of urban poverty (although there is more intense black rural poverty than intense black urban poverty) affects the black and Hispanic population to a greater extent than most of the white population. However, as the following section indicates, large numbers of the urban poor are white.

The Aged

The aged—those people over 65 years of age—comprise an increasingly dependent population that is often urban. Of course not all old people are in poverty.) Whereas only 4 percent of the population in 1900, about 4 million people, was over 65, the over-65 population is now more than 22 million in number, or between 10 and 11 percent of the nation's population.[45] While the total national population doubled between 1915 and 1970, the population over 65 doubled between 1943 and 1970.[46] In part, this population increase is the result of improved medical care and resultant longevity, and in part, this phenomenon reflects the aging of a large age-cohort group.

The aged tend to cluster in urban industrial states such as California, Florida, Illinois, New York, Ohio, and Pennsylvania. Hispanics and the nonwhite poor and the aged poor share many of America's cities. The services required by this bimodal, largely economically nonparticipant population in our central cities are very expensive. The young (largely Hispanic and nonwhite population) need education, recreation, and health services; the aged often need expensive health care and social services as well as recreational services. To some extent, the costs of services to the aged and, to a much lesser extent, to the young poor have been assumed by the federal government in full or in part. Most notably, Medicare and Medicaid provide a minimum level of health care for many of the aged and/or the poor; the Supplemental Security Income Program (SSI) and the Aid to Families with Dependent Children Program (AFDC) provide means-tested financial assistance; and the Old Age, Survivors, Disability, Health Insurance Program (OASDHI) provides financial assistance based upon social insurance payments to retired workers, survivors, the disabled, and their related beneficiaries. Some social services for the elderly are provided by the federally funded public assistance–related social service programs as well as by U.S. Administration on Aging sponsored programs—both of which are financed on a matching-grant basis. However, federal payments for Medicare and Medicaid do not cover the complete cost of health care services; thus, states, cities, and counties often have to bear substantial costs for health care services, including the establishment of health service facilities. SSI payments are also frequently supplemented by state payments. Social services programs for the elderly also require state and local revenues. Given the limited availability of city, county, and state revenues, such state and local funds for health and welfare services are often unavailable or insufficiently available for adequate provision of service.

The financial problems of these government units are becoming more severe as the economically productive, tax-paying middle class, the white working class, and industry have retreated from the central city, leaving behind the young and the aged who cannot afford the health and social services they need. The question then arises: Should the society at large provide services to these groups? Are these urban residents citizens of the United States, and as such should other American citizens maintain services for them? Many of the needy have moved into the cities from other jurisdictions, thus freeing the other jurisdictions from the need to provide them services. If the broader citizenry refuses to assist the urban jurisdictions in caring for the needy, what effects will be felt by the rest of the nation? Though the answers to these questions are not completely clear, it is apparent that a central city that refuses to maintain business district services, for example, will inconvenience industry and the executives who work in the city but often live outside the city. Similarly, a default by a major city is feared by many investors and bankers who recognize the possible repercussions on the nation's bond market and the nation's banking system. In 1975, Arthur Burns, then chairman of the Federal Reserve Board, expressed apprehensiveness about the possible effects of a New York City default. He said at one point that he might support federal assistance to the city to avert a default if the financial markets began to "deteriorate noticeably." [47]

A Profile of Poverty

For 1977, the Bureau of the Census established a "low income" or poverty threshold of $6,191 a year for a nonfarm family of four. This index, based upon the U.S. Department of Agriculture's Economy Food Plan, reflects estimates of differing consumption requirements of families, relating to size, composition, sex, age of family head, and farm or nonfarm residence. Because the Economy Food Plan was based on an estimate of a nutritionally minimal diet, this poverty threshold may be considered a conservative estimate of human needs. [48] With this caution in mind, one can note that in 1977, 24.7 million persons lived in consumer units with incomes below the poverty threshold. Almost 9 percent of all white Americans, 31.3 percent of all black Americans, and 22.4 percent of all Hispanic Americans fell below this poverty threshold. Families with a female head of household accounted for almost 50 percent of all low-income households. The proportion of black persons in female-headed households in poverty is greater than for white or Hispanic families. Thus 39 percent of poor, white families are headed by females, while approximately 70 percent of poor, black families are headed by females. On a proportional basis, children under 18 years of age constituted about 40 percent of the poverty level population. Approximately 36 percent of the white population below the poverty level were under 18 years of age compared to almost 50 percent of all low-income blacks who were within this age category. At the other end of the age spectrum, aged poor persons constituted over 12 percent of those individuals with incomes below the poverty line.[49]

In summary, then, there is a disproportional likelihood of poverty among the black, the young, and the members of a female-headed household, even though there are numerically more poor white, male-headed households in this country than any other kind. The figures cited, however, very likely underestimate the number of persons deprived of basic physical and social necessities.

The seriousness of these poverty conditions can be seen in the results of a study released by the National Center for Health Statistics in 1976. The Center analyzed conditions in nineteen of the nation's largest cities. They found that persons living in *urban poverty areas*, and in particular members of minority groups, experience poorer health than the residents of more affluent areas. This study, which covered the period 1969–71, defined an urban neighborhood as "impoverished" if at least 20 percent of the residents lived in consumer units with yearly incomes of less than $3,743 for a family of four. More specifically, the study found that people in poverty had death rates of between 50 and 100 percent higher from accidents, suicides, and murder than residents of nonpoverty areas. For poor nonwhites, the death rate was 46 percent higher than for whites. Illegitimate birthrates were considerably higher in poor neighborhoods than in nonpoor areas, as were infant mortality and lack of prenatal care. Tuberculosis rates were also much higher among residents of poor areas than among the more affluent, with the tuberculosis death rate three times higher for whites and twice as high for blacks. The obvious conclusion of this study was suggested by Dorothy Rice, the director of the Center, when she noted that: "Living in a poverty area is shown to increase the odds against enjoying good health, and being in a racial minority worsens the odds."[50] These conditions do not seem to have been corrected in the years since this study was completed. In fact, the U.S. Public Health Service suggested, on the basis of a health interview study it reported on in December 1978, that: "Just as people with lower incomes had more acute conditions, they also had more disability days than the more affluent. People 45–64 years of age in families with less than $5,000 incomes had 3 times the number of restricted-activity days per person than those in families with incomes of $15,000 or more per year."[51]

Can the Urban Crisis Be Considered a Racial Crisis?

Between 1960 and 1970, the population of central cities did not change significantly, while the suburban population increased about 34 percent; however, between 1970 and 1976, the central city population declined by 3.4 percent (to 60.7 million), while the suburban population increased 10.3 percent (to 81.8 million).[52] In 1976, the proportion of the nation's population living in central cities was about 29 percent, while the proportion of the population living in the suburbs was almost 39 percent. Increasingly, it has been the poor and particularly the nonwhite and Hispanic poor who have concentrated disproportionately in the central cities. However, nonwhites, Hispanics, and poor people do live in some of the suburbs of our metropolitan areas. (In 1976, blacks living in suburbs represented 6.5 percent of the suburban population and about 39 percent of the central city population.) The median income level is lower for persons living in central cities than for those living in the suburbs. In 1977, these levels were $14,677 in central cities of over 1 million people and $15,192 in the central cities of less than 1 million people. In the suburbs of these cities, the comparable figures were $20,110 and $17,252, respectively.[53] During this same year, black median income in the larger central cities was $10,012 and in the smaller central cities it was $8,922. In the suburbs of these cities, the comparable figures for blacks were $13,104 and $12,858.[54] On the average, Hispanics fared a little better than blacks. In the central cities of the larger SMSAs, the median income for Hispanics was $10,026, and in the central cities of the smaller SMSAs, their median income was $10,866. The corresponding figures for the suburban Hispanic population was $14,301 in the suburbs of the larger SMSAs and $12,273 in the suburbs ringing the smaller central cities.[55]

Generally, black populations are concentrated in cities of between 50,000 and 500,000 people. These cities are the medium-sized centers such as Atlanta, Georgia, and Birmingham, Alabama, or "close-in suburbs" like East Orange, New Jersey, and Chester, Pennsylvania. Similarly, Hispanic populations have moved into such cities too. Often these cities have substantial problems with numerous low-income residents and public welfare dependency.[56] In addition, such cities have often experienced general declines in population size as well as an exodus of their middle class constituency, thereby depriving them of vital revenues. The extent of racial and cultural change in our cities has been both recent and rapid. Impoverished rural blacks and Hispanics have moved into both northern and southern cities. This has been accompanied by the movement of the white working class and middle class away from the central cities. Thus, for example, between 1960 and 1970, the white population of New York City declined by 9.3 percent, while the black population increased by 53.2 percent.

Within the nation's SMSAs, the vast majority of the black and Hispanic population live within central cities; a minority of the metropolitan area whites live in these cities. Thus, as industry and the middle class continue to move from the central cities, the poor have continued to move into central cities. These cities, with their shrinking and inadequate financial resources, have been unable to meet the educational, health, and social service needs of a large dependent population. The cities have waited for new and enlightened federal initiatives to help them meet this crisis, but only palliatives have been provided to enable them to continue. New substantial federal initiatives have not yet been forthcoming. In 1974, the Supplemental Security Income Program (SSI) was implemented. Basic minimum payments to the needy aged, the blind, and the disabled are being met by the federal government under the provisions of this program. However, the largest group of aided needy people, primarily dependent children and their needy mothers (AFDC), was not included in this federal program. Their aid is still provided on the basis of matching federal formula grants to the states, with some states requiring some local funding as well. Also, federal aid to education has constituted a minor portion of expenditures for public primary and secondary schools. In fiscal 1975, $4.7 billion was appropriated for aid to public elementary and secondary education.[57] By fiscal 1980, the figure had increased modestly to $7.73 billion.[58] In communities where there is sufficient wealth to tax for the provision of good schools, this limited federal addition poses no problem. In some areas, however, much more is required to raise the schools to an educational par with the "better" suburban schools. Essentially, public school expenditures are state and local expenditures. It was estimated that total public elementary and secondary school expenditures were $61,100,000,000 in 1975.[59] Thus, the federal role, while welcomed and needed, is quite restrained.

As noted previously, one group of poor moving into the cities and contributing to the urban crisis is the elderly. Some of the elderly who live in cities, however, are native to the cities. These people have spent their lives in the cities and are now either emotionally or economically unable to leave. Many of the elderly, who spent their working years in suburbia, but are now unable to cope with suburbia's requirements for landscaping, home repairs, and the need to maintain and drive an automobile, are now "retiring" to the cities. Because an individual at this time of life often has limited income and substantial health costs, another low income group with substantial social service needs is adding to the "urban crisis."

However, since a large segment of the central city population is non-white and Hispanic and since nonwhites and Hispanics are more likely than whites to be poor, middle class criticisms of the central city's problems are often placed in the context of *race*. Thus, it is not unusual to hear the urban crisis referred to as a racial crisis. If the nonwhite and

Hispanic population of central cities continues to increase as the white population continues to depart for the suburbs, then the urban crisis may be seen by an ever-increasing number of people as a racial crisis. But it is not just the white population that is leaving the cities; middle class nonwhites and Hispanics also are leaving. Thus, it may be more accurate to describe the crisis of the cities as a *class crisis* rather than a *racial crisis*. Poor Hispanics, nonwhites, and the white aged are being left in the older cities, while the working class and the middle class are moving to the suburbs and to the smaller cities of the nation.

Current Dilemmas Relating to Urban Change

Decay of the Central City and the Rise of the Suburbs

One of the most critical factors in the urban crisis is the decay of the central city. In an in-depth study of America's cities prepared by TEMPO, the General Electric Company's Center for Advanced Study, it was estimated that between 1966 and 1975 American cities would generate a significant revenue gap. In part the decay of the central cities is due to the needs of those who live in the cities matched with the improbability that the cities can raise the necessary revenues to cope with their problems. The TEMPO report noted that revenue needs in fact reflect an interweaving of factors concerned with social change, politics, and governmental finance. More specifically, they noted that the aging of the cities, the limited local revenues to finance city services and improvements, and the movement of industry and people out of high tax jurisdictions all have intensified the revenue gap problem for American cities.[60]

In 1978, the Congressional Budget Office also completed a study, *City Need and the Responsiveness of Federal Grants Programs*, that considered the contemporary condition of American cities. They determined that urban need could be examined on three dimensions, which they identified as: social needs, economic decline, and fiscal problems.[61] They further identified the cities that had problems relating to each of these indicator sets and found that "regardless of the dimension of need, large cities in the Northeast and Midwest appear deeply troubled. Other groups of cities have some serious problems, but in comparison, they are limited in scope and number."[62]

The suburbs have fared somewhat better, although often at the price of excluding the lower classes and creating affluent private developments accompanied in many places by a minimum of needed public services. Indeed, a report published by the United States Commission on Civil Rights noted that the movement of the white middle class from the central cities to the suburbs has brought many of the suburbs unparalleled wealth and prosperity while generating growing demands on the central cities for services for the poor and the suburban commuters.[63]

The populations of suburban communities *tend* to remain less embroiled in the dilemmas and crises of the central cities. However, increasingly as some older suburbs are becoming more urbanized, the problems of the central city are moving out—in somewhat smaller scale—to the suburbs. Also, newer suburban communities have often resisted the development of local services, such as sidewalks, sewers, and hospitals (but generally *not* schools), because they fear developing their own "urban·crisis," or becoming too citylike.[64] Some suburbs resist metropolitan solutions to the problems of the central city. Daniel Elazar has speculated that such resistance reflects an American attitude that

> the American urban place is a non-city because Americans wish it to be just that. Our age has been the first in history even to glimpse the possibility of having the economic advantages of the city while rejecting the previously inevitable assertion of citified living, and Americans apparently intend to take full advantage of the opportunity. To do so, they are relying on the traditional spirit and mechanisms of federalism, ranging from the maintenance of territorial democracy to the encouragement of governmental fragmentation. If we wish to make a realistic approach to our real urban problems, we would be wise to begin with that fact of life.[65]

Administrative Integration of Megalopolis

Though the city has sprawled into metropolitan areas and metropolitan areas are now sprawling into the megalopolis, the governmental administrative machinery in these areas remains virtually unchanged. Thus government structures that evolved to deal with the needs of often separate and discrete units still operate in an environment in which there often is a need for greater interaction in planning and development. But does structure really matter that much, or is it political will and resource allocation that need to be changed? If the latter needs alteration, then perhaps the former will need to change, too. The architectural notion that form follows function should probably apply to government as well as to buildings. If form does follow function, then new forms of administrative and policy-making units of government will have to be developed, because the separate units now operating are unable to fulfill the function of urban government; the existing units have shown themselves incapable of delivering essential services.

Inasmuch as the optimum form will vary from place to place, perhaps forms could vary. Some areas may best be served by county government, and other areas might better be served by "metro" government. Of course, political hurdles would have to be overcome before structure could be changed. Integration of government roles into more comprehensive units often meets opposition because voters and their elected officials are unwilling to give up what they see as their separate power bases. Suburban communities do not want to become embroiled in the problems of the cities. City politicos do not want the city to drown in a "sea of suburbs"; they do not want their power base to become lost among a larger maze of articulated suburban interests. For example, the prospect of organizing a "metro" government for Atlanta and the surrounding suburban areas was as much opposed by Atlanta political leaders as it was by suburban politicos. The Atlanta political community foresaw the decline of their own power if the city became part of a larger governmental unit. More precisely, some of the black leaders saw the end to their political power just as they were gaining political momentum. The mayor in Atlanta is black; it is unlikely that the chief executive in an Atlanta "metro" government would be black.

The obvious benefits of new governmental forms—be they single county, multicounty, or interstate (authority)—seem reasonably clear. There would be a broader tax base upon which to draw revenues for the delivery of public services. Also, integrated services—such as police, fire, sanitation, pollution abatement, hospitals, roads—would help eliminate unnecessary duplication, and could even lead to more systematic program planning and development.

Response of the Nation

The 1960s and early 1970s were a period of rapid growth in federal, state, and local budgets. In part these increases were a reflection of the very steep inflation the nation experienced during some of these years. For example, between 1970 and 1975, the real increase in the value of federal aid to subnational governments was 54 percent—not 107 percent, which a simple reading of the data might lead one to believe.[66] Thus, not all of the expansion in state and local spending could be attributed to inflation. Some of the increases in budgets reflected significant expansion in service delivery by these jurisdictions.

By fiscal 1979, federal grants to states and localities were approximately $82 billion, an increase of less than 1 percent from the previous year. However, between 1958 and 1978, the annual average increase in federal grant-in-aid outlays to subnational governments had been 14.6 percent. By 1979, federal grants-in-aid amounted to over 25 percent of total state and local expenditures, compared to 22.9 percent of these expenditures just four years earlier in 1975 (see Table 1).[67] Total state and local expenditures have increased too. Thus in fiscal 1975, states expended $95.7 billion and localities spent $80.3 billion; comparable figures for 1979 were $145 billion and $125 billion.[68]

Three-quarters of federal intergovernmental grants are either project grants, which provide states or localities a percentage of the cost of a particular project, or formula grants, which provide states or localities a percentage of funds according to a formula established by law. However, some block grants as well as general revenue-sharing grants are now

Table 1 / FEDERAL AID OUTLAYS IN RELATION TO TOTAL AND DOMESTIC FEDERAL OUTLAYS AND TO STATE–LOCAL EXPENDITURES, SELECTED YEARS 1960–79

| | | Federal Aid as a Percent of. | | |
	Amount (millions)	Total Federal Outlays	Domestic– Federal Outlays	State– Local Expenditures
1960	$ 7,020	7.6	15.9	14.7
1970	24,018	12.2	21.1	19.4
1975	49,832	15.3	21.3	22.9
1977	68,415	17.0	22.7	26.4
1979 (est.)	82,129	16.6	22.1	25.4

Source: Advisory Commission on Intergovernmental Relations, *Significant Features of Fiscal Federalism 1978–1979 Edition* (Washington, D.C.: U.S. Government Printing Office, May 1979), Table 51, p. 77 (selected years only).

available to states and localities. Under the State and Local Fiscal Assistance Act of 1972 and the 1976 amendments to this act, the federal government divides a sum of money among the states on the basis of formulas. Within guidelines established by the legislation, states and localities can determine how they will spend this revenue. With its weak federal oversight of state and local spending of those funds, this act was consistent with the policy of "permissive federalism" enunciated by the then Republican administration. This act was their attempt to respond to the urban crisis without adding to what they considered the already excessive power of the federal government. The words of President Nixon, who was instrumental in the passage of this act, demonstrate this concern. In his 1971 State of the Union Address, he asserted that the federal government was "so strong that it grows muscle-bound" while states and localities were approaching "impotence." [69] In his 1973 Second Inaugural Address, he reiterated: "Abroad and at home, the time has come to turn away from condescending policies of paternalism—of 'Washington knows best.' " [70] President Nixon asserted that revenue sharing was intended to "combine the efficiencies of a centralized tax system with the efficiencies of decentralized expenditure." [71]

Like revenue-sharing funds, block grant money is distributed on the basis of formulas. Within a broad functional area, the receiving jurisdictions—states and localities—are able to use these federal funds according to their own priorities with only limited federal restraints. The amount of flexibility varies among the block grants. At the present time there are five block grant programs: Partnership for Health Act (enacted in 1966); Omnibus Crime Control and Safe Streets Act (enacted in 1973); Housing and Community Development Act (enacted in 1974); Social

Services Amendments (Title XX) of the Social Security Act in 1935 (enacted in 1974); and Comprehensive Education and Training Act (enacted in 1973).[72]

By 1978, direct federal aid to cities made up 54 percent of the revenues of economically hard-pressed cities: Buffalo, 76 percent; Newark, 64 percent; Cleveland, 60 percent; St. Louis, 56 percent; Philadelphia, 54 percent; Phoenix, 50 percent; Baltimore, 46 percent; Chicago, 42 percent; Atlanta, 40 percent; Los Angeles, 40 percent; Boston, 30 percent; Denver, 26 percent; Houston, 24 percent; and Dallas, 18 percent.[73] Furthermore, the Advisory Commission on Intergovernmental Relations reported that in 1978 city dependence on federal aid ranged from 63.3 percent of budgets in selected Frostbelt cities to 51.9 percent in selected Sunbelt cities.[74]

Permissive federalism's response to the urban crisis has been criticized by some people for its lack of the necessary national leadership. For example, in a proposal presented to the American Assembly at Columbia University, it was suggested that major metropolitan areas be designated "national cities" and be dealt with directly by the federal government.[75] Similarly, Daniel P. Moynihan suggested that a number of contemporary urban problems require an active federal policy. These urban problems include the "poverty and social isolation of minority groups in the central city," and "imbalances in industry, transportation, housing, social services and similar elements of urban life."[76] Other urban problems include the fragmented and obsolescent metropolitan governmental structures, the current inequalities in public services within various regions of metropolitan areas, the lack of systematic research and statistics concerning urban problems, and the need to protect the esthetics and natural resources of the city.[77]

When he became president, Jimmy Carter stated his own personal commitment to a national urban policy. He appointed a cabinet-level Urban Task Force that made numerous proposals, which, had they been implemented, would have provided some basis for a national urban policy. However, Carter's proposed urban policy was of a limited nature. It included support for limited "countercyclical" revenue-sharing funds for some cities with high unemployment rates. It also included limited support for welfare reform involving an increase in the proportion of federal funding for the AFDC program and for public employment of AFDC heads of household. Furthermore, it included support for temporary public employment and for work training under the Comprehensive Employment and Training Act. These recommendations certainly did not represent a major federal financial commitment to assist economically troubled cities.[78] Moreover, many of the proposals have died in congressional committees or were not even introduced in Congress. Proposals that have passed have been "scaled-down" in scope. Carter did, however, articulate the position that a national urban policy with a significant federal role is needed because metropolitanism is a national phenomenon whose components and end products are national problems.

CONCLUSION

The central cities of our nation increasingly provide less employment for their low-skilled and unskilled residents. At the same time, however, many white-collar jobs provide employment for a middle class that has left the cities for the suburbs. Also, between 1973 and 1976, employment in the suburbs increased 7.9 percent while central city employment declined 2.5 percent. In particular, manufacturing jobs declined in some central cities.[79] For instance, between 1970 and 1975, employment in New York City declined by 8 percent. This decline was particularly heavy in the apparel industries. Moreover, the effect of this decline on lower income employees is more acute than these figures indicate because an increasing proportion of the "manufacturing" jobs are really nonproduction, mainly white-color, positions.[80] Accompanying this shift has been a growth in white-collar office jobs in areas such as retail trade, services, finance, and government.

Besides New York, other central cities have severe socioeconomic problems. For example, Cleveland, Buffalo, Boston, and Pittsburgh have exhibited the characteristics of "depressed urban areas": low median family income, high out-migration, and prospects for sudden downturns in the employment rate.[81] Although low-skilled jobs in manufacturing increasingly are being replaced by technology, low-skilled manufacturing jobs still exist. However, industrial development has been increasingly a suburban phenomenon. In many cities there has been a net outflow of industry—especially the kind that has traditionally employed low-skilled workers.

The growth of cities has resulted in the development of massive social and economic resource needs. To capitalize a mass transportation system or to maintain a public welfare program is extremely expensive. Furthermore, the economics of dense urbanization with problems of transportation congestion and high real estate values has resulted in some movement toward the less densely populated suburbs and smaller cities of the country. As a result of these developments, industry often leaves the central city, the middle class moves to the suburbs, and many central cities are becoming poorer. Some of the problems of metropolitan areas might be resolved by metropolitan governmental units. However, social and political cleavages make such solutions difficult. In addition, the decentralized tradition of the federal structure has acted as a barrier to such political reform. The problems of urban areas have been addressed by Congress. However, more extensive national urban linkages are needed if we are to prevent the crisis of urban America from afflicting all of America.

REFERENCES

1. James Rosenau, "Introduction: Political Science in a Shrinking World," *Linkage Politics* (New York: Free Press, 1969), pp. 44–45.
2. Statement by William H. McNichols before the Joint Economic Committee (September 24, 1975), quoted in *The New York Times* (September 25, 1975), p. 1.
3. George E. Hale and Marian Lief Palley, "Federal Grants to the States—Who Governs?" *Administration and Society*, 11 (May 1979), 24–25. This excerpt from "Federal Grants to the States—Who Grants?" by George E. Hale and Marian Lief Palley is reprinted from *Administration and Society*, Vol. 11, No. 1 (May 1979), 24–25 by permission of the Publisher, Sage Publications.
4. John C. Bollens and Henry J. Schmandt, *The Metropolis: Its People, Politics and Economic Life* (New York: Harper & Row, 1975), p. 48.
5. Some attempts to adjust governmental structure to metropolitan needs are discussed on pp. 75–78.
6. Bollens and Schmandt, op. cit., p. 51.
7. This section relies heavily on Marian Lief Palley and Howard A. Palley, "National Income and Services Policy in the United States," in *Analyzing Poverty Policy*, ed. by Dorothy B. James (Lexington, Mass.: Lexington Books, 1975), pp. 242–44.
8. *The Washington Post,* March 16, 1976, p. A8.
9. William L. Henderson and Larry C. Ledebur, *Urban Economics: Process and Problems* (New York: John Wiley, 1972), p. 13.
10. Lewis Mumford, *The City in History* (New York: Harcourt, Brace and World, 1961), pp. 454–55.
11. U.S. Bureau of the Census, *Statistical Abstract of the United States: 1971,* 92nd edition (Washington, D.C., 1971), p. 829.
12. Daniel J. Elazar, *The Metropolitan Frontier: A Perspective on Change in American Society* (Morristown, N.J.: General Learning Press, 1973), pp. 1–19.
13. Jean Gottman, *Megalopolis: The Urbanized Northeastern Seaboard of the United States* (New York: Twentieth Century Fund, 1961), p. 3.
14. Advisory Commission on Intergovernmental Relations, *Urban and Rural America: Policies for Future Growth* (Washington, D.C.: U.S. Government Printing Office, 1968), p. 14.
15. U.S. Department of Health, Education, and Welfare, Public Health Service, *Health—United States 1978* (Hyattsville, Maryland, 1978), p. 137.
16. Philip M. Hauser, "Population Composition and Trends," in *Toward a National Urban Policy*, ed. by Daniel P. Moynihan (New York: Basic Books, 1970), p. 28.
17. U.S. Department of Health, Education, and Welfare, Public Health Service, *Vital Statistics in the United States, Natality, Vol. 1* (Washington, D.C., 1969), pp. 1–8.
18. *Urban America—Policies and Problems* (Washington, D.C.: Congressional Quarterly, 1978), p. 8.
19. U.S. Bureau of the Census, *Historical Statistics of the United States, Colonial Times to 1957* (Washington, D.C., 1960), p. 14.
20. Hauser, op. cit., p. 31.
21. U.S. Bureau of the Census, *Statistical Abstract of the United States: 1972,* 93rd ed. (Washington, D.C., 1972), p. 18.

22. *Health–United States 1978,* op. cit., p. 139.
23. *Urban America,* op. cit., p. 8.
24. Inscribed on the pedestal of the Statue of Liberty, written in 1883. Italics added for emphasis.
25. Quoted in Irving Howe, *World of Our Fathers* (New York: Harcourt Brace Jovanovich, 1976), p. 76.
26. *Historical Statistics of the United States, Colonial Times to 1957,* op. cit., pp. 56–57.
27. See, for example, Blake Fleetwood, "The New Elite and an Urban Renaissance," *The New York Times Magazine* (January 14, 1979), 16–26, 34.
28. *Urban America,* op. cit., p. 8.
29. Ibid.
30. *The New York Times* (February 18, 1979), p. 16.
31. U.S. Bureau of the Census, Population Estimates and Projections, *Current Population Reports,* Series P–25, No. 643 (Washington, D.C.: U.S. Government Printing Office, January 1977).
32. Most Latin Americans, whether predominantly Caucasian, Indian, or Mestizo, are characterized by the U.S. Census Bureau as "white." To some degree this leads to an overestimate of the extent to which Americans are Caucasian. See U.S. Bureau of the Census, *Current Population Reports,* Series P-20, No. 224, "Selected Characteristics of Persons and Families of Mexican, Puerto Rican, and Other Spanish Origin: March 1971" (Washington, D.C.: U.S. Government Printing Office, 1971), p. 7.
33. *The New York Times* (February 18, 1979), p. 16.
34. Ibid.
35. Neal R. Peirce and Jerry Hagstrom, "The Hispanic Community—A Growing Force to Be Reckoned with," *National Journal,* 11 (April 7, 1979), 554.
36. *The New York Times* (February 18, 1979), p. 16.
37. Ibid., pp. 1 and 16.
38. Congressional Budget Office, *Barriers to Urban Economic Development* (Washington, D.C.: U.S. Government Printing Office, May 1978), p. 1.
39. Reported by Neal R. Peirce, "Dealing with the New Urban Pinch," *The Washington Post* (January 26, 1979), p. A15.
40. *The New York Times,* October 19, 1975, section 4, p. 1.
41. E. Franklin Frazier, *The Negro Family of the United States* (Chicago, Ill.: University of Chicago Press, 1966), p. 255.
42. U.S. Department of Labor, Office of Planning and Research, *The Negro Family: The Case for National Action* (Washington, D.C., March 1965), p. 59.
43. Ibid., pp. 5–6. Indeed the study notes that the middle class black family "puts a higher premium on family stability and the conserving of family resources than does the white middle class family." (p. 6)
44. University of Pennsylvania, interview with Director of Minority Recruitment, September 5, 1974.
45. *U.S. News and World Report* (April 1978), duplicated reprint.
46. U.S. Congress, House, *Problems on Aging, Hearings* before a Subcommittee of the Committee on Government Operations, 92nd Cong., 1st Sess., 1971, pt. 1, p. 219.
47. *The New York Times,* November 12, 1975, p. 1.

48. U.S. Senate, Select Committee on Nutrition and Human Needs, *Poverty, Malnutrition and Federal Food Assistance Programs: A Statistical Summary,* 91st Cong., 1st Sess., 1969, pp. 18–19.
49. U.S. Bureau of the Census, *Current Population Reports,* Series P-60, No. 116, "Money Income and Poverty Status of Families and Persons in the United States: 1977 (Washington, D.C.: U.S. Government Printing Office, July 1978), pp. 3 and 20.
50. *The Wilmington Morning News,* March 24, 1976, p. 12.
51. *Health—United States 1978,* op. cit., p. 231.
52. *Money Income and Poverty Status . . . 1977,* op. cit., p. 6.
53. Ibid.
54. Ibid., p. 7.
55. Ibid., p. 8.
56. Executive Office of the President, Office of Management and Budget, the *Budget of the United States Government: Fiscal Year 1975* (Washington, D.C.: U.S. Government Printing Office, 1974), p. 109.
57. National Education Association, *Estimates of School Statistics, 1974–75* (Washington, D.C.: National Education Association, 1975).
58. *Congressional Quarterly* (January 27, 1979), 119.
59. *Estimates of School Statistics, 1974–75,* op. cit.
60. "Is the Big City Problem Hopeless?" *U.S. News and World Report,* 64 (June 24, 1968), 61.
61. Peggy L. Cuciti, *City Need and the Responsiveness of Federal Grants Programs* (Washington, D.C.: Congressional Budget Office, 1978), p. xii.
62. Ibid.
63. U.S. Commission on Civil Rights, *Equal Opportunity in Suburbia* (Washington, D.C.: July 1974), p. 1.
64. Daniel J. Elazar, "Are We a Nation of Cities?" in *A Nation of Cities,* ed. by Robert A. Goldwin (Chicago: Rand McNally, 1968), p. 100.
65. Ibid., p. 114.
66. Advisory Commission on Intergovernmental Relations *Categorical Grants: Their Role and Design* (Washington, D.C.: U.S. Government Printing Office, 1977), p. 32.
67. *Congressional Quarterly* (January 27, 1979), 115.
68. Advisory Commission on Intergovernmental Relations, *Significant Features of Fiscal Federalism, 1978–79 Edition* (Washington, D.C.: U.S. Government Printing Office, 1979), p. 79.
69. Michael D. Reagen, *The New Federalism* (New York: Oxford University Press, 1972), p. 97.
70. *The New York Times,* January 21, 1973, section 1, p. 40.
71. Reagen, op. cit., p. 98.
72. Advisory Commission on Intergovernmental Relations, *In Brief. The Intergovernmental Grant System: An Assessment and Proposed Policies* (Washington, D.C.: U.S. Government Printing Office, 1978), pp. 8–10.
73. Neal Peirce, "A Fresh Approach to the Cities," *The Philadelphia Inquirer* (March 27, 1978), p. 7A.
74. Reported in *The New York Times* (January 21, 1979), p. 33.
75. Sigmund G. Ginsburg, "When the Students Meet the City," *City,* 6 (Winter 1972), 20.

76. Daniel P. Moynihan, "Toward a National Urban Policy," in *Toward a National Urban Policy,* ed. by D. P. Moynihan (New York: Basic Books, 1979), pp. 9–11.
77. Ibid., pp. 12–25.
78. *The New York Times,* January 3, 1979, pp. A1 and A7; *The New York Times,* January 4, 1979, p. A13.
79. *Barriers to Urban Economic Development,* op. cit., p. 1.
80. Dick Netzer, "New York City's Mixed Economy: Ten Years Later," *The Public Interest* (Summer 1969), 195.
81. Cuciti, op. cit.

The Urban Electorate

INTRODUCTION

Redress of the urban crisis depends to a considerable extent on the development of political alignments within the cities, the metropolitan areas, the states, and the nation. If the local jurisdictions cannot or will not solve the problems of the central cities and other "urbanized suburbs," then other more inclusive government jurisdictions may be forced to provide the necessary policy leadership to retain the cities as viable economic, social, and political entities. (Many of the generalizations made about central cities can also be made about the older, often heavily urbanized, suburbs as well.) As we observed in the first chapter, the problems facing the cities should not be ignored by noncity residents or industries. The economic, social, or political disequilibrium in the cities reverberates across the nation and causes problems for all Americans, either directly or through their institutions.

The flight of industry and the middle class from many of the older central cities and the concurrent influx of poor people has left the central cities with insufficient resources to maintain traditional urban services much less provide the additional services required by an increasingly dependent population. But while the cities alone cannot manage, help from larger units of government is not immediately forthcoming. In metropolitan counties divided between central city interests and suburban interests, the suburban interests often minimize county assistance to the central city. Within many state legislatures, the representatives of suburban populations operating with representatives of traditionally conservative rural and small town electorates have developed political alignments that sometimes have been able to block policies geared to meet the specific needs of central cities.

Instances of suburban–small-town–rural alignments against the central city may stem from the victim-blaming attitude described in Chapter 1 as well as from a triple-fear phenomenon: a fear of deterioration of services to high income suburbanites, a fear of new taxes by suburbanites of various income ranges, and a fear of vulnerability to the decline of public order associated with the central city.[1] In addition, the provincial ideology of some suburbs often leads to a lack of sympathy with urban needs. Robert Wood observed that

> the more closely suburbs are studied, the more genuine their claim to provinciality appears. In many essential qualities many suburbs seem like small towns much more impervious to modern life than is commonly supposed.[2]

This description of suburban reluctance to assist central cities cannot, however, be taken as evidence of the homogeneity of the suburbs. Suburban districts do not necessarily take a conservative stance in supporting a low level of public expenditure. Nor are suburbs easily characterized. There are rich suburbs and working class suburbs. There are suburbs with mixes of the rich, the poor, and the working class similar to those found in major central cities. There are Democratic suburbs and there are Republican suburbs. The particular social, ethnic, and economic background of particular districts determines the political positions of particular suburbs. Also, in light of the increasing political, social, and economic problems of central cities, large numbers of individuals have migrated to increasingly urbanized suburbs. Government financial subsidies, increased employment opportunities, and the superhighway-automobile nexus have led to the increased urbanization of the suburbs. By 1980, almost 40 percent of the American population lived in suburbs. These new urbanites—outside the central cities—represent a significant ingredient in the problem of urban policy development.

Some manifestations of these settlement patterns can be seen in the variability of political preferences among suburban voters. Thus the conservative-voting suburban congressional districts around the city of Chicago include the Thirteenth Congressional District northwest of Chicago, the Fourteenth Congressional District including most of DuPage County, and the Seventeenth Congressional District encompassing the suburbs of Chicago Heights and Park Forest. On the other hand, the suburban Tenth Congressional District (encompassing Evanston, Winnetka, and Skokie), while not heavily Democratic, elected a liberal Democrat to Congress in 1976 and 1978.[3] Suburban Baltimore County, Maryland's Second Congressional District, repeatedly elects Clarence D. Long, a moderate Democrat with a 65 percent ADA vote rating. (The ADA—Americans for Democratic Action—is a politically liberal organization that ranks the congressional voting records of members of Congress from 0 to 100, based on their liberalism.) At the same time, the Baltimore/Washington, D.C., suburban Fourth Congressional District, supports Congresswoman Marjorie S. Holt, a conservative Republican who has voted against federal support for the development of sewers and who received a 5 percent ADA vote rating.[4]

Despite these divergent trends and the difficulties of mobilizing Washington's support for urban assistance programs, the past unwillingness of contiguous units to help the cities leads us to believe that the problems of the central cities probably would be best dealt with at the national level, removed from the state and local interests that are frequently unsympathetic to the resolution of urban problems and particularly central city problems. Suburbs show a perhaps natural unwillingness to help "bail out" the central cities with their severe fiscal problems. In the following pages, the subgroups of the urban electorate will be considered to understand more completely the fragmentary nature of political participation and how it affects urban decision making.

Urban Areas and Unmet Public Needs

Inasmuch as central cities represent the nerve centers of business, government operations, universities, hospitals, and art and cultural activities, they are necessary for our vitality as a nation. Increasingly, however, they have fallen into disrepair as centers of living. This phenomenon has been accompanied by the departure of essential elements of the city tax base. As noted earlier, the middle class has fled and large corporations continue to leave for the suburbs.[5] Thus between 1970 and 1975, northeastern central cities lost employment at an average annual rate of 2 percent and midwestern central cities experienced average declines of 1.6 percent. Some of these jobs moved to the suburbs; other jobs moved to other sections of the country; other positions just disappeared with the onset of more advanced technologies. (At the same time, it should be noted that the average employment increases were 3.2 percent in southern central cities and 1.6 percent in western central cities.[6]

The erosion of the city's tax base, accompanied by shifting population settlement patterns, has not provided conditions conducive to dealing with the city's serious human resource problems—caused in large measure by inadequate resources and a resultant breakdown in social cohesion. The limited resources available to the cities has led to insufficient services, particularly affecting poor groups, which are disproportionately black, Puerto Rican, Mexican-American, and American Indian. Inadequate funds for physical and social services has led to deterioration of urban social structure within many central cities and has affected the functioning of public schools as well as the delivery of other essential public services. One result of this deterioration is the development of a social pathology indicated by a high incidence of drug addiction and assaults on persons and property.

The rate of violent crime increased significantly all across the country in the decades of the 1960s and 1970s, especially in central cities— though these rapid increases did seem to level off as the 1970s drew to a close. Thus the *Gallup Opinion Index* in 1978 reported a public perception of less crime, which is corroborated by the FBI's Uniform Crime Statistics for the same period.[7] This is not intended to suggest that there is no crime in American cities. Quite to the contrary, the crime statistics are staggeringly high (see Table 1), with people in larger urban areas having greater fear of crime than residents in less populated areas. If one looks at the data more closely, it becomes apparent that nonwhites perceive more crime than whites. This is, of course, largely a function of their own separate experiences. Thus in May 1978, when the Gallup organization asked "Is there more crime in this area than there was a year ago, or less?," 42 percent of whites responded yes, while 49 percent of nonwhites responded yes.

Table 1 / CRIME VICTIMIZATION
(in percentages; in a previous twelve-month period)

City Size	Property Vandalized	Money or Property Stolen	Home Broken into or Attempt Made	Assaulted or Mugged	Car Stolen	Total Victimized at Least Once
1,000,000 and over	11	9	7	1	2	23
500,000–999,999	11	9	7	2	1	27
50,000–499,999	13	7	4	3	2	24
2,500–49,999	10	9	5	1	1	21
Under 2,500, rural	8	5	4	1	*	17

Source: *The Gallup Opinion Index* (May 1978), p. 28.
*Less than 1 percent.

At the same time, the pressure to resolve urban problems by providing adequate employment opportunities and services (schools, recreation, and so forth), which might lead to a decline in the social pathology noted previously, remains unlikely. In the face of a divided urban constituency and often resistant rural and suburban constituencies, expectations for action at the state and local levels appear dim. These unresolved urban problems could be a social-political time bomb with the potential for undermining social peace in the United States.

But the dominance of suburban and rural interests in state legislatures is only part of the problem. The competitive nature of the states also acts as a barrier to the alleviation of urban problems. One example of such competition was illustrated in this display at the airport terminal in Salt Lake City: "Utah is a free port state, no property tax on inventory held for out-of-state shipment. If stored in California, the tax would add more than 20 percent to your storage cost each year." [8] Also, in 1971, the New York State Legislature cut the Aid to Families with Dependent Children (AFDC) allowance by 10 percent and reduced the state commitment for financial assistance to local governments because, as then Lieutenant Governor Malcolm Wilson noted, New York State "has gone as far as it can [with regard to taxation] without destroying its competitive position with other states." [9] Other states, such as Mississippi, have even reduced their income tax in the hope of attracting industry. [10]

The breakdown of social cohesion is being reinforced by the economic decline of the central cities. Although not all such cities are advancing toward their economic fall, even cities that have maintained their economic viability have not been able to muster sufficient political support for reallocation of resources to assist their needy. Thus, some central cities have experienced a net economic decline, but this experience has not been uniform. For example, between 1965 and 1975, New York City, Baltimore, New Orleans, Philadelphia, and St. Louis all had steep declines in their net employment base. However, during this same ten-year period, San Francisco, Nashville, Jacksonville, Indianapolis, and Denver all experienced net increases in their employment base. It is important to note too that whenever the national unemployment rate increases, it increases more steeply in the central cities of the metropolitan areas than in the suburbs or other smaller communities of the nation. [11] Thus the Bureau of Labor Statistics reported that in 1977 the total U.S. unemployment rate was 7 percent. The average unemployment rate in suburbs was 6.3 percent and in nonmetropolitan areas it was 6.6 percent. However, the comparable rate for central cities was 8.7 percent and for central city poverty areas it was 14.9 percent. (The same types of differences appear if one selects any other year in the decade of the 1970s for observation.) [12]

Some cities still exhibit population growth, though these cities are not immune to problems of poverty and unemployment. In fact, there has been a geographical shift in population. In 1950, only one of the nation's ten largest cities (Los Angeles) was located outside the midwest or northeast. By 1975, five southern and western cities were among the top ten cities in population—Los Angeles, Houston, Dallas, San Diego, and San Antonio.[13] Other cities in the southern part of the nation have also experienced population as well as economic expansion. For example, Atlanta, Georgia, has grown into a major economic center. On the other hand, cities such as New York, Chicago, Philadelphia, Cleveland, Baltimore, St. Louis, Detroit, and Washington, as well as some smaller cities, have experienced both population and economic losses.[14] Most often, as noted in Chapter 1, the population movement out of these cities has been of the white middle class with a concomitant increase in these cities of a nonwhite and Hispanic disproportionately dependent population. This net out-migration has deprived many cities of the fiscal capacity to meet the needs of a population increasingly disadvantaged.

Many central cities have simultaneously experienced social and fiscal decline. They have lost substantial portions of their middle class population while simultaneously failing to expand their industrial tax base. The counties and states have not been able to meet the challenge to maintain the central cities' viability. Strong and innovative national leadership might be able to meet this challenge. The beginnings of the development of national infrastructure to deal with the social problems of the city were found in President Johnson's War on Poverty and Model Cities Programs. These programs facilitated the development of governmental structures for housing, education, health, and welfare programs for low income residents in many urban areas. Although the Johnson "Great Society" programs were curtailed in the 1970s, it appears that only national-urban policy linkages, which recognize the apparent interdependencies of units within the American political system and are characterized by strong congressional and presidential leadership, will be able to advance urban social and physical developments in the years ahead.

Group Interests and Political Participation

The different groups that comprise the urban electorate respond differently to urban policy issues. In this section, we will begin to examine the perspectives of different groups of urban residents to understand better the political cleavages that exist in and around our cities. When considering the various segments of the urban electorate, it is important to remember that specific groups often *tend* to live in certain kinds of political jurisdictions—working class, very poor, nonwhites and Hispanics in the central city, and the middle class in the suburbs. However, a tendency is not a universal statement. There are white, nonwhite, and Hispanic middle class residents of cities, and there are working class, very poor, nonwhite and Hispanic residents of suburbs.

In February 1979, 78 percent of respondents to a Gallup Organization Opinion Poll question regarding whether or not one favored or opposed a constitutional amendment that would require Congress to balance the federal budget each year favored such an amendment (12 percent opposed and 10 percent had no opinion).[15] Of those people who claimed that they supported such an amendment, several interesting demographic differences were apparent when they were asked what programs they would be willing to see cut back to facilitate a balanced budget. There was, as would be expected, a relationship between income level and attitudes toward reduced spending for public welfare. Among those persons interviewed for this poll, 66 percent of those with family incomes of over $20,000 per year supported cuts in federal spending for welfare if there was a need to cut the budget to bring it into balance. However, among those respondents who reported family incomes of under $5,000, only 44 percent supported such a cut. Looking at racial data, 59 percent of whites and only 27 percent of nonwhites favored such a cut to balance the federal budget. If one observes the responses of those questioned in relation to where they lived, it becomes clear that residents of large cities were less likely to want to see federal welfare expenditures reduced (44 percent in favor) than were small city and rural respondents (56 percent and 61 percent). Finally, regarding political party identification, 44 percent of Democratic Party–identifying respondents as opposed to 66 percent of Republican and 57 percent of independent-identifying respondents favored cutting federal welfare expenditures if the federal budget had to be balanced.[16]

There is also a contemporary concern for the general decline in the quality of urban life. A report of the National League of Cities and the United States Conference of Mayors concluded: "America's cities are smothering in garbage, and 46.5 percent will run out of places to dump their trash within five years. . . ."[17] The result of such concerns is a preference (expressed in Gallup Poll interviews of residents of cities of one-half million or more people) of only one respondent in five for living in cities rather than in suburbs, small towns, or farms.[18] Eighty percent of the respondents in that survey preferred not to live in cities.

Not even in the central cities themselves is there agreement among the citizenry on policy and program priorities. Part of the central city electorate votes against social programs deemed necessary by other elements of the population. For example, predominately white working class central city residents may minimize their public service needs and instead seek political promises of no tax increases and strong police action for crimes against persons and property. At the same time, the central cities' nonwhite constituencies may be concerned with the budgeting of ghetto schools and public housing as well as nondiscrimination in employment, housing, and access to public education on a nonsegregated basis. In 1978, there were sixteen black members in the United States House of Representatives. The uniformity of their support for social priorities suggests strong support for such positions in the black community. In a document they issued, "Key National Policy Issues for 1978: The Congressional Black Caucus Legislative Agenda," the essential problems they isolated as requiring immediate attention were:

The exceptionally high rate of unemployment which continues in the nation as a whole;

The disproportionate jobless rate among minorities in particular;

The continuing discrimination against black persons and other minorities; and

The continuing inadequacies in health, education, welfare, housing, social services and many other aspects of a decent quality of life for all of the nation's citizens.

The positions of the Black Caucus seem to be congruent with the high level of personal discontent with the quality of life expressed by nonwhites (nonurban as well as urban) in a 1979 Gallup Poll. When asked whether on the whole they would say they were satisfied or dissatisfied with the quality of their own life, nonwhites expressed dissatisfaction to a much greater extent than whites, as is indicated by the data in Table 2.

Table 2 / OUTLOOK TOWARD PERSONAL LIVES (IN PERCENT)

Race	Satisfied	Dissatisfied	No Opinion
White	80	18	2
Nonwhite	57	45	4

Source: *The Gallup Opinion Index* (March 1979), p. 3.

The different concerns of the nonwhite poor and the working class white does not imply, however, that there is no room for cooperation. In fact, black-white coalitions have developed in some cities and have fostered the development of municipal administrations geared to emphasizing public investments needed to resolve urban problems. However, in many more cases, white voter concerns in the cities have resulted in opposition to higher taxes and to the public expenditures needed to deal adequately with the health, education, and welfare of the residents of the central cities. This latter condition led, for example, to the mayoralty victories in 1972 and 1976 of Frank Rizzo of Philadelphia, Frank Yorty of Los Angeles (1969), Frank Stenvig of Minneapolis (1969, 1975), and Frank Perk (1971) and Dennis Kucinich (1977) of Cleveland.

To assume that divisions within our cities and between the cities and suburbs have no class base is to fall prey to an oversimplification of political analysis. Though divisions often appear to be along racial or ethnic lines, the root of group separateness is most often class. In the next section, we will consider the role of political activity by members of the urban electorate (suburban as well as city) in trying to effect change in their geographic areas. For the purposes of this discussion, we will consider five separate urban (not necessarily central city) constituencies: the nonwhite minorities, the white working class, the middle class, the poor, and the rich.

The Nonwhite and Hispanic Poor Electorate

Although not all nonwhites and Hispanics are poor, our discussion of nonwhite and Hispanic voting patterns will focus on the patterns of the nonwhites and Hispanics who are poor, both because poverty is disproportionately high among nonwhites and Hispanics and because their problems highlight certain urban issues such as the need for compensatory or desegregated public schools, bilingual and bicultural education programs, nondiscriminatory employment practices, and adequate health and welfare services. In 1977, almost 25 million people were living in consumer units with incomes that fell below the poverty level.[20] Whereas 50 percent of poor white families living in metropolitan areas lived in central cities, the comparable figure for nonwhites and Hispanics was 80 percent.[21] Insofar as nonwhites and Hispanics perceive their problems to be different from those of the largely white working class, their voting patterns tend to be different.

• VOTING PATTERNS

To assume that all nonwhites and Hispanics have similar interests or that they vote consistently as a block would be to oversimplify American voting behavior, but nonwhites do *tend* to support the more socially and economically liberal candidates. Since nonwhites and Hispanics are in the majority in an ever-increasing number of American cities, their political power to elect candidates sympathetic to their problems should be considerable. In fact, it is not. Although nonwhites and Hispanics are a large *potential* electorate in cities, the number who *actually* vote is often much less. In fact, the likelihood of voting declines as income declines. Thus the power of the poor in cities is much less than their numbers would indicate. As a result, mayors and council members who do not necessarily sympathize with the concerns of poor nonwhites and Hispanics sometimes serve as their elected spokespersons.[22]

Some election data will highlight the differences in voting among different groups. According to 1976 Election Survey data collected by the Gallup Organization, nonwhites tended to support Jimmy Carter for president. They gave him 85 percent of their votes while giving just 15 percent of their votes to President Ford. White voters, however, preferred Ford to Carter, casting 52 percent of their ballots for Ford and just 46 percent of their ballots for Carter.[23] In fact, with the exception of the 1964 Goldwater-Johnson race in which a majority of both whites and nonwhites supported President Johnson, in all of the presidential elections since 1952 a majority or plurality of the white voters have supported the Republican candidate and a majority of nonwhite voters have supported the Democratic candidate.[24] Some insight into this presidential election voting split can be found by looking at a Gallup Poll question asked of the members of their sample population after the 1976 election. The respondents were given a list of groups in the population and were asked "whether you feel that [a] group would be better off with Ford as the next President, or with Carter as the next President." Nonwhites perceived that manual workers, the unemployed, welfare people, blacks, and "people like yourself"—all classifications that disproportionately account for the nonwhite population—would be better off with Mr. Carter as President.[25] Thus the nonwhite vote for Carter can be viewed as an indication that these voters believed that he advocated social programs that would be of benefit to them.

In the 1978 elections, low voter turnout among blacks remained a problem that hindered the full exercise of political influence by black Americans in several elections. Now that voting registration barriers have been eliminated in the South, many blacks still fail to register or to vote. The Atlanta-based Voter Education Project estimated a 10 to 15 percent gap between the registration of black voters and white voters registered in the South. While the number of black officeholders in the South has increased since 1969, when 0.01 percent of elective officeholders were black, still less than 3 percent of elective officeholders in the South are black. In Houston, in 1978, low black turnouts contributed to the defeat by Republican William Clement of the more liberal Democratic candidate for governor, John Hill, and to the victory of conservative Republican Senator John Tower over Democratic challenger Robert Kreuger. However, in Louisiana, strong black voter turnout helped to elect Democrat Claude Leach to victory over Republican Jimmy Wilson in Louisiana's Fourth Congressional District, which includes the city of Shreveport.[26]

Black voting has on occasion been significant as an antivote against city officials considered racist or indifferent to the black community. Black turnout in Chicago's mayorality primary was sufficient to give Jane Byrne a victory over the city's Democratic machine candidate in February 1979. In November 1978, blacks in Philadelphia, responding to what they considered racist appeals by Mayor Frank Rizzo, voted in sufficient numbers to defeat a city charter amendment that would have allowed Rizzo to seek reelection.

In at least two 1978 elections, black voting led to the election of Republicans. In Mississippi, Mayor Charles Evers of Fayette, running as an independent for the Senate, received 95 percent of the black and 23 percent of the total vote. This was a sufficient drain on the traditional black Democratic support to lead to the election of the Republican senatorial candidate. Similarly, black support for a black independent candidate contributed to the election of a Republican in Mississippi's Fourth Congressional District. However, black support was critical for the election of several liberals in 1978, including Governor Hugh Carey in New York (who received 83 percent of the black vote), Governor William Graham in Florida (who received 84 percent of the black vote), and Senator Carl Levin in Michigan (who received 91 percent of the back vote).[27]

Increasingly, the practitioners of urban politics and political coalitions will need to take into account the largest growing ethnic population, Hispanics. As of yet, however, Hispanics have exhibited little political clout. They do have a measure of local influence in San Antonio, Texas, with its majority of residents of Mexican ancestry; and Cubans in the Miami, Florida, area support a Puerto Rican mayor. However, in New York City, with its large Latin population, the only Hispanic official, until his 1979 resignation, was a mayoral appointment, Deputy Mayor Herman Badillo. One significant influence of the Hispanic population has been manifested in the support provided for the federal government's subsidization of bilingual education programs—primarily geared to Spanish-speaking pupils.[28]

According to a 1976 study by the Southwest Voter Registration Education Project, the primary reason for the relatively low political impact of Hispanics has been low voter registration.[29] According to this study, in 1976 there were 6.3 million Hispanics of voting age; 23 percent of this population were not citizens. Of the 4.9 million Hispanics eligible to vote, only 55 percent registered to vote. Of those registered, only 69 percent voted in the 1976 presidential election.

• COALITION BEHAVIOR

Black and Latin voters are often significant partners in an urban coalition with what Edward Banfield and James Q. Wilson have called the "public-regarding" middle class.[30] These are a subgroup of middle class voters throughout the nation who support the delivery of public goods and services for the benefit of the community at large, even if they can provide themselves with these services privately. The public-regarding middle class would support improved public health facilities, for example, even if they could afford private care, since the public good would be served. Banfield and Wilson have suggested that white Anglo-Saxon and Jewish middle class members are predisposed to being public-regarding, while working class members are essentially private-regarding in that they are more predisposed to maintaining their private needs than to supporting public needs. Banfield and Wilson can be accused of oversimplifying in the development of their categories; but whatever the limitations of their typology, some political participants among the white middle class do tend to be public-regarding.

Since central city electorates are becoming increasingly nonwhite and Hispanic and since some middle class whites support improved public delivery of more adequate services to the poor community, it is not surprising that both nonwhite and white mayors in some cities are expressing strong social concerns. This coalition has elected black mayors, such as Andrew Hacker of Gary, Indiana; Maynard Jackson of Atlanta, Georgia; Kenneth Gibson of Newark, New Jersey; and Coleman Young of Detroit. Black and Puerto Rican voters played a vital part in the second election of Mayor John V. Lindsay of New York after he was denied renomination on the Republican ticket and ran as the standard bearer of New York State's Liberal Party.[31]

Recently, there has been an effort by Hispanics to join in coalition with blacks. M. Carl Holman, president of the National Urban Coalition, and Raul Yzaguirre, President of the National Council of La Raza, have set up a Working Committee on Concerns of Hispanics and Blacks. They have convened meetings of twenty-four national and congressional leaders from the black and Hispanic communities. This joint committee has agreed to support public financing of political campaigns as a measure for increasing minority representation in Congress. The committee supports increased expenditures for the food stamp program and opposes the balanced budget amendment aimed at curtailing federal social programs. Black leaders within the committee have agreed not to issue statements on illegal aliens without prior discussion with Hispanic leaders. In addition, they have agreed to support bilingual, bicultural education.[32]

Another coalition has developed in some cities and has been able to support successfully candidates for public office. In some cases, the poor nonwhite and Hispanic voters have joined with the poor white and white working class voters to elect public officials. In these cases, the nonwhite, Hispanic, and white populations have been able to overcome race hatred and fear of each other to rally around a candidate who has articulated support for "race-cutting" and sometimes "class-cutting" issues. A study of New Orleans politics, for example, reported the success of a coalition between blacks and lower income whites in that city during the 1960s in both local and national election campaigns. Using voting behavior in five key elections, the presidential elections of 1960 and 1964, the congressional elections of 1964 and 1966, and a councilmanic election in 1967, Allen Rosensweig found a strong negative correlation between class and liberal support.[33] Ongoing success of a black/white coalition, such as the one described in New Orleans, sometimes has been undercut by low voting participation by blacks. For example, in 1964 in Harris County, Texas, 94 percent of the blacks voted for President Johnson but only 35 percent of the voting age black population voted.[34] For a group to be effective as a political force, members of the group must vote. If they do not vote, then elected officials may not feel the need to be as responsive to their demands as they are to demands of those who do vote.

Coalitions formed along class lines are not necessarily just a southern phenomenon. In his successful 1973 Los Angeles mayoralty campaign, Thomas Bradley, a black candidate, was able to forge this type of coalition. He supported development of parks and beaches and took positions against commercial exploitation of urban space by oil companies and construction interests. At the same time, he stressed his experience as a former policeman and denounced street crime. This strategy enabled him to win about 50 percent of the white vote, a slight majority of the Mexican-American vote, and 90 percent of the black vote—the latter vote comprising only 18 percent of the city's vote.[35] In April 1977, Mayor Bradley was reelected, polling more than 59 percent of the city's vote. Blacks still constituted less than 20 percent of the voters in this election.[36]

Even if coalitions are successful in electing mayors sympathetic to the problems of the city's poor, the ability of local leaders to cope with these problems remains limited. The cities' resources continue to dwindle as the flight of the middle class and industry erodes the tax base. Imposing new and higher taxes on those who remain only exacerbates the problem because it encourages further flight, and while the cities clearly cannot survive on their own, little help is forthcoming from the state legislatures. Thus, when there is increased political representation of the poor, it does little to make up for the cities' lack of the financial base needed to provide services while remaining fiscally viable. Though the cities cannot survive well alone within the states, insufficient help is forthcoming from the state legislatures. Also, despite the increased political representation of the poor, often nonwhite and Hispanic residents of the central city, the cities lack the financial base needed to retain their fiscal viability while meeting their substantial service needs.

The White Poor in Urban Areas

Just as all nonwhites and Hispanics are not poor, so too not all the poor are nonwhite. Similarly, not all the poor live in the cities. White poverty is found in such nonurban areas as West Virginia and Kentucky. Although poverty in these areas is not an urban phenomenon, it contributes to the city's problems because the lack of opportunity in small towns and rural areas results in urban in-migration and new tax burdens on the central cities.

Poor whites in West Virginia and Kentucky often lack local political power. Local machines controlling judgeships, the sheriff's office, and the schools have used legal penalties and control over welfare grants and school lunches to control the white poor; in these activities, such local "bosses" often act in coalition with the coal mining companies headquartered in Pennsylvania, New York, and New England.[37] Describing the local political process in Mingo County, West Virginia, a local community organizer commented: "[T]hey're just a bunch of small time crooks, . . . and not half as bad as the *real* crooks in Appalachia. A lot of them don't live here and never have. They come from the Golden Triangle in Pittsburgh and from Wall Street." [38]

Through a lack of social organization and often clear political direction, the poor whites in such areas have not been able to develop programmatic responses to meet health, housing, and employment needs. Indeed, the people who control local political structures and newspapers often have been aligned with financial and mining interests, more concerned with profits and production than with meeting the social needs of the community. This lack of social organization and opportunity results in poor white in-migration to cities such as Chicago, Illinois; Detroit, Michigan; Akron, Ohio; and Baltimore, Maryland. The cities then must bear the burden of providing income and services to people who often cannot cope unassisted in an urban environment. Frequently, their rural home jurisdictions did not provide them with the necessary training to find employment in a technologically based industrial society. The city becomes responsible for caring for the poor and needy; the rural areas often vote for candidates—both state and national—who oppose aid to the cities. Thus, there is a clear interdependence of jurisdictions with respect to such population movement with inadequate policy linkages developed to cope with what has become the "city's problem."

Also, segments of the white working class have, with the presence of national economic slumps, increasingly become the white poor. In the mid-1970s, 25,000 of New York's 87,000 construction workers were out of work: One unemployed New York City construction worker noted that regarding the spending money left after receiving his $95 per week unemployment benefits: "I used to put $30 on the bar, on a day when it would rain or something, or after work and never worry about it. Now I gotta get through a whole week on $30." [39] In this case also, a national problem has become the "city's problem."

The White Working Class: Ethnic and Nonethnic

The white working class communities in our large cities and increasingly of our suburbs, represent a political input of great importance. Insofar as the people in these neighborhoods tend to participate in the electoral process, they represent a political force with which local decision makers must contend. In the past, as a result of the relatively high level of political participation by some white ethnic-identifying working class groups, the ethnically "balanced ticket" evolved in some large cities with large ethnic population enclaves. An ethnically "balanced ticket" will have people running for public office who represent the major ethnic groups in a political jurisdiction. For example, in many East Coast cities, slates are comprised of a Jew, a black, an Italian-American, and an Irish-American. Irish-Americans, Italian-Americans, and Jewish-Americans still represent a significant portion of the political leadership of some of our major cities. Their constituencies are still very cohesive; they vote in force and often have well-organized and long-standing political organizations.

In cities that maintain partisan as opposed to nonpartisan electoral systems, the Democratic Party has historically been the party of the white working class voters. In the past decade, however, as issues with racial overtones have come to the forefront of city politics, the white working class in some cities has sometimes defected from the Democratic Party to support more conservative candidates of other political parties. In cities that have nonpartisan local elections, the same voting patterns prevail. When issues with racial overtones reach the forefront of politics, the white working class often will support a conservative candidate.

When discussing the white working class, which is predominately a central city group, it is important to note that in many eastern and midwestern cities, this group is often, with the exception of the Irish, characterized by Eastern and Southern European ethnic identifications—Polish, Italian, Russian, Hungarian—and Catholicism. All working class members are not, however, Catholic ethnic identifiers. Also, some segments of the white working class are moving into the suburbs; thus there are now working class suburbs. Often the residents of these communities have political behavior patterns not unlike those working class residents of the central cities. In the discussions that follow, the working class (on the basis of 1978 data) will be defined as members of households with family incomes within the income range of $11,000 to $18,000. However, as income is not the sole determinant of class identification and class style, these inferential limits are by no means absolute determinants of the class grouping we are discussing. Also, the income range of the white working class, as well as those of other population subgroups must constantly be readjusted because of inflation. U.S. Bureau of the Census data indicated that in 1978, assuming an average family of four, over 14,700,000 of the nation's 57,215,000 million families had incomes that fell between $11,000 and $18,000 a year.[40] (The figures that were selected as the range for identifying the working class were derived from U.S. Bureau of Labor Statistics calculations on urban family budgets. The lower figure was the average lower budget for an urban family of four; the higher figure was the average intermediate budget for an urban family of four.)[41]

The white working class tends to be liberal on many economic "bread-and-butter" issues, such as Social Security, minimum wage laws, and health care delivery programs. They tend to be conservative on AFDC grants ("the welfare"), integrated housing, and public school education policies—issues that relate to socioeconomic class and often are overshadowed by questions of race. They also tend to be conservative on "life-style" issues,[42] such as liberal abortion policies, smoking marijuana, and the use of hard drugs. Thus, where "counterculture" and certain racially oriented issues are not involved, members of the white working class tend to vote liberally. However, as we noted before, where such issues are involved, this liberal voting predisposition is replaced among significant numbers of white working class voters with support for conservative candidates. This characteristic could be seen clearly in 1972 in the voting split in white ethnic working class areas. In Baltimore, Maryland, these areas tended to support the liberal congressional candidate incumbent, Paul S. Sarbanes, while not providing electoral support for liberal presidential candidate, Senator George S. McGovern. (In 1976, Sarbanes was elected to the U.S. Senate; his congressional seat was taken by Barbara Mikulsky, also a liberal Democrat.) McGovern was identified with the "counterculture," although he did not espouse it, and he was also identified with the position of forced racial integration in public education and public housing. Congressman Sarbanes received overwhelming support in the heavily Polish and Bohemian ethnic sections of Baltimore City's First Ward, the Greek section of the Twenty-sixth Ward, and the heavily Italian Second Ward. At the same time, these areas supported Richard M. Nixon in his bid for reelection as president. The trend of working class support for the conservative presidential candidate, Richard M. Nixon, was also revealed by the November 1972 CBS Election Day Survey. Of blue collar respondents, 54 percent voted for Nixon and 44 percent voted for McGovern. Of respondents with a union member in the home, 48 percent voted for Nixon while 50 percent voted for McGovern. Of Catholic respondents, a substantially working class group that had never given a national Republican candidate a majority of its vote, Nixon received 53 percent of respondents' votes while McGovern received only 46 percent of their votes.[43] Postelection Gallup survey data indicated that blue collar (manual) workers—traditionally Democratic Party voters—supported Nixon over McGovern by 57 to 43 percent.[44]

At times this tendency to turn to conservative candidates on particular social issues has led to support for conservative candidates for other political offices. In 1970, Republican-Conservative Senator James Buckley was elected to the U.S. Senate from New York State in part on the basis of the substantial Roman Catholic working class support he received in New York City. Such white working class conservatism was revealed by the portion of the vote for Buckley coming from traditional Democratic voters. In the Thirty-fourth Assembly District (Maspeth and Sunnyside) of New York City's borough of Queens, which contains a high proportion of working class residents of Irish, German, and Eastern European extraction, Buckley received 56 percent of the votes cast.[45] In 1976, in an effort to prevent this "backlash" defection, Democratic Party leaders supported a centrist Catholic senatorial candidate, Daniel Patrick Moynihan. Their strategy was to promote candidates who would counter Buckley's appeal to blue collar voters while not being rejected by more liberal Jewish voters. In defeating Buckley, Moynihan was able to reduce substantially Buckley's support in Irish and Italian areas in Brooklyn and Queens, while running very well in Jewish areas of New York City and receiving substantial but less enthusiastic support among black voters.[46]

The voting phenomenon that New York's Democratic politicos were able to counter is sometimes labeled "white backlash." It is based on a concern by white working class voters for social peace on the streets and in the schools, as well as for a concern with low taxes in the face of the declining purchasing power of their income. Also, such voters are concerned with the stability of their neighborhoods, in terms of class and ethnic makeup. Thus, the movement of nonwhite middle class residents into white neighborhoods is viewed as the initial stage of an influx of low income nonwhite residents who may ultimately alter the ethnic character of the neighborhood. The nature of this perceived threat can be illustrated by Slovak-black relations on Cleveland's East Side in the early 1970s. The problem with which Slovak residents expressed the greatest concern was the presence of social violence not previously experienced, to any great extent, in their neighborhood:

> A telephone booth on the corner of ... [a] street had been damaged so often that it was removed. A mailbox had been burglarized on the day Social Security checks were to come. A doctor had installed a peep hole in his door and had gone to irregular office hours to thwart robbers. A mentally retarded boy whose joy was a paper route had to give it up after his collections were stolen and his paper thrown into the street. Somody's Delicatessen closed between 2:30 and 4 each afternoon to avoid harassment from Audubon [high school] students.[47]

Despite these political tales, it is significant to note that in the 1976 presidential campaign, when the social issues faded into the background, the Democratic Party, with a candidate who was perceived by some to be the more economically liberal hopeful, once again became the party of choice of the ethnic-identifying working class. In fact, 59 percent of blue collar workers voted for Jimmy Carter. The basic "bread-and-butter" liberalism of the disproportionately working class Catholic population also is confirmed by National Opinion Research Center (NORC) data. Using such NORC data, Andrew Greeley determined that Catholics were on the average liberal on the traditional New Deal issues such as jobs, government intervention, income equalization, and Medicare. They were not liberal on civil rights issues such as legalization of marijuana, pornography, rights of criminals and radicals, nor on racial issues such as welfare for blacks, school integration, and housing integration.[48]

Middle Class Suburbanites

Suburban residents may be very affluent, middle class, working class, or poor. Consequently, it is not surprising that they do not clearly represent one political attitude. Middle class suburbanites can, however, be counted on to participate in the political process—and in particular to vote—more than the poor residents of the central cities. Overall, while not clearly definable in terms of either electoral behavior or class, suburbs tend to be more middle class than the central cities, which, as we have noted earlier, tend to be home for the poor. With the preceding qualification kept in mind, we would note that many of the children of the urban ethnic and nonethnic working class today are middle class suburbanites. To the extent that they often "blame the victim" and maintain a "siege" psychology, their votes are often cast for candidates opposed to social expenditures for the cities. Also, residents of class-stratified middle and upper income suburbs tend to oppose the movement of the poor, white and nonwhite, into their areas. (Residents of working class suburbs respond in a like manner.) Often they vote for candidates who will act to support their economic and social distance from the central cities.

The quality of suburban services is highly variable. Many suburbanites have sufficient income to buy services such as membership in private swimming pools. Other more essential services often must be purchased, too, since they are not publicly provided. For example, garbage collection is often privately franchised. The result, at times, is limited support for high-quality public services. Opposition to expanded public services is often based on grounds of opposition to increases in local taxes. Thus in *some* suburbs, needed school appropriations sometimes have great difficulty being passed because of local opposition to increased property taxes. At the state level, representatives of such suburbs, as well as rural representatives, often vote against fiscal measures aimed at improving the quality of life in the central cities.

At times, difference in class orientation and policy interest may differentiate policy positions of suburbanites and central city residents. In a study of five Wisconsin cities, Milwaukee, Madison, Green Bay, Racine, and Kenosha, it was found that the "social distance" between the suburbs and the central cities is distinctive. Between smaller cities and surrounding suburbs, such social distance tends to be smaller. The largest urbanized area studied was Milwaukee, Wisconsin. Thus, the greatest status differences between the suburbs and the city were found in the Milwaukee area. Thomas Dye found that such status differences affected policy orientations such that:

> More dollars were spent on educating the average school child in the suburbs of Milwaukee and Madison than were spent on the average child in these central cities. Sixteen of the 18 suburbs of Milwaukee County spend more per pupil for operating their public schools than the City of Milwaukee. Four of Madison's seven suburbs spent more per pupil than Madison.[49]

The residents of these suburbs tend to have higher than average social status. Parents with high social status have high aspirations for their children, which were translated into greater concern with the operation of the school system and higher per pupil education expenditure.[50]

It costs more to have an adequately functioning central city—given the complexities of such a city, as well as the problems of the city's population—than most cities can raise. Also, it costs more per capita to provide adequate services in such a city than it costs to run a socially well-developed suburb. The result of differential attitudes and the different situational needs of cities and their suburbs is that suburbanites spend more of their locally derived revenues than do city residents on education. City residents, however, spend more on other municipal services, which are at times unavailable in the suburbs, or are purchased privately.[51] Compared to central cities and rural areas, middle and upper income suburbs have lower degrees of educational need, a more adequate resource base for financing education, lesser competing demands for revenues; yet relative to their needs, they have had greater support from their states and from the federal government for expenditures.[52] Also, central cities have a lower fiscal capacity than suburbs and thus a lower tax effort expenditure ratio in comparison with suburbs.[53] Because of land acquisition costs, insurance rates, and nonprofessional personnel costs, the central cities bear a higher cost than suburbs in the provision of most services, including education, sanitation services, fire and police services, as well as other municipal services. Overall, the central cities lack the relative tax resources often available to the suburbs. Moreover, the complexity of municipal services is greater in the central cities, which must provide services to the needy as well as maintain the more traditional services, than it is in the suburbs. These differences lead to the development of a different cultural view and a differing perception of political realities by political leadership in the suburbs and the central cities.

The Rich and the Superrich

Whether they live in the central cities or in the outlying areas, wealthy individuals, corporate executives, local bankers, and the like have had an impact on local politics stemming from their own expertise, prestige, and the power to provide or withhold financial support from candidates for local and statewide office. The question that comes to mind is who benefits from the influence of these individuals. Is their participation in local political and service activity, for example, an extension of corporate welfarism? What are their expectations of the candidates they choose to support for state and local office? To generalize about a group of individuals is, of course, to oversimplify. But inasmuch as trends appear among people with like characteristics, we can discuss *predispositions*. The predisposition of the very rich is often to support candidates and policies that will maximize their own monetary advantage and corporate interests.

Not only do the rich vote in elections, provide support for candidates, and run for public office, but they also often provide the manpower and funding for private service delivery, and by so doing maintain their own advantaged position in society. By working with the private sector, the wealthy are facilitating a situation—however inadequate the state of public services—that can operate as a counterpoise to the public sector and thus help to keep the public sector from taking over the delivery of some of these services. If the government provided the multitude of services that private agencies now provide, either spending priorities would have to be altered (an unlikely occurrence given our concerns with national security) or taxes would have to be increased through the elimination of tax loopholes or the imposition of new taxes.[54]

In either case, the rich might have to pay more than they do now. (President Kennedy observed the paradox that oilman John Paul Getty in the early 1960s had an income of over $1 billion a year and paid only a few thousand dollars in taxes.[55]) Furthermore, the tax interests of this class are based in part on limiting demands for government spending. This runs counter to increased government participation in the delivery of services to the cities. Inasmuch as the wealthy and the super-wealthy have been able through their financial support of candidates and their control of significant private sector decision making to have disproportionate influence on municipal and state policies and related national policies, they have been able to affect the priorities of public expenditure.

At times the influence of the wealthy in state and local politics may be substantial and obvious. In other situations it is less predominant and more subtle. Several illustrations of substantial and obvious influence by the wealthy on state and local politics can tell this story more clearly.

Edward W. Ball, head of the billion-dollar Alfred I. DuPont estate in Florida, had an important influence in local and state politics within that state. In discussing this influence, the late Mayor of Miami, Robert King High, once testified: "You can hardly drive 50 miles in Florida—in any direction—without encountering some facet of the DuPont estate." [56] Ball also was a leading proponent of a sales tax rather than an income tax in Florida; his success in this advocacy in large part resulted in the state's current regressive tax structure.

The inordinate political influence of the Wolfe family in Columbus, Ohio, is almost a caricature of the role of the wealthy in some major American cities. The Wolfe family started out by founding the Wolfe Wear-U-Well Shoe Corporation. They then went on to gain control of the newspaper the *Dispatch,* and to form Banc-Ohio, a holding company with twenty-two central Ohio banks. They now also control the Ohio Company, a large securities underwriting firm, considerable farm land, radio and television stations and the Neil House, Columbus' leading hotel as well as other real estate. According to a local businessperson in Columbus, this economic power is translated into political power:

[T]he Wolfe clan is involved in all that transpires. You bank with them, you may rent from them, you hire your employees through their newspapers, you advertise your goods in their papers, you get your view of the world from the news they carry in their newspaper and on their television station.[57]

They also maintain close connections to politicians, especially the Republicans.

The great political influence of the wealthy is further evident in the campaign expenditures of some of the nation's political leaders. For example, in 1976, when he was a contender for a Senate seat from Pennsylvania, Senator John Heinz spent $2.2 million of his own funds to help defray campaign costs. This, of course, gave Heinz, who was a relative political unknown, the media and organization advantage that was necessary for victory.[58]

It is also appropriate to note the more anonymous influence of corporate wealth on state and local political decisions. In response to the Electoral Reform Law of 1974, which limits individual contributions to presidential, senatorial and congressional primaries and elections, special interests have organized into a variety of political action committees (PACs). Ironically, this law, in effect since 1976, has increased the political influence of corporate and trade association interest groups.

In general, in 1978 a greater share of funds from corporate PACs was contributed to Republican than to Democratic candidates. In fact, through October 23, 1978, 61 percent of corporate PAC contributions were made to Republican candidates. The total "special-interest" breakdown of contributions during the 1978 campaign through October 23, 1978, according to the Federal Election Commission, included $8.8 million in corporate PAC contributions to Senate and House candidates; $10.7 million in Trade Association contributions (such as those of the Realtors Political Action Committee, and the Automobile and Truck Dealers Election Committee); $9.4 million in labor union contributions and $3.1 million in other special interest group contributions (such as those of the American Medical Association Political Action Committee).[59] Fred Wertheimer, the senior vice-president of Common Cause, predicted the rise of the PAC mechanism would lead to the "total domination of the political financing system by corporate PAC's [by 1984]."[60] Major corporate PACs in 1978 included those of the International Paper Company, Standard Oil Company of Indiana, Dart Industries, American Family Corporation, General Electric Corporation, Eaton Corporation, Union Camp Corporation, United Technologies Corporation, and the Union Oil Company.

In terms of pure industrial power, in 1977, the top 500 industrial firms in the United States controlled 83 percent of all manufacturing and mining assets in the United States. Less than 3 percent of American industrial corporations controlled over 80 percent of industrial assets.[61]

They also controlled many hotels and department stores. The impact of major industries on commercial and industrial activity in urban areas and on the quality of urban life is clearly determined by the location of such private-sector activity and by such events as the impact of gasoline availability and pricing activity on urban life. Mayors and local officials have learned to respect this institutional power.[62] In Toledo, Ohio, a committee of local businesspersons and government officials persuaded the Owens-Illinois Corporation, a glass and container manufacturer, to build their new headquarters in the downtown Toledo redevelopment area. This commitment, in part, led to a federal commitment of $12 million in federal matching funds for street and park development and a state and local commitment for urban redevelopment of $13 million. The power of corporate and commercial interest on local urban decision-making will be a central dimension of state and local political decision-making in the 1980s.

CONCLUSION

The problems and policies of urban government are integrally linked to the texture of the urban community and the orientation of economic and class interests within urban areas. The 1960s and 1970s were marked by the frequent flight of urban manufacturing and commerce from the larger central cities and by the flight of the predominantly white middle class from these same areas. Less dense urban areas have experienced substantial growth, but despite these trends, the major central cities have remained formidable cultural and commercial centers. With decreasing employment opportunities for the poorly skilled and the working class, the quality of central city urban life has declined. A shrinking financial base has resulted in poorer educational, recreational, and social services. With increased poverty, crimes against persons and property have increased.

Movement to the suburbs has not been without problems. The limited financial base of suburban communities has led to problems regarding financing of education, inadequate public transportation, inadequate water supply and sewage services, and inadequate fire and police protection for many suburban communities. Also, suburbanites who are often refugees from the central cities may fear taxes necessary to finance adequate services.

Within central cities, middle-sized cities, and very urbanized suburbs, the poor and their middle class allies may demand improved services. Middle class and working class residents who fear tax increases more than poor services may support conservative, "no tax increase" candidates. In part, the movement of traditionally Democratic urban voters of working class backgrounds to support conservative candidates for national office in the 1970 and 1972 elections was a reflection of this trend. After 1974, when inflation became the primary issue for a vast proportion of these voters, they tended to support more liberal candidates for congressional and state offices—though even the more liberal candidates seem to feel constrained increasingly by considerations of fiscal responsibility and concerns about big government. In terms of group interests, the poor white, nonwhite, and Hispanic constituencies have indicated a potential for coalition in support of greater social spending for the cities. However, in some cities and counties, black registration and voting have been too low to provide for an effective black-Hispanic-white coalition to meet urban crises.

Moreover, within state legislatures, positions relating to urban problems are fragmented among suburban and central city interests. Often legislative suburban/rural majorities will not favor policies to ease the problems of central cities and the often older urbanized suburbs. Because suburban voters often prefer low tax policies, or tax policies that do not ease the city overburden, legislatures may reflect these concerns regarding the funding of public services. In this alignment, the suburbs may reflect the middle class and working class constituencies who fear taxes more than they desire public services and who feel that they are able to pay their own way in the sense that they prefer to repair their cars rather than finance an adequate mass transit system. Indeed as we have noted, many central city white working class residents also fear taxes more than they desire municipal public services.

Wealthy families and corporate interests often use their influence to maintain poorly financed state and local services for urban areas. Even when such sources make generous contributions for community services, as is true of the DuPont family in urban New Castle County, Delaware, a parallel low level of public service and/or the politically unresponsive decision-making process of foundation trusts and wealthy individuals leaves needed public services (and private services) in cities and suburbs in an uncoordinated and inadequate condition. In some instances, the commercial and communications interests and wealth of individuals may control small- and medium-sized communities. Corporations—national and multinational—often have shown more concern with their private profits than with urban needs.

The thrust of this chapter has been to point to the need for national leadership to meet both the educational, health, welfare, and employment needs as well as the physical service needs of urban America. In other words, since neither the states and localities nor wealthy individuals or corporations have been able to solve the problems of urban America, and since there are substantial cleavages within the urban electorate, perhaps a stronger federal role in funding as well as planning is now necessary to prevent the further deterioration of the urban condition and its effects on other sectors of the national system.

REFERENCES

1. Edward C. Banfield and James Q. Wilson, "Cleavages in Urban Politics," in *Politics in the Metropolis,* ed. by Thomas R. Dye and Brett W. Hawkins (Columbus, Ohio: Charles E. Merrill, 1967), pp. 47, 53.
2. Robert C. Wood. "Republics in Miniature," in Dye and Hawkins, ibid., p. 332.
3. Michael Barone, Grant Ujitusa, and Douglas Matthews, *The Almanac of American Politics* (Boston: Gambit, 1977), pp. 238–40, 244–45, 250–51.
4. Ibid., pp. 360–61, 364–65.
5. *Nation's Cities,* 10 (February 1972), 13–14. This account notes that between 1965 and 1972, New York lost the headquarters of twenty-two very large companies, including Shell Oil, Pepsi-Cola, Universal Oil, and Johns Manville.
6. *The Fiscal Outlook for Cities,* ed. by Roy Bahl (Syracuse, N.Y.: Syracuse University Press, 1978), p. 9.
7. *Gallup Opinion Index* (May 1978), p. 25.
8. Terry Sanford, *Storm over the States* (New York: McGraw-Hill, 1967), pp. 26–27.
9. Neal R. Peirce, *The Megastates of America* (New York: W. W. Norton, 1972), p. 36.
10. Charles N. Fortenberry and F. Glenn Abney, "Mississippi: Unreconstructed and Unredeemed," in *The Changing Politics of the South,* ed. by William C. Havard (Baton Rouge: Louisiana State University Press, 1972), p. 517.
11. *The Fiscal Outlook for Cities,* op. cit., p. 10.
12. Ibid., p. 95.
13. *Urban America: Policies and Problems* (Washington, D.C.: Congressional Quarterly, 1978), p. 8.
14. Ibid.
15. *Gallup Opinion Index* (March 1979), p. 23.
16. Ibid., p. 26.
17. *Cities and the Nation's Disposal Crisis* (Washington D.C.: Office of Urban Services of the National League of Cities and the U.S. Conference of Mayors, 1972).
18. *Gallup Opinion Index* (December 1972), p. 21.
19. Congressional Black Caucus, *For the People,* 3 (1978), 1.
20. See Chapter 1 for a discussion of "Profile of Poverty," pp. 17–18.
21. U.S. Department of Commerce, Bureau of the Census, *Money, Income and Poverty Status of Families and Persons in the United States: 1977,* Series P-60, No. 116 (Washington, D.C., July 1978), pp. 3–4.
22. For a more complete discussion of voting patterns among the poor, non-white populations, see Joyce Gelb and Marian Lief Palley, *Tradition and Change in American Party Politics* (New York: Thomas Y. Crowell, 1975), Chapter VI.
23. *Gallup Opinion Index* (December 1976), p. 17.
24. Ibid., pp. 16–17.
25. Ibid., pp. 22–25.
26. *The New York Times,* November 13, 1978, p. A21.
27. *The New York Times,* April 1, 1979, p. E5.

28. Robert Lindsey, "U.S. Hispanic Populace Growing Faster Than Any Other Minority," *The New York Times,* February 18, 1979, pp. 1 and 16.
29. Neil R. Peirce and Jerry Hagstrom, "The Hispanic Community—A Growing Force to Be Reckoned With," *National Journal,* 11 (April 7, 1979), 550.
30. Edward Banfield and James Q. Wilson, "Public-Regardingness as a Value Premise in Voting Behavior," *American Political Science Review,* 58 (December 1964), 885–86.
31. See Howard A. Palley, "The White Working Class and a Strategy of Coalition for Social Development," *Social Service Review,* 47 (June 1973), 249.
32. Peirce and Hagstrom, op. cit., p. 552.
33. Allen Rosensweig, "The Influence of Class and Race on Political Behavior in New Orleans: 1960–1967," M.A. Thesis, University of Oklahoma, cited in Chandler Davidson, *Biracial Politics: Conflict and Coalition in the Metropolitan South* (Baton Rouge: Louisiana State University Press, 1972), p. 214.
34. Ibid., p. 90.
35. *The New York Times,* May 31, 1973, p. 17.
36. *The New York Times,* April 7, 1977, p. A22.
37. Robert Coles, *Migrants, Sharecroppers, Mountaineers* (Boston: Little, Brown, 1971), pp. 197, 287.
38. Ibid.
39. Pete Hamill, "The Rise of the Workless Class," *The Village Voice,* October 17, 1974, p. 5.
40. *Money Income and Poverty Status of Families and Persons in the United States: 1977,* op. cit., p. 2.
41. U.S. Department of Labor, Bureau of Labor Statistics, *News* (USDC: *79–305*) (Washington, D.C., April 29, 1979), p. 1.
42. See Herbert J. Gans, *The Urban Villagers* (New York: Free Press, 1962), pp. 27–28; Gelb and Palley, op. cit., Chapter II.
43. "CBS Election Day Survey," *National Journal,* 4 (November 11, 1972), p. 1733.
44. *Gallup Opinion Index* (December 1972), 8.
45. *The New York Times,* November 5, 1970, p. 31.
46. Maurice Carroll, "Moynihan Defeats Buckley for New York Senate Seat," *The New York Times,* November 3, 1976, p. 19.
47. Paul Wilkes, "As the Blacks Move In, the Ethnics Move Out," *The New York Times Magazine,* January 24, 1971, p. 11. © 1971 by The New York Times Company. Reprinted by permission.
48. Andrew M. Greeley, "Catholics and Coalition: Where Should They Go," in *Emerging Coalitions in American Politics,* ed. by Seymour Martin Lipset (San Francisco: Institute for Contemporary Studies, 1978), pp. 286–87.
49. Thomas R. Dye, "City-Suburban Social Distance and Public Policy," *Social Forces,* 44 (September 1965), 103.
50. Ibid.
51. Ibid., p. 106.
52. Joel S. Berke and John J. Callahan, "Serrano v. Priest, Milestone or Millstone for School Finance," *Journal of Public Law,* 21 (1972), 47.
53. Ibid., p. 62.
54. This problem is discussed at length in Philip M. Stein, *The Rape of the Taxpayer* (New York: Vintage, 1974), pp. 381–97.
55. Ibid., pp. 7–8.

56. Peirce, op. cit., p. 490.
57. Ibid., p. 331.
58. *The Washington Post,* November 4, 1976, p. A21.
59. See Maxwell Glen, "At the Wire Corporate PAC's Came Through for the GOP," *National Journal,* 11 (February 3, 1979), 174–77.
60. Ibid., p. 174.
61. *The New Republic,* 180 (June 23, 1979), 2.
62. Robert Reinhold, "New Teams, New Attitudes Run the Nation's City Halls," *The New York Times,* June 17, 1979, p. E4.

The Economic
and Fiscal Conditions
of Urban America

INTRODUCTION

As we have seen, metropolitan areas usually consist of a central city, often some satellite cities, and a ring of suburbs that traditionally provided bedrooms for the city. Increasingly, however, suburbs are developing as integrated residential and industrial clusters around the city. As industries and the middle class migrate from the central city, the poor, young, and old, remain. This population often is disproportionately nonwhite and Hispanic. These remaining groups tend to be the least productive from a perspective of capital generation and growth, though the most expensive from the vantage point of required social welfare services. These social costs generate serious problems relating to the provision of services to the central cities at a time when it is becoming increasingly more expensive to develop good services. As the middle class and industry leave, who is to pay?

Given the mobility of the American people and the significant population shifts of the past twenty-five years, many of the urban poor are recent migrants from other sections of the country. A cogent argument may be made that the residents of the communities to which these migrants move should not be made to bear the costs required to support and educate them. These costs should equitably be incurred by the residents of the whole nation.[1]

The pages that follow will contain some discussion of the economic and fiscal consequences of the flight from the central cities. In particular, the economic impact of this exodus on many of the central cities will be considered. To understand more fully the fiscal problems that have afflicted many urban jurisdictions, the effects of the existing taxing system and the proliferation of government units will be examined to see how these two conditions have interacted to sustain an urban crisis in the United States. Given the constraints of political organization, the mechanisms for fiscal allocation will be discussed to determine whether there might be a more equitable and adequate way to allocate resources for urban America.

Intergovernmental Fiscal Relationships

Metropolitan areas have become balkanized and fragmented. Municipal deficit areas—those areas of low income residents and declining commerce—are increasingly separate from the jurisdictions where new industry and commerce are locating, as well as from the upper and middle income bedroom communities. This separation threatens the social balance in these jurisdictions. Such social balance had served an important purpose. The Advisory Commission on Intergovernmental Relations (ACIR) has suggested:

> By far the most important social function performed by the great "balanced" municipalities was political in the Aristotelian sense—that of keeping the public peace by moderating the competing demands of the various classes that comprise the urban body politic.[2]

Simultaneously with this expanding balkanization, the central city has been forced to provide costly services with the concomitant development of large municipal payrolls that often outstrip municipal resources. The demands made on the older central cities for high-cost services such as education and health as well as the demands being made on the suburban communities for new schools, roads, water and sewer extensions have often forced these local jurisdictions to enlarge their payrolls and budgets at a rate faster than that of the national government.[3]

Between 1950 and 1978, state-local revenues had increased by over

1,000 percent. During this 28-year period, these revenues had increased from $23 billion to $224 billion.[4] Though the amount sounds large, such financing still has not been adequate to meet urban needs. The amount of money that local jurisdictions can raise through taxation, as well as the types of taxes that can be utilized, is limited. Local jurisdictions generate most of their tax revenue from the property tax, though some local governments use sales taxes and limited income taxes.

Politics in 1978 began to take a turn away from the continued expansion of the property tax as a local revenue source. On June 6, 1978, Californians voted overwhelmingly in support of Proposition 13—a constitutional amendment that among other things rolled back local property taxes and restricted severely any future increases in such taxes. California's lead in reducing the local property tax bite was followed by Nevada and Idaho. Other states—Alabama, Missouri, North Dakota, and South Dakota—passed somewhat different provisions to limit such taxation.[5] Also, state and local income taxes compete with the federal income tax and the relative tax levels in other jurisdictions, and the amount of revenue that can be raised at the state or local level with this tax mechanism, is thus politically limited. The other tax mechanism that states and localities often use is the general sales tax. States share this revenue source with local areas for functions such as welfare and education. As a result of these conditions, it is not surprising that state and local bonded indebtedness increased from $24 billion in 1950 to $221 billion in 1975.[6]

City governments have increasingly received more of their revenues from federal and state sources. In fiscal 1977, such intergovernmental sources provided local governments with $42.5 billion, a $3.5 billion increase over the previous year. Of this revenue, just over $13.5 billion came from the federal government[7]; the remainer came from the states. The greatest amount of state aid to localities goes for public welfare (31.6 percent), followed by education (21.9 percent), general local government support (18.4 percent), and highways (11.6 percent). The largest amount of federal aid was appropriated for revenue sharing (34.6 percent), urban renewal and housing (8.9 percent), and education—excluding independent school districts—(2.7 percent). Before the enactment of general revenue sharing legislation in 1972, state governments had provided 86.1 percent of the intergovernmental aid received by local governments; by fiscal 1977, this proportion of aid had been reduced to 70.2 percent.[8] In fiscal 1975, municipal general expenditures for public welfare were almost $3.8 billion; education expenditures were almost $6.1 billion; hospital expenditures were approximately $3.56 billion.[9] These expenditure levels were reached even though, in many areas, a significant share of public welfare expenditures is financed by state (or state and county) rather than municipal revenues and public education is financed mainly through taxes collected from special school districts rather than from municipalities.

The burden of public welfare and educational expenditures on urban areas is most apparent where a substantial portion of such costs falls directly on the local jurisdiction—especially the central city. For example, in fiscal 1975 in New York State, the payment of 19.2 percent of all public welfare costs was the responsibility of local jurisdictions. California's local jurisdictions paid 24.6 percent of public welfare costs, Minnesota's local governments paid 28.6 percent of these expenditures, and New Hampshire's local jurisdictions covered 27.6 percent of these costs. Other states had different fiscal arrangements with their local governments for the payment of public welfare costs.[10]

Similarly, education expenses sometimes fall on local governments rather than special school districts. In such situations, municipalities are often responsible for some of the costs. In Rhode Island, for example, in fiscal 1975, 55.7 percent of revenues for primary and secondary education were locally derived. This amounted to $143 million out of a total of $257 million spent on public primary and secondary schools in that state. Because school districts spent only 2.5 percent of the direct general costs in Rhode Island, municipalities and townships were left with the remaining local revenue obligations.[11] When counties or special districts, which are not necessarily coterminous with the city boundaries, are responsible for covering local costs, the fiscal problem for the city is not as severe as when the city itself—either as a municipality or as the major or only population concentration in the county—is the jurisdiction mandated by the state to cover service delivery costs. For example, New York City has the latter problem because the state treats it as a fiscally responsible county for the purposes of providing local welfare funds. In addition, it is treated as a school district for the purposes of raising local revenues for schools. Despite significant infusions of state aid, New York City has had trouble remaining financially solvent, in part because of its high degree of local fiscal responsibility.

The fiscal dilemmas of the central cities are characterized by at least three discrete trends. First, high cost citizens are concentrated in the central cities; the cost of services they need outstrips the revenue resources of these cities. For example, Essex County, New Jersey (which includes the city of Newark), spent 27 percent of its local revenues in fiscal year 1971 on public welfare, whereas only 9 percent of New Jersey's general revenues were spent on public welfare throughout the state.[12] In November 1975, Maryland attempted to reduce costs by cutting $12 million in its medical assistance program; this aid was available to the 427,100 welfare recipients and other medically needy persons in Maryland. The cuts restricted hospital in-patient care, dental services, podiatry services, visual care, and medical supplies. The impact of this cut fell most heavily on the services available in Baltimore, which has 60 percent of Maryland's Medicaid recipients. Secondly, with its disproportionate number of high cost students, the central city has less own source revenue to spend on the education of such students than the wealthier suburbs. Finally, municipal services for high-cost citizens, greater population density, and the need to provide services for commuters force the central cities to spend more than most suburbs for police, fire protection, and sanitation services.

In 1975, per capita expenditures for all municipalities were $358.65. However, larger jurisdictions had higher per capita expenditures than smaller jurisdictions. Thus jurisdictions with 1,000,000 or more people spent $844.44 per capita compared to $193.55 per capita in those municipalities with fewer than 50,000 people (see Table 1).

If the cities try to raise revenues, their industrial and commercial enterprises may seek to relocate elsewhere. The same reality exists, to some extent, when suburbs consider increasing their tax rates. Also, high cost state programs, such as New York's Medicaid Program of the late 1960s, lead to threats by industry that they will leave the state. In New York State, some industries threatened to relocate if this revenue absorbing program was not curtailed. The Medicaid Program in New York was curtailed in the face of these threats.[13]

The movement of commerce and industry from highly urbanized areas was illustrated by a study conducted by the Center for Urban Policy Research of Rutgers University. This study showed that the highly urbanized New Jersey counties of Essex (which includes Newark) and Hudson (which includes Jersey City) would continue to lose commerce and industry in the 1970s while the less urbanized counties of Bergen, Middlesex, Union, and Monmouth would continue to gain employment opportunities.[14] This pattern also was noted in a study conducted by the National League of Cities. This study cited the following reasons for industry's leaving major central cities: (1) taxes in these cities were too high, and around every central city were dozens of tax jurisdictions with much lower tax rates; (2) land in the central cities is too expensive and too difficult to assemble; (3) traffic jams eliminated the central-city advantage of easy access; and, (4) cities cannot provide physical safety.[15] As a result of these problems, the nation's major metropolis, New York City, lost the headquarters of companies such as Universal Oil, Johns Manville, American Can, Shell Oil, Cyanamid, Pepsi-Cola, and Flintkote.[16]

Such central city decline also results in declining employment opportunities for blue collar workers. A 1977 report of the Advisory Commission on Intergovernmental Relations noted that in 1972 the central cities of the metropolitan areas of the Northeast had 81.1 percent of the manufacturing employment that they had in 1963. (From 1960 to 1975, they had lost, on the average, 3.2 percent of their total population.) In the Midwest, the comparable figure for manufacturing employment was 103 percent. (However, from 1960 to 1975, their population had increased on the average of 13.5 percent.) Such cities as Chicago, St. Louis, and Akron sustained severe job losses. Also, Philadelphia and Bridgeport lost an average of 19 percent of their manufacturing jobs and Newark, New Jersey, lost 37 percent of its manufacturing jobs during this fifteen year period.[17]

Table 1 / AVERAGE ANNUAL RATE OF GROWTH IN PER CAPITA EXPENDITURE, AND SELECTED OTHER ITEMS, BY CITY POPULATION—SIZE GROUPS, 1962–75

City Size	Per Capita Expenditures, 1962	Per Capita Expenditures, 1975	Annual Average Rate of Growth in Per Capita Expenditures, 1962–75	Per Capita Aid, 1962	Per Capita Aid, 1975	Annual Average Rate of Growth in Per Capita Aid, 1962–75	Aid ÷ Own-Source Revenue, 1962	Aid ÷ Own-Source Revenue, 1975	Number of Cities, 1962	Number of Cities, 1975
All municipalities	$113.56	$358.65	9.20%	$22.66	$144.76	15.27%	25.85%	65.1%	—	—
1,000,000 +	219.11	844.44	10.89	49.50	437.83	18.22	28.50	90.5	5	6
500,000–999,999	166.49	531.95	9.30	39.53	216.68	13.94	32.23	71.5	17	20
300,000–499,999	124.06	413.96	9.65	25.11	156.07	15.07	27.08	60.76	21	20
200,000–299,999	126.87	395.31	9.05	22.59	153.57	15.83	23.53	64.22	19	17
100,000–199,999	122.73	340.66	8.13	23.24	118.60	13.35	24.43	54.56	68	95
50,000–99,999	111.25	295.62	7.75	19.11	90.76	12.68	22.21	46.55	180	229
Less than 50,000	63.16	193.55	8.98	10.44	62.84	14.75	21.23	47.07	17,690	18,130

Source: ACIR Staff computations based on data from U.S. Department of Commerce, Bureau of the Census, *Compendium of City Government Finance in 1962* and U.S. Department of Commerce, Bureau of the Census, *Compendium of City Government Finances in 1975*, various tables.

The national and international organization of industry and commerce in the United States permits many industries to play the role of restrainer of public development at the local and state levels. When an industry has a component in a city and its employees have no strong ties to the city because they are "company citizens," not local citizens, public service development does not have to be a major concern of the company elite. If costs increase too much, inasmuch as the management group is not associated in any long-term sense with the city, the company can leave with minimum difficulties for their management employees. This may cause economic dislocation for the city but not for the company or for most of the members of its management. Indeed, their ability to move is facilitated by the fact that a number of major companies in the United States are multinational or foreign-owned. Prominent multinational corporations include the IBM Corporation and Unilever.[18] Acquisitions of American holdings by major foreign companies include Certain-teed Products Corporation by Saint Gobain (France), Computest Corporation by Siemens (Germany), Dearborn-Storm Corporation by Trafalger House Investments (England), Franklin Stores Corporation by Standard and Chartered Banking Group (England), Grand Union Company by Cavenham Limited (England), and Travelodge International, Inc., by Trust House Forte Ltd. (England).[19]

Given the high costs—translated, this means taxes—of services such as public welfare or pollution control, a state unconcerned with public development needs may provide a better home for business in terms of its profit picture. Also, the internal complex of politics within the states and, indeed within the cities, may effectively restrain social programs and civic improvements. The public often seeks simple solutions to complex problems. It may for example be satisfied with a diet of state and local law-and-order statements by public officials, as one could witness with the popularity of Mayor Frank Rizzo in Philadelphia in the 1970s. Or, the public may support rollbacks on property tax rates or lids on state spending. This was the case in 1978–79 when voters in perhaps a dozen states supported a variety of taxing and spending limits.[20]

How States and Local Jurisdictions Tax

Total governmental expenditures in the United States for 1978 amounted to $685 billion. State and local government expenditures amounted to $224 billion.[21] At the state level, the largest expenditures in recent years have been for education, public welfare, and highway construction and maintenance. Because the costs of these services have increased substantially, the states have been seeking new sources of revenue. The mechanism they have used most often is the tax structure. From 1959 to 1969, state governments introduced thirty-six new taxes, and raised existing taxes 376 times.[22] As noted previously, however, a movement to curtail state and local taxing and spending surfaced in 1978. In fact, in

1978, twenty-one states cut taxes amounting to around $2.4 billion. Increases in taxes in eight other states amounted to a total gain in taxation of only $200 million in those states.[23] Because state taxation is not very elastic (that is, there are restrictions on its ability to expand), by the late 1960s and early 1970s, federal aid had become the most important single source of state revenue, followed by state general sales and income taxes. In fiscal 1975, 30.9 percent of all state tax collections were derived from general or gross receipts sales taxes and 23.5 percent of their tax collections came from individual income taxes.[24]

The most expensive service provided by localities is usually education, though often special school districts have the responsibility for the delivery of this service. Nevertheless, it is often the largest expenditure for municipalities, too. Police protection, highways, welfare, fire protection, and hospitals also receive substantial appropriations from local jurisdictions. As cities increase in population, they spend a higher proportion of their budgets on education, welfare, health, and housing and a lesser proportion on highways, police, firefighting, and sewage services.[25] It was estimated by the ACIR that in fiscal 1978, 85.1 percent of the forty-seven largest cities' (excluding New York City) own source general revenue came from federal and state aid. Federal aid was estimated to be 49.7 percent of these cities' own source general revenue, and state aid was estimated to represent 35.4 percent of these revenues. The state figure includes unsegregatable federal aid that passes through the state.[26] The significance of "external" aid can be seen if one considers the changes from 1957 to 1978. Table 2 provides such an analysis of federal aid for fifteen selected cities.

State and local taxes may be progressive or regressive. Progressive taxes take a greater percentage of income from those with higher incomes; regressive taxes take a greater percentage of income from those in lower income brackets. Income taxes are most likely to be progressive taxes, while sales taxes are always regressive. Other taxes are tied to the benefit that is provided. Examples of this type of tax include special assessment taxes, earmarked for sewer and water use, educational assessments for meeting school expenses, and gasoline taxes earmarked for highway maintenance. Cities may also impose user charges such as bridge tolls for maintenance of bridges and roadways. States increasingly have also sought to gain revenues through lotteries in which revenue collected is earmarked for specific areas such as education or services for the elderly. However, as we have noted previously, for most state governments, the general sales tax is the largest tax revenue source. Thirty states levy general sales taxes. Municipalities in twenty-six states are authorized by state law to collect city sales taxes. In some states, cities share the revenues of state-collected sales taxes. Although a sales tax is regressive, its incremental impact on the individual taxpayer often increases its acceptability, especially when it is a municipal tax, because it shifts some of the tax burden to tourists and commuters (see Table 3).

Table 2 / DIRECT FEDERAL AID AS A PERCENT OF OWN-SOURCE GENERAL REVENUE, SELECTED CITIES AND FISCAL YEARS, 1957–78

City	Fiscal Years				Exhibit: Per Capita Federal Aid [2]	
	1957	1967	1976	1978 Est.	1976	1978 Est.
St. Louis	0.6%	1.0%	23.6%	56.1%	$86	$228
Newark	0.2	1.7	11.4	64.2	47	291
Buffalo	1.3	2.1	55.6	75.9	163	239
Cleveland	2.0	8.3	22.8	60.3	65	190
Boston	*	10.0	31.5	30.2	204	219
Unweighted averages	0.8	4.6	29.0	57.3	113	233
Baltimore	1.7	3.8	38.9	46.4	167	225
Philadelphia	0.4	8.8	37.7	53.8	129	204
Detroit	1.3	13.1	50.2	76.8	161	274
Chicago	1.4	10.9	19.2[1]	42.1	47	117
Atlanta	4.3	2.0	15.1	40.0	52	167
Unweighted averages	1.8	7.7	32.2	51.8	111	197
Denver	0.6	1.2	21.2	25.9	90	150
Los Angeles	0.7	0.7	19.3	39.8	54	134
Dallas	0	*	20.0	17.8	51	54
Houston	0.2	3.1	19.4	23.8	44	71
Phoenix	1.1	10.6	35.0	58.7	57	117
Unweighted averages	0.5	3.1	23.0	**33.2**	61	105
Unweighted average of 15 cities	1.1	5.2	28.1	47.5	95	179

Source: ACIR staff computations based on U.S. Bureau of the Census, *City Government Finances in 1957, 1967, and 1976.* Estimated city own-source general revenue for 1978 based on annual average increase between 1971 and 1976. Direct federal grants to each city for fiscal 1978 based on (a) ACIR staff estimates of the federal stimulus programs for 1978 and (b) Richard Nathan's estimates for all other federal aid in fiscal 1978 as set forth in his testimony before the Joint Economic Committee on July 28, 1977. Printed in Advisory Commission on Intergovernmental Relations, *Significant Features of Fiscal Federalism, 1976–77 Edition,* 3 (Washington, D.C.: U.S. Government Printing Office, 1977).

* Less than 0.05 percent.

1 Percentage based on federal aid excluding general revenue sharing. Funds withheld pending judicial determination.

2 Based on 1975 population.

Forty states levy income taxes on individuals and/or corporations. Municipalities in eight states also levy such taxes. State taxes are not as steeply progressive as the federal income tax; municipal income taxes are less progressive because they are usually levied on a flat percentage basis. Municipal income taxes may tax residents, nonresidents employed in cities, or both.

Table 3 / THE STATE AND LOCAL REVENUE SYSTEM, 1976

Federal aid	20%
Sales and gross receipts tax	19%
Property tax	18%
Income tax	11%
Charges and miscellaneous general revenues	15%
All other revenue (includes utility, liquor store, and insurance trust revenue)	13%
All other taxes	4%

Source: Advisory Commission on Intergovernmental Relations, *Significant Features of Fiscal Federalism, 1976 Edition, Vol. I, Trends* (Washington, D.C.: U.S. Government Printing Office, 1976), p. 34.

While states have increasingly relied on sales and income taxes, property taxes constitute more than two-thirds of the locally collected revenues.[27] Property taxes apply to *real property,* such as land and buildings and *personal property,* such as automobiles and washing machines or stocks and bonds. Taxes result from *assessment,* which is an estimate, first, of the cash value of the property and, secondly, of the rate at which the assessed property may be taxed. Thus, a homeowner's house and property may be assessed at a cash value of $60,000. The rate of assessment may be 20 percent of $60,000 or $12,000. The rate of taxation may be 5 percent of $12,000 or $600. Wide variations exist among states and localities regarding the cash value of property, the assessment rate, and the tax rate.

There are some limitations on the revenues that can be raised by using the property tax. Certain properties may be nontaxable and therefore will be waived from the tax rolls. Churches, state facilities such as universities, and federal landholdings such as army bases or building complexes are exempt from state and local property tax. These facilities are frequently concentrated in older, often deteriorating cities. For example, over half of Newark, New Jersey's developed property is tax exempt. Another problem with the property tax is its regressive nature. It falls much more heavily on poor families than on higher income groups.[28] It also has been criticized as a deterrent to property improvement because higher valued property will have a higher tax assessment.

Often states and localities cannot develop sufficient sources of funding through taxation. "Pay as you go" arrangements may not seem feasible, since inflation may increase building costs over a period of time or urbanization may increase property valuation over a period of time. Thus, states and localities may resort to borrowing. Borrowing takes two main forms: general obligation bonds and revenue bonds. General obligation bonds are backed by the jurisdiction's taxing and revenue powers. Usually they have been issued at a moderate rate of interest as investors feel that they are generally unlikely to be defaulted. Revenue bonds are supported by the returns of the project undertaken, such as highway, bridge, or tunnel tolls. They are considered by investors to be of somewhat greater risk and thus are usually offered at a somewhat higher interest rate. Borrowing is usually limited by state constitutional or statutory debt limits and by state requirements regarding public referendums. Such state and local government bonds are termed *municipals*. The revenues received from such bond interest are exempt from the federal income tax, thus encouraging investors to purchase these bonds. As central cities and urbanized suburbs have turned increasingly to borrowing to meet their service needs, more and more of their revenues are earmarked for servicing bonded debt.

Very large debts may undermine the financial viability of states and localities. Increased reliance on bonded debt in states and localities is due, in part, to payments that must be made to meet burgeoning state and local employee payrolls and to meet the service needs of states and localities. Just such a condition had actually undermined the financial stability of New York City by 1975.[29] According to the U.S. Bureau of the Census, at the end of fiscal 1975, state and local governments in Alaska, Connecticut, Delaware, the District of Columbia, Hawaii, Nebraska, New York, and Washington had average per capita debts of over $1,500.[30] As for the cities themselves, in 1976 Boston had a per capita debt of $1,145.61; Pittsburgh had a per capita debt of $817.50; and San Francisco had a debt of $808.43 per capita.[31]

The revenue sources available to local jurisdictions clearly lack the elasticity of the federal income tax and federal corporate tax. Indeed, federal revenues have become an indispensable element in financing state and local projects. Also, state and local revenue sources are often more regressive than the federal income tax. Finally, as state and local revenue sources fail to expand to meet their fiscal needs, they often resort to bonded indebtedness. If this device is used excessively, too great a portion of state and municipal revenue may be needed merely to pay back the interest and principal of bonded obligation, and states and localities may have insufficient funds to meet current service commitments as a result. If that happens, they must cut back commitments to education, fire and police protection, and other essential services or request increased federal assistance for state and local governmental functions. An interesting case of just such a situation arose in Illinois in 1971. In that year, Governor Richard B. Ogilvie successfully sought a broad interpretation from the U.S. Department of Health, Education, and Welfare for the possible state use of federal funds for social services. He requested funds for state welfare programs from the federal government because he did not want to appeal to a resistant state legislature, nor did he want to set stricter eligibility standards for welfare programs or lower cash payments in welfare categorical programs, as would have been necessary without additional money. Ultimately, Illinois received $188 million in federal social service grants for fiscal year 1972, an amount that more than compensated for the expected state deficit in the welfare expense area. (This amount was $163.5 million more than Illinois had initially received for fiscal year 1971.)[32]

The Proliferation of Governments

It seems reasonably clear that because of the extent of urban decay and the complexity of urban problems, necessary and meaningful programs for the alleviation of these conditions will be very costly. Only by recognizing the relationship between different structural and social dimensions of urban problems and the need for a national perspective and strong national initiatives, can an adequate resolution be found in terms of urban public policy.

Part of the problem facing local jurisdictions with high program costs and low revenue expectations has been caused by proliferation of government jurisdictions with separate taxing powers. Within the fifty states in 1977, there were 3,042 counties, 18,862 municipalities, and 16,822 townships. In addition, there were 15,174 school districts and 25,962 special districts for such purposes as urban water supply, fire protection, sewage, and school buildings. There were a total of 79,862 local governments within the fifty separate states for an average of 1,597 governmental units per state (see Table 4). Though there has been a continuing decline in the number of school districts, there has been a continuing increase in the number of special districts for land-use development and sewer development. Such districts increased by over 300 percent in the twenty-five years from 1942 to 1977.

Several reasons are often offered to explain the multiplicity of governmental units in this country. It has been argued that special districts were created because the established governmental units were not able to meet adequately the new and changing problems of urbanizing areas. For example, water districts were developed that provided services to larger areas than just a town; often, unincorporated areas surrounding incorporated towns and cities are included in service districts. Developing fiscal units broader than existing municipalities often made it more economically feasible to provide services.

Though they have declined in number in the past thirty years, school districts are still the most numerous type of special district. Historically, in many areas, very small school districts developed because of transportation limitations for children. More recently, districts have been consolidated to provide education from kindergarten through twelfth grade. These districts are often not coterminous with municipal government boundaries. In part, this was done to include unincorporated areas into the districts, as well as to minimize the potential of school jurisdictions being taken over by municipal government. Special districts for schools have been especially popular since many people want the education

Table 4 / Number of Governmental Units by Level of Government, 1942–77

Level of Government	1942	1952	1957	1962	1967	1972	1977
U.S. government	1	1	1	1	1	1	1
States	48	48	48	50	50	50	50
Local governments	155,067	116,694	102,279	91,186	81,248	78,218	79,862
Counties	3,050	3,049	3,047	3,043	3,049	3,044	3,042
Municipalities	16,220	16,778	17,183	18,000	18,048	18,517	18,862
Townships	18,919	17,202	17,198	17,142	17,105	16,991	16,822
School districts	108,579	67,346	50,446	34,678	21,782	15,781	15,174
Special districts	8,299	12,319	14,405	18,323	21,264	23,885	25,962

Source: U.S. Bureau of the Census, Census of Governments: 1967, 1972, and 1977, Vol. 1, Governmental Organization.

function close enough to permit them to be able to participate in educational decision making. If a unit of government is big and complex and distant from the serviced population, participation in the decision-making process is often more difficult than it is in a geographically closer structural unit.

• SEVERAL FORMS OF MUNICIPAL GOVERNMENT

The structure of local government can be a factor affecting the kinds of political decisions made at the local level in urban areas. Thus, it is pertinent to review some of the basic forms of municipal government, since such forms may have an impact on decisions affecting urban areas. As noted elsewhere, municipalities derive their prerogatives from state constitutions and state legislative actions. Municipal charters derived from the states vary among the states in certain respects. The most common form of charter is the *general act charter*, which provides that municipalities falling into certain size classifications will possess the same combination of structures and powers. Charters that permit municipalities within certain size classifications to choose among a variety of organizational forms and powers are termed *optional charters*. State charters that grant a specified set of powers and organizational forms to a specific municipal area are termed *special act charters*. Finally, some state constitutions allow cities to draft and approve their own basic governmental forms. This procedure is known as *constitutional home rule*. While home rule permits cities to determine their governmental form, the state can still limit the ability of cities to regulate, to provide services, and to generate revenues.

There are three basic forms of municipal government in metropolitan areas: the *mayor-council form* of government, the *commission form*, and the *council-manager form*. The mayor-council system is most popular in the larger cities. This structure is the only form of government found in American cities with a population of over 1 million. Commission government is found in cities of various sizes with the exception of the largest cities. Council-manager forms are common in cities with less than 1 million population, but not in very small cities.

Mayor-council forms of government are characterized by a separation of powers between the executive (the mayor) and the legislature (the city council). Mayor-council government has three variations: the strong mayor form, the weak mayor form, and the mayor with a chief administrative officer (CAO) form. The weak mayor form is called that because it gives little administrative power to the mayor. Under this form, both legislative and administrative powers are exercised by the city council. The council is usually elected on the basis of city ward jurisdictional areas; it may appoint a number of city administrators; council members may serve on a number of municipal boards and, in some cases, have responsibility for preparing the city's budget. Mayors under this system are weak because many boards, commissions, and city administrators are not under the mayor's direct control. The mayor shares significant administrative authority with the city council. In addition, some administrators are not under direct mayoral control because they are elected at large. One commentary on American municipal government has noted, and perhaps understated: "Given the complexities of the modern urban situation, the weak mayor form is not well suited to the development of policy leadership in city government. Power and responsibility are widely diffused. . . ."[33] However, even though Chicago has a weak mayor-council form of government, control of the Democratic Party organization in that city permitted Mayor Richard J. Daley to play a commanding role in city government in the 1960s and 1970s.

The concern for providing political leadership in urban policy formulation has led to a general preference for the strong mayor-council form of government in large American cities. Under the strong mayor-council form, mayors are directly elected; they usually have responsibility for preparing the city budget, appointing top-level administrators, and supervising city administrators. The mayor often presides over the city council's meetings and usually has a veto over actions of the city council. Thus, the governmental structure permits such a mayor to play a central role in policy initiation and program development. However, as the public administrator Robert Moses has noted: "First-rate men can make third-rate machinery run well, and a third-rate man can wreck the best machinery."[34]

One device used to help the mayor sort out and control administrative responsibilities has been the position of chief administrative officer (CAO). This official is usually appointed by the mayor and may be subject to removal by the mayor. In some cities, the city council must approve appointment and/or removal. The CAO, working under the general supervision of the mayor, directs the daily administrative activities of the city. He or she may appoint some department administrators, although usually the approval of the mayor is necessary for such appointments. The CAO's function frees the mayor for the general policy leadership and conciliation roles that often require much of an urban mayor's time.

The commission form of government is found in about 6 percent of our cities, all of which have populations of over 5,000.[35] Under this form of government, elected commissioners constitute the legislative and executive body for the city. Individually, such officials serve as department heads for various city operating units. The commission form assumes, not always correctly, that political leaders possess a substantial amount of political competence and technical knowledge; in addition, it fails to clearly establish an accountable executive leadership.

A more popular form of government than either the mayor-council or commission form is the council-manager plan. Under this system, an elected city council provides political and policy-making leadership; administrative functions are carried out by a professional city manager appointed by, removable by, and accountable to the city council. Under this system, the manager may appoint and remove department heads, prepare the city budget for council consideration, and supervise the operation of municipal activities. By 1979, 55 percent of all American cities with over 5,000 people operated under the council-manager form. Over half the American cities with populations between 25,000 and 250,000 have this form of government. It is the predominant form of government in metropolitan suburbs around such major cities as New York, Chicago, St. Louis, and Los Angeles.[36] Often the mayor is not popularly elected in this system; instead the council designates one of its members to serve as mayor. The duties of the mayor are generally limited to presiding at meetings of the municipal legislature and to serving a ceremonial role. The city manager provides a technocratic function concerned with professional management, administrative accountability, and economic efficiency. The manager operates with some success in relatively homogeneous, small and medium-sized, essentially middle class, metropolitan suburbs. This type of community often lacks intense political cleavage based on municipal issues. Since the city manager, as an appointed professional administrator, is not in a good position to provide policy leadership in heterogeneous urban areas where different economic and class cleavages must be resolved or ameliorated, a council-manager system in such communities can foster a paucity of needed public policy initiatives.

• COUNTY GOVERNMENT AND SPECIAL DISTRICTS

In addition to the municipal governments, the counties and the special districts are also important jurisdictions in the governance of urban areas. The traditional functions of the county under state constitutions and statutes include collecting taxes and fees, maintaining roads, recording land titles, administering certain health and welfare functions, and providing some judicial functions in areas not located within municipal jurisdictions. Often county government consists of elected supervisors with an elected or appointed chief supervisor. Most counties maintain the long ballot electing a county clerk, treasurer, sheriff, county attorney, and other officers, thus tending to promote divided government and reducing the likelihood of unified policy leadership. County functions are usually designated by the separate states and are limited to the specified areas just noted. Within these areas, counties have administrative and legislative powers. The legislative powers fall essentially into the financial and regulatory areas. The financial powers include levying taxes and borrowing money, as well as appropriating revenues. Regulatory powers include establishment of land-use zoning and enforcement of land-use codes, as well as enforcement of fire-safety codes and liquor licensing. A few urbanized suburban areas have expanded the uses of the county and now maintain the county as a unit for governing unincorporated areas, using forms similar to the mayor-council forms of municipalities.

Baltimore County, Maryland; New Castle County, Delaware; and St. Louis County, Missouri; all use the county for such urban governance. Also, in recent years, several major cities—including Detroit, Cleveland, and Louisville—that have been caught in fiscal squeezes have seen some of their services assumed by their counties. For example, during the 1970s, Cleveland turned over its sewers, mass transit, port authority, jails, and health and welfare systems to a city-county system that diminished the power of both the city council and the mayor to regulate services for citizens. George L. Fortes, President of the Cleveland City Council, observed: "You can see that all we're going to end up with is police and firemen. And those are the services the county doesn't want anyway."[37]

Finally, some essential municipal functions are governed by special districts, which serve a single purpose, such as providing school services, fire protection, sewers, and water conservation. Chicago has carried the special district as far as creating a Chicago Park District to administer parks, museums, theaters, and zoos. A major advantage of maintaining special districts has been the flexibility of the unit—it may be single county or multicounty or it may not follow county boundaries at all. In addition, the district has taxing power solely related to the provision of the special service. Thus, in addition to its flexibility, the special district system has the advantage of having a separate budget. The result of the budget separation is that the function governed by a special district does not lose out to alternative programmatic areas in municipal budget decisions—though the taxpayers may choose to limit the district's spending or borrowing. However, even given the advantages just noted, the fragmentation associated with the proliferation of government jurisdictions may be more negative than positive in its effects since such fragmentation tends to undermine priority determination and rational policy planning in urban areas and thus reinforces some of the problems associated with the crisis of urban America.

• LIMITATIONS OF THE PREVALENT FORMS

Because of their effects on leadership patterns and planning styles in urban areas, the existing forms of municipal government do not provide optimal structures for urban governance. Their inadequacies are due in large measure to the fragmented structure of government in American urban areas, which is sometimes intensified by the lack of strong executive leadership.

Intense demands are made on mayors for special leadership skills to meet the needs for social change. However, the realities of urban political life make it difficult for mayors to perform both effectively and consistently as chief executives. As a result, a paradox arises because of fragmentation of authority and dispersal of power in the formal structure of government of American urban areas. In the larger cities, governmental authority is dispersed among federal, state, county, and city jurisdictions. Frank Yorty, former mayor of Los Angeles, complained that the mayor of Los Angeles has no authority over many important urban policy areas. The school board is independently elected, the welfare program is county operated and state funded, the city housing authority is an independent authority, transit system development is under state authority, and the health department is part of a county structure.[38] In Los Angeles, as well as in other cities, authority is also dispersed among the mayor, the council, and the various independent officials, boards, and commissions designated by the electorate to deal with specific services and functions.[39] In addition, the entrenchment of a well-institutionalized municipal civil service often limits executive policy leadership in the cities. Stringent civil service rules covering entrance to positions, promotion, and seniority for all but the highest administrative levels reduce the flexibility of political leadership to promote programmatic innovation. This has led one political analyst to comment that the impact of such civil service bureaucracies has led many cities to "become well-run, but ungoverned."[40]

The structure and lines of authority of urban government limit the implementation of the strong programmatic leadership needed to deal with the economic and social problems of urban areas. To a significant extent, such constraints are related to the forms of municipal government structure (particularly, weak mayor systems), the fragmentation of governmental authority in metropolitan areas, the number of independent officers and commissions chosen in urban areas, the proliferation of special districts, and the nature of municipal civil service systems.

Alternative Methods of Fiscal Allocation

That the present system of urban governance is not providing necessary services equitably to the population is a generally accepted conclusion. Political jurisdictional splintering has, in fact, led to a division of the tax resources of metropolitan areas and has often left the central cities and sometimes the suburbs with insufficient resources to provide needed services. Because the traditional organizational forms have not been able to provide necessary services to urban populations, other mechanisms have evolved. It is useful at this point to understand these approaches and to understand some of their limitations. In part, the failure of the alternatives to be acceptable to the separate city and suburban jurisdictions has led to the continued fiscal splintering of urban areas and thus to the need for more inclusive policy linkages.

Four Basic Approaches

Four general approaches to the problems of urban fiscal management that do not require political consolidation or major reorganization have been tried:[41]

1. New operating agencies have been superimposed on the existing governmental structure.
2. Functions and responsibilities have been shifted to territorially broader limits.
3. Metropolitanwide financing has been used to support services.
4. Federal and state action has been taken to redistribute income.[42]

The first approach utilizes special districts. The second can be seen in county assumption of some functions. In twenty-one states, for example, public welfare services are administered and partially funded by county jurisdictions. The third method has been attempted when county or metropolitanwide taxing agencies are developed to collect and distribute funds to local units through the use of an equalization formula. In Canada, the Toronto area uses this approach for education. The final alternative leads to income redistribution by the reallocation of revenue at the federal or state level. Thus, in some states local school districts are almost totally state funded. Also, in recent years increased pressure has been placed on the federal government to assume total funding of public welfare.

In addition, some structural reorganizations that could affect fiscal resource allocation have received particular attention. In particular, metro-government and councils of government (COGs) have been utilized in various forms with that end in mind. In the pages that follow, these two systems will be described.

Metrogovernment

The underlying assumption for supporting metropolitanwide government is that such a form would provide for a more socially, politically, and fiscally balanced urban metropolitan area. In other words, the financial base would be broader and therefore funding for services would be more available to the city. Also, better services, integrating the needs and the demands of both city and suburb, could be more adequately met.

Two basic types of metropolitan government have been implemented: (1) the two-tier approach, and (2) the single-level approach. In *the two-tier system,* one new and unified level of government is established to handle functions that concern the entire area, and local jurisdictions are left to provide the functions that concern mainly the localities. The metropolitan county, federation, and metropolitan special district are the three forms of the two-tier system. These forms are semiconsolidations in that not all functions of government are consolidated in the upper tier. *The single-level approach* requires complete consolidation. A consolidation implies the merger of two or more units of government with equivalent legal status. The result of this process is a new government. Consolidation has taken three forms: (1) a county has been completely merged with its cities; (2) a county has been merged with its cities, but the county retains some of its functions; (3) some but not all the municipalities in a county are merged.[43]

Some implementation of metropolitan government has taken place since World War II. In 1947, Baton Rouge, Louisiana, partially merged its metropolitan functions with East Baton Rouge Parish. In 1953, the municipality of Metropolitan Toronto was created by the provincial parliament of Ontario (Canada), forming a federation of the city of Toronto and twelve surrounding suburbs. In Florida in 1957, Miami and Dade County adapted a two-tiered metropolitan government with limited application of the principle of federation, and, in 1962, the City of Nashville, Tennessee, consolidated with Davidson County into a single metropolitan areawide government.[44] The most recent attempt to operate a metropolitan government has been in the Portland, Oregon SMSA, where in 1978 a two-tiered government was established. The Portland SMSA has about 1 million people and takes in parts of three counties. The Portland Metropolitan Service District is the regional government tier with authority in land use, air and water quality, transportation, water supply, sewerage, waste disposal, and cultural activities. The municipal, county, and other local jurisdictions are the second tier, and will continue to provide such basic services as police protection and schools.[45]

Advocates of metropolitan government claim that such government enables a broader community to think through and resolve local areawide problems, and that metropolitan government would eliminate geographic, social, and economic fragmentation in areas such as education, housing, health services, transportation, and land use. A survey conducted after the first year of the Nashville metropolitan government's operation showed that a large majority of the voters did believe knowing who to call or see when they had a problem was easier under the combined government than it was under separate city and county government.[46] Moreover, developing metropolitan government as a fiscal system would, in the words of Luther Gulick, create a situation in which "the wealth, power and credit of the area as a whole may be mobilized for the solution of the overall problem of the area."[47] The advocates of metrogovernment may be correct, but they have had limited success in implementing their credo. Of course one could argue that even if metrogovernments were developed, the increasing interdependence of jurisdictions would still demand more extensive federal policy linkages. After all, environmental pollution does not respect metropolitan area boundaries any more than it respects state lines.

Regional Planning Agencies and Councils of Government

Whereas metrogovernments have not been very popular as organizational mechanisms to govern our urban areas, Regional Planning Agencies (RPAs) and Regional Planning Commissions (RPCs) are organizations with advisory responsibility for comprehensive planning that have been widely accepted. To date, they have been concerned primarily with land-use planning or the coordination of local plans. RPAs and RPCs have three basic forms. The oldest form is the county planning commission, dating back to 1922. In addition, there are city-county planning commissions and multijurisdictional planning commissions. The latter form is the most prevalent kind of planning commission. It is sponsored by two or more municipalities and/or counties. Members of these commissions and agencies are citizens appointed by the state government or the involved localities.[48]

Another type of regional organization is the Council of Government (COG). The governing boards of COGs are comprised predominately of the chief elected officials of the participating political jurisdictions; part of their funds come from local public sources.[49] They coordinate programs and they have legal status to receive funds and provide for staffing. These bodies perform a number of functions. For example, COGs are used as vehicles for metropolitanwide planning, governance, and administration in the Atlanta, Kansas City, and New York metropolitan areas and in the metropolitan areas in Texas. The functions of COGs range from the planning and development of highways, parks, and sewers (in Atlanta and its suburbs), to land-use planning (in the New York City region). One of the most powerful COGs currently in operation is the Twin Cities Metropolitan Council (in the St. Paul–Minneapolis Metropolitan Area). This council, established in 1967, has its own tax base, the power of review over all federal aid projects, and the control over metropolitan-wide concerns such as transit, parks, airports, and sewage. Its members are selected by the governor of Minnesota.[50] Such organizations temper to a certain extent the potential for fragmentation in the metropolitan area. It is important, however, to remember that while COGs have some powers of governance, they are essentially coordinating and planning bodies, and as such they are a confederal form.

Barriers to Consolidation

Intrastate and suburban/central city cleavages have with few exceptions prevented the formation of metropolitan governments. The suburban voters often do not want to be burdened by the problems or the fiscal pressures that confront the city. The cities often do not want to be absorbed in a "sea of suburbs." In Georgia, for example, if Atlanta had merged with its primarily white suburbs, then its majority nonwhite population would have lost the political power they had finally gained with the election of their first black mayor in 1973.

Furthermore, because good transportation and communication make it unnecessary for industry to be centralized in one location to operate effectively, it seems unlikely that metropolitan government could ensure as much of a social and fiscal balance as its advocates claim.

Finally, suburban counties often view the central city as a fiscal liability. Thus, in 1974, suburban delegates to the Maryland State Legislature threatened to filibuster moves to provide more state funds to alleviate Baltimore's fiscal problems.[51] Conversely, the cities sometimes see their suburbs as a drain on their resources. In 1975, Hartford, Connecticut, used legal actions to block its suburbs from collecting over $4 million in federal community development funds. The city claimed it needed the funds for housing the poor and the aged more than the suburbs needed the money for the roads, sewers, and parks they planned to build; the suburbs had not applied for funds to house the needy. The suburbs threatened to retaliate when funding questions relating to the city arose in the state legislature. Nicholas Carbone, the majority leader of the Hartford City Council, observed that the suburbs could not do too much to retaliate against the City of Hartford since they were not supporting it at a level commensurate with either its needs or their heavy reliance on the city and its services. For example, of the 116,000 jobs in Hartford, 70,000 were filled by nonresidents, while of the 98,000 jobs in the suburbs, only 18,700 were held by Hartford residents; three-quarters of the patients at Hartford Hospital were suburbanites; and only 40 percent of the students at Trinity College (Hartford) were from the city. Furthermore, over 90 percent of the region's poor live in the city, and the city has insufficient decent housing for these people. The suburbs are not providing housing for the needy. In fact, in several of the region's suburban communities, housing for the poor is all but prohibited by zoning restrictions.[52]

The fiscal plight of the cities is due in some measure to central city/suburban cleavages. In the suburban cities with populations between 15,000 to 50,000, the services and functions their people most want include quality education for their children, good fire protection service, and good police protection. The suburban constituencies try to get other less popular services from the central cities without paying for them, or they try to have some other level of government provide them. The core cities cannot afford to perform all the services of government while they continue to permit suburban governments to provide only limited services.[53] If we maintain this unequal condition without having a more inclusive jurisdiction—presumably the national government—assist with major forms of relief, many cities will fail to meet their obligations to their own citizens as well as to the citizens of their regions.

The Role of the States in Fiscal Allocation

Fiscal relief for urban problems at the state level has not been sufficiently forthcoming in part because, at the state level, the economic and social grievances of the cities are often those of politically and numerically weak minorities such as the aged, the poor, and the economically marginal working class. States, however, do provide some revenue to local governments. In fiscal 1976, in fact, about 35 percent of all municipal revenue in the nation's forty-seven largest cities was from state sources.[54] However, adequate fiscal relief for cities from the states is not perceived to be a realistic goal.

Governors and state legislatures may fear raising taxes will drive business from their states. They may also believe that a greater state financial commitment to the vast physical and social needs of urban areas will undermine the credit ratings of the states and lead to fiscal chaos. Such concerns among Massachusetts decision makers resulted in budgetary cutbacks in a wide range of social and physical services in the mid 1970s. The Advisory Commission on Intergovernmental Relations emphasized the problem of states' fears of potential loss of industry in the following terms: "No Governor proposes a major tax change, and surely no legislature adopts one, without considering how the enactment may affect the State's standing compared to that of neighboring and competing states."[55]

Moreover, the essential independence of states in determining their tax levels, the varying cultural and political backgrounds of the states, as well as the nature of interstate competition, result in wide variation among the states in the extent of taxing and the type of taxes used. The range of tax rates among the states is clearly very broad. Thus, in 1977 at the high end of the tax-paying scale, the state of Alaska and its local governments collected an average of $2,296 per person; a New Yorker's state and local tax bill per capita was an average $1,252; and an average Californian's tax bill was $1,089. At the low end of the scale, Arkansas collected the least taxes—$494 per person (see Figure 1).

Though it is becoming more difficult to fund programs at the state and local level, overall state and local tax revenues have increased faster than the inflation rate and many states and localities have made substantial tax efforts to meet public needs. However, as the Advisory Commission on Intergovernmental Relations has indicated, governors and legislatures fear that more adequate appropriations to deal with urban (and indeed rural) problems will place them at a competitive disadvantage in offering locations to manufacturing and commercial enterprises seeking low taxes, and thus at a disadvantage in providing jobs for the people of their states.

The Federal Role in Fiscal Allocation

Given the inelasticity of state and local tax resources, some additional fiscal relief at the national level is probably necessary to substantially alleviate the plight of the cities. At the present time, federal funds to states and localities are often categorical grants. These require the states to provide matching funds for specific programs—such as highways, education, sewers, and water systems. The same political conditions that have thwarted state and local initiative in social programming also thwart

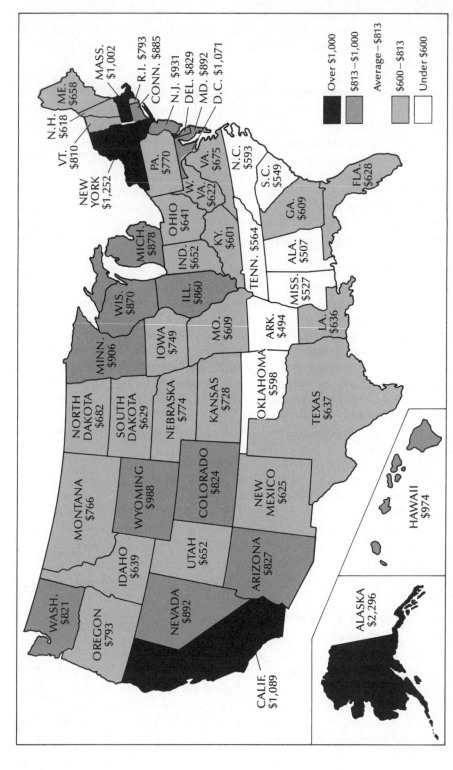

Figure 1 State and Local Per Capita Tax Burden in Fiscal 1976–77. (Reproduced with permission from *State Tax Levies*, published and copyrighted by Commerce Clearing House, Inc., 4025 W. Peterson Avenue, Chicago, Illinois 60646.)

the states' ability to obtain and use matching federal funds. The states with the least-developed social programs are usually the states least willing or least able to provide the maximum funding to receive the optimal federal grant. Furthermore, to some extent, the political forces operating in states and localities operate nationally as well. Therefore, though industries usually do not threaten to leave the nation as they may do in cities and states, they influence the national tax structure and spending priorities. Furthermore, voters who oppose state and local spending for social benefit programs often oppose national spending for these programs, too.

The State and Local Fiscal Assistance Act of 1972 and its 1976 amendments (revenue sharing), which provide "untied" monies to all state and general purpose local jurisdictions, was hailed by its supporters as a source of fiscal relief to urban areas. Under the initial legislation, Congress authorized $30.2 billion, which did not have to be matched by state and local jurisdictions, to be used over a five-year period for a variety of purposes. The 1976 amendments authorized an additional $25.6 billion to state and local governments through the 1980 fiscal year. In fiscal 1978, state governments received $2.3 billion and local governments received $4.5 billion in revenue sharing money. This distribution was very similar to the funding splits of previous years. (For example, in 1977, the states received $2.3 billion and the local governments received $4.4 billion.[56]) Almost thirty-nine thousand state and general-purpose local governments receive their share of the funds, based upon either of two distribution formulas. One of the formulas considers five factors—population, urban population, relative per capita income, tax effort, and state personal income tax collections. The other formula considers population, tax effort, and relative per capita income.

Revenue sharing has not, however, provided the degree of fiscal relief for which urban political leaders had hoped. In addition, the act does not establish national goals, so that the direction of funding is subject to many diverse local interests, including the interests of commercial and industrial groups who often exhibit little concern for basic issues of health or social services. Also, the amount of revenue provided many local jurisdictions is not sufficient to meet their revenue needs.

Richard P. Nathan and Charles F. Adams provided some insight into how revenue sharing funds have been utilized. They studied the expenditure patterns of twenty-nine cities, as well as several other jurisdictions, and they found that the smaller cities used about 75 percent of their revenue sharing funds to expand service programs (often building projects). Cities with populations of over 100,000 used over 50 percent of their revenue sharing money for tax relief or to avoid borrowing.[57] In fiscal 1977, the largest expenditure of federal revenue sharing funds by the 38,758 units of state and local governments that receive these funds was for education (19 percent), followed by police protection (14.4 percent) and highways (12.4 percent).[58] (See Table 5.)

Table 5 / REVENUE SHARING EXPENDITURES BY STATE AND LOCAL
GOVERNMENTS REPORTED TO THE BUREAU OF THE CENSUS,
1976–77

Category	Actual Expenditures (thousands of dollars)	Percentage
Airport	$ 7,963	0.1
Corrections	166,652	2.5
Education	1,248,437	19.0
Finance/general admin.	327,675	5.0
Fire protection	523,467	8.0
General public building	261,719	4.0
Health	476,732	7.3
Highways	799,024	12.2
Hospitals	138,542	2.1
Housing/urban renewal	17,627	0.3
Interest and general debt	55,811	0.9
Libraries	79,722	1.2
Natural resources	27,455	0.4
Parks and recreation	247,588	3.8
Police protection	942,809	14.4
Public welfare	165,699	2.5
Redemption of debt	90,214	1.4
Sanitation and Sewerage	370,877	5.7
Utility systems	79,281	1.2
Others	527,400	8.0
Total	$6,554,694	100.0

Source: U.S. Department of the Treasury, Office of Revenue Sharing (Washington, D.C., March 1979), p. 8.

In addition to revenue sharing, the federal government does provide some other non-categorical, non-matching grant revenues that particularly aid the cities: Community Development Block Grants (CDBG), Comprehensive Employment and Training Assistance (CETA), Antirecession Fiscal Assistance (ARFA), and Local Public Works (LPW). In fiscal 1978, these programs along with general revenue sharing had outlays of $21.4 billion of which approximately 90 percent went to local governments.[59] The need for a greater federal role in urban politics does not imply that it is not already substantial. In fiscal 1979, over $82 billion of a total national budget of almost $560 billion was allocated for federal grants to states and localities.[60] In fact, some critics of big government claim that the federal presence is already too large. Among the 1980 presidential candidates, both Republican Ronald Reagan and Democrat President Jimmy Carter held to this perspective. These presidential hopefuls did not accept the view that national interdependence requires additional significant national policy linkages to improve conditions for urban life. It is our view, however, that at the present time federal funding is inequitable and insufficient, and integrative program development remains a goal. However, the federal presence is a reality. This presence has been manifested through the total and partial funding of some local programs, as well as through revenue sharing. A variety of regulations have also been imposed by the federal government in policy areas as diverse as education and air pollution. Furthermore, matching grants-in-aid for specific programs do have some federal regulations attached to them. Finally, it should be noted that five of the more recent additions of cabinet-level departments—Housing and Urban Development (1965), Transportation (1966), Energy (1977), Education (1980), and Health and Human Services (1980)—are examples of national government involvement in areas with significant urban impacts.

CONCLUSION

The contemporary urban area must cope with unique political, economic, and fiscal problems. Metropolitan areas often are fragmented in terms of political jurisdictions and, indeed, perception of community interest. Suburban districts often have restricted service interests related to schools and to fire and police protection. Often they are unenthusiastic about accepting their share of high-cost/high tax services such as social services for needy groups, highly capitalized transportation services such as subways and buses, and the hospital services that have traditionally developed within the central cities. Demands by public administrators and central city mayors for an end to the fragmentation of metropolitan areas have led to the advocacy of metropolitan government and metropolitan Councils of Government (COGs). Such jurisdictional units seek more coordinated planning and administration as well as more centralized funding of services. The centrifugal forces within metropolitan areas, however, often lead to resistance to such inclusion in metropolitan areas. The class cleavages within central cities, as well as the disparities of interest between central cities and suburbs, have left some major cities in dire economic and social circumstances. Similarly, the financial needs of urban suburbs for education, health, and police protection are often unmet.

While the more united funding offered by metropolitan government or increased state aid to central cities and suburbs might relieve some urban problems, the inelasticity of local and state revenue sources makes it difficult for metropolitan jurisdictions and states to meet urban needs from state and local revenue sources. Increasingly, such jurisdictions demand more assistance from the national government. There is ongoing debate regarding whether such assistance should carry specific national requirements or be given to states and localities without "strings." Also, the level of federal spending clearly has not been sufficient to relieve fiscal crises in many of the central cities. Detroit Mayor

Coleman Young testified before the congressional Joint Economic Committee that Detroit was in a desperate financial condition and faced potential bankruptcy unless federal or state assistance was forthcoming. Young observed: "Detroit may find itself in the same situation as New York, and there will be others. Philadelphia will not be far behind, nor will Boston, San Francisco and some others." [61] Because many states are also suffering financial difficulties, the need for increased federal assistance to cities seems necessary.

In addition, civic boosterism as a solution for urban ills ceases to be an adequate solution for urban fiscal crises. Manufacturing and commerce often move from the central city and urban suburbs to exurban areas because of the high costs of operation and transportation difficulties. Attracting such enterprises by offering tax benefits deprives urban areas of needed revenues. Furthermore, many of these are national or multinational corporations with little sense of obligation to locality. Thus, it appears increasingly necessary to accept national interdependence with regard to meeting urban social and economic needs. Such policies will require greater national financial support and prescriptions for meeting the social and economic priorities of both the central cities and the suburbs.

REFERENCES

1. For a discussion of the most equitable revenue level, see The President's Task Force on Suburban Problems, *Final Report,* ed. by Charles M. Haar (Cambridge, Mass.: Ballinger, 1974), p. 70.
2. Allen D. Manvel, *Urban America and the Federal System* (Washington, D.C.: Advisory Commission on Intergovernmental Relations, 1969), p. 9.
3. John Feild, "Federal Funds and Local Leadership," *City,* 4 (October–November 1970), 62.
4. U.S. Bureau of the Census, *Statistical Abstract of the United States: 1977,* 98th edition (Washington, D.C., 1977), 276; Advisory Commission on Intergovernmental Relations, Significant Features of Fiscal Federalism, 1978–79 (Washington, D.C.: U.S. Government Printing Office, 1979), p. 7.
5. "States Tackle Tough Fiscal Issues," *Intergovernmental Prospective,* 5 (Winter 1979), 8–10.
6. U.S. Bureau of the Census, *Statistical Abstract of the United States, 1977,* op. cit.
7. Peggy L. Cuciti, *City Need and the Responsiveness of Federal Grants Programs* (Washington, D.C.: Congressional Budget Office, 1978), p. 43.
8. *National Journal,* 11 (August 12, 1978), 1299.
9. Advisory Commission on Intergovernmental Relations, *Significant Features of Fiscal Federalism, 1976–77 Edition, Vol. 3, Expenditures* (Washington, D.C.: U.S. Government Printing Office, 1977), pp. 26, 39, and 42.
10. Ibid., p. 31.
11. Cuciti, op. cit., pp. 23 and 26.
12. Calculations based on data in U.S. Bureau of the Census, *State Government*

Finances in 1971, Series G-71, No. 3 (Washington, D.C.: U.S. Government Printing Office, 1972), pp. 19, 31.

13. Neal R. Peirce, *The Megastates of America* (New York: W. W. Norton, 1972), p. 36.

14. *The New York Times, Jersey Edition,* December 3, 1973, pp. 81–82.

15. "Municipal Bootstraps," *Nation's Cities,* 10 (February 1972), 15.

16. Ibid., 14.

17. Data reported by Cuciti, op. cit., pp. 24–27.

18. Jacques G. Masonrouge, "The Myth of Multi-Nationalism," *The Columbia Journal of World Business,* 9 (Spring 1974), 7–11.

19. Winsor H. Watson, Jr., "Global Role of U.S. Stock Exchanges," *The Columbia Journal of World Business,* 9 (Spring 1974), 43.

20. *The New York Times,* June 4, 1979, p. B15.

21. *Significant Features of Fiscal Federalism, 1978–79,* op. cit., p. 7.

22. David R. Berman, *State and Local Politics,* 2nd ed. (Boston: Holbrook Press, 1978), p. 246.

23. "States Tackle Tough Fiscal Issues," op. cit., 15.

24. Murray S. Stedman, *State and Local Governments, Second Edition* (Cambridge, Mass.: Winthrop, 1979), p. 390.

25. John W. Jack and Paul C. Reuss, "Financing Municipal Government: Fiscal Challenge of the Seventies," *Municipal Finance* (February 1971), 141–48.

26. *Significant Features of Fiscal Federalism 1976–77, Edition . . . ,* op. cit., p. 10.

27. Berman, op. cit., p. 252.

28. Advisory Commission on Intergovernmental Relations, *A Circuit Breaker on Property Tax Overload* (Washington, D.C.: U.S. Government Printing Office, 1969).

29. Berman estimates that 70 to 80 percent of most state and local budgets are devoted to public employees' salaries and fringe benefits. Berman, op. cit., p. 216. Additional discussion of the New York City fiscal crisis is included in supra, Chapter 11.

30. Figures cited by Stedman, op. cit., pp. 402–03.

31. *Moody's Analytical Overview of 25 Leading U.S. Cities* (New York: Moody's Investor's Service, 1977), p. vii.

32. Martha Derthick, *Uncontrollable Spending for Social Service Grants* (Washington, D.C.: The Brookings Institution, 1975), p. 69.

33. Leonard E. Goodall and Donald P. Sprengel, *The American Metropolis* (Columbus, Ohio: Charles E. Merrill, 1975), p. 56.

34. Cited in Claudius O. Johnson, Daniel M. Ogden, Jr., H. Paul Castleberry, and Thor Swanson, *American State and Local Government* (New York: Thomas Y. Crowell, 1972), p. 276.

35. Alan Klevit, "City Councils and Their Functions in Local Government," *Municipal Year Book, 1972* (Washington, D.C.: International City Managers Association, 1972), p. 15.

36. *Municipal Year Book, 1979* (Washington, D.C.: International City Management Association, 1979), p. 98.

37. *The New York Times,* November 9, 1979, pp. A1, A16.

38. "A Big City Mayor Speaks Out," in *Social Science and Urban Crises,* ed. by Victor B. Picker and Herbert S. Graves (New York: Macmillan, 1971), p. 160.

39. Alexander George, "Political Leadership and Social Change in American Cities," *Daedalus,* 97 (Fall 1968), 1196.

40. Theodore J. Lowi, "Machine Politics—Old and New," *The Public Interest,* 9 (Fall 1967), 86.
41. See John C. Bollens and Henry J. Schmandt, *The Metropolis* (New York: Harper & Row, 1975), pp. 233–35, for discussion of these points.
42. Ibid., p. 233.
43. A good discussion of metropolitan reorganization can be found in Alan Shank and Ralph W. Conant, *Urban Perspectives: Politics and Policies* (Boston: Holbrook Press, 1975), Chap. 4. Also see Bollens and Schmandt, op. cit., Chaps. 11, 12, 13.
44. Daniel R. Grant, "Trends in Urban Government and Administration," in *Urban Politics and Problems,* ed. by H. R. Mahood and Edward L. Angus (New York: Charles Scribner's Sons, 1969), p. 57.
45. *The New York Times,* March 22, 1979, p. A16.
46. Daniel R. Grant, "Metro's Three Faces," in Picker and Graves, op. cit., p. 147.
47. Luther Gulick, "Needed: A New Layer of Self Government," in *Urban Government,* ed. by Edward C. Banfield (New York: Free Press, 1969, rev. ed.), p. 154.
48. For a more detailed discussion of RPCs and RPAs, see Advisory Commission on Intergovernmental Relations, *Regional Decision-Making: New Strategies for Substate Districts* (Washington, D.C.: U.S. Government Printing Office, 1973), p. 50.
49. Ibid.
50. Norman Beckman, "Metropolitan Area Trends and Developments," *Municipal Year Book, 1974* (Washington, D.C.: International City Management Association, 1974), p. 13; *The Washington Post,* September 16, 1975, p. A17.
51. Bill Richards, "Baltimore: A City in Deep Trouble," *The Washington Post,* March 5, 1974, p. B9.
52. *The New York Times,* November 17, 1975, pp. 33, 51.
53. "The Cities Are Trying to Do Too Much," *Nation's Cities,* 10 (February 1972), 38.
54. *Significant Features of Fiscal Federalism, 1976–77 Edition, Vol. 3, Expenditures,* op. cit., p. 10.
55. Advisory Commission on Intergovernmental Relations, *Measuring the Fiscal Capacity and Effort of State and Local Areas* (Washington, D.C.: U.S. Government Printing Office, 1972), p. 1.
56. "In Washington: Not Many Answers," *Intergovernmental Perspective,* 5 (Winter 1979), 32.
57. Richard P. Nathan and Charles F. Adams, *Revenue Sharing: The Second Round* (Washington, D.C.: The Brookings Institution, 1977).
58. U.S. Office of the Treasury, *Sixth Annual Report of the Office of Revenue Sharing* (Washington, D.C., March 1979), p. 8.
59. Cuciti, op. cit., p. xiii.
60. *Congressional Quarterly* (January 27, 1979), 110.
61. *The Washington Post,* February 26, 1976, p. A1.

PART TWO

The next chapters consider the delivery of three separate services to urban populations and the national urban policy linkages that have evolved to facilitate their delivery. The policy areas to be discussed are education, public welfare, and police services. Each of these service areas has developed primarily as a public sector activity with strong traditions of localism. Only in the provision of public welfare have strong national urban policy linkages developed—though it can be argued that federal involvement in that area has still not been sufficient to meet urban needs. Education and police services have remained primarily local activities with major fiscal support and administrative decision making being retained by local jurisdictions.

In the next three chapters, each of these services will be described separately to determine the adequacy of the existing delivery of the service and the role of the various levels of government—local, state, and national—in providing the service. The position presented in the education and public welfare chapters is that many national decision makers have not sufficiently accepted the maintenance of both high quality and adequately available services as a national responsibility. Police services remain primarily a local responsibility, and it is argued in Chapter 6 that to alter this focus might lead to the destruction of the delicate balance between freedom and order in our democratic society.

Education and
the Local Tradition

INTRODUCTION

In the United States, we have a long tradition of support for public education dating back almost to the beginning of the Republic. This tradition has placed great emphasis on local policy determination, which over time has been hemmed in by overall state supervision of the school calendar, teacher qualifications, and curriculum areas. The federal government, until quite recently, had almost no positive role in public urban education. In fact, not until after World War II was there any significant federal involvement in public education. The first major contemporary education policy linkage can be traced to the Supreme Court's 1954 decision in *Brown* v. *the Board of Education of Topeka* (347 U.S. 483), in which the 1896 "separate but equal" doctrine of *Plessey* v. *Ferguson* (163 U.S. 537) that reinforced legal segregation of schools (*de jure* segregation) was declared unconstitutional. The effects of this decision were first felt in the South since that was the home of the dual school system. But over the long term, this decision has had a significant effect on urban areas. The political environment changed when the 1954 decision declared that separate was not equal. Since 1954, other cases questioning the constitutionality of residentially based segregated schools in urban areas have been brought into federal courts, and decisions requiring redistricting in urban areas have been handed down. Another major national-urban policy linkage was developed in 1965 when the enactment of the Elementary and Secondary School Act provided the first significant federal funding to urban public schools. Though this funding has been quite limited, it has helped alleviate some of their problems.

The federal inroads into public urban education were stimulated considerably by the inability of essentially locally based and funded public primary and secondary schools to provide fair shares of educational opportunity to all citizens. Two thrusts in public education that have attempted to equalize opportunity have been (1) increased state funding and supervision of public school systems, and (2) increased federal support for public education. Though movement toward greater equality among school districts—particularly between central cities and wealthy suburbs, and between wealthy suburbs and less wealthy suburbs and rural areas—has been supported by federal and state courts and by congressional legislative action, the establishment of equality between school systems is complicated by the class segregation that divides our urban areas into affluent, less affluent, and poor areas. Since the property tax is the primary source of local revenue for public schools, the obvious paradox is that school systems with less severe educational and social problems have the highest tax base and can afford the best faculties and best facilities. The central cities and highly urbanized suburbs with the greatest educational challenges and the highest levels of services competing for municipal revenues cannot, by themselves, afford the specialized educational facilities and services needed to provide equal educational opportunities for their children.

Urban schools are the focus of other social cleavages of our society. Civil rights organizations, particularly the National Association for the Advancement of Colored People's (NAACP) Legal Defense and Educational Fund, have successfully urged federal courts to provide greater equality of education by dispersing predominately white middle class students from less highly urbanized areas among predominately black, Hispanic, and poor central city students. This has led to city-suburban conflict regarding "forced" busing, the sanctity of the neighborhood school, and problems related to educating a student body of diverse social and educational backgrounds, as well as the heating up of "the American dilemma" of racial conflict. In addition, beginning in the late

1960s and continuing into the 1970s, concern has been expressed in urban areas with neighborhood control of city public schools. This notion has conflicted with the concern of educators for the professional autonomy of classroom teachers and their need for job security in an increasingly politicized atmosphere. In practice, local urban parent groups have accepted the mandates of state and municipal boards of education. What they have often sought is greater influence over the personnel who administer and teach in local schools. At times, conflicts have reflected the ethnic succession of newer groups into urban schools. In such instances, community concern has been expressed that principals and teachers be of the same ethnic or racial background as the student population. That is, the subject of employment has sometimes been at issue. A less controversial concern of newer immigrant Hispanic, French-Canadian, and Portuguese groups is the need for respect and understanding of the foreign culture in educating immigrants and the children of immigrants. Also, a primary concern of families where English is at best a second language is the need for bilingual education and bilingual teachers. A similar concern with the need for inclusion of materials relating to black culture has been made by local leadership in many black communities.

Given the problems of funding urban schools and the role of the courts in enforcing urban area school integration, it is clear that the problems of local public education and policy responses for public education have increasingly become problems for state and national policy, even if federal funds for education are still too limited to meet urban needs. After the historical context of localism in education within the American system is considered, this chapter will review current issues affecting urban public education and the social context of the issues. Several areas of conflict will be discussed. Busing and neighborhood control of education within metropolitan areas and the need for an equitable tax base for public school systems will be considered. In addition, the state and federal response to the needs of urban education and the challenge of providing equal educational opportunity within the urban context will be discussed.

History of Education in the United States: A General Background

In 1785, the Continental Congress set aside land in the Northwest Territory for a common school system. As a result of this congressional decision, a common school system developed early in the frontier area of the upper Midwest. Following the public support for education implied by the Northwest Ordinance, the older states of the northeastern United States established free common schools in the early part of the nineteenth century. By 1850, the *principle* of the free elementary common school at public expense had been established in every northern state,[1] and by 1875, every state had established a public school system.[2] It was not, however, until 1918 that compulsory education was the law in all states.[3]

The movement to establish common schools was culminated by the desire of some educators and other citizens to establish statewide systems of free, tax-supported, nonsectarian, and state-supervised schools. In 1834, Pennsylvania established free elementary education. Indiana (1852), Ohio (1853), Illinois (1855), Vermont (1864), and New York (1867) followed the lead of Pennsylvania. A uniform free system was then established in Connecticut and Rhode Island in 1868, Michigan in 1869, and New Jersey in 1871. Before these free systems were established, parents were charged for their children's education. For example, in New York State (and other states as well) a "rate bill"—a tax on parents—was in effect until 1867 when the state legislature abolished it.[4] The New York State Legislature then appropriated $821,371.32 for public education.

The first public schools in the United States were local, and they were supported principally by local subscriptions. As Elwood Cubberley notes of the late-eighteenth and early-nineteenth-century public schools:

Communities or neighborhoods which wanted schools and were willing to pay for them could easily meet and organize a school district, vote to levy a school tax on their own property, employ a teacher and organize a school. On the other hand, communities which did not desire schools or were unwilling to tax themselves for them could do without them, and let the free school idea alone.[5]

State involvement in public education varied in the separate states. The first state government to become involved was New York, which established the Board of Regents in 1784 to oversee schools. The New York experience laid the foundation for educational oversight in other states.[6] Other states had other kinds of involvements in education during the early years of public education. In 1797, Massachusetts granted land endowments to approved academies. (Academies were quasi-public or private secondary schools.) In 1783, Georgia created a system of county academies. New York extended state aid to its academies in 1813, having placed them under state inspection as early as 1784. Maryland chartered many academies between 1801 and 1817, and authorized lotteries (as did North Carolina) to provide them with funds.[7] State funding of public school systems as well as state supervision of public education gradually increased throughout the nineteenth century. By 1850, ex-officio state school officials had been appointed in seven of the then thirty-one states. By 1861, there were ex-officio state officials in nine states and regular state school officials in nineteen of the thirty-four states.[8] Such officials collected data and tried to assert some control over local schools. In addition, they tried to introduce some degree of uniformity in local school practices. Issues of state enforcement in the nineteenth century included the role of local taxation as supplementary to state aid; enforcement of systematic requirements for teacher certification; oversight of curriculum such that state-required subjects were taught in the schools; and the development of mechanisms to require schools to adhere to a full school-year calendar.

Public high schools were established somewhat later than elementary schools. Thus, public high schools did not exist until 1821, when Boston opened its first publicly supported high school.[9] By 1840, only about 50 public high schools existed throughout the country.[10] During these early years, the private academies provided the main form of college preparatory education. In the latter half of the nineteenth century, high schools gradually became part of the state public school systems, and state and local funds and taxation gradually extended to cover the support of public high schools.

As public involvement in education increased, inequality of provision became a more serious problem. The concern with the unequal ability of local jurisdictions to provide equitable educational opportunity to its children was apparent to some educational analysts as early as the 1930s. In 1934, Cubberley noted an apparent need for some assistance to local jurisdictions to maintain more equal educational opportunity. He recognized that interjurisdictional linkages in educational policy were needed if we were to maintain equal educational opportunity for all our children in the face of differential taxing capabilities of jurisdictions. During the early 1930s, an average of 85 percent of school costs were covered by local school districts. Thus, the first demand for aid from *other* jurisdictions was directed to the states. However, even when states assumed 15 percent of school costs, the ultimate necessity for more overarching assistance was recognized. For example, Cubberley wrote:

> With the continuing growth of tax inequalities and the continued increases in cost for schools there [was] an urgent demand that the State should assume a much greater percentage of the annual maintenance burden.[11]

At that time he also asserted:

> Only through some form of federal aid, with a view to the equalization of educational opportunity up to a certain determined minimum length of school term, attendance, teacher quality, and expenditure, can the disparity [between the states] in ability to maintain schools be remedied within any reasonable period of time.[12]

Local School Boards

Throughout the years of their development, public schools have been largely local operations, funded and supervised primarily by local governing boards. More specifically, local school districts are operated by local school boards that have substantial authority and whose members are elected by the residents of the school district. Within almost all states, a lay state board supervises and exerts a degree of control over these local systems. A state school official, either elected or appointed, works closely with the lay state board. The number of people on local boards of education varies, though elected membership is usually kept to nine or less. The method of nominating local board members varies greatly. They may be nominated by petition, primary election, individual announcement, citizen committee, mass meeting, or school district meeting. Members are usually elected, though they may be appointed by the mayor and council, county commissioners, city manager, or by a self-perpetuating board. The term of office for members varies from one year to several years. Authorities in educational administration recommend that the *election* of members be at large rather than by wards, on a nonpartisan rather than a partisan basis, and for relatively long overlapping terms of office. Qualifications for holding office are usually that a member must be at least twenty-one, a legal voter, and a resident of the school district. In major cities, members of school boards traditionally tended to be prominent business and professional people, with a marked tendency for exclusion of members of lower and middle socioeconomic groups. In some suburban communities this is not as true because a homogeneous middle class district will have by necessity a school board with middle class membership. In recent years, however, members of minority groups and organized workers have served on school boards to a greater extent.[13]

A board must usually address itself to four specific types of functions and powers (though they often have some discretionary powers, too). They are usually responsible for:

1. Developing and improving the educational program.
2. Selecting the chief administrative officer and providing a staff.
3. Providing funds and facilities.
4. Maintaining good community relations.[14]

School boards can be divided into two categories on the basis of their fiscal relationship to city governments. Some school boards are fiscally independent; that is, they have the authority to raise and spend funds without the consent of the municipal government. Other school boards, however, are actually departments of some other political jurisdiction, such as a city, and therefore depend on that other jurisdiction for their budgets.[15]

The History of Revenue Sources for Local School Districts

The base of financial support for public education traditionally has been the local property tax. In many areas, however, this revenue source was inadequate to provide education appropriate for the student population. The areas most affected by this problem are central city districts with declining tax bases and increasing educational problems, though less affluent suburbs also have difficulty raising sufficient local revenue to support good schools. This condition was intensified by the anti-property tax pressures that arose in the late 1970s, which caused local jurisdictions some difficulties in raising local revenues for their schools. For example, in Ohio, almost 60 percent of school bond issues were rejected in 1978.[16] Another state that experienced the political effects of this phenomenon was California, where a statewide referendum was passed that reduced local property tax rates. Consequently, for the first time in American history, data for the 1978–79 school year show that state funding of education actually exceeded local contributions and rose to over half of the costs incurred by school districts.

Though new, this change in the pattern of funding had been gradually evolving throughout the 1970s. Put in somewhat different terms: the national average of state support for schools is now about 50 percent, but the actual amount varies from state to state. For instance, in Nebraska, 19.4 percent of public school funding for the 1977–78 school year was provided by the state, while in Hawaii, 93.5 percent of such funding was statewide. The funding ratio often has caused a persistent and troublesome problem and has led many states to develop equalizing formulas for sharing educational costs with localities. Increasingly, states with tax-poor jurisdictions have some provision in their educational support programs to equalize the available revenue across the state's school districts. These provisions tend to provide for allocations related inversely to the wealth of the local school district. Thus, state equalization formulas have tended to benefit central city and poorer suburban school districts which have limited taxing ability and high need.

The problem of uneven taxing abilities and its effect on equality of educational opportunity has led to some state judicial actions. Several court rulings in the 1970s have challenged the methods used to finance public education. These court decisions[17] have forced legislatures in the affected states to develop other sources of revenue for local school districts and to seek methods for more equitable allocation of available funds. A national reassessment of taxing for schools has not, however, been mandated by the federal courts. In its decision in *San Antonio Independent School District et al.* v. *Rodriguez* (411 U.S. 1 [1973]), the Supreme Court held that disparities in methods of financing public schools did not violate the Fourteenth Amendment of the Constitution (more specifically, the Equal Protection Clause). The majority of the court, though recognizing the inequities in the educational system, held that state legislatures, not the national courts, must correct them. Within a year of the Supreme Court's decision, many state legislatures and state courts became the centers of pressures for such redistributive policies. States as geographically separate as New Jersey and California have been affected by state court decisions requiring the alteration of the fund raising mechanisms for their school districts.

The condition of unequal resources can be brought into sharp relief if one considers the per child tax assessments in different school districts. In 1973, Englewood Cliffs, an affluent suburban community in northern New Jersey, had $145,000 worth of assessed property for every child being publicly educated in the school district. Newark, however, a New

Jersey central city within a short commuting distance of Englewood Cliffs, had only $19,000 of assessed property value for each public school student. The result of this phenomenon is that Newark must tax itself proportionately more heavily than Englewood Cliffs for its public schools; Englewood Cliffs, with its relatively lower tax rate can spend more of its own revenues per student than Newark.[18] Similarly, in Cuyahoga County, Ohio, the per pupil tax assessments in 1974–75 ranged from $260,014 in Cuyahoga Heights down to $14,404 in Olmsted Falls. The costs per pupil ranged accordingly from $2,067.76 for Cuyahoga Heights down to $886.34 for Olmsted Falls.[19]

Distribution of Resources

In 1976, there were approximately 50 million students enrolled in all public and private elementary and secondary schools in the United States. Over 44.3 billion of these students were enrolled in the 16,376 operating public school districts of the nation.[20] By 1976, over 28 percent of all youth attending public schools were enrolled in school districts with more than 25,000 students. In a study of twenty large central city school districts—with enrollments totalling almost 4.5 million children—that were surveyed by the National Center for Education Statistics of the U.S. Department of Health, Education, and Welfare, it was estimated that in fiscal year 1977 these cities spent in total about $9.2 billion on education (see Table 1). There has been a notable recent increase in revenues made available to big-city school districts by the states and, to a lesser extent, by the federal government. Thus in 1968 only 38 percent of big-city school systems had per pupil finances equal to or more than their state's average. By 1975, this figure had increased to 78 percent.[21] Though at first glance there appears to be an equitable distribution of funds to these districts, it has not been sufficient to meet the special needs of big city schools.

In part this insufficiency of funds for central city school districts is related to the changing problems of its constituents. Increases in low-income youth, often of black, Puerto Rican, and Mexican background, are providing a new challenge to the urban public schools at a time when municipal revenues are becoming increasingly strained. For example, in 1978 the National Center for Education Statistics reported that mean achievement scores for seventeen-year-olds in schools are 2.78 from the mean for whites, −16.44 for blacks, and −11.42 for Hispanics.[22] Given the disproportionate number of often low-income blacks and Hispanics in central city schools, the education problems should appear reasonably apparent. To use Chicago as an illustration, in 1977, one-fifth of its residents were receiving public welfare assistance, and 42 percent of the children attending that city's public schools came from families at or below the poverty level. The average child in the eighth grade was two years behind the national average in reading achievement.[23] The U.S. Office of Education has reported that city school systems are faced with increased demands for services, since they have had thrust upon them tasks that strain the capabilities of their present structures.[24]

In 1968, central cities spent on the average 95 percent of what suburbs spent on public education. By 1975, however, these same jurisdictions were expending on the average 113 percent of what the suburbs spent. This change has been due to the availability of increasing amounts of federal and state money, which has led to a higher expenditure level for many urban school districts. Title I of the federal Elementary and Secondary Education Act of 1965 has been a factor contributing to these higher urban expenditures, which in some instances have exceeded suburban levels.[25] However, these expenditures have not been sufficient to overcome the disparities faced by low-income children in urban settings. Rehabilitating old schools and developing new structures is very costly in the central cities. Also, public housing, government installations, and religious facilities that are usually located in central cities are not subject to property taxes, and thus yield little revenue for educational purposes.[26] Students suffer class barriers, often reinforced by discrimination, to educational success which underplay the importance of education and which often do not provide parental or peer-group support for the achievement of educational goals.[27] These conditions develop when little opportunity for success in the educational system is perceived in the collective experience of poor inner-city populations.[28] All of these factors make urban education more difficult and successful urban education more expensive.

The federal government's response to the fiscal needs of education, and more specifically urban education, has not been great. In fact, prior to 1965 and the passage of the Elementary and Secondary School Act, federal aid to public education did not have much impact on public education in urban America. Even with the 1965 law, the legislative policy linkage is weak, and the value of localism in education is the pervasive perspective of large numbers of educators.

Current Legislative Linkages[29]

In 1862, Congress passed the Morrill Act (the so-called Land Grant College Act), which provided assistance to states if they developed postsecondary educational programs in agriculture and home economics. After the enactment of that legislation, the federal government did very little to support public education until 1965 when the Elementary and Secondary School Act was passed. Even since then, federal involvement in education has been limited. To a considerable extent, any federal-urban linkage has been circumscribed by the tradition of localism in public education and a fear among educators and parents that increased federal aid will bring unwanted federal regulations and restrictions on

Table 1 / SELECTED STATISTICS ON PUBLIC ELEMENTARY AND SECONDARY SCHOOLS IN 20 LARGE CITIES COMPARED WITH THE UNITED STATES TOTALS, 1976–77

	Fall Enrollment							Average Annual Salary[2] for:	
	Total	Kindergarten—Grade 8[1]	Grades 9–12 and Postgraduate	Classroom Teachers	Pupils per Teacher	Total Expenditures[2] (in thousands)	Current Expenditure per Pupil in Average Daily Attendance[2]	Other Professional Educational Staff[3]	Classroom Teachers
City									
1	2	3	4	5	6	7	8	9	10
United States	44,335,000	30,012,000	14,323,000	2,193,000	20.2	$74,806,266	$1,578	$15,199	$13,347
20 large cities, total	4,491,458	(4)	(4)	(4)	(4)	9,234,008	(4)	(4)	(4)
Baltimore, Md.	159,038	113,088	49,950	8,240	19.3	264,334	1,756	14,841	13,489
Boston, Mass.	91,973	(4)	(4)	(4)	(4)	276,926	(4)	(4)	(4)
Chicago, Ill.	524,221	370,060	154,161	2 23,081	2 22.7	1,218,789	2,333	17,623	5 17,302
Cleveland, Ohio	122,727	84,905	37,822	5,303	23.1	224,603	1,837	18,991	14,588
Dallas, Texas	141,407	98,249	43,158	6,668	21.2	213,823	1,451	16,000	13,600
Detroit, Mich.	236,279	174,544	61,735	8,847	26.7	408,696	1,770	19,132	18,617
Houston, Tex.	210,025	152,222	57,803	9,237	22.7	259,202	1,403	14,000	12,250
Indianapolis, Ind.	82,102	56,832	25,270	3,524	23.3	130,095	1,578	18,638	12,930
Los Angeles, Calif.	601,429	408,373	193,056	2 28,700	2 21.0	1,275,145	1,769	6 20,100	17,399
Memphis, Tenn.	120,322	83,849	36,473	5,675	21.2	132,100	1,124	13,324	12,060
Milwaukee, Wis.	109,151	73,998	35,153	5,366	20.3	226,931	2,352	21,802	19,296
New Orleans, La.	93,364	64,167	29,197	4,380	21.3	135,247	1,530	(4)	7 11,399
New York, N.Y.	2 1,097,445	2 721,222	2 376,223	2 51,980	2 21.1	2,615,700	2,607	6 24,400	6 19,000
Philadelphia, Pa.	260,787	175,818	84,969	13,957	18.7	669,643	2,685	16,505	15,959
Phoenix, Ariz.	2 177,204	123,374	2 53,830	7,969	2 22.2	275,431	1,360	15,384	13,510

Table 1 / CONTINUED

City	Fall Enrollment			Classroom Teachers	Pupils per Teacher	Total Expenditures[2] (in thousands)	Current Expenditure per Pupil in Average Daily Attendance[2]	Average Annual Salary[2] for	
	Total	Kindergarten —Grade 8[1]	Grades 9–12 and Postgraduate					Other Professional Educational Staff[3]	Classroom Teachers
1	2	3	4	5	6	7	8	9	10
St. Louis, Mo.	82,804	58,307	24,497	3,082	26.9	132,346	1,832	19,000	13,000
San Antonio, Tex.	65,929	45,958	19,971	[2]3,202	20.6	80,785	1,283	18,100	12,751
San Diego, Calif.	120,667	83,052	37,615	[2]5,400	[2]22.3	234,848	1,554	[6]20,000	16,767
San Francisco, Calif.	68,736	44,086	24,650	[2]4,100	[2]16.8	213,311	2,377	[6]19,000	17,239
Washington, D.C.	125,848	89,925	35,923	6,057	20.8	246,053	2,060	19,256	16,460

Source: U.S. Department of Health, Education, and Welfare, National Center for Education Statistics, *Statistics of Public Elementary and Secondary Day Schools,* Washington, D.C. (Fall 1976).

1 Data include nursery schools and kindergartens operated as part of the regular public school system.

2 Estimated.

3 Includes salaries of curriculum specialists, counselors, librarian/media and remedial specialists only. Salaries of classroom teachers, supervisors, and principals are not included except as otherwise footnoted.

4 Data not available.

5 Includes salaries for assistant principals, counselors, psychologists, social workers, speech therapists, supervisors, and consultants.

6 Salary data reported as median salary.

7 Includes salaries of assistant principals, librarians, and counselors.

99

local school districts. (To some extent, this fear has been proven justified because the federal government has required compliance with civil rights and affirmative action guidelines to be eligible for its aid.) Also, federal aid, when it has been forthcoming, has been limited. Assistance to revenue-needy urban and other poor districts has been inadequate to overcome the inequalities in educational opportunities provided children in these areas in contrast to the more affluent suburban areas.

Between 1862 and 1965, there were some federal initiatives in education (though not particularly urban education), but they were small and piecemeal. The Smith-Hughes Act of 1917 provided matching funds to states for vocational education in public schools. The Lanham Act of 1940 authorized federal funds for the construction, maintenance, and operation of schools in areas that had increased populations due to the presence of federal defense facilities. Such areas still receive federal assistance for their schools. Perhaps the major pre-1965 education-related legislation was enacted by Congress in 1944. At that time, the Serviceman's Readjustment Act ("GI Bill of Rights") was signed into law. Similar laws were passed in 1952 (for Korean veterans) and in 1966 (for Vietnam veterans). These laws have had a significant effect on American education—though not specifically on urban education—as well as on social and economic relationships. In their annual report, the Veterans Administration reported that in 1974 alone, the program provided $3.269 billion in educational assistance to over 2.3 million veterans. Many veterans were able, as a result of their opportunity to complete their advanced education, to make radical changes in their life work and socioeconomic status.

World War II not only led to the GI Bill and the education of millions of individuals who otherwise might not have had an opportunity for education, it also resulted in a sharp rise in the birth rate. In the 1950s, a resultant sharp rise in public school enrollment occurred. Since school construction, however, had dropped during the depression of the 1930s and had almost stopped during World War II, more classrooms were needed for the returning veterans and for their children. The federal government did almost nothing to meet these construction costs. It also did not provide the revenues to maintain the structures or to staff the classrooms. In fact, there was very little federal initiative in funding education from 1945 until the 1960s. In part, this federal inaction can be tied to other political problems. The question of federal aid to education had become enmeshed with other sociopolitical conflicts. All individuals who discussed federal aid had to address themselves to the question of whether federal aid should be made available to racially segregated schools and whether aid should be available to private schools as well as to public schools, with no restrictions relating to a school's religious affiliation. Problems arose as to whether or not aid to education, if it was granted to church-related schools, would violate the principle of separation of church and state. Significant numbers of representatives and senators simply blocked any legislation that would provide aid to public schools but not private schools. Consequently, no aid to education bills were passed during this period. Also, whenever a bill reached the House Education Committee, then Representative Adam Clayton Powell (Democrat, N.Y.), who represented New York City's Harlem area in the House of Representatives and was chairman of that committee, would amend the bill to provide that aid be denied to school districts maintaining segregated schools. This amendment ensured that no bill would come to a vote in the Senate, since it would be filibustered to its death. The social-political divisions tied to segregation and provision (or nonprovision) of aid to parochial schools in the post–World War II era thus effectively limited the development of a program of federal assistance to public schools.

The limited federal education legislation enacted during this period was directed more at higher education than public elementary and secondary education. For example, the National Science Foundation Act passed in 1950 was directed at promoting scientific research, though it did provide for training institutes for elementary and secondary school science teachers and for elementary and secondary school curriculum revision projects. Public Law 81-815 for school construction and Public Law 81-874 for operating expenses provided grants to federally impacted areas (a continuation of the Lanham Act). The Cooperative Research Act of 1954 authorized the U.S. Office of Education "to make contracts and cooperative arrangements with colleges and universities for joint studies of educational problems." Although this legislation was only modestly funded, it established the principle of federal funding for educational research under the control of the U.S. Office of Education. The National Defense Education Act of 1958, passed in reaction to the Soviet Union's successful launching of Sputnik I in 1957, provided funds to improve education in science, mathematics, and foreign languages. In 1963, the Higher Education Facilities Act (HEFA) and the Vocational Education Act were both enacted, and in 1964 the Library Construction and Services Act was signed into law. The HEFA was directed to colleges and universities to help meet construction costs. The Vocational Education Act was geared to meeting the needs of postsecondary students who did not want to attend college but wanted postsecondary vocational training. The Library Construction and Services Act authorized grants for library construction and operation.

In 1965, Congress passed the Elementary and Secondary School Act (ESEA) and the Higher Education Act (HEA). These two laws represented the largest expansion in the federal role in education to date and the ESEA represented the first meaningful aid for public elementary and secondary education. Both bills affect urban populations; but to limit the scope of our discussion, we will consider only the ESEA because the HEA will not directly benefit a child unless he or she is able to make it through the elementary and secondary schools.

The Elementary and Secondary School Act

The federal Elementary and Secondary Education Act of 1965 was signed into law in April 1965. Its major urban education provision, Title I, provides a national-urban policy linkage aimed at providing federal funds for local projects to help educationally deprived children. By 1980 there were a total of fifteen separate titles in this law, which addressed a variety of educational problems ranging from Indian education and bilingual programming to administrative concerns such as the outlining of the duties of state education agencies.[30]

Until May 1980, the Office of Education of the Department of Health, Education, and Welfare administered these programs. Now these programs are administered by the Department of Education. Though much of the funding has been used for educational programs in urban areas with severe social and economic deprivation, the legislation provides substantial program flexibility for state and local authorities, and in so doing it provides for considerable program differentiation. Each time the law has been extended by Congress—the most recent extension was enacted in 1978 and is for five years—the basic thrust of the original legislation has been kept intact. However, the range of funded activities has been expanded. For example, the 1978 five-year authorization provided funds for a new program of grants to states and school districts to improve instruction in the basic skills.[31]

Representative William D. Ford (Democrat, Michigan) noted in discussing the origins of Title I of the Act: "I recall vividly that we carefully avoided putting a definition of 'educationally deprived' in this piece of legislation as it is used in that section." [32] Just as eligibility was vaguely defined, program options were also left nonspecific both in the law and in its administrative regulations. Consequently, the range of program benefits accruing to the low-income student population has varied considerably from school district to school district. ESEA funds have been used for a variety of programs including the establishment of reading skills centers, teaching English as a second language to native Spanish-speaking pupils, and improving reading achievement in the elementary grades in poor areas.[33]

The problems these funds are often used to address are quite serious. Consider the case of Spanish-speaking children, a predominantly urban population. In a major study of schools in Arizona, California, Colorado, Texas, and New Mexico conducted by the United States Commission on Civil Rights, it was found that approximately 40 percent of the Mexican-Americans who enter first grade in those states never graduate from high school. According to estimates made by school principals, in the eighth and twelfth grades, 40 percent of Chicano students were two or more years behind grade level and about two-thirds were reading six months or more below grade level. Similarly, according to several authoritative reports, the Puerto Rican dropout rate is among the highest and their achievement levels among the lowest in the country. According to the Philadelphia Board of Education, the dropout rate for Puerto Rican students for the 1977–78 school year was almost 15 percent. Further, the Board of Regents of the State of New York reported that during the early years of the 1970s, in a random sample of schools with high concentrations of Puerto Ricans, 81 percent of fifth-grade and 86 percent of eighth-grade Puerto Rican students in New York City were reading below their grade level.[34]

Bilingual education does not appear to have improved educational gains. In fact, the results of the first national evaluation of the impact of federally funded bilingual education programs (now Title VII of the ESEA), a study of 11,500 students in 150 schools, completed nine years after the enactment of the first federal bilingual education legislation, showed that the Hispanic children in these programs did less well on English reading and vocabulary tests than the Hispanic children who remained in English-speaking classes.[35] Though these findings are disappointing, it is perhaps important to note this report's observation that: "These negative findings do not mean that bilingual education is an unworkable idea."[36] Future programming efforts and evaluations will need to be focused on such educational activities. Funding of bilingual education has continued as the size of the nation's Hispanic population and other non-English-speaking groups has increased.

There have been some educationally positive achievements associated with the programs funded with ESEA monies. Thus the National Institute of Education determined that first graders whom they studied in an effort to evaluate the effectiveness of Title I of the ESEA made average gains in reading of twelve months and average gains in mathematics of eleven months in the seven-month period between their fall and spring testing; third graders gained eight months in reading and twelve months in math. Another study, completed for the U.S. Office of Education, also found that Title I programs were retarding or preventing the relative decline in achievement among disadvantaged children.[37]

Problems of Accountability

Since the Elementary and Secondary School Act was enacted in 1965, accountability procedures for monitoring the use of federal funds and the effectiveness of their use by local school districts has been questioned. Often the data on use of funds have been aggregated for counties, effectively eliminating information on the use of funds in particular schools. Robert J. Goettel, Associate Director of the Educational Finance and Government Program at the Syracuse University Research Corporation, in February 1973 told the General Subcommittee on Education and Labor of the Education and Labor Committee of the House of Representatives that a reasonable and rational system of accountability was lacking in the U.S. Office of Education and, often, at the local level. He observed:

It is clear in most large school districts that the entire school-by-school resource allocation question is simply not handled in any systematic way.
Rochester, New York, is an example of a district which has made considerable effort to budget and account for most of the general State and local
resources that go to the schools, but the Federal resources are not built
into that system. . . . [C]urrent New York State accounting procedures make
it difficult to tie local and Federal aid accounting together. . . .[38]

Despite the inability in many jurisdictions to account for the specific
use of federal money, it is clear that the funds provided school districts
with concentrations of educationally deprived children have relieved
some fiscal pressure on urban school districts with slum schools. However, the extent of federal involvement should not be overstated. As of
fiscal year 1977, *all federal expenditures to public elementary and secondary school* education amounted to less than 9 percent of the total
cost of such education (see Table 2).

One final point ought to be made regarding federal assistance to
public schools. To retain eligibility for federal monies—be they Title I
funds, other ESEA funds, Vocational Training funds, or money from any
other federal government program such as the school breakfast and
lunch program—school districts must comply with federal government
civil rights, affirmative action, and other procedural guidelines. These
compliance requirements are a backdoor policy linkage that force all
school districts—urban as well as nonurban—to maintain certain minimum program and policy standards.

Current educational issues that relate to urban educational policy include: the provision of an equal opportunity for educational achievement
in public schools regardless of the individual's economic background, the
development of a public school system in which local government neither
explicitly, nor by indirection, fosters racial segregation, and the establishment of an "appropriate" level of community participation with neigh-

Table 2 / PERCENTAGE OF REVENUE RECEIVED FROM
THREE LEVELS OF GOVERNMENT FOR
PUBLIC ELEMENTARY AND SECONDARY SCHOOLS

School Year	Federal Sources	State Sources	Local Sources
1957–58	4.0	39.4	56.6
1965–66	7.9	39.1	53.0
1971–72	8.0	40.2	51.8
1976–77	8.4	43.6	48.1

Source: Data for 1957–58, 1965–66, 1971–72 were adapted from U.S. Department of Health,
Education, and Welfare, National Center for Education Statistics, *Revenues and Expenditures
for Public Elementary and Secondary Education, 1975–76;* and adapted from the Committee on
Education Finance, National Education Association, *Financial Status of Public Schools, 1973,*
p. 73. Data for 1976–77 were derived from Advisory Commission on Intergovernmental Relations, *Significant Features of Fiscal Federalism, 1978–79 Edition* (Washington, D.C.: U.S. Government Printing Office, 1979), p. 19. Reprinted by permission.

borhood educational programs in urban areas. (What level of community participation would be appropriate is a matter of much controversy.) The following section deals with these areas as problems of urban education. Particular attention is paid to national-state and urban policy linkages. Also examined are the community, professional, and governmental dimensions of the issue of community participation in urban public schools.

Some Current Problems

The Problem of Equity between School Districts

The educational problems facing the populations of our central cities have not been solved through the recent limited involvement of the federal government in the area of education. Despite federal aid to education, the educational achievement of children attending schools in the affluent suburbs exceeds that of the children of our urban ghettos. The reason for this disparity in achievement can be traced to several factors. It would be naïve to underestimate the role of the family as a socializing agent for children. Education as a positive value is often more pervasive in a middle class home than in a poor home, since the middle income family has more than likely derived social and economic benefits from education and since the poor family has not, and does not usually have such expectations. As a result, middle class children will be more likely to have a positive view of school. They also are more likely to be encouraged at home and assisted at home with their work. The skills necessary for academic success are more evident in a middle class home than in a poor slum home. That is, the need for delayed gratification (necessary for studying), standard verbal skills, and standard (that is, middle class) group behavior patterns are taught by middle class parents to their children. These skills are indispensable for success in school. When children raised in a slum area are deficient in these skills, they are more likely to become behavior problems and to develop school learning disabilities.

If one accepts the notion that a child raised in a poverty area often enters school with a deficiency relative to the middle class child, then it is easier to view more extensive compensatory education programs as one solution to the problem of educational inequity. In other words, if the notion of relative deficiency is accepted, it leads to greater acceptability of the premise that children who have little likelihood of success in school must be given additional assistance. However, the programs developed in urban areas have not been sufficient to so equalize opportunity. In part, this insufficiency is due to the limited funding of the Elementary and Secondary School Act, which is the primary educational

Table 3 / ELEMENTARY AND SECONDARY EDUCATION

(in millions)

	1978	1979	1980
Services for the Disadvantaged ESEA Title I:			
Regular program	$2,735	$3,078	$3,078
New concentration provision	—	+258	+400
Education for the handicapped	724	977	1,028
Desegregation assistance	326	332	354
Bilingual education	144	159	174
Education Quality/Basic Skills	28	28	37
General Support Activities			
Impact aid	805	816	528
Vocational education	642	682	682
School libraries	168	180	168
All Other	416	437	431
Total	$5,988	$6,947	$6,880

Source: *Washington Social Legislation Bulletin,* 26 (February 26, 1979), 1.

aid legislation. Other federal aid programs such as the programs to assist federally impacted areas, Head Start programs, and vocational education programs do not add substantially to the federal aid provided to elementary and secondary schools (see Table 3). (Such fiscal 1980 federal assistance amounted to less than $7 billion.) Also, long-range evaluation will be needed to determine the effectiveness of the programs. Adequate evaluations of successes and failures of these programs have been limited. Money alone will not solve all the problems associated with unequal education. However, since ongoing significant compensatory funding of relevant educational programs has not been widely available to date, it is one alternative that should be considered.

As noted earlier in this chapter, local real estate taxes were for many years the primary source of income for schools. This resulted in differential expenditure patterns between central cities and their economically varied suburbs. For example, in 1972, Detroit had a school population that was 65 percent black and minority group background. The Detroit suburb of Dearborn was 1.3 percent black and minority background; Bloomfield Hills, 1.1 percent black and minority background; and Grosse Pointe, 0.3 percent black and minority background. A 1972 amicus curiae brief to the Supreme Court in the case of *San Antonio Independent School District et al.* v. *Demetrio P. Rodriguez et al.,* supported by the Council of Great City Schools which represented the twenty-three largest school districts in the United States, observed:

On Seventh grade achievement tests, Dearborn students score in the 87th percentile nationally, in Bloomfield Hills in the 98th percentile; in Grosse

Pointe, in the 97th. Detroit's seventh graders score at the bottom, in the first percentile. Per student assessed valuation in 1968–69 in the three suburbs ranged from nearly $24,000 to over $42,000. In Detroit, it actually fell from $20,000 in 1960 to $16,500 in 1968. The suburbs with their easily educable middle and upper class children spent $965 to $1,056 per student. The City of Detroit was able to spend only $756 per student, even with federal aid. This inverse relationship of need to resources existed despite the fact that the city taxed itself for education at double the statewide average rates and its total tax rate was substantially higher from that of any suburban jurisdiction.[39]

As the tax base for central city schools has diminished, and the needs of central city schools have increased, pressures have been brought to bear on state and national authorities to fund these schools. The states have responded, but given the unequal resources of the states, they have aided urban school districts differentially. As we noted previously, the federal-urban linkage regarding equalization of educational opportunity has been quite limited. The states have been complying to demands for educational funding at least as much in response to suburban demands as to city demands, and the states' funding has not eliminated the inequality we have been discussing. Despite the use of equalization formulas within many states, differences between states as well as differences within states regarding the extent of funding for urban educational programs have not been fully eliminated, though progress has been made.

School Integration

Perhaps at this time it is necessary to consider some of the alternative solutions that have been proposed to overcome the inequitable distribution of resources relative to needs between various school districts within our metropolitan areas. In particular, in this section we will consider the integration (both forced and unforced) of school populations between more and less affluent areas. It can be argued in this context that where such integration has been mandated, the national-urban policy linkage has been quite substantial. The federal courts have set policy by which local jurisdictions have had to abide. More particularly, the federal courts have required that equal educational opportunity *cannot* be denied students on the basis of race. In this sense, a significant policy linkage has been implemented. This discussion will focus on the integration process as it affects the black population. Discussion of other disproportionately poor urban groups—most notably Hispanics—will not be included because the court litigation regarding desegregation of schools has not been focused on groups other than blacks.

The 1954 Supreme Court decision in *Brown* v. *the Board of Education of Topeka et al.* stated that separate schools for white and nonwhite students are not equal. In the years following the Brown decision, many of the legally segregated school districts (located primarily in the South) were forced to replace their dual school systems with just one school system for all students regardless of their race. The 1954 decision did not, however, address itself to the segregation that exists within school districts caused by residential housing patterns or by gerrymandering of school attendance zones. That is, the 1954 decision was addressed to *de jure* segregation and not *de facto* segregation. Given the migration of nonwhites (often poor) into central cities and of middle class whites (and increasingly the white working class) into the suburbs ringing the central cities, racial ghettos have developed in many of the nation's urban schools and de facto segregation has become increasingly prevalent. In the 1970s, the Supreme Court began to respond to de facto segregation. In 1971, the Supreme Court decided in *Swann* v. *Charlotte-Mecklenburg Board of Education* (402 U.S. 1) that "[i]f school authorities fail in their affirmative obligations . . . judicial authority may be invoked." In this particular case, the court held that the school district in and around Charlotte, North Carolina, had to integrate its schools even if they had to bus children. In its 1974 decision *Millikan* v. *Bradley* (94 S.Ct. 3112), the court held that Detroit and its suburbs did not have to maintain a system of cross-busing between central city and suburban school districts to facilitate the desegregation of the Detroit schools. In so ruling, it stated that

> [b]efore the boundaries of separate and autonomous school districts may be set aside by consolidating the separate units for remedial purposes or by imposing a cross-district remedy, it must first be shown that there has been a constitutional violation within one district that produces a significant segregation effect in another district. . . .

Thus, since Detroit's schools were not segregated as a result of the actions of Oakland and Macomb counties, "they were under no constitutional duty to make provisions for [Detroit's] Negro students."

These Court decisions provided for the legal acceptance of two separate, but not disparate concepts. First, in order to desegregate schools within a school district, children can be assigned to schools outside their neighborhood. However, cross-district school assignment is not an acceptable method of eliminating de facto segregation *unless* the other districts were responsible in some way for the segregation of the predominately nonwhite district.

The purpose of sending children to schools outside their neighborhood (which often requires busing) is to provide racial integration and by extension enhance social class integration. It is intended also to provide more equitable educational opportunities for central city, largely nonwhite students vis-à-vis the more affluent, often suburban children. Nonwhites are more likely to be attending central city schools, which are not believed to be as good as the middle class city schools or the suburban schools that many white children are attending. The central city students do not perform as well on standardized tests, nor do they have college acceptance rates as high as those of middle class city or suburban students. As a result of these factors, busing within districts or between districts to achieve racial balance is seen as a possible solution to educational inequity. There is certainly no shortage of arguments and data to support the effectiveness or lack of effectiveness of both voluntary integration and compulsory (usually by busing) integration. The proponents point to data that show increased achievement for nonwhite students and maintained performance levels for white students when integration occurs. Opponents of integration attack long bus trips as detrimental to the health of children and they point to studies that show no increased performance and even decreased performance by bused children.[40]

For many school districts, it is no longer a question of whether integration of de facto segregated public schools is good or bad. Rather, many school districts are implementing school desegregation plans under court order. In 1975, Boston was involved in a citywide integration plan and shortly thereafter Louisville, Kentucky, integrated its schools with those of the surrounding Jefferson County system. The immediate outcome of such school desegregation programs is often as fraught with anger and animosity in the North as it was a decade earlier in the South. The Boston integration controversy was acrimonious; not only were there parent pickets and organized political activity to try to stifle the neighborhood cross-busing, but there were also bloody student riots. Conditions deteriorated so much that during the fall of 1975, Federal District Court Judge W. Arthur Garrity placed the Boston school system under federal court receivership in an attempt to remove the schools from the political arena. On the other hand, busing came peacefully to Detroit. In January 1976, more than 21,000 students were bused with little turmoil. There were no screaming parents, no helmeted police officers, and almost no school pickets in the city when the integration order went into effect. Richard Salem, the midwest regional director of the Community Relations Service of the United States Department of Justice, referred to the implementation of the Detroit busing plans as "a piece of cake."[41] Similarly, in 1978, court-ordered cross-district busing in New Castle County, Delaware (Wilmington and its suburbs), and districtwide busing in Los Angeles were accomplished peacefully and calmly.[42] In Seattle, busing was instituted without the involvement of the federal courts.

Regardless of the political atmosphere surrounding court-ordered integration of de facto segregated schools, the collective actions of government bodies—the courts, federal administrative agencies, school boards, and legislatures—have required many urban school districts in both the North and the South to integrate their schools and may lead to more interdistrict school integration as well. The actual integration effects of the desegregation process have not been universally successful in the major urban areas. Thus, in 1967, Detroit's public school system was 50 percent nonwhite; by 1977, this school system was 85 percent nonwhite. Philadelphia's public school system was 60 percent nonwhite in 1967; by 1977, it was 70 percent nonwhite. Chicago's public school system was 60 percent nonwhite in 1967; New York's, 50 percent nonwhite; and Los Angeles's, 50 percent nonwhite. By 1977, Chicago's public school system was 75 percent nonwhite; New York's, 70 percent nonwhite; and Los Angeles's, 65 percent nonwhite. Some areawide desegregation efforts, however, have been more successful. In 1968, 40 percent of nonwhite students nationally attended public schools which had populations that were almost entirely nonwhite. Desegregation, either on a voluntary or court-ordered basis, had reduced this figure to 15 percent in 1978. This reduction was facilitated by the more successful desegregation efforts in the South and in the smaller cities and towns in the Northeast and Midwest.[43]

Who Should Control the Schools?

Given the frequent inability of urban school systems to meet educational needs and the difficulties that such schools have faced in dealing with the issue of racial imbalance, perhaps the only rational public policy alternative is one that recognizes local and especially urban problems as national problems requiring national support. One further educational policy question raised in recent years at first blush might sound contradictory to national support for education, but upon closer reflection clearly is not antithetical. Increasingly, central city parents have been wanting greater control over their schools. In the parlance of this movement, they have been demanding community control over their own schools and their children's education. As Mario Fantini and Marilyn Gittell observed:

> America's economic and political institutions no longer provide ready access for new groups. Demands for decentralization and community control are a reflection of that general political circumstance. The movement represents an effort by powerless groups to become a part of the system, and at the same time, to make the system more responsive to their needs. They seek a means of shared responsibility in the allocation of the resources of the society.[44]

In many ways, these parents are demanding what middle class parents have had for many years. Insofar as suburban school districts have school boards to which the citizens elect representatives, and these school boards provide oversight to their boards of education, parents have been able to maintain oversight, too. Also, middle class—often suburban—parents are not usually intimidated by school authorities. Through their parent associations, they have been able to maintain an ongoing surveillance over their children's schools.[45]

It can be argued that the suburban community control of schools is rational since it provides a neat fit into the funding unit—that is, the school district. Similarly, it can be contended that community control of central city schools is not quite as rational since the community in this latter instance is not contiguous with the funding unit, but only a section of it, since most often the funding unit is the city or a section of the county. This latter argument is not entirely a cogent one since substantial sums of money are made available to some small town and suburban school districts from their respective states and from the federal government (even if these funds are insufficient in many instances).

An example of this phenomenon can be found in Delaware. Delaware provides approximately 70 percent of all funds for the operation of public elementary and secondary schools in the state.[46] Local school boards are required to raise whatever other funds they deem necessary to maintain their schools. One can thus argue that the State of Delaware is the primary funding unit for its school districts. However, local school boards, which represent the citizens residing within the district, are policy-making bodies (within the limits of a state-mandated curriculum, teacher certification, and attendance regulations).

What the outcome of demands for community control of city schools will be is still in question. In part the reason for this unclear position can be related to the politics of education and the character of urban succession patterns. Thus, though poor often nonwhite and Hispanic children are increasingly becoming a majority in central city schools, the teaching and administrative staffs are middle class (either by background or by virtue of education and current status) and often are of different ethnic backgrounds. Many of these educators have gained job security in their positions because of established tenure rules. Also, with the expansion of teacher unionization, teachers are protected by union contracts. The unions may provide a united front against parent groups seeking to influence the schools' educational programs over which traditionally teachers and administrators have had a major influence. In some instances, urban parents claim that the teachers are often too different from their children to be effective in developing a meaningful curriculum for them. Such urban parents want to control their own schools through local school boards and choose their administrators and teachers. Ironically, often unionized teacher groups by their high level of political organization may develop candidate slates that are subsequently elected as the dominant group within local school boards, as has been the case in New York City. (Unfortunately, in 1980 only 9 percent of parents eligible to vote in New York City district school board elections exercised their franchise.[47]) The union is concerned that parental control or local control situations would eliminate professional discretion and academic freedom for educators, and would destroy employment security for them, too. A conflict between teachers and advocates of greater community control reached the explosive level in New York City in 1969. An experimental community-controlled neighborhood school board that wanted to control personnel decisions illegally dismissed teachers. In response, the United Federation of Teachers went on strike for three months.[48] The eventual downfall of this local board, in the Ocean Hill–Brownsville section of Brooklyn, was its failure to recognize the governmental structure within which it operated. The city is a creature of the state; the local governing board could only exercise its powers provided it did not arbitrarily exceed its authority, which was limited in this instance by the authority of the New York City Board of Education and the New York State Department of Education.

CONCLUSION

We have reviewed the historical tradition of local public education at the elementary and secondary level in the United States and have noted that within our federal tradition, education has been essentially a state-supervised local responsibility. The role of the federal government in education has been limited, and to date there have been just a few significant national-urban policy linkages in education because interdependence of jurisdictions in education has been difficult for the American voter to accept. Americans have traditionally coveted their right to govern their own schools. Regardless of the fiscal problems to which this situation has led, Americans continue to fear national involvement. In fact, the national policy linkages that they have experienced have often made them even more fearful of national government intervention. Thus, compliance with civil rights and affirmative action guidelines often has been enforced because of local school boards' concerns that federal funds will be withheld if they do not abide by federal regulations. Also, the federal courts have acted in some metropolitan areas to enforce integration of schools, often to the despair of middle class and working class residents.

Today, urban education is the center of class-based conflicts. Areas of current dispute include policy formulation by the local school systems in terms of relative roles of educational administrators, professional teachers' unions, and neighborhood groups. A further area of controversy relates to civil rights litigation and the effects of de facto racial segregation patterns on the schools. Finally, concern has been raised with the need for establishment of statewide taxing equity for schools. We have discussed the structural difficulty of providing such equity in the face of the reliance of school districts for their local funding on the property tax, which provides its greatest yield in affluent suburbs. Federal and state funding of public elementary and secondary education has increased, although the federal funding still remains quite limited. This relatively new development has occurred in part because of the need for provision of multiple social and physical services, especially in central cities, at a time when there is insufficient municipal revenue to meet the challenge of contemporary urban education. Certainly, many of the problems relating to urban education have yet to be solved.

A particularly interesting question that has not been considered in this chapter relates to the size of the cohort to be educated. Between 1950 and 1970, the number of elementary and secondary school-age children increased 70 percent; but, the estimated 1979 school-age population was 11 percent lower than in 1970, and it is expected that during the decade of the 1980s, there will be a further 10 percent decline. Despite this drop in school-age population, federal spending for elementary and secondary education increased 25 percent after accounting for inflation during the eight years prior to 1979.[49] Will funding levels be raised or even maintained as the number of children requiring education declines? We cannot say, but what is clear, however, is that Americans believe that education provides an opportunity by which the economically deprived can move into the mainstream of American society. As long as belief in the value of education is a prevailing value in this nation, the question of quality education in the urban context for whom, determined by whom, and involving what governmental level will remain a politically viable public policy issue.

REFERENCES

1. Elwood P. Cubberley, *Public Education in the United States* (New York: Houghton Mifflin, 1934), p. 163.
2. Lawrence A. Cremin and Merle L. Borrowman, *Public Schools in Our Democracy* (New York: Macmillan, 1956), p. 91.
3. Chris A. DeYoung and Richard Wynn, *American Education,* 7th ed. (New York: McGraw-Hill, 1972), p. 169.
4. Cubberley, op. cit., pp. 200–05.
5. Ibid., p. 213.
6. Carroll Atkinson and Eugene T. Maleska, *The Story of Education* (Philadelphia: Clinton Books, 1965), p. 201.
7. Elwood P. Cubberley, *The History of Education* (Cambridge, Mass.: The Riverside Press, 1920), pp. 654–57.
8. Cubberley, *Public Education,* op. cit., p. 216.
9. Cremin and Borrowman, op. cit., p. 84.
10. Cubberley, *Public Education,* op. cit., p. 259.
11. Ibid., p. 738.
12. Ibid., p. 744.
13. DeYoung and Wynn, op. cit., pp. 130–33.
14. Ibid. For a good general discussion of local school boards, also see Joel Spring, *American Education* (New York: Longman, 1978), pp. 81–116.
15. DeYoung and Wynn, op. cit., p. 169. The authors note that "while political scientists usually favor the latter (that is, fiscally dependent boards), educational writers prefer the fiscally independent school board" (p. 132).
16. *1978 Congressional Quarterly Almanac* (Washington, D.C., 1979), p. 556.
17. For example, in *Serrano* v. *Priest* (1971), the California Supreme Court held

that the education of children could not be a function of wealth, other than the wealth of the entire state.

18. *How to Save Urban America,* ed. by William A. Caldwell (New York: New American Library, 1973), pp. 152–53.
19. Spring, op cit., p. 225.
20. U.S. Bureau of the Census, *Statistical Abstract of the United States, 1978,* 99th Edition (Washington, D.C., 1978), p. 135.
21. U.S. Department of Health, Education and Welfare, National Center for Education Statistics, *The Condition of Education, 1978 Edition* (Washington, D.C., 1978), p. 78.
22. Ibid., p. 94.
23. Gary Orfield, *Must We Bus?* (Washington, D.C.: The Brookings Institution, 1978), p. 193.
24. H. Thomas James, James A. Kelly, and Walter I. Garms, *Determinants of Educational Expenditures in Large Cities of the United States,* Cooperative Research Project No. 2389 (Washington, D.C.: U.S. Department of Health, Education, and Welfare, Office of Education, 1966), p. 17.
25. Raymond C. Hummel and John M. Nagle, *Urban Education in America* (New York: Oxford University Press, 1973), p. 178.
26. Carl Thornbald, "A Summary of the Fiscal Impact of a Concentration of Low Income Families in the Public Schools—A Study of Public Housing in Chicago in 1962," in U.S. Congress, House of Representatives, Committee on Education and Labor, *Elementary and Secondary School Act Hearings,* before the General Subcommittee on Education, 91st Cong., 1st Sess., March 1969, p. 5.
27. Ralph W. Tyler, "The Federal Role in Education," *The Public Interest,* 34 (Winter 1974), 168. Also see James Coleman et al., *Equality of Educational Opportunity* (Washington, D.C.: U.S. Office of Education, 1966).
28. For additional discussion of this point, see supra, pp. 105–106.
29. The discussion in this section relies heavily on material presented by Norman C. Thomas, *Education in National Politics* (New York: David McKay, 1975), pp. 19–27.
30. *1978 Congressional Quarterly Almanac,* op. cit., p. 558.
31. Ibid.
32. U.S. Congress, House, Committee on Education and Labor, *Elementary and Secondary Education Amendments of 1966, Hearings,* before the General Subcommittee on Education, 89th Cong., 2nd Sess., March 1966, pt. 1, p. 143.
33. In Philadelphia, programs of this nature were provided for a school population of 289,000 composed of 59.8 percent black pupils and 2.8 percent Spanish-surnamed pupils. The pupil population of Philadelphia had 40 percent of the disadvantaged pupils in the State of Pennsylvania. See U.S. Congress, House of Representatives, Committee on Education and Labor, *Elementary and Secondary Education Amendments of 1973, Hearings,* before the General Subcommittee on Education and Labor, 93rd Cong., 1st Sess., February–March 1973, pt. 2, p. 1630.
34. Information regarding Philadelphia was made available by Michael H. Kean, Executive Director for Research and Evaluation, Philadelphia Board of Education, Philadelphia, Pennsylvania, September 1979; U.S. Congress, Senate, Committee on Labor and Public Welfare, *Education Legislation, 1973, Hearings,* before the Subcommittee on Education, 93rd Cong., 1st Sess., October 1973, pt. 7, p. 2615.

35. Study cited by Orfield, op. cit., p. 225.
36. Ibid.
37. *1978 Congressional Quarterly Almanac,* op. cit., p. 560.
38. U.S. Congress, House, Committee on Education and Labor, *Elementary and Secondary Education Amendments of 1973, Hearings,* before the General Subcommittee on Education, op. cit., January–February 1973, pt. 1, p. 476.
39. Cited in U.S. Congress, House, Committee on Education and Labor, *Oversight Hearings on Elementary and Secondary Education, Hearings,* 92nd Cong., 2nd Sess., September–October 1972, pp. 262–63.
40. A sharp debate of the arguments regarding integration appeared in *The Public Interest* in 1972 and 1973. See David J. Armor, "The Evidence on Busing," *The Public Interest,* 28 (Summer 1972), 90–126; Thomas F. Pettigrew, Elizabeth L. Useem, Clarence Normand, and Marshall S. Smith, "Busing: A Review of 'The Evidence'," *The Public Interest,* 30 (Winter 1973), 88–118.
41. *The New York Times,* January 27, 1976, p. 1.
42. Jeffrey A. Raffel, *The Politics of School Desegregation* (Philadelphia: Temple University Press, 1980).
43. Robert Reinhold, "25 Years After Desegregation, North's Schools Lag," *The New York Times,* May 17, 1979, p. B11.
44. Mario Fantini and Marilyn Gittell, *Decentralization: Achieving Reform* (New York: Praeger, 1973), p. 7.
45. For a discussion of this problem, see ibid., pp. 40–55; Kevin Cox, *Conflict, Power and Politics in the City: A Geographic View* (New York: McGraw-Hill, 1973), pp. 31–36.
46. *1973 Delaware Abstract* (Dover, Del.: State Planning Office, 1973), p. 103.
47. *The New York Times,* June 26, 1980, p. B6.
48. Diane Ravitch, *The Great School Wars, New York City, 1805–1973* (New York: Basic Books, 1974), p. 320–78.
49. *1978 Congressional Quarterly Almanac,* op. cit., p. 114.

Public Welfare and Individualism

INTRODUCTION

Welfare programming in the United States is primarily a public sector activity. Though a proliferation of private charities and agencies also provide care to the poor and the needy, the government has traditionally assumed the primary responsibility for providing for the poor. Thus any discussion of welfare in urban America must focus on public sector activities. A second characteristic of welfare in America is that it was born of a tradition of localism and individualism. The localism has been the nemesis of numerous urban jurisdictions which, despite an increasing federal involvement, are finding it more difficult to maintain reasonable public assistance payment levels to poor mothers and children. The individualism that underlies the welfare function is still very much alive and affects the public response to demands for welfare reform.

The federal government's involvement in public welfare has increased over the years. In fact, despite the tradition of localism, the federal role in the delivery of public welfare income and services has become substantial. In the early years of the Republic, the national government was not involved in public welfare. Not until the New Deal was any major role carved out by the federal government. Since that time, however, the role of the federal government in public welfare has increased to the point where it is now substantially involved in the two major public assistance income programs, Supplemental Security Income (SSI) and Aid to Families with Dependent Children (AFDC). The national government provides basic funding levels for SSI, which supplies benefits to the needy aged, the disabled, and the blind; these funds may be optionally supplemented by the states. Federal variable grants-in-aid to the states provide part of the funds for AFDC, a states' program for needy mothers and children. A General Assistance category, maintained by some states and localities for people who do not qualify for AFDC or SSI, receives no federal funds, but this tends to be a small category. In addition to SSI and AFDC, the federal government also supplies funds for some service programs. The Department of Health and Human Services is responsible for administering these programs. Prior to May 1980 these programs came under the jurisdiction of the Department of Health, Education, and Welfare.

Despite the increased federal role in public welfare, the states and localities still must provide substantial monies for public welfare programming. More specifically, though federal income and services grants help defray the costs of categorical public assistance (of which AFDC is the major program), these programs cost states and localities substantial sums. Thus in fiscal 1977, these jurisdictions spent almost $9 billion on these programs. This represented about 33 percent of the total cost of all such public assistance programs. Although state funds represent an increasing proportion of the state and local funding of public welfare, fairly high local expenditure levels for public welfare are found in some urban states. Thus in 1977, local contributions were over 15 percent of total cost in Minnesota (21.7 percent of total expenditure), New York (20.3 percent), California (17.7 percent), Indiana (17.7 percent), and Ohio (17.7 percent).[1] Public aid in some urban jurisdictions represents over 20 percent of the total operating budget. Some cities and urban counties have been forced by state action to reduce their welfare payment levels in the wake of the inflationary spiral of the decade of the 1970s. When welfare payment levels are low to begin with and no welfare recipient really makes money on welfare, reductions are difficult to make.

Although states and localities clearly need even further federal support for welfare programs, public attitudes toward these programs and their recipients make such increased involvement difficult. The prevailing belief, especially among many noncity dwellers, is that if a local jurisdiction has a welfare problem, it should solve its own problem. To some extent, this narrow-gauge view, which does not take into account the interdependence of units within our nation, was broken down with the implementation of SSI in 1974. However, individualism and racism operating together have made this an unpopular program for national political leaders to consider nationalizing. Assistance to mothers and children is often seen as aid to the "unworthy poor" both because of the assumption that somewhere there is a father who should be working to support his family and because of the disproportionate number of nonwhites receiving this assistance. Also, because AFDC is the most costly welfare program, opponents of a strong national presence do not want the national government to assume a greater share of its costs, since that might reduce the local role and increase the national role in welfare income and service programs. These attitudes have resulted in a recognition that a policy linkage in public welfare policy at the national level would reduce the costs for urban jurisdictions while standardizing income and services for millions of poor mothers and children. Such change, however, has been stalled by contemporary proponents of localism.

The following sections contain a discussion of the historical and theoretical underpinning of the American public welfare system. The discussion emphasizes the traditions of localism and individualism that have acted as the baseline from which all our subsequent programming efforts have derived. After these assumptions are set forth, we will describe the present public welfare system, analyzing its initial development and then its growth and development as a partially nationally funded program with strong state and local options retained. Finally, some of the contemporary problems that require a legislative response will be posed to show how interjurisdictional linkages, especially between the federal government and states and their urban population centers, could help solve the fiscal dilemma caused in part by the public welfare program needs that face urban jurisdictions.

The History of the Development of the Public Welfare System

Public welfare, like the other human resource areas under discussion in this volume, has a history of local responsibility. To understand more fully the public welfare system in the United States and its roots in localism, we must examine the history of the system. To do this effectively, it is necessary to consider both the political and religious roots[2] of the delivery of assistance to the poor. Very briefly then, let us look at these two forces in history to see their effects on public welfare in contemporary America.

Reinhold Niebuhr, in *The Contribution of Religion to Social Work,* suggested that: "Calvinism has never been able to overcome the temptation to regard poverty as a consequence of laziness and vice, and therefore to leave the poor and the needy to the punishment which a righteous God has inflicted upon them." [3] The United States developed as a Protestant nation, with underlying beliefs in individualism and the Protestant work ethic. All the programs that have evolved to aid the poor have been predicated on this Calvinist assumption. William Ryan, in his more recent volume, *Blaming the Victim,*[4] has suggested that Americans "blame the victim" in the sense that the poor are seen as being responsible for their own poverty. In a more traditional Calvinistic sense, idleness is sin. Those who do not work with industry show signs of a "lack of grace." [5]

The religious values that blamed individuals for their own condition were secularized first by the British in the sixteenth century—after it became a Protestant nation—with the evolution of local regulations and restrictions. The Elizabethan Poor Laws of 1597 and 1601 provided for local governments to assume responsibility for their impoverished residents; they provided for the exclusion or regulation of people likely to become paupers; they also provided for the development of charitable trusts to assist the poor.[6] The American colonists patterned their regulations after these poor laws. The colonists granted their local governments the responsibility to provide assistance to the poor. They also gave their officials the power to establish residency requirements for relief eligibility and to aid only the "worthy poor," who in a period where unemployment was not a problem were defined to be the old, the sick, and women and children who had lost the male breadwinner. Anyone else could be excluded, because "[i]ndustry and thrift were considered critical and poverty a sign of the lack of both." The New England colonies copied the English regulations to such an extent that their relief statutes closely resembled the English Elizabethan Poor Laws—except that they contained no provision for the development of charitable trusts.

By the time of the American Revolution, many towns and cities attempted to deal with the poverty that had developed in their midst (in part due to the inability of the cities to absorb economically the increasing urban population) by developing two major methods for dealing with the poor: the workhouse or almshouse (indoor relief), and the more dominant form of relief, assistance to the poor in their own homes (outdoor relief). Both forms of relief were kept at low levels of adequacy and the system often retained an unpleasant and harsh form. During the nineteenth century, indoor relief increased in popularity and many local jurisdictions built almshouses or workhouses. This latter approach put those deemed able to work; in so doing, it responded well to the religious underpinning of the welfare system, which assumed that many people were poor because they did not want to work and that their "idleness breeds sin."

The large eastern seaboard cities, such as New York, Philadelphia, Boston, and Charleston, preferred almshouse relief in this early period.[7] In 1824, New York State enacted a County Poorhouse Act which stipulated that all counties in New York State were to erect one or more poorhouses. Support for these institutions as well as support for its residents was the responsibility of the county. Until 1860, indoor relief was the dominant response to poverty in other (particularly eastern) states, too. In 1824, Massachusetts had 83 almshouses. By 1839, it had 180 almshouses, and by 1860, the total had increased to 219.[8] By 1860, however, outdoor assistance became the main form of public assistance. This change in the nature of relief services was due in large measure to the high cost of sustaining an almshouse and the unsanitary conditions and confinement associated with indoor relief.

In 1857, the President of the Philadelphia Board of Guardians of the Poor concluded that outdoor relief was less expensive and more humane than almshouse relief. Also, the Report of the 1857 New York State Senate Select Committee to Visit Charitable and Penal Institutions contended that a

> more efficient and economical auxiliary in supporting the poor, and in the prevention of pauperism, consists, in the opinion of the Committee, in the proper and systematic distribution of *out door* relief. Worthy indigent persons should, if possible, be kept from the degradation of the poor house, by reasonable supplies of provisions, bedding, and other absolute necessaries in their own homes. Half the sum requisite for their maintenance in the poor house would often save them from destitution and enable them to work in their households and their vicinity, sufficiently to earn the remainder of their support during the inclement season when indigence suffers the most, and when it is most likely to be forced into the common receptacles of pauperism, when it rarely emerges without loss of self respect and a sense of degradation.[9]

Indoor relief, with all of its degradation, did not die easily. In the late nineteenth century and early twentieth century, the voluntary Charity Organization Society (COS) movement was influential in having some cities abolish outdoor relief. In 1900, cities of over 200,000 population that gave no public outdoor relief included New York, Philadelphia, Brooklyn, St. Louis, Baltimore, San Francisco, New Orleans, Washington, Kansas City, and Louisville. Cities of over 200,000 that did provide public outdoor relief were Milwaukee, Detroit, Boston, Buffalo, Minneapolis, Newark, Cleveland, Pittsburgh, Jersey City, and Cincinnati.[10] The COS movement argued that indoor relief could be combined with instruction of the poor and was therefore more beneficial. They also believed that very limited relief grants would encourage the dependent to rehabilitate their lives. They did not emphasize the influence of economic and social

Table 1 / TOTAL WHITE INMATES: 1,509

Children	111
Hospital and Lunatic	718
Old Men's Infirmary and Incurable Section	188
Male Working Wards	79
Mechanics Wards	42
Old Women's Asylum and Incurable Section	256
Women's Working Ward	71
Nursery with Women	21
Nursery with Children	23

Source: Benjamin J. Klebaner, "Public Poor Relief in America, 1790–1860," *Social Problems and Social Policy: The American Experience.* Reprinted by permission of Arno Press, Inc., 1976.

conditions in creating poverty and their impact on the lives of the poor. One could argue that in some ways the early COS movement provided the intellectual roots for the social work movement of the late nineteenth century with its concern for rehabilitation of the individual poor. In the words of Niebuhr, if "Calvinism" is replaced by "the COS movement" then the COS movement regarded "poverty as a consequence of laziness and vice." However, unlike the Calvinists, the COS movements' adherents wanted to rehabilitate individual poor people so that they would not be left to "the punishment which a righteous God has inflicted upon them."

Advocates of almshouse care often assumed that there was a large group of able-bodied poor. In reality, however, most of the residents of the almshouse were not in a position to work. The classification of inmates in Philadelphia's Blockley almshouse in 1848 gives some indication of this circumstance. Of 1,509 white inmates, only 192 men and women—about 12 percent of the inmate population—were able to work (see Table 1).

The role of states and localities in the provision of assistance to the needy was set for eighty years by the famous Pierce Veto of 1854. Concerned with the care of the insane in local institutions and the inadequacy of state efforts to provide adequate care, Dorothea Dix, a famous social reformer of this era, was successful in influencing Congress to pass a bill that would have provided federal land grants to the states to help pay for mental hospitals established by the states. The measure would have allotted 12.25 million acres of land; 10 million acres for the mentally ill, and 2.25 million acres for the deaf, the dumb, and the blind. In vetoing the bill, President Franklin Pierce emphasized the local character of the relief function. He asserted:

I cannot find any authority in the Constitution for making the Federal Government the great almoner of public charity throughout the United States. ... It would in the end be prejudicial rather than beneficial to the noble offices of charity, to have the charge of them transferred from the States to the Federal Government.[11]

Increase in the Role of the States

The Pierce Veto delayed national activity in the welfare area until the 1930s and the passage of New Deal legislation. But even then the tradition of state and local activity shaped the nature of national intervention. The role of state authority in public welfare increased during the second half of the nineteenth century. In 1863, the Commonwealth of Massachusetts established a Board of State Charities to oversee local relief. In addition, this board was given the authority to reorganize various state charity institutions. The 1863 act also permitted the investigation of conditions for support of the poor in cities and towns, as well as in county institutions and institutions that received partial or full state funding.[12] By 1874, nine states had established Boards of Charities with state authority to oversee state and local welfare activities, as well as private charitable institutions.[13] It was the State Boards of Charities that eventually metamorphized into State Public Welfare Departments that served to control and consolidate public welfare functions in the states. The first such department was established in Illinois in 1917; by the 1930s most states had consolidated different aspects of welfare services and had state welfare departments, and not charity boards, to oversee, though not control, local public (as well as private) welfare functions.

Not until after World War I did state provision of public assistance emerge as a discernible pattern in the states. State laws providing public aid were, in fact, not enacted until the 1920s and 1930s. By 1926, Connecticut, Maryland, New Jersey, Texas, and Utah had developed state laws providing aid limited to widowed mothers termed "mother's aid." In the same year, six states—Colorado, Maine, Nevada, New Hampshire, Rhode Island, and Washington—enacted laws to provide aid, generally for mothers with dependent children. In twenty-seven states, such laws had various limitations. Such aid limitations included: "[a] mother whose husband is dead; deserted; divorced; totally incapacitated physically or mentally; imprisoned; or in an institution for the insane, feeble-minded or epileptic."[14] Six states had no such mother's aid program. In states that had the program, mother's aid was not mandatory but available at the option of the county or municipality and paid for locally.[15] It was not until the 1930s that such laws became compulsory and partially state funded. Similarly, by 1930, nineteen states had implemented old age pension laws. Such laws prior to 1930 also had been optional and paid for at the local level. After 1929, these laws were increasingly made compulsory and also were partially funded at the state level.

It is apparent that the state response to the needy was very much consistent with the traditional views of poverty. Thus the "worthy poor" were defined and then aided; and when states first entered the public assistance arena, they were reinforcing the maintenance of local options and prerogatives for helping the "worthy poor." At this stage in American development, there was no clearly articulated and accepted view of a national responsibility to assist poor American citizens. Clearly the notion of interregional or even intraregional interdependence was not well established for the delivery of public welfare assistance. The basic assumptions regarding "poverty as sin" and local responsibility, as reinforced by the federalism of the constitution and underlined by the Pierce Veto, were quite vital at the onset of the depression of the 1930s despite unprecedented levels of unemployment, sharp declines in the gross national product, and the shattering of the national and international banking and money markets.

The Social Security Act and the Development of the Contemporary Public Welfare System

In the wake of the depression, the federal government treaded where the state and local jurisdictions were unable to move. One such problem area was meeting the fiscal needs of providing for the depression poor. As one commentator observed: "Soaring expenditures, a limited local tax base, and statutory and constitutional restrictions on tax rates and debt often added up to almost complete fiscal inability to cope with hitherto unimagined volumes of urgent human need." [16] The recognition of obvious linkages between jurisdictions became so clear that emergency measures had to be taken. The questioning of the federal government's right to act in behalf of localities in order to ameliorate the crisis was not particularly relevant since the alternatives were clearly federal actions or no actions. When Roosevelt took office in 1933, he took immediate action to rectify the dislocations caused by the depression. The Roosevelt administration established the Federal Emergency Relief Administration to provide for the income needs of the depression's destitute. The Federal Emergency Relief Administration provided federal grants-in-aid to the states for unemployment relief. From November 1933 to April 1934, a work relief policy was undertaken by the federal Civil Works Administration (CWA) which provided temporary work for about 4 million able-bodied unemployed persons. This program was operated directly by the federal government. A subsequent, basically federally funded and administered, work relief program was adopted in 1935 and lasted until 1942.[17]

It appears evident that one of the forces motivating Franklin Roosevelt in his support for relief programs was political self-interest. There were clear indications of a potential for cracks in the political coalition he had fashioned in the 1932 and 1934 elections. Radical labor unionists, the organizations of the unemployed, supporters of Huey Long, Townsenites, and Coughlinites were all critical of national government inaction in responding to the poverty and unemployment of the depression. There was fear of more widespread discontent, too. To overlook these political forces and the concern they gave Roosevelt and his loyal supporters would be an error of omission. Frances Piven and Richard Cloward have observed that "relief arrangements are initiated or expanded during the occasional outbreaks of civil disorder produced by mass unemployment." [18] Though this condition may not always prevail, it certainly did occur during this period in American history.

By 1935, Roosevelt sought to limit the federal role in public assistance. In many ways, he was as bound to the tradition of localism in public welfare as outspoken opponents of federal intervention. In an executive order of May 6, 1935, terminating the Federal Emergency Relief Administration, Franklin Roosevelt commented that "the federal government must and shall quit this business of relief." [19] However, the role of the federal government in public welfare, although limited and circumscribed by state program administration, was cemented by the Roosevelt-sponsored Social Security Act of 1935. There were two basic components of this law: social insurance and public assistance. The *social insurance* component of the law was established as a national insurance program for aged retirees under the direction of the Social Security Administration. Thus, this part of the income maintenance system was conceptualized as a federal program. (Unemployment insurance was also instituted by the 1935 law. The unemployment compensation programs were to be developed basically as state programs.) The *public assistance* component of the Social Security Act of 1935 was developed so that states would receive federal grants-in-aid that would be matched by the states to fund public assistance payments to the needy. The categories of needy were aged, blind, and dependent children (later amended to be families with dependent children). [20] These categories of poor were the traditional "worthy poor." Resource standards for eligibility were determined by the states. In the public assistance programs, payments as well as eligibility varied from state to state. [21]

The assumption of this two-pronged approach to income maintenance was that public assistance would provide aid for the poor. There was more poverty during the depression than in any other period of the twentieth century, with estimates of unemployment as high as 25 percent of the work force. It was expected, however, that as people gained coverage in the social insurance system and as that system expanded its protection against various social risks, the public assistance programs would become residual categories. That is, the older person would be eligible to receive old age insurance benefits; the child without a parent to provide support would receive survivor's insurance, and the disabled worker would receive disability insurance; the worker unemployed because of fluctuations in the marketplace would receive unemployment insurance. When restricted to the specified categories of need, public assistance was imagined to be needed by only a small group of people not eligible for social insurance payments. It became apparent in the 1950s and 1960s that there were many more poor people either not eligible for social insurance or inadequately assisted by social insurance than Franklin D. Roosevelt, his advisors, or congressional leaders responsible for the passage of the law ever anticipated.

The federal grants authorized to the states fell into three categories of dependent and needy persons: the aged (Old Age Assistance—OAA), the blind (Aid to the Blind—AB), and dependent children (Aid to Dependent Children—ADC). To qualify for such grants, states had to submit a plan specifying that the state program would be "in effect in all political subdivisions of the state, and if administered by them be mandatory upon them." [22] Initially, the federal matching grant was 50 percent of total revenue expended for the categories of Old Age Assistance and Aid to the Blind. For Aid to Dependent Children, the federal matching grant was 33⅓ percent of total revenues *excluding any payment to the caretaker.* An important concession made before the Senate Finance Committee in its consideration of the initial bill has had an important effect in shaping and limiting the role of the federal government in the public assistance area. Senator Harry Byrd of Virginia was concerned about the provision that states could receive federal grants for old age assistance only if their plans maintained federal assistance at an income level sufficient to provide the aged recipient "a reasonable subsistence compatible with health and decency." [23] This provision would permit federal authorities to determine whether state payment levels for old age assistance were adequate. After Byrd successfully raised the specter of federal supervision to determine whether states provided such a reasonable subsistence level, this limitation on the prerogatives of the states was removed from the bill.[24]

The New Deal belief that with the growth of social insurance, the need for public assistance would diminish and eventually wither away did not come to pass. Following World War II, the OAA rate indeed dropped by one third, but the ADC rate increased sharply. Also, overall federal public assistance income and services grants increased sharply, rising from $439 in 1946 to $1 billion in 1950, to about $5 billion in 1970, and to over $19 billion in 1976.[25] State and local expenditures for such assistance had also risen to almost $9 billion in 1976. In 1950, approximately 2.2 million women and children received Aid to Families with Dependent Children (AFDC). Between December 1969 and December 1978, the average number of persons receiving AFDC increased from just over 6 million persons to over 10.3 million persons.[26]

Outline of the Current Problem

The administration of public welfare programs, particularly AFDC, has been uneven and inadequate.[27] Eligibility as well as levels of payment vary from jurisdiction to jurisdiction. Although every state maintains an AFDC program, they have relative independence in determining whether and how much they will participate in such federal-state programs. Thus, the extent of a state's participation is often a question of political will or economic wealth. In addition, even the national standards that have been established do not ensure that programs will be adequate because it has been difficult to force states and localities to comply with such standards. Therefore, program differentiation, even when not mandated by law, has been able to flourish. For example, federal regulations require that states participating in the AFDC program maintain a current standard of basic financial needs. Compliance with this regulation has been difficult to enforce. Definitions of basic need vary from state to state; the standard on which states base their payments varies too. In addition, in many states, AFDC payments are a portion of basic need and not total defined basic need.

One additional parameter of the welfare problem relates to the population shifts of the past two decades. While such population shifts have been discussed earlier in a more general context, they are particularly relevant to a discussion of the welfare problem. Congruent with this movement has been an increase in the social needs always associated with the in-migration to cities of poor white or nonwhite populations. Simultaneous with this movement has been the outmigration of the middle class and industry to the suburbs and other regions. The city's welfare problems have been seen increasingly as racial problems and thus race and poverty have often been grouped together in policy considerations. This makes policy changes more difficult to achieve.

That the severe economic and social problems of the nonwhite urban ghetto are a key national policy issue was underscored by data concerning Los Angeles County, California. According to data released by the Economic and Youth Opportunities Agency of Los Angeles in 1969, 1.4 million of the county's 7.2 million people (19 percent of the population) were poor. The racial or ethnic ghettos and barrios, such as South Central Los Angeles and East Los Angeles, contained 7 percent of the county's population and 31 percent of its poor. The proportion of the poor in the black community (34.5 percent) and the Mexican-American community (25.7 percent) was much greater than that of the white (Anglo) community (16.8 percent).[28] The nature of racial and ethnic poverty in the Los Angeles area was further emphasized by a 1965 study conducted by the Welfare Planning Council of the Los Angeles Region. This study grouped into contiguous units those 1960 census tracts in which over 20 percent of the population had a family income of less than $4,000 per year. The study divided such units into eleven poverty areas within Los Angeles County. The results of this study were summarized in an article by Richard H. Brown. He noted that:

> All of these areas are characterized by high density of poor people, higher number of dependents supported by relatively fewer people with jobs, high

rates of male unemployment, higher residential density, dwellings with above average rates of deterioration, high percentages of welfare recipients, high rates of medical indigence, infant mortality, and communicable diseases, high rates of crime and juvenile offenses, and low levels of educational attainment. . . . [T]ypically they are Negro or Mexican-American slums.[29]

By 1977, 10.7 percent of individuals below the poverty level lived in metropolitan areas and 15.8 percent lived in central cities. Of those individuals in poverty, 61 percent were found in metropolitan areas (38 percent in central cities and 23 percent in suburban areas). While this data reflects a slight decrease from 1970 in the percentage of persons in poverty in metropolitan areas, this decrease is in suburban areas and the number of those individuals in poverty in central cities has actually increased since 1970.[30] The U.S. Bureau of the Census has noted that the Hispanic population in the United States is more concentrated in metropolitan areas than either the white or black population. This Hispanic population is more evenly divided between central cities and suburbs than the black population which is still more heavily concentrated in central cities.[31] It is also a population in high risk of poverty. Just over 23 percent of Spanish-origin families were in a poverty status in 1976. Poverty status for those of Mexican origin was 22 percent; Puerto Rican origin, 38.8 percent; and Cuban origin, 19.6 percent.[32] Such circumstances particularly affect the public assistance system. As Duncan MacIntyre observed:

A large and badly underprivileged minority, underemployed and heavily unemployed, is now resident in New York and other big cities that long have had liberal public assistance policies. Negroes, and . . . Puerto Ricans and Mexican-Americans, are emerging as a large public assistance beneficiary group, in the big cities the dominant beneficiary group. Their stake in public assistance, whether it involves supplementation or full relief, AFDC or General Assistance, is enormous, for low as some public assistance grants are, great as is the amount of unmet need, PA still, literally, can mean the difference between starvation and some kind of existence.[33]

It is becoming more and more apparent that a stronger federal role will be required to cope with the public welfare burdens of our urban jurisdictions. It is becoming increasingly clear that state and county welfare departments cannot do the job without a stronger federal presence.

Funding Patterns and the Effect of General Revenue Sharing

In many urban areas, public assistance is a shared county and state function, though in some states public assistance is totally a state activity. When states require local participation, the extent and exact nature of the local (most often county) involvement will depend on state law. Thus, local participation is a state option; the nature of the participation is state determined, too.

In a few major cities, especially where city and county lines are identical, public assistance represents a substantial portion of municipal expenses. For example, in 1975, New York City's public assistance expenditures amounted to $2.887 billion (24.8 percent of the city's general expenditures; New York City encompasses five counties); in San Francisco, public assistance expenditures amounted to $132.481 million (22.6 percent of the city's general expenditures); in Denver, Colorado, such expenditures amounted to $43.456 million (14.5 percent of the city's general expenditures).[34] When county jurisdictions are broader than municipalities, the tax base is often broader and thus the proportion of the local budget earmarked for welfare is proportionately less. For example, in Cook County, which encompasses Chicago, public welfare expenditures amounted to 4.9 percent of the county's general expenditures; in Wayne County, Michigan, encompassing Detroit, the public welfare budget amounted to 3.9 percent of the county's general expenditures.[35] The proportion of total jurisdictional expenditure for public welfare programs would have been higher had the jurisdiction been smaller. These counties are highly urban and the county expenditures for public welfare require the residents of large cities and in-close suburbs to pay sufficient countywide taxes to meet these public welfare needs. Regardless of whether the county or the municipality is charged with financing public assistance, the burden of support for public assistance is on communities—municipalities being worse off than counties—which are sometimes fiscally unable to meet this need without increasing state or federal revenue.

State and local funds provided $17,282,500,000 for public aid (Public Assistance including Medicaid, Supplementary Security Income, and Food Stamp Programs) payments in fiscal 1977. In fiscal 1970, the comparable level was $6,839,200,000. Thus, in the seven-year period from 1970 to 1977, state and local effort had more than doubled.[36] In 1950, only $1,393,000,000 had been expended from state and local revenues for public welfare programs. The level of federal fiscal involvement has increased substantially, though it does not meet fully the needs of dependent populations or eliminate the fiscal burden of local jurisdictions. In fiscal 1977, the federal outlay for public aid payments was $35,146,-100,000, of this amount, $2,315,800,000 was expended for social services; SSI had a federal outlay of $5,272,900,000. In 1950, federal public assistance income payment outlays were $1,097,200,000. (There were no outlays for social services in 1950, and SSI was not funded until fiscal 1974). In 1960, federal outlays for public assistance income payments had increased to $1,857,700,000. It was not until 1970, when $4,465,200,000 was expended by the federal government for public assistance income payments, that the impact of federal fiscal involvement was really felt. However, even the 1977 federal allocation of almost $11.8 billion for public welfare income payments (including SSI payments) did not begin to reduce state and local costs which amounted to almost $8.6 billion in 1977, though federal payments did represent 67 percent of total overall public aid costs in fiscal 1977.[37] Moreover, the amount of benefits cities and counties can provide is limited because of the level of state standards for payment as well as the levels of state contribution.

Under AFDC, these standards continue to vary widely. In December 1978, the average monthly payment per recipient of AFDC by state (and the Commonwealth of Puerto Rico) varied from $123.22 in Hawaii, $117.97 in New York, and $108.25 in Massachusetts to $38.03 in Alabama, $34.53 in Texas, $25.66 in Mississippi, and $11.76 in Puerto Rico.[38]

General revenue sharing funds for social services have made little impact on increasing support for social welfare expenditures by urban communities.[39] In a study conducted by the U.S. General Accounting Office on the use of revenue sharing funds by 250 local governments, it was determined that by the end of the 1973 fiscal year only 2 percent of such funds had been used for the delivery of social services to the poor and the aged.[40] Such spending is sometimes the function of cities and sometimes the function of counties. Of those funds, $8.7 million was for cities with populations of between 500,000 and 1,000,000 and $11.1 million was for counties with populations of over 1,000,000 persons.[41] These expenditures represented (and still represent) only a minor portion of the money spent in all categories for operations and maintenance of activities supported by revenue sharing funds. General revenue sharing funds expended for social services to states and localities continue to be of minor consequence. In fiscal 1977, 2.5 percent of total revenue-sharing funds, or $165.7 million, was expended by states and localities for social services.[42]

Welfare, Urban Politics, and Urban Resources

As noted previously, the costs associated with public assistance increased substantially in the late 1960s and 1970s. These costs mounted as a result of increased participation in the programs as well as increased levels of payments. To a great extent, these costs have burdened central cities and urban counties. For example, between 1960 and 1966, public assistance in Baltimore increased by 300 percent, accounting for three-fourths of the increase in public assistance for Maryland. Frances Piven and Richard Cloward have attributed increases in the case loads to the success of federally funded advocacy services such as legal services and neighborhood service centers. The increase in such services was, according to Piven and Cloward, a strategy of the Kennedy and Johnson administrations to appeal to urban black voters. In addition, it was in part a response to the discontent of urban blacks that had crystallized into major urban disorders. Also, in the second half of the sixties, fear of the various Black Power groups mounted in many urban areas. Piven and Cloward have suggested that:

[By 1960] the Kennedy Administration began to cast about for . . . ways of strengthening its base in the cities.

It was no small problem. A way had to be found to prod the local Democratic Party machinery to cultivate the allegiance of urban black voters by extending a greater share of municipal services to them, and to do this without alienating urban white voters. It was this political imperative that eventually led the Kennedy and Johnson Administrations to intervene in the cities, and that intervention had much to do with creating the welfare explosion.[43]

Federal programs (such as those established under the Economic Opportunity Act of 1965), promoted advocacy services that often focused on the need for more adequate welfare services. These efforts also spurred on voluntary groups such as the National Association for the Advancement of Colored People's (NAACP) Legal Defense and Educational Fund and the National Welfare Rights Organization (NWRO) to focus on information and advocacy services with respect to public assistance.

In addition, the welfare explosion was in part due to the increased number of poor persons residing in the major urban areas of our nation. In 1970, in fifteen of the eighteen major metropolitan areas, very low income households (with earned and unearned incomes of less than $3,000 a year per family) constituted 10 percent or more of the total population. It is very difficult simply to dismiss such large numbers of people. Indeed, as the 1970s progressed, evidence mounted that a growth in the number of very low income households occurred in urban areas. By 1975, very low income households accounted for 15.8 percent of the population of St. Louis, 15.6 percent of the population of Baltimore, and 14.5 percent of the population of Boston.[44] While the U.S. Bureau of the Census has not recently provided more detailed data regarding urban poverty in specific cities, it has, as noted earlier, provided more general data regarding the persistence of urban poverty.

Other factors also led to the increased welfare loads of the 1970s. The recipient population for AFDC, the largest public assistance category, changed in the post–World War II period. Increasingly, the eligible urban poor were mothers and children suffering from economic insecurity as a result of desertion and illegitimacy. In 1969, in 43.3 percent of AFDC families on the welfare roles, the father was divorced or legally separated from the mother, separated informally, or had deserted the family. The male head of household deserted in 15.9 percent of AFDC cases. In the same year, illegitimacy accounted for 27.9 percent of the families receiving AFDC.[45] (In reaction to this situation, an Office of Child Support Enforcement was initiated in August 1975, in order to help collect child support payments from absent fathers.) More recently, a 1977 study showed that female-headed families are heavily concentrated in central cities of metropolitan areas, particularly in the larger SMSAs.[46] While fewer such families are found in suburban rings of SMSAs, their concentration there is also considerable.

Table 2 / RELATIONSHIP BETWEEN EARNINGS OF AFDC MOTHERS, AFDC
GRANT LEVELS, AND CASE LOADS PER 1,000 POOR PERSONS
IN THE POPULATION FOR 11 CITIES

	1	2	3	4
	Median Best Wages[1]	Grant Level	Difference between 1 and 2[2]	Case Load per 1,000 Poor Persons
New York, N.Y.	$274.56	$278.00	$ 3.44	200.7
Philadelphia, Pa.	237.60	213.00	24.60	84.1
Providence, R.I.	264.00	266.00	− 2.00	76.1
Chicago, Ill.	265.00	279.00	− 15.00	72.5
San Jose, Calif.	315.04	221.00	94.04	71.8
Phoenix, Ariz.	230.56	134.00	96.56	41.7
Rochester, N.Y.	281.60	278.00	3.60	40.9
New Orleans, La.	220.00	116.00	104.00	39.7
Atlanta, Ga.	221.76	125.00	96.76	36.4
Memphis, Tenn.	220.00	120.00	100.00	32.0
Raleigh, N.C.	220.00	144.00	76.00	23.7

Source: "Report of Findings of Special Review of Aid to Families with Dependent Children in New York City," transmitted to the House of Representatives Committee on Ways and Means by the U.S. Department of Health, Education, and Welfare, and the New York Department of Social Services on September 24, 1966, pp. 43 and 84.

[1] Self-reported, highest wages of AFDC mothers as reported in survey interview.

[2] Columns 3 and 4 have a statistically significant correlation of −0.57.

Since the framers of the Social Security Act had expected welfare categories to become residual as participation in the social insurance programs became widespread, they included no plans in this original blueprint for economic insecurity caused by desertion and illegitimacy. Thus AFDC, with its variable federal grants-in-aid to the states, continues to increase in scope and in cost to the federal government, to the states, and to numerous urban jurisdictions.

Finally, welfare rolls have increased partly because the monetary levels of the grants have increased. As the dollar value of AFDC grants has increased, higher levels of income eligibility have been established; this has resulted in higher case loads in many cities. Indeed, according to 1970 testimony of then Secretary of Health, Education, and Welfare, Robert H. Finch, before the Senate Committee on Finance, case loads were particularly high in New York City, in Providence, Rhode Island, and in Chicago, where the grant level exceeded the "median best wages" reported by AFDC mothers.[47] Secretary Finch presented AFDC case loads in eleven cities to validate this relationship (see Table 2 for the data).

Public Welfare Today

Current public welfare programs in the United States can be divided into income programs and service programs. Income programs provide financial assistance to the poor and needy (these programs do *not* include social insurance). At the present time, SSI is funded directly by the federal government with states often supplementing the basic federal benefit; AFDC is funded by the federal government and the states and localities; and General Assistance is funded by some states and cities. The small General Assistance program aids only some of those cases that are ineligible for either a federally funded or subsidized welfare category. Thus, the two major public welfare programs depend on federal funding either for direct and in many cases nearly total support (SSI) or for partial funding (AFDC). As a result of this funding phenomenon, we will consider the evolution of the federal programs in some detail. Service programs provide "income-in-kind." That is, money payments are not provided; instead, services such as day care or "meals on wheels" are provided to poor people who are defined as eligible for aid. Federal funds are available on a matching grant-in-aid basis to the states and, by extension, to the local jurisdictions for these programs.

Income Programs

Public welfare as a federal-state, sometimes local, program endeavor has undergone a number of changes as it has evolved to its current form. Many of the changes have occurred as a result of changes in the federal laws and program regulations. An important change is the broadening of eligibility to include more categories of poor people. For example, in 1950, Congress authorized a new federal category, Aid to the Permanently and Totally Disabled (APTD). In the same year, a *caretaker grant* was added to the Aid to Dependent Children category. In 1958, the principle of variable matched grants was established. The *variable* formula permitted higher rates of federal subsidization of welfare costs in states with "limited fiscal capacity." In 1960, the category of Medical Assistance to the Aged was established for medically needy elderly citizens. In 1962, the principle of federal support of state programs of Aid to Families with Dependent Children (formerly termed Aid to Dependent Children) was *permanently* established where dependency was due to the unemployment of a parent rather than the breakup of the family (known as AFDC-U). In the same year, federal grants were made available in cases where AFDC children were placed in foster homes by the courts. In 1967, the principle of an income "work incentive" was also established by federal provisions that allowed mothers who work to keep an initial $30 of income, plus work expenses out of each month's earnings, plus one third of additional earnings up to a state need standard, and still maintain their entitlement for some AFDC benefits. Under this program, an eligible caretaker who refused work would have the caretaker grant reduced from the AFDC benefit. This procedure—usually unenforced—represented an element of federal compulsion that local welfare administration usually evaded or avoided.

The federal role in subsidization of the public welfare system continued to expand, too. Two key alterations of the federal role were the 1962 authorization of 75 percent federal payment of state rehabilitation and preventive services, related to AFDC programs, if approved by the federal Bureau of Family Services, and the 1965 Medicaid amendments which provided a broad mandate for federal support of state medical assistance programs for those falling within the criteria of medical need.

Increasingly during the 1960s and 1970s, both the state and the federal commitment for meeting income and service needs of the poor has increased. With this increased commitment, the revenue burden of public welfare, as we have noted, has required high levels of federal expenditure as well as expanded state and local revenue involvement. This latter condition has led state and local officials to urge greater federal assumption of welfare costs. Increased urbanization of the poor, particularly in central cities, plus the fiscal limitations of state and local governments has led to numerous bipartisan appeals by the nation's governors for a fiscal takeover of public welfare by the federal government. At the 1969 National Governor's Conference, it was resolved by a 49 to 1 vote that there be

> substitution, on a phased basis, of a federally financed system of welfare payments for the current federal-state program for the aged, blind, disabled, and dependent children, and including also the general assistance programs now financed by the states themselves. Eligibility and grants would be determined by the federal government; the system should include realistic income exemptions to provide incentives for persons to seek employment. Adequate day care for children of working mothers and an expanded federal job training program should also be assured . . .
>
> Transfer of the present Old Age Assistance, Aid to the Permanently and Totally Disabled, and Aid to the Blind programs [would be made] to the Social Security Program, with payments being made from federal general revenues to the Socal Security Trust Fund to cover the increased cost.[48]

Subsequently, representatives of American municipalities also called for increased federalization of public welfare policy using as their rationale the contention that welfare dependency was a problem national in scope. The National Municipal Policy adopted by the Congress of Cities noted that

> National solutions are needed to meet social problems which ignore state and local political boundaries . . . Welfare in America has become a national problem that requires national solutions. The welfare program should be altered and expanded to encompass more of those in need, provide a national minimum standard of assistance, and eliminate demeaning restrictions to help recapture the rich human resources presently wasted by a system that creates and perpetuates dependency.[49]

• FAMILY ASSISTANCE PLAN [50]

The Social Security Amendments of 1972 provided a greater fiscal role for public assistance to be assumed by the federal government under the

Supplementary Security Income Program. SSI was developed as an alternative to a far more inclusive program proposal, known as the Family Assistance Plan (FAP), which would have nationalized all public welfare programs. Though this proposal was not adopted, it is an interesting program to examine and to understand. The political constraints within which its supporters operated are also of interest to urban policy analysts who wish to know better how the political system operates in the public welfare arena. Thus, at this juncture it is useful to turn our attention to FAP and the unsuccessful movement of the early 1970s to nationalize public welfare.

The original FAP proposal was made by President Nixon in 1969. It provided a minimum federal cash payment for needy aged, blind, and disabled adults as well as for families with children with incomes below a specified level. Eligible families would have included the working poor with steady or unsteady employment in low-paying jobs as well as families with no employment income.

The President's Urban Affairs Council recommended the development of FAP as a way of eliminating the very low AFDC payment levels maintained by some states. In addition, the plan was to relieve state and local governments of their present contributions to AFDC. Perhaps the chief argument for the enactment of such a program was that FAP would help families remain intact. This argument is contained in the following statement by the Urban Affairs Council:

> No longer will fathers have to leave their families in order to support them. No more will poor persons be driven out of one section of the nation by inadequate or even punitive welfare legislation, and forced into crowded and hostile cities. It is no accident that of the 16 to 18 states [with the lowest payment levels] in which state payments will be eliminated by the Family Security System, only *one* has taken advantage of the AFDC-U program first enacted in 1961, under which a family with an unemployed father is eligible for benefits.[51]

The FAP proposal provided that the first $720 of a family's yearly earnings would be excluded from consideration when reducing cash benefits. One-half of earnings over $720 up to a specified cut-off point ($3,970 for a family of four) would also be excluded from the reduction in subsidy. For the low income aged, blind, and disabled, the proposal established a minimum payment of $90 per person per month to be provided under the existing federal-state administrative structure. Thus, the initial Nixon proposal included a national Family Assistance Plan and national eligibility and payment standards for the aged, blind, and disabled.

The thrust for a national welfare policy in a conservative administration requires some additional comment. John Osborne, a Washington political observer of the Nixon administration, stated that part of the thrust toward reform in this area was the president's "genuine conviction" that the American public assistance system was "an utter disaster." In addition, concern with rising welfare roles and concomitant family breakdown affected both conservatives and liberals. Seeking a new approach was a popular action. Daniel P. Moynihan, a presidential urban affairs advisor (now a U.S. senator from New York State), in a 1969 memo to President Nixon, noted:

> From the most conservative to the most liberal ranks, an amazing number of members [of Congress] agree that AFDC must go. Thus, I would argue that if you move now, you will dominate the discussion. Congress will be discussing your proposal. It hardly matters what form it takes, or how many times we change our position in the process. The end result—if you wish it to be—will be your change.

Finally, the issue of rising local taxes made a federal program offering some fiscal relief popular. An unnamed Nixon administration official has been cited as noting:

> The extent of public concern over welfare was important. The increase in costs and recipients, and local politicians using this as a political scapegoat for rising taxes, produced a public reaction which demanded change. Local politicians have been using welfare as a scapegoat for years. Reagan uses it. The problems of California are much bigger than welfare but [Governors] Reagan, Rockefeller, Ogilvie and others have been using it as a scapegoat for rising [state and local] taxes, so there was a demand that something be done.

A later version (1972) of the initial Nixon proposal was adopted in the House Ways and Means Committee and was generally referred to by its House Bill number, H.R.1. In H.R.1., provision was made for federalizing the categories of Aid to Families with Dependent Children as well as Old Age Assistance, Aid to the Blind, and Aid to the Permanently and Totally Disabled. This bill also maintained the provision for benefits to intact and working poor families with an employed head of household. A four-person family with employed members was to retain eligibility for benefits until its income reached $4,140. (The basic program payment for a four-person family with no income was set at $2,400 per year with no eligibility for food stamps.) After an initial disregard of $720 per year of earned income, the tax rate on subsequent earned income beyond that amount for recipients of this aid was set at 67 percent.

This 1972 proposal provided for administration of income supplements for eligible working poor families by the Department of Labor under the Family Assistance Plan program. H.R.1 would have replaced the existing AFDC program by a two-part federal program: (1) The Family Assistance Plan (FAP) segment would be administered by the Department of Health, Education, and Welfare and would serve families with no employable members. (2) The Opportunities for Families (OFF) was to be administered by the Department of Labor and would serve families with an employable member. Under this program, a family member deemed employable and referred for work training or employment referral would be penalized for failure to accept work or work training by reduction from the grant of the portion allotted to such an employable family member. Finally, the three adult welfare categories would be replaced by one federal program administered by the Social Security Administration. Yearly federal benefits of $1,800 would be provided for covered single individuals without income, and $2,400 per year would be provided for eligible couples with supplementation left optional to the states.

The Family Assistance Program proposal was ultimately defeated. The issues relating to this defeat were somewhat complex. Conservatives feared the program would be too costly for the federal treasury; many liberals feared that the benefit levels were not high enough; some liberals and many black leaders feared that the work requirement potentially would be too punitive to the poor and nonwhite. In addition, some figures indicated that the program would actually provide less federal financial assistance to many progressive states with fairly advanced payment levels for AFDC programs.[52]

Regarding such opposition, President Nixon was to note in a March 2, 1973, press conference:

> [W]ith regard to Family Assistance, I thought at the time that I approved it . . . that it was the best solution to what I have termed . . . the "welfare mess." I believe that it is essential that we develop a new program and a new approach to welfare in which there is a bonus not for welfare but a bonus, if there is to be one, for work. The Family Assistance Program I thought then, and I think now, is the best answer.[53]

More recent proposals have been less ambitious. In May 1979, President Carter proposed a moderate welfare reform sharply scaled down from a more comprehensive but legislatively unacceptable 1977 proposal.[54] The 1979 proposal would have established a national minimum benefit level of AFDC and food stamp payments at 65 percent of the national poverty line. This would have established a 1979 payment level of $4,654 a year to all low-income 4-person families. States with low AFDC payment levels would not have to increase their revenues because the increased revenue requirements would have been met by the federal treasury. This provision would primarily have helped the thirteen states (mostly southern) where combined AFDC and food stamp benefits were below 65 percent of the poverty level. Increased federal support also would have taken the form of a 10 percent increase in the federal share of matching federal-state payments under the basic AFDC program, which would particularly have benefited New York and California, as well as a $200 million block grant fund to assist states in meeting emergency needs of families. The aged, blind, and disabled recipients of SSI who live alone would have received additional cash benefits in lieu of food stamp coupons for which they had eligibility. (This provision was aimed at cutting down on the number of persons eligible for food stamps who do not receive them.) All states would have been required by national law to provide AFDC benefits to two-parent families in which the primary wage earner is unemployed. This mandate would have only been for a period of two months. The plan would also have increased the number of public service jobs available to welfare recipients, including the creation of 375,000 such jobs available only to welfare recipient family heads. Also, the plan called for a small increase in tax credits available to the working poor. This modest proposal was "shelved" by the Congress in 1980 due to its reluctance to tackle the welfare issue during an election year.

• SUPPLEMENTAL SECURITY INCOME PROGRAM

Despite the defeat of FAP, the provision to develop a uniform federal benefit for the needy blind, disabled, and aged on a means tests basis—a provision less controversial and less costly—was passed by Congress in October 1972. Aid to Families with Dependent Children remains a state program with federal variable grants-in-aid provided states to meet some of the cost, and with the level of payments to the states dependent on state per capita income. Supplemental Security Income, which is a totally federal program (which *may* be supplemented by the states), was set up for all aged, blind, and disabled individuals whose reportable resources were less than $1,500 per year ($2,250 for a couple per year). The federal yearly guaranteed income for eligible persons without income as of July 1980 was $2,856 for an individual and $4,284 for a couple.

States are free to supplement these payments and by 1977, forty-two states and the District of Columbia made some supplemental payments to individuals either above the federal payment level or on an eligibility basis varying from federal eligibility standards. A further initiative under this program provides that states may enter agreements for federal administration of state supplemental benefits, a factor further reducing state costs of public assistance. By October 1, 1977, sixteen states and the District of Columbia had chosen federal administration of their optional supplementary programs. The state's optional supplementation in cases of federal administration refers in all cases to the dollar amounts above the federal payment level that the states provide to eligible clients. The states that have entered into this agreement are California, Delaware, Hawaii, Iowa, Maine, Massachusetts, Michigan, Montana, Nevada, New Jersey, New York, Pennsylvania, Rhode Island, Vermont, Washington, and Wisconsin.[55] Under the federally administered optional supplementation program, agreements specifying payment amounts and accepting federal eligibility criteria are entered into with the Secretary of Health and Human Services. In return, the federal government assumes the cost of administering the programs and guarantees that for states entering into such agreements, the state's fiscal liability will initially be limited to the state's 1972 expenditures to aid the aged, blind, and disabled.[56] (However, subsequently states may not reduce optional payment levels that have been established.) Although the federal government guaranteed initially to limit states' fiscal liability at the 1972 calender year level for optional supplementation only if the federal government administers the program, as of October 1, 1977, twenty-six states administered directly or supervised county administration of their own optional programs, thereby retaining the right to establish their eligibility requirements and payment levels. Those states in which determination of eligibility criteria and payment levels are made by the state administration include Alaska, Arizona, Connecticut, Florida, Illinois, New Mexico, Oklahoma, and Oregon. States in which eligibility requirements are established by the state agency, but county departments determine actual eligibility and payment amounts, include Alabama, Colorado, Indiana, Maryland, Minnesota, North Carolina, and Virginia.[57]

Services Programs

In 1962, the Kennedy administration sponsored public welfare amendments that initiated a category of grants to the states and, by extension, to local jurisdictions for social services. This category of aid became an adjunct to the cash-support grants (AFDC, OAA, AB, and APTD) and Medical Assistance for the Aged grants that were already in operation. Prior to 1962, some federal funding had been available for services, but the funds were incidental, and the federal government did little to encourage the states or their local jurisdictions to provide services to public assistance recipients. Abraham Ribicoff, then Secretary of Health, Education, and Welfare, told President Kennedy that the department sought to reorient "the whole approach to welfare from a straight cash handout operation to one in which the emphasis is on rehabilitation of those on relief and prevention ahead of time." [58] The 1962 amendments provided that federal funds (with no ceiling set) be available to the states to provide services to welfare recipients; it authorized federal payment of 75 percent of the cost—which was a very high rate of federal participation. Previously, matching grant-in-aid money was rarely above 50 percent federal participation. The law did not define services: it merely stated their purpose. It referred to self-support, self-care, strengthening family life, and reducing dependency as the goals of the services.[59] Thus, federal funds were authorized, but services were not mandated nor were levels of adequacy defined. The 1967 Social Security Amendments went on to specify that states had to provide childcare services and family planning services to people who were in work-training programs funded under the 1967 act. This, in effect, mandated two types of services that states had to provide.[60]

Although the 1967 amendments had limited specificity, the law was vague regarding services because it lacked definitions. Furthermore, it authorized the purchase of services from various state agencies, and authorized the delivery of services to former and potential welfare recipients, as well as to existing recipients. By 1970, it was apparent to some observers of the public welfare system that these vague definitions were leading states and, by extension, their localities to seek money from HEW for a wide variety of services that were not all clearly supportive of the intent of the law. HEW approved much of the state and local spending. By the early 1970s, federal spending for these often vaguely defined services to vaguely specified recipients had reached nearly $2 billion. States and their local jurisdictions saw their opportunities to develop service programs with federal funds, and they took them. The programs that developed within the separate jurisdictions were often very different from each other (that is, legal aid services, health clinics, day care, family planning, training programs, and so on). Also, some states and their local governments received considerably larger proportions of the funding (in relation to their population or needs) than other states. Thus because the service programs permitted considerable state and often local discretion, they promoted inequities between jurisdictions while increasing expenditures for services at an unprecedented rate. The 1962 amendments had promoted localism and, some might argue, inequities in public welfare programming at considerable cost. Thus, the 1962 amendments (and the 1967 amendments as well) reinforced the tradition of localism and in so doing undermined the development of a national social services policy in our federal system. The perhaps sad commentary often made of this program is that the lack of interdependence via national planning and/or national administrative oversight eventually led to the placing of a limit on national spending for public assistance–related social services even though integrated planning might have facilitated the utilization of this source of revenue for needed services to populations in many service-poor urban jurisdictions.

An interesting use of the monies made available by the 1967 amendments was the purchase of care by state departments of welfare from other state agencies concerned with programs such as mental health, education, drug abuse, alcoholism, and corrections. Most purchase of care was for day care, which was consistent with the intent of the law.[61] But some states, most notably Illinois and New York, tried to purchase a much wider range of services. At one point, Illinois officials suggested that social service grants for services to adult prison inmates was justified since their incarceration was "responsible for family breakup which results in the family remaining outside needing to go on AFDC rolls."[62] In New York State, welfare officials proposed purchases from state agencies as seemingly unlikely as the Department of Commerce and the State University, as well as from the more obvious state agencies such as those dealing with education, aging, narcotics control, and the like. In fact, New York and Illinois accounted for 70 percent of the almost $1 billion increase in service grants between 1971 and 1972.

Requests for social service grants received by HEW for fiscal 1973 totalled $4.7 billion. Nine states had projected increases of over 1,000 percent. This rapid expansion of state spending of federal grant money, as well as questions of program responsibility and the apparent excesses of the program, led the Secretary of Health, Education, and Welfare to ask who would kill the goose that laid the golden egg. Ultimately, it was Congress that brought social services spending under tighter controls.[63]

In reaction to the rapid increases in spending for welfare-related state and local services, Congress, in the State and Local Fiscal Assistance Act of 1972, included limits on federal spending for welfare-related services; these amendments also specified more precisely eligibility for receipt of services as well as types of services that could be funded under this law. Public assistance–related social services were limited to $2.5 billion per year. The money was to be allocated to the states for specific services on the basis of population, still using a 75 percent federal matching grant basis for the allocations to the states for most social services. Two years later, in 1974, the Social Services and Child Support Amendments (Title XX of the Social Security Act) were passed by Congress and signed into law by President Ford. These amendments returned some discretion for welfare-related services to the states and, by extension, to their localities, and provided greater state discretion in the provision of services to nonwelfare recipients. Among the social services that may be provided to both welfare and some nonwelfare recipients are day care and after-school care for children so that mothers can accept job training and retain employment; chore services for an elderly couple who might otherwise have to go to an institution; referral services for unemployed teenagers to community agencies that specialize in job training; and the provision of halfway houses for drug-addicted youth who need treatment and a supportive environment.

The greater program flexibility provided by the 1974 amendments, particularly as they relate to poverty needs found disproportionately in central cities and urbanized suburbs, helped reduce somewhat the fiscal burden to these jurisdictions and allowed them to develop social services for local needs. The broader income limits for eligibility for services also has enabled urban areas to contain, though not substantially reduce, the size and expense of welfare case loads by maintaining supportive and preventive services such as day care and employment counseling. It also has enabled them to reduce the costs of caring for dependent persons; for example, by providing chore services for the elderly, the need for expensive institutional care for them can be reduced.

This legislation does not, however, take into account the higher proportion of poverty-related needs in highly urbanized areas; though the more populous states, which have the highest concentrations of urban population, do receive the highest allotments. For fiscal year 1976, California received $245.5 million of such Title XX funds, Pennsylvania received $141.75 million, and Texas received $140.5 milion. On the other hand, smaller states, which may also have urban poverty concentrations, may receive such inadequate funding that they may not be able to provide services for their poor residents, particularly the urban poor. Thus, for fiscal year 1976, Nevada received $6.5 million, Delaware received $6.75 million, and the District of Columbia received only $9 million.

In 1976, additional amendments to Title XX were enacted. These provisions allowed states the option to establish more liberal eligibility standards for social services. More specifically, states may determine eligibility for social services on a group basis except for nonmigrant child care services and family planning services, the latter having no federal eligibility requirement at all. The group basis requires that states opting to use this criteria must determine that "substantially all" people who receive the service are members of families that have monthly gross incomes of not more than 90 percent of the state median income for a family of four, adjusted according to family size. ("Substantially all" was later defined by federal regulation as 75 percent.) Other provisions of the 1976 amendments provided for an increase in federal funds for child care services from 75 percent to 100 percent of cost. In 1980, a federal funding ceiling for social services was adopted which ranges from $2.7 billion in fiscal 1980 to $3.3 billion in fiscal 1985. Two hundred million dollars was made available to the states for child day care in fiscal 1980 and fiscal 1981 with no state matching funds requirement.

Not only is there an overall limitation of federal funding for Title XX, but also each state has a revenue ceiling based on the size of its population in relation to the population of other states. In general, most services are still funded by federal matching of state expenditures on a federal-state proportion of 75-25 matching formula. For family planning services, federal revenue provides 90 percent of the matching funds. In addition, as we have noted, a portion of child care services is fully reimbursed by the federal government too. There is now federal funding for services with more federal regulations than existed in the 1960s. However, the available funds are limited. Also, the federal government, constrained by a tradition of localism in the delivery of public welfare income and services has not played the role of integrator either by performing the public-assistance-related service delivery role itself or by ordinarily requiring states to provide specified services at specified levels of adequacy or by mandating that available services be distributed equitably.

CONCLUSION

The rising costs for public assistance and the increased public assistance case loads can be attributed to a number of phenomena:

1. The economic and social problems of new largely nonwhite inmigrant groups—black, Puerto Rican, and Mexican—who have settled in the inner-city areas of the central cities and the ghettos of older suburbs led to increased dependence on public assistance.

2. Patterns of advocacy as well as information services, established by the War on Poverty strategy, helped to increase the welfare constituency.
3. Patterns of social pathology resulting in family breakdown, desertion, and illegitimacy have led to the increase in the urban and close-in suburban welfare load.
4. The increased monetary level of assistance grants, in the AFDC category, at times has outstripped the wages for jobs welfare clients could expect realistically to hold.
5. The number of programs, categories, and services under federally subsidized public assistance titles has undergone a continual increase since the initial passage of the Social Security Act of 1935, and this, of course, also has increased costs.

Since cities, suburbs, and states are often competing fiscal units, the increased monetary burden of public assistance has led to increased state and local demands for federal assumption of welfare functions. A beginning in this area has been made with the institution of the Supplementary Security Income program. Urban needs and limited urban fiscal resources will probably lead to further incremental developments in this area in the 1980s.

REFERENCES

1. Advisory Commission on Intergovernmental Relations (ACIR), *Significant Features of Fiscal Federalism, 1978–1979 Edition* (Washington, D.C.: U.S. Government Printing Office, May 1979), p. 24.
2. This analysis was suggested by Joe R. Feagin, *Subordinating the Poor* (Englewood Cliffs, N.J.: Prentice-Hall, 1975), Chap. 2.
3. Reinhold Niebuhr, *The Contribution of Religion to Social Work* (New York: Columbia University Press, 1932), pp. 15–16, cited in ibid., p. 16.
4. William Ryan, *Blaming the Victim* (New York: Vintage Books, 1971).
5. Feagin, op. cit., p. 22.
6. An excellent discussion of the development of the English Poor Laws is provided in Karl de Schweinitz, *England's Road to Social Security* (New York: A. S. Barnes, 1961), pp. 39–47.
7. Blanche D. Coll, *Perspectives in Public Welfare* (Washington, D.C.: U.S. Department of Health, Education, and Welfare, 1969), pp. 30–31.
8. Walter I. Trattner, *From Poor Law to Welfare State* (New York: Free Press, 1974, p. 55.
9. Coll, op. cit., p. 32.
10. Ibid., p. 58.
11. Cited in Ralph E. Pumphrey and Muriel W. Pumphrey, *The Heritage of Social Work* (New York: Columbia University Press, 1961), p. 133.
12. Ibid., p. 143.
13. Ibid., p. 163.
14. Coll, op. cit., p. 80.

15. Ibid.
16. Duncan M. MacIntyre, *Public Assistance: Too Much or Too Little* (Ithaca, N.Y.: New York State School of Industrial and Labor Relations, Cornell University, 1964), p. 14.
17. Ibid., p. 17.
18. Frances Fox Piven and Richard A. Cloward, *Regulating the Poor* (New York: Vintage, 1971), p. xiii.
19. Cited in Arthur J. Altmeyer, *The Formative Years of Social Security* (Madison, Wisc.: University of Wisconsin Press, 1966), p. 16.
20. Aid to the Permanently and Totally Disabled was added in 1950.
21. Marian Lief Palley and Howard A. Palley, "National Income and Services Policy in the United States," in *Analyzing Poverty Policy,* ed. by Dorothy B. James (Lexington, Mass.: Lexington Books, 1975), p. 245.
22. Social Security Act as Amended, Title I, Sec. 2(a).
23. Altmeyer, op. cit., p. 39.
24. Ibid.
25. Alfred M. Skolnik and Sophie R. Dales, "Social Welfare Expenditures, Fiscal Year 1976," *Social Security Bulletin,* 40 (January 1977), 6. Also see Gilbert Y. Steiner, *Social Insecurity: The Politics of Welfare* (Washington, D.C.: The Brookings Institution, 1966), p. 31.
26. *Social Security Bulletin,* 38 (January 1975), 63; U.S. Department of Health, Education, and Welfare, Social Security Administration, *Public Assistance Statistics, December, 1978.*
27. This section relies heavily on Marian Lief Palley and Howard A. Palley, "A Call for a National Welfare Policy," *American Behavioral Scientist,* 15 (May–June 1972), 681–95.
28. Richard H. Brown and M. Nichols, *Subemployment in Los Angeles* (Los Angeles, Calif.: Economic and Youth Opportunities Agency, 1969), cited in Richard H. Brown, "Economic Development as an Anti-Poverty Strategy," *Urban Affairs Quarterly,* 9 (December 1973), 171.
29. Ibid., pp. 171–72.
30. U.S. Bureau of the Census, *Current Population Reports,* Series P-23, No. 75, "Social and Economic Characteristics of the Metropolitan and Non-metropolitan Population, 1977 and 1970" (Washington, D.C.: U.S. Government Printing Office, 1978), p. 17.
31. Ibid., p. 5.
32. U.S. Bureau of the Census, *Current Population Reports,* Series P-20, No. 329, "Persons of Spanish Origin in the United States: March, 1977" (Washington, D.C.: U.S. Government Printing Office, 1978), p. 15.
33. MacIntyre, op. cit., p. 86.
34. U.S. Bureau of the Census, *County and City Data Book, 1977,* A Statistical Abstract Supplement (Washington, D.C.: U.S. Government Printing Office, 1978), pp. 629, 725.
35. Ibid., pp. 131, 239.
36. Alma McMillan, "Social Welfare Expenditures Under Public Programs, Fiscal Year, 1977," *Social Security Bulletin,* 42 (June 1979), 6.
37. Ibid., pp. 4–6.
38. *Public Assistance Statistics, December, 1978,* op. cit.
39. See pp. 81–82 for a more detailed discussion of revenue sharing.
40. Comptroller General of the United States, U.S. General Accounting Office,

Comptroller General's Report to the Congress: Revenue Sharing—Its Use and Its Impact on Local Governments, Washington, D.C., April 25, 1974, p. 20.

41. Ibid., p. 47.
42. U.S. Department of the Treasury, *Sixth Annual Report of the Office of Revenue Sharing* (Washington, D.C., March 1979), p. 8.
43. Piven and Cloward, op. cit., p. 256.
44. *The New York Times,* October 28, 1975, p. 33.
45. 117 Cong. Rec. 46907 (1971) (remarks of Senator Russell H. Long).
46. U.S. Bureau of the Census, *Current Population Reports,* Series P-20, No. 326, "Household and Family Characteristics, March, 1977" (Washington, D.C.: U.S. Government Printing Office, 1978), p. 36.
47. U.S. Congress, Senate, Committee on Finance, *Family Assistance Act of 1970, Hearings,* 91st Congress, 2nd Sess. (April–May 1970), pt. 1, p. 201.
48. Gilbert Y. Steiner, *The State of Welfare* (Washington, D.C.: The Brookings Institution, 1971), p. 333.
49. "Our Nation's Obligations to Its Cities," *Nation's Cities,* 9 (March 1971), 12.
50. This section relies heavily on the account of FAP presented by M. Kenneth Bowler, *The Nixon Guaranteed Income* (Cambridge, Mass.: Ballinger, 1974). Unless noted otherwise, all quotations in this section were cited by Bowler.
51. Daniel P. Moynihan, *The Politics of a Guaranteed Income* (New York: Vintage, 1973), p. 162.
52. An extensive discussion of the interplay of interest groups with Congress in the FAP proceeding is contained in ibid., pp. 236–347.
53. *Congressional Quarterly,* 31 (March 10, 1973), 516.
54. "Scaled-Down Carter Welfare Plan Announced," *Congressional Quarterly* (March 26, 1979), 1013–14; *U.S. News and World Report,* 86 (June 4, 1979), 42.
55. U.S. Department of Health, Education, and Welfare, Social Security Administration, "Supplemental Security Income: Compilation Based on Selected Characteristics of Optional State Supplementation Programs, October, 1977," *Research and Statistics Note,* Note No. 9 (August 23, 1979), 4.
56. The expenditure level is calculated on the basis of the amount of the cash payment an individual with no other income would have received in January 1972, under an approved plan for aid to the aged, blind, or disabled, plus a factor for readjusting income levels without increasing total state expenditure in calendar 1972, plus a factor for the bonus value of food stamps.
57. *Research and Statistics Note,* Note No. 9, op. cit.
58. Martha Derthick, *Uncontrolled Spending for Social Service Grants* (Washington, D.C.: The Brookings Institution, 1975), p. 7.
59. Ibid., pp. 7–8.
60. Ibid., p. 12.
61. Ibid., p. 45.
62. Letter, Harold O. Swank to Donald F. Simpson, December 30, 1970, quoted in ibid., p. 47.
63. Ibid., pp. 71–76.

Police Services in a Democratic Society

INTRODUCTION

The American criminal justice system is comprised of three discrete but not totally inseparable parts: police services, the court system, and correctional facilities. Our federal system has both civil and criminal codes at national, state and local levels. The bulk of both civil and criminal jurisdiction is state and local, and thus the bulk of criminal justice activity is designated as rightfully within the domain of the states and localities. This is not to suggest that this dual system leads to a total separation of criminal justice procedures. In fact

[c]rime control requires effective intergovernmental relations. The geographic spread and mobility of crime as well as the sharing of criminal

justice responsibilities among Federal, State and local governments have a significant impact on the intergovernmental dimensions of effective crime control.[1]

Several questions relating to the effects of federalism as well as the role of democratic theory come to mind when discussing jurisdictional interrelationships in crime control. Protection against crime as well as fighting crime are seen as largely local functions. Indeed, these functions have a local origin in the United States and the vast majority of Americans—both liberals as well as conservatives—still assume that the criminal justice system must be retained as a local function. Indeed the single most distinctive characteristic of the organization of police services in the United States is the extent to which it is decentralized. If criminal justice functions are centralized and thus concentrated in one jurisdiction, the fear that a national police state will be created will be always present. Yet some coordination of functions must be (and in fact is) maintained. The Federal Bureau of Investigation (FBI) keeps criminal records; the federal government provides funds for equipment and training for police; and in some cases, federal court decisions supercede state court decisions. All these federal activities seem appropriate even in a federal system where we guard closely our freedoms against federal police power. In an interdependent system, all facets of a system's development, maintenance, and control must have some linkages. In our criminal justice system, these are minimal linkages. They seem appropriate given the need to communicate information, to maintain local forces, and to combat the ability of criminals to move with relative ease between jurisdictions.

In the other chapters in this volume, it has been argued that additional national-urban linkages need to be developed to solve many of the urban problems that are both cause and effect of the crisis of urban America. Crime is a crisis, also. However, it might be unwise to build stronger linkages between government jurisdictions in combating crime except for general constitutional oversight by the federal courts over the criminal justice system and the continued provision of federal funds for equipment and training. To call for national controls for a criminal justice system (except perhaps for police and corrections training) might be tantamount to calling for a national police force. A national police force concentrates too much force in the hands of too few people. Such force might then be used not to protect citizens but to coerce them into supporting a government that does not act to maintain and build the values of a democratic society.

In the sections that follow, we will be looking at one aspect of the criminal justice system in urban America—the police. The police provide an essential safety service. They also represent the first step in the criminal justice system, and are the most visible part of the criminal justice system. In addition, they represent the internal enforcement arm of the government. Though the other elements of the criminal justice system are of equal importance in maintaining order in society, the limitations of space make it feasible to consider only the role of police as providers of a safety service. Of course, there are other safety services that could be considered instead of police. Sanitation services or fire protection and prevention could be examined. It seems, however, that police are the most visible public personnel in most communities. Also, they are most central to the maintenance of order in society. Without a fine balance between freedom and order, the other problems we are considering pale into less central positions in our collective political consciousness.

Organizationally this chapter will differ from the previous presentations on urban public policy areas. This chapter will commence with a discussion of the origin of localism in police services in our federal system. Also considered will be the organization of urban police forces as well as some of the pervasive characteristics of the members of urban police forces, because the police officer has considerable discretion within a paramilitary system to legitimately define and then maintain order. Several of the contemporary problems regarding the delivery of police services, which have arisen as a result of the complexities of our highly mobile industrial society, will also be examined. Among the issues that will be considered is the role of the police as maintainer of social peace and order. Finally, there will be a discussion of attempts by both the states and the national government to support, coordinate, and oversee police services.

A Historical Perspective on Local Police Jurisdictions

The function of the police in seventeenth-century England and in their American colonies was largely voluntary and essentially local in both scope and jurisdiction. Thus, the police services then did not resemble the uniformed police departments that exist in contemporary urban areas. In the early years of the Republic, some areas maintained private arrangements for protection. For example, colonial New York (New Amsterdam, until 1664), Philadelphia, and Boston maintained the institution of the night watch (per diem evening watchmen). They each also had constables to maintain order and apprehend criminals. The office of constable was considered of minor status: "[O]f seventeen chosen in Boston in 1743, only five agreed to serve, ten paid fines for refusing, and two were excused without fine." In New York the night watch varied in different periods "depending upon whether the citizens' fear of disorder or dislike of paying taxes was greater at any given time." [2]

The lack of an American tradition of an organized police force stemmed in large measure from English fears of despotic control that might arise if an organized police functioned as a standing army. English fears were related to the seventeenth-century actions of Oliver Cromwell's major generals who attempted to close England's theaters and taverns.

Also Protestant England's fears that the Catholic King James might use the army to undermine Protestantism reinforced English antipathy to nationally organized military or police forces. Finally, the Parliamentary aristocracy wished to limit centralized military forces in order to maintain their own position of authority vis-à-vis the king. Fear of authoritarian power in the hands of a central government was also apparent among those American colonists who rebelled against the British government. The American fear of strong and/or centralized police powers was institutionalized to some extent by the Constitution which established the United States as a federal system. Thus the states as well as the national government developed both civil and criminal codes, and the states' authority over the daily activities of their citizenry was considerable. Fear of central control led to an even further decentralization of authority as the states created towns, counties and other local jurisdictions, and granted their "creatures of government" some of the reserved power granted to the states by the Constitution. Among the areas of authority divested by the states to local jurisdictions often were police functions.

The American Local Tradition in the Nineteenth Century

The tradition of the night watch and the unsalaried police constable was generally maintained in urban areas until the 1830s.[3] However, one general exception to this style of police control arose earlier. In the major cities of the South, the white population feared that revolts might erupt among members of the large slave population. Thus, the cities of Charleston, Savannah, and Richmond maintained both foot and mounted patrols to prevent the congregation of slaves.[4] Such patrols were in fact substantial items in their respective municipal budgets.

During the 1830s and 1840s, it was becoming apparent that American society had grown both more heterogeneous and more prone to numerous serious crimes. Cleavages had developed in the major cities of the United States between whites and blacks, Irish and native born, Protestants and Catholics, and beer drinkers and prohibitionists.[5] Antiabolitionist rioting occurred in 1834; between 1834 and 1837, rioting related to antiabolitionist and anti-Irish/anti-Catholic feelings occurred in Boston; in the 1830s and 1840s, rioting caused by tensions similar to those that affected Boston's population occurred in Philadelphia, too. In 1838, racial rioting in Philadelphia resulted in many deaths. Similar riots broke out again in 1842. Events like these led many city residents to demand that police forces be better organized to control riots as well as other threats to social peace. Also, highly publicized homicides in the 1830s and 1840s led to increased demands for better organized urban police systems.[6]

By 1844, New York City had established a police department. Police officers were appointed for one-year terms upon nomination by a member of the city council. They had to live in the ward in which they served.

A chief of police was selected and given limited supervisory powers.[7] One certainly can argue that New York City's first "official" police force was hardly professional and that it was clearly rooted in a system of political spoils. It was, however, the harbinger of today's well-organized, bureaucratized, and sophisticated police departments.

By 1848, Philadelphia had established an independent police force of thirty-four men, while retaining the night watch. The establishment of this police force did not, however, eliminate antiblack and antiabolitionist rioting. Proponents of urban-suburban consolidation used the civil unrest as the basis for extending the city's geographic boundaries. They argued that Philadelphia's political jurisdiction had to be expanded to enable local Philadelphia police to control potentially troublesome activities in areas along Philadelphia's suburban fringe. In 1854, the Pennsylvania legislature changed Philadelphia's charter so that its boundaries were extended from approximately 2 square miles to nearly 130 square miles. Over the objections of Irish immigrants, this police force initially appointed only native-born Americans. However, soon thereafter the police force was integrated to include Irishmen.

In 1823, Boston's aldermen created the office of Marshal of the City. Benjamin Pollard served as the first marshal from 1823 to 1836, assisted by one or two deputies. During that time, he concerned himself less with the criminal law than with the municipal public health regulations. However, crime and disorder continued to increase. Thus, in 1838, the Massachusetts General Court allowed the City of Boston to appoint a number of policemen to serve under the authority of the Marshall. Their function was to suppress riots. The night watch, essentially low-paid casual labor, continued to exist. It was not until 1854 that the Boston police and watch departments were consolidated into a single police force.[8]

Police and Politics

For the most part, the city police forces of the 1840s and 1850s were appointed for limited terms by political officeholders. These jobs represented party patronage, and a change of party fortunes would result in the loss of position for local policemen. Therefore, police were often very much involved in partisan political activity. Indeed, in a number of cities, chiefs campaigned and sometimes policemen themselves were directly elected. Cincinnati elected all its policemen; for a time, Philadelphia, San Francisco, Chicago, and Cleveland elected their police chiefs; Brooklyn elected captains as well as its chiefs of police.[9]

American egalitarian ideology influenced the initial resistance by the citizenry to a uniformed police force. In fact, uniforms as a symbol of efficiency and authority did not come into vogue until the 1850s and 1860s. Also, early urban police forces were highly decentralized. A number of cities followed New York's model of having the city wards constitute separate patrol areas with little overall administrative supervision by the chief of police.[10] While such a procedure allowed responsiveness to local community pressures, it provided little administrative efficiency with respect to public accountability for police services. In the late 1850s demands arose for police to expand their functions to include control of activities other than violent crime and rioting—such as public intoxication, gambling, and prostitution. When new laws were enacted in these areas, policemen tended to enforce them in a limited manner and to develop working relationships with saloon keepers, commercialized vice, and professional criminals. These early police did not try to shut down vice; all they attempted to do was prevent excesses.[11] This perspective on the discretionary (often corrupt) role of the police was not limited to the urban centers of Boston, New York, and Chicago, but applied to western towns such as Abilene, Wichita, and Dodge City as well.

The main function for which police were held accountable was maintaining civil order. In discussing criminality in New York City in the early 1870s, Charles Loring Brace observed that the level of violent crime was higher than that of European cities:

> They [New York City's criminals] rob a bank, when English thieves pick pockets; they murder, where European proletaires cudgel or fight with fists; in a riot they begin what seems about to be the sacking of a city, where English rioters merely batter policemen or smash lamps.[12]

The Later Nineteenth Century and Early Twentieth Century

In the 1860s, while seeking reform of urban police corruption, some rurally dominated state legislatures required that police administrators be appointed by the state legislatures. Such a pattern of state control lasted in Detroit from 1865 to 1885. In Missouri, the St. Louis and Kansas City police departments were under state control from the early 1860s into the early 1900s. State control brought little improvement in urban police services. What was perhaps most involved in the politics of state control of police forces were cleavages based on alignments that were rural versus urban, Republican versus Democratic, native-born Protestant Americans versus immigrants, often Catholics, from Ireland and Southern and Eastern Europe. In most cases, the cities regained control of their police forces in the first decades of the twentieth century.[13] By the 1870s, the major American cities all had police forces based on the consolidation of police services and abolition of the night watch. By the early 1900s, the unified police force had been institutionalized in most urban areas. Over time, such forces came under the direct administrative control of a commissioner or chief, frequently an appointee of the mayor, sometimes selected by the mayor with the consent of the city council, and sometimes directly elected by the citizens.

Initially, police commissioners were responsible to mayors and city councils. This relationship involved such early commissioners in partisan political activities. In the late nineteenth century, many large cities established lay police boards in an attempt to insulate the police from partisan politics and urban corruption. However, such boards also became involved in urban corruption. Perhaps the classic example of police corruption was in New York City in the 1880s. In response to apparent widespread police corruption, the New York State legislature established the Lexow Committee to investigate corruption. The committee found that corruption was widespread in New York City despite the existence of a police board. The Commission went on to charge that whenever the New York City Democratic political organization, known as Tammany Hall, controlled the majority on New York City's police board, voter fraud was rampant in New York City elections. As a result of such corruption, police boards eventually were abolished in the first two decades of the twentieth century, and ultimate police authority became centered in either a single professional police chief or a nonprofessional civilian commissioner. By 1920, of 52 cities with populations of over 100,000 people, only 14 police departments were still administered by police boards.[14]

The Call for Local Police Reform at the National Level

A landmark effort to reform police practices and professionalize police was the 1931 report of the National Commission on Law Observance and Enforcement (the Wickersham Commission). The Commission's analysis led to some professionalization efforts by local law enforcement agencies. The Wickersham Commission found that the average police commissioner's term of office was too short to provide substantial security (and independence) in his position.[15] The Commission also felt that future efforts should be made to educate, train, and discipline prospective officers so that inefficiency and corruption among patrolmen could be eliminated. Furthermore, the Wickersham Commission felt that most police forces in large cities (over 300,000 population) lacked communication systems and equipment adequate for effective law enforcement.[16]

The process of developing modern and technologically effective city and suburban police forces has been only partially accomplished, however. This fact was observed in a more recent report by the President's Commission on Law Enforcement and the Administration of Justice. This report observed that as recently as 1967,

> [s]ome cities, counties, and States have taken great strides in streamlining their operations through reorganization and increased use of technology and the use of modern techniques to detect and apprehend criminal offenders. Others are on the threshold of modernization. But many departments remain static. And it is these that obviously constitute a burden on the machinery of justice, and are detrimental to the process of achieving a truly professional police service.[17]

Furthermore, the presidential Commission reported with some concern that over 70 percent of the nation's police departments had set the high school diploma as the minimum educational requirement for employment.[18] Six years later in 1973, the National Advisory Commission on Criminal Justice Standards and Goals articulated the view that a truly professionalized police force requires a college-level professional police curriculum for police with specializations to accommodate the varied needs of patrolmen, specialists, and managers. This Commission also saw the development of an appropriate police educational program as a major task facing educators, police, and other criminal justice administrators.[19]

The Delivery of Police Services: Organization and Functions

It has been emphasized thus far that the delivery of police services has local origins and that we have retained this local base for the provision of police services even as we have increased national involvement in the delivery of other services. It should not be surprising, then, that there are more than 20,158 separate police agencies[20] in states and localities in the United States with almost 557,000 law enforcement officers[21] (of whom 83.7 percent are local), ranging in size from New York City's force of 24,895 (in 1977), to one-member constabularies. These law officers make most of the approximately 10 million arrests a year.[22] Needless to say, the huge number of jurisdictions and the variety of their organizational forms and sizes makes it impossible to catalogue all of the organizational forms in one chapter. It is possible, however, to consider general forms. Thus *types* of urban systems will be considered to develop a sense of what factors influence the organization of urban police forces.

Regardless of an urban police force's organizational form, J. Edgar Hoover, the head of the FBI for over forty years, believed that both urban and rural police forces should be expected to (1) protect life and property, (2) preserve the peace, (3) prevent crime, (4) detect and arrest violators of law, (5) enforce laws and ordinances, and (6) safeguard the rights of individuals.[23] Of course, police perform other functions, as well. Specifically, they are responsible for regulating traffic, combating vice and gambling, and trying to cope with juvenile delinquency. In some places, they are also responsible for various licensing, inspecting, and administrative tasks.[24] To perform these services, police are organized into local police forces with varying forms of bureaucratic controls.[25] The type as well as the extent of control over the police by political authority varies with the size of the jurisdiction and the level of government jurisdiction. Although cities and counties are but legal creatures of the states, most states have granted local jurisdictions control over their police activities and they permit them to operate without state interference. Thus, local autonomy reigns and state involvement in local police activities is in most areas limited to an oversight function.

In most cities, the police department is the largest agency under the direct control of city hall. When the mayor is the chief executive, he or she usually controls the police department. The mayor's power depends upon four factors: (1) the power to appoint the police chief, (2) the existence of a special police commission serving as a buffer between the mayor and the police, (3) the degree of police unionization, and (4) the degree of police civil service protection. If there is a commission form of government, one of the commissioners is usually responsible for the police function.[26] Although the ultimate sanction for law enforcement is found in state law, authority over the police for both policy formulation and administrative direction most often resides with the city council and the city's executive. Thus, the chain of command begins with the patrolman on the beat, moves up through the command channels to the administrative chief (or board or commission), and finally ends with the mayor, a city commission, or the city manager. As a general rule, the council approves the appointment of the department head, may investigate police actions, and might be responsible for disciplining or dismissing the chief administrative officer of the police department. The chief administrative officer of the police department is usually a chief of police, a director of public safety, or a collective police commission.

Where there is a chief, he is generally the highest ranking civil servant in the department by virtue of his position as chief, and he has some hierarchial structure operating under his control.[27] He is expected to provide departmental leadership and to represent the department in its relations with the city administrative officials, the city council, and the community.[28] Since a local director of public safety need not be a civil service officer, he may be employed to provide supervision over the civil service–protected police chief, or to bring outside talent to the civil service–related local police department. In many states, the director of public safety is a coordinator who supervises a statewide department that oversees functions such as state police, alcoholic beverage control, motor vehicle inspection, state fire inspection, weights and measures, and civil defense. A third administrative form is based upon variations of a police commission. A commission is usually comprised of a small group of part-time officials appointed by the chief executive or the city council with duties akin to that of a civil service commission—that is, it develops rules and regulations and administers personnel matters. One variant of the commission limits this body to serving only as an appeal body for personnel and disciplinary matters. A more extensive form of the commission provides this body with direct statutory control over the entire operations of a department.[29]

If a jurisdiction has a police chief, his role will depend to a considerable extent upon the type of jurisdiction in which he is operating. In small departments, there will most often be very little social distance between the chief and the patrolmen. As departments become larger, the organizational structure becomes more complex and the social distance between the chief and the patrolmen increases. However, in the larger and more complex organizations, the multiple supervisory levels enable the chief to maintain effective controls over the rank-and-file police units. The chief in these larger departments must depend upon the information provided him by his subordinates in the chain of command.[30] This chain of command is often paramilitary in character and many of the most common titles are of military origin. The usual titles, beneath the chief, in order of rank are captain, lieutenant, sergeant. Next in rank are detective, patrolman and patrolwoman (ranked according to grade), matrons, clerks, and other civilian employees.[31]

In addition to the chain of command, some reasonably standardized organizational units are also used by police departments, though not all departments use the same terms. The larger the department, the more complex the organization; smaller units do not have systems as complex as the model about to be explained! In large departments, personnel are assigned to functional divisions. The largest organic unit in a large department is a bureau. The bureaus are comprised of a number of divisions. A division has either a departmentwide function or a specialized activity. Divisions with district stations are most often headed by a chief; divisions with no district stations are most often headed by a captain. When a department is very large, there will be additional specialization within the divisions along functional lines. These functional subdivisions are known as sections. For example, a large detective division may have sections to investigate different classes of crimes. The head of a section may be a lieutenant; but if a section is small and the responsibility limited, a lower ranking officer may be in charge. If further specialization is required within a division, the personnel may be divided into offices or desks. The primary purpose of these designations is to facilitate assignments and to direct people to locations. If this is the sole purpose of a desk or office, there may not be a person in charge. If there is some specific activity, such as office of public information, then there will be a person designated to oversee the office.[32] In large departments, it is the chain of command built into the organization that provides information to the police chief who cannot be in daily contact with the local law enforcement officers.

One additional point must be made and perhaps emphasized. Though there are formal systems of accountability operative for police forces—for example, the department is ultimately responsible to elected officials and internal review mechanisms operate in many departments[33]—external pressures operate to keep police departments in line too. Public opinion, the media, citizen groups, and the courts are always ready to criticize if they do not approve of individual or collective police behavior. Also, the threat of court actions is always present if the police violate the law. Finally, though civilian review boards are not presently popular, the threat of their becoming popular instruments for public oversight of the police is always present.

County Services and Metropolitan Consolidation

In addition to the town and city police organizational units that have been considered, other levels of local government, often encompassing developed urban areas, also provide police service in diverse organizational forms. For example, the county provides public safety services through the office of the sheriff to both rural sections of the county and to unincorporated urban areas. A few counties, most notably St. Louis and Los Angeles Counties, offer police services on a contractual basis to municipalities within their boundaries. Some cities provide contract arrangements to smaller bordering jurisdictions,[34] although these are exceptional situations.

There has been some movement toward metropolitan city-county consolidation of police services in recent years, but it has had limited acceptance so far. The support for consolidation comes from individuals who believe that departments comprised of fewer than ten sworn officers are too small to be efficient. There is, in fact, a considerable range in the sizes of the thousands of local police forces; the vast majority, however, have been very small.

The 1972 Census of Governments study, *Local Governments in Metropolitan Areas,* notes the average size of such forces and particularly observes that smaller police units proportionate to population size are found in smaller SMSA areas. In all SMSAs, the average number of full-time equivalent employees engaged in police protection functions was 23.9 per 10,000 population. In SMSAs with populations of 1 million or more, this average figure was as high as 27.7; in SMSAs with populations between 500,000 to 999,999, this figure was 20.5; and in SMSAs with populations between 300,000 to 499,999, the comparable figure was 18.9. In the smallest SMSAs, the comparable figure was 16.9.[35]

A 1978 study also indicates that the size of a police department (including both uniformed and nonuniformed personnel) is still positively related to city size. The number of full-time paid personnel per 1,000 population in cities of over 1,000,000 population was 4.55; in the 500,000–1,000,000 size city category, the number was 3.24; in the 100,000–250,000 category, the number was 2.26; and in the smaller size cities, the ratio of such personnel per 1,000 population hovers around 2 (see Table 1). In addition, by far the largest number of cities reporting were those with a population of below 25,000.

In fiscal 1976, the seventeen largest SMSAs accounted for a disproportionate amount of expenditures for criminal justice activities. Indeed, these SMSAs spent approximately $5.7 billion on criminal justice activities, including police activities. This expenditure amounted to 47 percent of the nation's local criminal justice expenditures in an area

Table 1 / FULL-TIME PAID PERSONNEL[1] POLICE DEPARTMENT

Classification	Number of Cities Reporting	Mean	Per 1,000 Population
Total, all cities	1,443	130	2.57
Population Group			
Over 1,000,000	4	10,212	4.55
500,000–1,000,000	12	2,166	3.24
250,000–499,999	26	930	2.66
100,000–249,999	73	319	2.26
50,000– 99,999	165	142	2.05
25,000– 49,999	354	69	1.97
10,000– 24,999	809	32	2.01
Metro Status			
Central	245	521	3.00
Suburban	800	55	1.95
Independent	398	42	2.08

Source: Carol A. Pigeon, "Police, Fire, and Refuse Collection and Disposal Departments. Manpower, Compensation, and Expenditures," *The Municipal Yearbook, 1979* (Washington, D.C.: International City Management Association, 1979), p. 174.
[1] Includes uniformed and nonuniformed personnel.

where 30 percent of the nation's population resided. Also, the seventeen largest SMSAs spent $3.655 billion directly on police protection. This amount was 47 percent of the national direct expenditure by local governments for police protection.[36] Furthermore, the local governments constituting these SMSAs employed 191,078 of the local government full-time equivalent employees in the police protection area or 41 percent of the total number of local government full-time employees working in this area.[37] All municipalities in the United States employed 374,225 or 80 percent of total local full-time equivalent workers in the area of police protection while counties accounted for 91,817 such employees or 20 percent of this amount. Of the total number of state and local full-time employees (556,926), state employees made up 90,884 or 16 percent.[38]

The States

The first regular state police force was established in the United States in Pennsylvania in 1905. After World War I, state police forces gradually developed in other states to cope with the problems associated with lawbreakers who went beyond the jurisdictional limitations of the localities in which the crimes had been committed. The state police units dealt primarily with the problems of automobile traffic and car thefts.[39] As of 1980, all states except Hawaii had a state law enforcement body. In most places, the state has had a limited role in the delivery of police services. In some states, the only state police function is highway patrol, and almost two-thirds of state expenditures for law enforcement is for traffic regulation. States do perform other relatively limited functions regarding police services. They aid localities in developing model laws and criminal justice systems. In some states, they have also been responsible for training, setting standards, and for providing administrative aid to localities. In recent years, however, there has been an upward drift of police responsibilities from localities to counties and states. The Advisory Commission on Intergovernmental Relations has noted:

> The division of police strength among state, county, and "other local" governments ... has been changing. In 34 states, the state police made up a greater proportion of the total force in 1967 than in 1957; in 31 states, the proportion of county police had increased in those ten years. Moreover, 17 states had over 40 percent of their police strength in state and county police forces as of 1967. ... The police function is still a local one, but there is a shift to police services on a more area-wide basis, and away from exclusive reliance on municipal protection.[40]

Given the proliferation and decentralization of police departments in urban areas, and the increasing suburbanization of our nation—with the resultant increase in suburban crime—the upward drift to more encompassing units such as the county or the state seems almost predictable.[41] However, this trend has been limited in scope, and the more local jurisdictions still provide the bulk of police services.

The Costs and Distribution of Services

As population increases, police costs rise faster than police strength. One can purchase more police personnel per dollar in rural than in urban areas because personnel costs are higher in more densely populated urban areas, a greater scope of protection is required, and police protection may be more capital intensive in more densely populated areas.[42] It has been estimated that approximately 85 percent of the total expenditures for police protection are allocated for wages and salaries. Thus, pay scales are significant in determining the total fiscal outlays.[43] In 1977, in cities with populations of over 1 million people, the average police pay scale ranged from $13,497 (minimum salary) to $17,303 (maximum salary) per year. In cities with populations between 100,000 and 249,999, the comparable scale was $10,889 to $13,266 (see Table 2).

In 1976, total state and local expenditures for police protection

Table 2 / AVERAGE ANNUAL SALARY SCALES OF POLICE, 1977

City Size	Average Minimum Salary	Average Maximum Salary
100,000–249,000	$10,889	$13,266
250,000–499,999	$11,768	$14,285
500,000–999,999	$11,675	$14,901
Over 1,000,000	$13,497	$17,303

Source: Data derived from U.S. Bureau of the Census, *Statistical Abstract of the United States, 1978*, 99th edition (Washington, D.C., 1978), Table 312.

amounted to over $9.5 billion. Local expenditures represented 82 percent of these outlays, or over $7.7 billion.[44] About 4 percent of the direct general revenues of state and local governments was spent on police protection (and corrections) in 1976.[45] More recently, a substantial sum of federal revenue-sharing funds has been used by state and local governments to support police services. In fiscal 1977, 14.4 percent of revenue-sharing funds or $942.8 million was utilized for such purposes.[46]

As far as distribution of police services is concerned, protection is better on the average in cities than in suburbs and better in suburbs than in county jurisdictions. Thus, in 1977, the average police protection to population ratio for cities was 2.1 per 1,000. In cities of over 250,000, the average police protection ratio was 2.8 per 1,000.[47] In 1977, the average suburban police protection ratio was 1.9 per 1,000. In contrast to the suburban and especially to the city ratio, the county police protection ratio is somewhat lower. Thus for the same year, counties with full-time sheriff's offices maintained an average police protection ratio of 1.7 per 1,000.

There has been some movement toward the increased use of civilian personnel in many police departments. In 1977, civilians accounted for 17.8 percent of city police personnel, up from 13.2 in 1972. Among the civilian police workers, 58.3 percent were women and 41.7 percent were men. (However, 97 percent of the sworn personnel in cities were men and 96 percent of sworn personnel in suburbs were men.)[48]

Profile of the Policeman

Jerome Skolnick, in *Justice Without Trial,* tried to outline a working personality of policemen. He suggested:

> (S)o far as exposure to danger is concerned, the policeman may be likened to the soldier. His problems as an authority bear a certain similarity to those of a schoolteacher, and the pressure he feels to prove himself efficient are not unlike those felt by the industrial worker. The combination of these elements, however, is unique to the policeman.[49]

Skolnick did not suggest that these were universal characteristics, but rather that they were behavior predispositions that seemed to prevail among members of police forces. Some observers of police behavior further suggest that police officers at times tend to display authoritarian characteristics.[50] Who become members of police forces? Why do they select police work as a career? These are important questions because police in contemporary society are the political system's legitimate purveyors of law and order. James Q. Wilson suggested:

> The patrolman's role is defined more by his responsibility for maintaining order than by his responsibility for enforcing the law. ... "(E)nforcing the law" is what he does when there is no dispute. ... Other agencies (the courts) will decide whether the suspect is guilty.[51]

Given Wilson's view that police are "maintainers of order," it becomes important to understand the background of the men and women attracted to police forces and how they define their order-maintaining roles, since maintaining order requires interpretation of the law and thus provides a wide discretionary range for law and order enforcement.

In the 1960s, police officers tended to have working class origins, high school educations or less, average intelligence, and a desire for security. Arthur Niederhoffer, who was a member of the New York City Police Department for over twenty years, has suggested that "only in his superior physical endowment does he stand above the crowd." [52] In an early study of the backgrounds of police recruits in New York City, it was estimated that 85 percent of the recruits came from working class homes. That is, their fathers worked in clerical or sales positions, service jobs, or as unskilled laborers. When recruits at the New York City Police Academy were asked why they chose to join the police force, the vast majority indicated that they wanted the security the position provided.

Also, there is some evidence that a high proportion of policemen have fathers or other relatives who worked on police forces. Studies in Chicago and New York City show that over one-third of the police officers in these departments had relatives employed in police work or related fields. In fact, family influence to choose an occupation may in part explain the predominance of some ethnic groups, especially the Irish, in many urban police forces. [53] One effect of this recruitment pattern is the difficulty of securing black recruits for police departments. Recruiting blacks to urban forces is also hampered by the requirement of most forces that recruits have no arrest records. It is hard to grow up in an urban black ghetto without some run-in, however slight, with the law. In a study of the Denver Police Department in the late 1960s, it was found that "the typical Denver policeman is white, Protestant, has at least a high school education, is married with two or three children, and has been raised in the western or north-central part of the United States." [54] Thus the Denver policeman was seen as an average person. Almost 25 percent of Denver's population is black or Spanish-surnamed, yet minority members made up only 5 percent of the force. [55] While recruitment efforts during the 1970s aimed at increasing the minority population in the police force generally had little impact on the racial makeup of many big-city police forces, some increases in recruitment did occur. In a few cities, such as Atlanta, Chicago, and Washington, D.C., the percentage of black officers had doubled between 1967 and the early 1970s. [56]

Recently, efforts to emphasize higher educational requirements for policemen have led to some indications that a new breed of policeman with new characteristics is being developed. A study by Mary Hageman of seventy police officers (police and detectives) found that the leading main reason (37.3 percent) for joining the police force within the sample was to do "something worthwhile," the second most important reason

(19.4 percent) was to "help the public," the third most important reason (11.9 percent) was related to "adventure and excitement," and only 9 percent indicated security as a main reason for selecting police work.[57] *Thus in this study, security seemed to play a much lesser role in determining career decision-making than earlier 1960 studies indicated.*[58]

Of entrants to police forces during the 1970–74 period, 39 percent had completed at least one year of college at time of entry. From 1965 to 1969, the comparable figure was 22 percent.[59] In 1974, almost 60 percent of police supervisors had at least one year of college background; 10 percent held B.A. degrees. In the same year, the comparable figure for line patrol officers was 47 percent with one year of college and 7 percent with the B.A. degree. Clearly the B.A. degree enhances promotion to supervisory positions in police departments.[60]

As of 1975, 43 percent of police chiefs in agencies with 400 or more employees had B.A. degrees; 34 percent of police chiefs in agencies with 75 or more employees held the B.A. degree. In very small police departments with fewer than 75 employees, only 13 percent of police chiefs held the B.A. degree. However, in such small departments, 39 percent of the police chiefs held two-year post–high school professional degrees.[61]

Moreover, the trend toward a better professionally educated police force continues to gather momentum. The Law Enforcement Assistance Administration (LEAA) National Manpower Survey of the Criminal Justice System projected in 1978 that, by 1980, 63.3 percent of all sworn police personnel would have at least one year of college. LEAA funding has encouraged this development. For fiscal 1975, 20.6 percent of the financing of Agency Academies, 13.2 percent of the funding of Academic Affiliates, and 19.6 percent of the funding of Regional/State Academies was provided by LEAA. Overall, LEAA provided 18.5 percent of the funding of all responding academies in fiscal 1975.[62]

Increasingly, the police, especially supervisory officers, reflect a level of professionalism related to the college degrees they have earned. To some extent, such higher education has increased the prestige of police enforcement as a profession, and it has especially increased the prestige of police leadership cadres. The esteem in which the public holds the police force, which once ranked low relative to other occupations, has improved. In a recent Gallup Poll that ranked occupations by the dimensions of honesty and ethical standards, 40 percent of respondents ranked police officers as having high or very high standards. Police officers were ranked sixth behind the clergy, medical doctors, engineers, college teachers, and bankers and ahead of lawyers, undertakers, and senators.[63]

The more highly educated police officers will most often succeed in advancing through the police hierarchy, while the people who remain as police officers on the streets tend to be less educated. These are the officers with whom citizens have the most continuous contact; they also tend to include the more authoritarian members of urban police forces.[64] It is important to note, however, that police recruits of working class backgrounds are on the average no more authoritarian in their personalities than other members of the working class, though the working class is on the average more authoritarian in personality and lifestyle than the middle class.[65]

In assessing police behavior, some observers of the police function emphasize the helping role of police officers as much more central to most police experience than an authoritarian enforcement role. Proponents of this view maintain that police are involved mostly in assisting people in trouble and in helping troublesome people. Rather than acting in an authoritarian manner, it is argued, they are involved in disaster prevention. As Bittner observes:

> I have seen policemen helping tenants in arrears gain access to medication which a landlord held together with other possessions in apparently legal bailment, I have seen policemen settling disputes between parents as to whether an ill child should receive medical treatment, I have seen a patrolman adjudicating a quarrel between a priest and an organist concerning the latter's access to the church. All this . . . compels the . . . inference that no human problem exists, or is imaginable, about which it could be said with finality that this certainly could not become the proper business of the police.[66]

A recent study indicates that when police do use coercive power, they react in varied fashion depending upon their own socialization and personality.[67] In a study of police behavior in Laconia, Illinois, William K. Muir found that less than 20 percent of the policemen observed exhibited authoritarian behavioral traits.

The Role of Discretion in Police Activity

The Advisory Commission on Intergovernmental Relations, in its report on the criminal justice system, suggested:

> [T]he police function is the frontal part of the criminal justice system. Its operation often determines the extent and scope of involvement of an individual with the criminal justice system. Much of the police function turns on the discretionary authority of the police.[68]

The options open to the police are varied. They may choose to arrest an individual and then practice "station house adjudication," or they may choose to formally book a lawbreaker.[69] With many laws on the books, they also have the option of determining for which minor infractions of the law they will arrest or not arrest an individual.

At least four factors affect police discretion: (1) the characteristics of a

Table 3 / FOUR KINDS OF DISCRETIONARY SITUATIONS

Nature of Situation	Basis of Police Response	
	Police-Invoked Action	Citizen-Invoked Action
Law Enforcement	I	II
Order Maintenance	III	IV

Source: James Q. Wilson, *Varieties of Police Behavior* (Cambridge, Mass.: Harvard University Press, 1968), p. 85. © 1968 by the President and Fellows of Harvard College. Reprinted by permission.

crime, (2) the relationship between the alleged criminal and the victim, (3) whether the police encountered an alleged wrongdoing, and the characteristics of the encounter, and (4) policies of the police department itself.[70] To put this into somewhat different terms, a police response is either a citizen-invoked or a police-invoked action; the situation will either call for law enforcement or order maintenance. Wilson has suggested four kinds of discretionary situations (see Table 3).

Type I and Type IV situations permit considerable discretion in police actions; Type I situations are amenable to department regulations while Type IV situations are not. Since Type III situations are police-invoked, they are by definition discretionary actions though they may be circumscribed by departmental control. Type II situations require the patrolman to function as a report taker and information gatherer unless someone has been caught by the victim or an onlooker. In these situations, he has little discretion unless the suspect is a juvenile; then he has considerable discretion subject to departmental policies and organization.

In all these situations, the police administrator along with the patrolman exercises varying degrees of discretion, which have been set to some extent by departmental regulations.[71] If the patrolman is authoritarian and if he is not tolerant of differences in demeanor, he may use his discretion to reprimand some individuals for legal infractions that he would leave unreported for other individuals. For example, often the well-dressed, middle class person is less likely to be stopped, frisked, and questioned on the street than the ghetto black. Similarly, the well-dressed, middle class individual is less likely than the sloppy teenager to get a traffic ticket for driving slightly above the speed limit. These are ordinary everyday examples of police discretionary behavior. With regard to police activity when on patrol, authoritarian behavior and even racial slurs are more likely to occur when police action is being taken in the face of ". . . outright hostility without [the policeman] having the formal authority to impose legal sanction."[72] Thus, situations that foster role insecurity for the police officer are most likely to result in authoritarian response.

Some Contemporary Police Problems

Police-Community Relations

In any discussion of police-community relations, it is important to bear in mind the background, training, and career socialization of police officers because some of the intergroup tension displayed in police-community relations draws heavily on these factors. It has been suggested that the "police seem to play a role in the life of minority people out of all proportion to the role they play in the lives of the dominant majority." [73] In fact, survey data indicate that ethnicity is an essential determinant of both the amount and the kind of contact people have with the police. [74] Blacks and other nonwhite minority group members tend to be wary of the police and feel that the police do not treat them with the same concern and respect with which they treat members of the white working class and the middle class. Such nonwhite populations often feel that they are being discriminated against by the dominant white policemen. This is not to suggest that nonwhite minority groups do not want police involvement in their communities. Quite to the contrary. In their study of Denver police, Bayley and Mendelsohn found that

> minority people ... desire more efficient police service. They deprecate a double standard in police operations with respect to both impartiality and conscientiousness of the police. Minority people do not want a "free ride" for minority lawbreakers. Quite the contrary, for it is minority people who suffer most from the criminal activity of minority persons. [75]

Police officers often are wary and suspicious of nonwhites, believing that they are more likely to be involved in criminal activities than are members of the dominant white middle class and working class. Policemen also believe that hostility against them is greater in nonwhite neighborhoods than in other areas; they are fearful that unpleasant situations may arise when they must deal with minority group members. Thus, police distrust of minority groups and minority distrust of police often results in very tense police-community relations in urban areas. Of course, not all police-community relations in urban America are tense. In white working class and middle class urban communities, police are seen as facilitators of justice; even if they do not aspire to have their children become members of the police force, their relations with the police are respectful and cordial. Tense relationships are more often found in nonwhite minority neighborhoods—most often in the most run-down ghetto communities of central cities and older suburbs—areas that have high crime rates and where nonwhites are the most frequent victims of crimes.

Some recent studies have confirmed the high rate of victimization by nonwhites. In a study of eight American cities, the Law Enforcement

Assistance Administration of the Department of Justice found that households headed by blacks and members of other minority races were more likely to have been burglarized than households headed by whites.[76] When LEAA conducted a similar study in the nation's five largest cities—Chicago, Detroit, Los Angeles, New York, and Philadelphia—the same patterns emerged. For example, in Chicago, blacks and other nonwhite groups were victims of "Robbery without Injury" at a rate of 30 per 1,000; the rate for whites was 14 per 1,000.[77]

Clearly, a significant community problem confronts the police in urban areas with nonwhite populations. A disproportionate amount of crime occurs in these areas; yet residents of these areas are distrustful of the police and question the quality of service they are receiving, and the police are skeptical about many of the residents of those areas. To improve the relationship between the police and the nonwhite communities, some police departments have established programs to seek minority views regarding police services. Some departments have provided their officers with training in race relations, community awareness, and ethnic history. Other departments have embarked on minority recruitment drives,[78] but minority police officers often confront different environmental constraints than other police officers when they try to perform their duties. The black policeman is often unable to perform his duties in white neighborhoods unless he is in uniform; in black areas he is often distrusted as a representative of "white law." [79]

Methods for hearing citizen grievances have been established in some jurisdictions in an attempt to overcome the distrust of the police. Some departments maintain quasi-judicial mechanisms with police officials presiding for hearing citizen complaints. No major American police department, however, currently has a citizen review board. In the 1960s, there was some support for community participation on police review boards. The support for these institutions tended to be strongest among nonwhites and social liberals. More conservative whites tended to oppose these boards seeing them as mollifiers of criminals. The police themselves opposed outside intervention in police activities. The first Police Review Board was established in Philadelphia in 1958. It was fought in the courts by the Fraternal Order of Police (FOP). Though FOP was not successful in its attempts at litigation, the board was abolished by executive order of the mayor in 1969. During its eleven-year existence, it had never been a very effective instrument of accountability to the community because it involved a cumbersome and slow process not supported by the police department.[80]

Similar opposition to review boards occurred in New York City, Minneapolis, Buffalo, and Baltimore, where leaders of the police organizations claimed that review boards constituted "grave threats to policemen," and "undermined their professionalism." [81] Indeed some scholarly critics also agreed that "community pressures" could undermine professional norms.[82] In general, the police have been quite successful in fighting the establishment and maintenance of these boards. In 1966, Mayor John V. Lindsay of New York City added four civilians to the New York Police Department Complaint Review Board; prior to 1966, it had been manned by three deputy police commissioners. The Patrolman's Benevolent Association (PBA) sought to force a referendum on the issue. Some of the most influential state politicos supported the review board (Senator Robert F. Kennedy, Senator Jacob K. Javits, and Mayor John V. Lindsay). When the issue came before the voters, they voted 1,313,161 to 765,468 to abandon the review board. The police had won. The patrolmen waged a battle against their bosses and they won. What is especially important about this event is that it taught urban police all over the nation that they had political power and could use it to bring substantial rewards.[83]

Since the New York City experience, police militancy has increased. Police have organized to gain better pay and working conditions, and the number of labor-management disputes has increased. In July 1969, for example, the police and fire department employees of Vallejo, California, left their jobs for five days. This was the first strike of uniformed employees in the history of the State of California. Police job actions have since occurred in hundreds of jurisdictions, both large and small, including Boston, New York, Minneapolis, Atlanta, and San Francisco, and Plant City, Florida, Chicago Heights, Illinois, and Poplar Bluff, Missouri.[84] By September 1978, almost 55 percent of 463,000 persons employed by local or county police departments belonged to a union or local association. At least 10,000 police officers were members of Teamsters locals. The Teamsters estimate that they bargain for police in about 225 municipalities.[85]

Crime in the Urban Setting

It is evident to most observers of contemporary urban problems that urban crime rates are very high (see Table 4), costs for preventing and reprimanding lawbreakers have been increasing, and that interjurisdictional mobility of lawbreakers has been on the uprise as well. Thus, it should not be surprising that there is some general concern about the appropriate governmental mechanisms and jurisdictions for managing police services, particularly in urban areas. Since concern with local autonomy is implicit in most public safety planning, little effort has been made to legislate linkage-building laws that reflect apparent interjurisdictional interdependence among police jurisdictions. (Interjurisdictional interdependence is increased due to the mobility of criminals that has been facilitated by modern transportation.) Furthermore, not all jurisdictions can manage equally well the high costs of crime prevention and control; these costs are especially high in large cities, which tend to have the highest crime rates,[86] and which may be least able to afford these costs. The need to maintain local control while equalizing protective

Table 4 / REPORTED AND UNREPORTED CRIME

City	Incidents Reported by Police and Published in the FBI Uniform Crime Reports	FBI Data: Incidents per 1,000 in the Population	Estimated Crime Incidents Projected from Impact Cities Crime Survey	LEAA Data: Incidents per 1,000 in the Population	Population
Atlanta	42,104	0.08	98,700	0.20	497,000
Baltimore	69,554	0.08	151,100	0.17	906,000
Cleveland	48,921	0.07	118,900	0.16	751,000
Dallas	64,876	0.08	166,500	0.14	844,000
Denver	47,704	0.09	139,800	0.27	515,000
Newark	35,423	0.09	493,300	1.29	382,000
Portland	35,736	0.09	93,700	0.24	383,000
St. Louis	64,890	0.10	95,800	0.15	622,000

Source: Rates drawn from statistics of the FBI Uniform Crime Reports and the Impact Cities Crime Survey of the Law Enforcement Assistance Administration. Data reported in *The New York Times,* January 27, 1974, p. 34. Also see Michael J. Hindelang, *An Analysis of Victimization Survey Results from Eight Impact Cities: Summary Report,* U.S. Department of Justice, Law Enforcement Assistance Administration, National Criminal Justice Information and Statistics Service (Washington, D.C., 1976 for later data showing subsequent general increases in criminal victimization in six of these cities, the exceptions being Denver and Newark.

services in politically and economically disparate jurisdictions has become the dilemma of contemporary police protection. Although some regional and state police services have been implemented, this dilemma has thus far not been totally eliminated.

There have been recent improvements in the provision of police services. Major problems that still must be dealt with, however, are the high crime rate and the inability to reduce or at least stabilize the crime rate in urban America without changing the basic distribution of police service. An additional problem is the sheer cost of crime. The National Commission on the Causes and Prevention of Violence estimated that for fiscal 1970 the annual cost of crime was equivalent to approximately 2 percent of our gross national product ($20 billion). By 1977, this cost had risen to almost $38 billion. This amount does not take into account the costs of family disruption, psychological damage, and economic hardship. The high incidence of crime—particularly urban crime—generates fear that leads to reduced use of cultural and recreational facilities, increases in segregation and racial conflict, and a faster rate of urban decay in some neighborhoods.[87] The criminal offender represents a high cost to society. In 1977, a violent crime—murder, forcible rape, robbery, or aggravated assault—was committed every thirty-one seconds; a property crime—burglary, larceny-theft, or motor vehicle theft—was committed every three seconds.[88] Also, the more than 1 million people held in state and local institutions at any one time represent maintenance costs as well as a net loss in social and economic productivity to society.[89]

The relationship of the crime rate to governmental jurisdictions and the nature of governmental mechanisms for maintaining and controlling the police systems also raise some complicated problems. First, crime is not stopped by city or county boundaries. Rather, crime is interjurisdictional and an extremely mobile activity. The criminal is very mobile. As Morton Grodzins wrote, "He may flee or fly across state boundaries, and he can plan a robbery in one state, execute it in another, dispose of his loot in a third, and look for sanctuary in a fourth." [90] Yet, in a federal system, all levels of government have legal and operational responsibilities, based on both divided and concurrent powers. Though there are both federal and state legal codes, most responsibilities for maintaining justice reside in the states and localities. In particular, the most responsibility for police services is borne by municipalities. This being the case, the multiplicity of jurisdictions makes it very difficult to provide regional police services though some areas have countywide police departments with primary law enforcement responsibilities. Also, some states bear a greater responsibility for police services than other states. In Alaska, Connecticut, Delaware, Rhode Island, and Vermont, the state has had a predominant role. Local governments have tended to predominate in California, Illinois, Massachusetts, Michigan, New Jersey, and New York.[91] Within most states, there is some cooperation between the separate police departments, but cooperation between states to control criminal activity is an area that has yet to be fully explored.

In other public policy areas, a role is seen for increased federal government involvement in the provision of services. Given the concern about concentrating legitimate force in a national police force and the resultant possibilities for repression and suppression of individuals and groups with divergent views, a strong federal police role does not seem to be a popular linkage. However, federal support for equipment and training and general minimum requirements for service does not necessarily represent an antidemocratic trend in American politics. Indeed some LEAA projects have encouraged the police to emphasize neighborhood approaches to the delivery of police services. LEAA has funded studies of neighborhood team policing efforts (that is, using more than one officer on a neighborhood assignment) in cities such as St. Petersburg, Florida; Los Angeles, California; Cincinnati, Ohio; and Albany, New York.[92]

Such experiments in neighborhood-oriented team policing as a mechanism for reducing urban crime have been inconclusive. A recent evaluation of team policing in Cincinnati published by the Police Foundation indicated that already favorable police-community relations changed little. Burglary was reduced, but other serious offenses were not affected. The Police Foundation concluded that team policing was "[no] worse than regular police practices . . . and is one reasonable option for change in police organization and practice." [93] In the next section of this chapter, the changing federal role in the delivery of police services will be considered.

The Changing Federal Police Role

A Limited Tradition

Federal law enforcement stems back to 1789 when a Revenue Cutter Service was established to curb smuggling. In 1836, police agents were authorized to function under the authority of the Postmaster General to deal with crimes involving postal regulations. Other important federal law enforcement functions established by Congress included internal revenue investigation and narcotics control. The Federal Bureau of Investigation was organized in 1924 within the Justice Department.[94] The jurisdiction of the FBI includes investigations of felonies related to stolen national property, kidnapping across state lines, fugitive felons, interstate movement of prostitutes, interstate gambling, the movement of autos across state lines, and the investigation of violations of federal civil rights laws.[95] All federal police jurisdictions are responsible to federal departments. For example, the Secret Service, which is charged with protecting the President and investigating counterfeiting and forgery of federal documents, serves within the Treasury Department. With the exception of the FBI, all civilian department agencies function under federal civil service regulations.

Current Federal Legislation

• THE OMNIBUS CRIME CONTROL AND SAFE STREETS ACT OF 1968

In the wake of the urban riots of the summer of 1967 and the spring of 1968, the national Omnibus Crime Control and Safe Streets Act of 1968 (Safe Streets Act) was passed. This act established the federal Law Enforcement Assistance Administration to provide federal assistance to state and local governments so that they might become more effective in the task of providing law enforcement services. Under the Safe Streets Act, LEAA was directed to accomplish the following tasks:

1. Encourage States and units of general local government to prepare and adopt comprehensive plans based upon their evaluation of State and Local problems of law enforcement.
2. Authorize grants to States and units of local government in order to improve and strengthen law enforcement.
3. Encourage research and development of new methods for the prevention and reduction of crime and the detection and apprehension of criminals.[96]

The principal form of assistance it provides are block grants to the fifty states and five territories. The amount a state or territory receives is based on relative populations.

Block grant programs are divided between *planning grants* and *action grants*. The planning grant program provides federal funding for 90 percent of the expenses of maintaining fifty-five state planning agencies (SPAs) that were established under the Safe Streets Act. The task of the SPAs is to formulate and submit to LEAA a comprehensive law enforcement plan and to administer a state plan within each state. Under the federal statute, SPAs must "assure that major cities and counties" are included among the recipients of the 40 percent of planning grant funds that must be "passed through" the SPA to units of local government.[97] This provision is intended to assure that some of the federal funds are used to help with urban crime problems. In most cases, action grants provide 75 percent of the funds necessary to carry out the criminal justice programs described in the plans submitted to LEAA by SPAs. The remaining 25 percent is provided by state and local matching contributions which may take the form of cash expenditures or goods and services. SPAs must pass through to units of local government a minimum of 75 percent of the LEAA action grant funds with "adequate assistance [being provided] to high crime areas and areas characterized by high law enforcement activity."

Under the Safe Streets Act, the states may establish their own law enforcement priorities and allocate block grant funds in accordance with these priorities. The LEAA's responsibility is to approve state plans and then to disburse block grants after being satisfied that the requirements of the Safe Streets Act have been met. Furthermore, LEAA has the responsibility for monitoring and evaluating state programs and for providing technical assistance to states and localities.

Finally, the Safe Streets Act provided for research, education, and training in law enforcement and criminal justice by establishing a National Institute of Law Enforcement and Criminal Justice. This institute's purpose is to encourage research and development to improve law enforcement and criminal justice, to disseminate the results of such efforts to state and local governments, and to assist in the development and support of programs for the training of law enforcement and criminal justice personnel. This part of the statute showed a movement toward the rise of the national government as a resource for providing standards of training and research for the development of improved levels of state and local law enforcement and criminal justice activities.

• SOME DEFECTS IN THE ADMINISTRATION OF THE 1968 LAW

Federal funds provided to states and localities most often specify minimum requirements for eligibility. LEAA grants are no exception to this general rule. However, some questions have been raised about the compliance controls maintained by LEAA. In setting guidelines for use of its block grants, the LEAA has apparently been lax in providing national leadership or guidelines for the development of programs to reduce crime or to improve the operation of the criminal justice system. So-called action funds have often been spent on projects only marginally related to the needs of the criminal justice system. In one case, the LEAA and the state of California approved a $75,000 block grant for the study of chronic learning problems among kindergarten children. Another grant allowed by LEAA was a State of New York request for $216,000 to finance a youth employment service project. A General Accounting Office review of the block grants in California and New York concluded that almost 30 percent of the federal action funds awarded by those states "had been applied to projects which are only tangentially related to the direct needs of the criminal justice system." [98]

A substantial portion of the LEAA block grants has been spent on hardware. A report of the U.S. House Committee on Government Operations noted that

> [t]ens of millions of block grant dollars have been spent on helicopters, airplanes, automobiles, firearms, ammunition, computer information systems, communications control centers, police radio equipment, electronic surveillance equipment, and a range of other hardware items.[99]

While such expenditures improve the technology of state and local professional police systems, congressional oversight hearings have noted instances in which police system technology has been approved and purchased without prior evaluation of its need. The same hearings revealed that the efficiency of purchasing could not be evaluated in situations where hardware was bought without competitive bidding. Thus, the congressional statutory requirement of comprehensive planning seems to have been frequently ignored by state and local police agencies, the SPAs, and the LEAA in the initial implementation of the LEAA block grant program.

• THE CRIME CONTROL ACT OF 1973

In 1973, Congress passed the Crime Control Act. This act assumes "crime is essentially a local problem that must be dealt with by state and local governments to be controlled effectively." [100] Whereas the 1968 law required local jurisdictions to submit applications for federal funds to SPAs, local governments or combinations of local governments with populations of 250,000 or more must now submit comprehensive local plans to the states when requesting funding. This provision represents an attempt by Congress to eliminate uncoordinated hardware spending and to require both planning and comprehensiveness in the activities of state and local police departments. Federal grants may range as high as 90 percent of the planning expenses incurred by state and local law enforcement units in developing comprehensive plans, and they may range as high as 100 percent for regional planning units concerned with law enforcement and criminal justice. Thus, by requiring local units with populations of 250,000 or more to develop comprehensive plans, the 1973 legislation recognized the increased importance of planning.

The provision for federal law enforcement action grants was continued under the 1973 act. In most cases, federal action grants to state and local governmental units constituted 90 percent funding of programs by the federal government. Federal money provides 90 percent of the funds in a number of areas, including implementation of programs to strengthen public protection, recruitment and training of personnel, public education relative to crime prevention and police-community relations, the development of crime prevention councils, the training of law enforcement and other criminal justice officers, and the establishment of a Criminal Justice Coordinating Council for a local government unit or combination of local government units with a population of at least 250,000. (Such coordinating councils are intended to improve planning and coordination of law enforcement and criminal justice activities.) Fifty percent federal funding is allowed for construction of physical facilities such as "local correctional facilities, centers for narcotic addicts, and temporary courtroom facilities in areas of high crime incidence." Under the legislation, each state must also develop a comprehensive juvenile justice program. Within these broad areas, the federal funds can be used by state and local jurisdictions to provide a wide variety of services. Congress's goals of assuring comprehensiveness in state plans in order to improve the overall system of state and local law enforcement and of avoiding unplanned spending of federal money seem to have been only partially accomplished by the 1973 legislation. A 1979 study found that state and local recipients of such block grants retained "substantial discretion in identifying problems, designing programs to deal with them and allocating resources" and that SPAs have played a "weak planning role." [101]

LEAA activities under the 1973 act have been aimed at improving the quality of local police and correctional personnel and strengthening local law enforcement agencies.[102] Among the pursuits supported by LEAA have been studies describing current investigative organization and practices, as well as those assessing the investigative effectiveness of different organizational forms, staffing arrangements, and investigative procedures.[103] A 1976 Twentieth Century Fund report summarized a number of worthwhile LEAA projects that have assisted local jurisdictions, including

> ... practical prescriptions on how to discourage burglars ... criminal victimization studies, which try to discover the real amount of unreported crime through random surveys of citizens and businesses; and [a city study] which documents the way in which—despite the 1972 Supreme Court decision guaranteeing indigents the right to counsel—the poor have been left out in the legal cold. . . .[104]

The Advisory Commission on Intergovernmental Relations noted that by 1975 LEAA was providing about 40 percent of its funding for police activities and that high crime areas (predominantly urban areas) were getting a higher share of federal funds than they had previously received under the program or than they would have been entitled to on a strict population basis.

With respect to training activities, the 1973 act also authorizes the Federal Bureau of Investigation to conduct or to assist in conducting training programs for state and local law enforcement officials, either at the Bureau's national academy or at local or regional training centers when such training assistance is requested by state or local government units. This provision shows the increased reliance on a national unit for fostering the development of training standards. However, it continues to emphasize local law enforcement.

Despite greater federal aid for the entire criminal justice system (not just police functions), the focus of this system remains the locality. In 1976, over 61 percent of criminal justice system expenditures were at the local level, while 26.4 percent were at the level of state government and 12.5 percent were at the level of federal government.[105] Of 1,080,000 full-time equivalent employed positions in the American criminal justice system, 708,000 were local, 272,000 were state, and the remaining 99,000 were federal.[106]

The Supreme Court and Law Enforcement

Several major Supreme Court decisions as well as numerous lower court decisions handed down in the past fifteen or twenty years have set procedural standards for state and local police. In 1961, the Supreme Court held in *Mapp* v. *Ohio* (367 U.S. 643) that materials gained from an illegal search and seizure could not be admitted as evidence in either state or federal courts. Two years later, in 1963, the Supreme Court, in its decision in *Gideon* v. *Wainwright* (372 U.S. 335), held that every defendant in a felony case in a state court was entitled to counsel even if he or she could not afford the fees. The decision in *Escobedo* v. *Illinois* (372 U.S. 473) handed down in 1964 provided further that in state courts, "when the process shifts from investigatory to accusatory . . . our adversary system begins to operate. Under the circumstances here, the accused must be permitted to consult with his lawyer." The logical extension of this doctrine was presented in 1966 in the decision in *Miranda* v. *Arizona* (384 U.S. 436). The Supreme Court held that the police in the separate states must, upon taking a person into custody, warn a person of the right to remain silent and to have a lawyer at the state's expense.[107] In the 1971 case of *Harris* v. *New York* (401 U.S. 222), the Supreme Court restricted the scope of the *Miranda* decision by ruling that statements obtained from a suspect in violation of *Miranda* safeguards could be used to impeach the credibility of the suspect if such a person chose to testify at his or her own trial. In January 1977, the Supreme Court again narrowed the scope of the *Miranda* decision by ruling in *Oregon* v. *Carl Mathiason* (429 U.S. 492) that *Miranda* warnings are not required when a suspect voluntarily agrees to go to a police station and admit to a crime while under closed-door questioning. In reviewing a Detroit, Michigan incident, the Supreme Court in June 1979, held in *Michigan* v. *Gary DeFillippo* (47 L.W. 4805) that the Fourth Amendment's Due Process Clause did not require suppression of evidence seized incident to a presumptively valid ordinance that was, however, later held unconstitutional. During the same session, the Court held in *Zackary C. Brown* v. *Texas* (47 L.W. 4810) that a pedestrian who had refused to identify himself to El Paso, Texas police officers, who had no reasonable suspicion to presume that the plaintiff had engaged or was engaging in criminal activity, could not, consistent with the Fourth Amendment, be arrested for refusal to identify himself.

In these as well as several other related decisions, the Supreme Court has set national standards for police behavior by mandating that the police in all government jurisdictions must protect the constitutional rights of "due process of the law" of those they arrest. The mandating of constitutional rights and clarification of the scope of these rights is perhaps one of the strongest and most important interjurisdictional linkages that the federal government has generated in the area of law enforcement.

CONCLUSION

Although the American tradition of localism in law enforcement makes it difficult to generalize about the delivery of urban police services, some observations can be made. Localism in police services is preserved because many Americans fear centralized and therefore concentrated police power. However, the increasingly apparent interdependencies of police jurisdictions require some policies to promote interjurisdictional linkages. To some extent, such oversight has been provided by the states and by the federal government. In particular, federal oversight has accompanied provision of federal funds to local police forces for training, equipment, and planning. In addition, the Supreme Court has mandated federal oversight of police activities.

REFERENCES

1. Advisory Commission on Intergovernmental Relations, *State-Local Relations in the Criminal Justice System* (Washington, D.C.: U.S. Government Printing Office, 1970), p. 5.
2. James F. Richardson, *Urban Police in the United States* (Port Washington, N.Y.: National University Publications, 1974), p. 5.
3. Watchmen were compensated on a per diem basis. Constables worked on a commission; the more arrests, the higher the constable's commission.
4. Richardson, op. cit., p. 19.

5. Ibid., p. 20.
6. William J. Bopp and Donald O. Schultz, *A Short History of American Law Enforcement* (Springfield, Ill.: Charles C. Thomas, 1972), pp. 34–35.
7. Richardson, op. cit., p. 24.
8. Ibid. p. 27.
9. Ibid., p. 28.
10. Ibid.
11. Ibid., p. 31.
12. Charles L. Brace, *The Dangerous Classes of New York* (New York: Wynkoop and Hallenbeck, 1872), p. 26.
13. Bruce Smith, Sr., *Police Systems in the United States,* 2nd rev. ed. (New York: Harper & Bros., 1960), pp. 186–87.
14. Raymond Fosdick, *American Police Systems* (New York: Century Book Co., 1920), pp. 108–9.
15. National Commission on Law Observance and Enforcement, *Report on the Police* (Washington, D.C.: Government Printing Office, 1931), pp. 5–7.
16. Ibid.
17. President's Commission on Law Enforcement and the Administration of Justice, *Task Force Report: The Police* (Washington, D.C.: Government Printing Office, 1967), p. 7.
18. Ibid., p. 10.
19. National Advisory Commission on Criminal Justice Standards and Goals, *Police* (Washington, D.C., 1973), p. 378.
20. U.S. Department of Justice, Law Enforcement Assistance Administration, National Criminal Justice Information and Statistics Service, *Sourcebook of Criminal Justice Statistics, 1977* (Washington, D.C., 1978), p. 36.
21. U.S. Bureau of the Census, *The Statistical Abstract of the United States, 1977,* 99th Edition (Washington, D.C., 1978), Table 311.
22. U.S. Department of Justice, Federal Bureau of Investigation, *Crime in the United States, 1977* (Washington, D.C., 1978), p. 233.
23. J. Edgar Hoover, *Should You Go Into Law Enforcement?* (New York: New York Life Insurance Co., 1961), p. 7.
24. Arthur Niederhoffer, *Behind the Shield* (Garden City, N.Y.: Anchor Books, 1967), pp. 11–12.
25. Alan Edward Bent, *The Politics of Law Enforcement* (Lexington, Mass.: Lexington Books, 1974), pp. 63–71.
26. Herbert Jacob, *Urban Justice* (Englewood Cliffs, N.J.: Prentice-Hall, 1973), p. 25.
27. The accompanying discussion is based upon Bent, op. cit., pp. 63–65.
28. O. W. Wilson and Roy Clinton McLaren, *Police Administration* (New York: McGraw-Hill, 1972), p. 28.
29. Bent, op. cit., 64–65.
30. Jacob, op. cit., p. 26.
31. O. W. Wilson, *Police Administration,* 2nd ed. (New York: McGraw-Hill, 1963, pp. 29–30. See also Wilson and McLaren, op. cit., pp. 56–59.
32. Wilson, ibid., pp. 30–31.
33. See pp. 166–67 for a discussion of internal police review mechanisms and the role of police employee associations.
34. John C. Bollens and Henry J. Schmandt, *The Metropolis* (New York: Harper & Row, 1975), p. 160.

35. U.S. Bureau of the Census, Census of Governments, *Local Government in Metropolitan Areas, 1972,* Vol. 5 (Washington, D.C., 1974), p. 169.
36. U.S. Department of Justice, Law Enforcement Assistance Administration and U.S. Bureau of the Census, *Expenditure and Employment Data for the Criminal Justice System: 1976* (Washington, D.C.: U.S. Government Printing Office, 1978), pp. 15–16.
37. Ibid., p. 15.
38. Ibid., p. 50.
39. The President's Commission on Law Enforcement and the Administration of Justice, *Task Force Report: The Police,* op. cit., p. 6.
40. Advisory Commission on Intergovernmental Relations, op. cit., p. 70.
41. U.S. Department of Justice, Law Enforcement Assistance Administration and U.S. Bureau of the Census, *Expenditure and Employment Data for the Criminal Justice System: 1976,* op. cit., p. 50.
42. Ibid., p. 71.
43. Bruce Smith, op. cit., p. 112.
44. *Statistical Abstract, 1977,* op. cit., Table 311.
45. Ibid., Table 482.
46. U.S. Department of the Treasury, *Sixth Annual Report of the Office of Revenue Sharing* (Washington, D.C., March 1979), p. 9.
47. The data on police protection ratios appeared in U.S. Department of Justice, Federal Bureau of Investigation, *Crime in the United States, 1977,* op. cit., p. 224.
48. Ibid., pp. 223–25.
49. Jerome Skolnick, *Justice Without Trial* (New York: John Wiley, 1966), p. 42.
50. The most inclusive concept of authoritarianism contains nine clusters of variables: (a) conventionalism, (b) authoritarian submission, (c) authoritarian aggression, (d) anti-intraception, (e) superstition and stereotypy, (f) power and toughness, (g) destructiveness and cynicism, (h) projectivity, (i) sex. T. W. Adorno, Else Frenkel-Brunswick, Daniel J. Levinson, and R. Nevitt Sanford, *The Authoritarian Personality* (New York: Harper & Row, 1950), p. 228. Cited by Niederhoffer, op. cit., p. 113.
51. James Q. Wilson, *Varieties of Police Behavior* (New York: Atheneum, 1970), pp. 16–17.
52. Niederhoffer, op. cit., p. 41.
53. Harlan Hahn, "A Profile of Urban Police," *Law and Contemporary Problems,* 36 (Autumn 1971), 450.
54. David H. Bayley and Harold Mendelsohn, *Minorities and the Police* (New York: Free Press, 1968), p. 3.
55. Ibid., p. 3.
56. Robert M. Fogelson, *Big-City Police* (Cambridge, Mass.: Harvard University Press, 1977), pp. 288–89.
57. Mary Jeanette C. Hageman, "Who Joins the Force for What Reasons: An Argument for 'The New Breed'," *Journal of Police Science and Administration,* 7 (June 1979), 207. Hageman also found that expressed attitudes by such policemen did not indicate a high degree of authoritarianism (208).
58. Neiderhoffer, op. cit., and Albert J. Reiss, Jr., *Career Orientation, Job Satisfaction, and Assessment of Law Enforcement Problems by Police Officers,* Field Survey III, Vol. 2 (Washington, D.C.: President's Commission on Law Enforcement and Administration of Justice, 1967).

59. U.S. Department of Justice, Law Enforcement Assistance Administration, Institute of Law Enforcement and Criminal Justice, *The National Manpower Survey of the Criminal Justice System,* Vol. 2, *Law Enforcement* (Washington, D.C., 1978), p. 18.
60. Ibid.
61. Ibid., p. 19.
62. Ibid., p. 40.
63. *Gallup Opinion Index* (January 1978), p. 8.
64. Niederhoffer, op. cit., p. 138.
65. Ibid., p. 159.
66. Egon Bittner, "Florence Nightingale in Pursuit of Willie Sutton: A Theory of the Police," in *The Potential for Reform of Criminal Justice,* ed. by Herbert Jacob (Beverly Hills, Calif.: Sage Publications, 1974), p. 30, Vol. III of Sage Criminal Justice System Annuals.
67. William Ker Muir, Jr., *Police: Streetcorner Politicians* (Chicago: University of Chicago Press, 1977), pp. 56–57. Also see Hageman, op. cit., 208.
68. Advisory Commission on Intergovernmental Relations, op. cit., p. 75.
69. Ibid.
70. Jacob, op. cit., pp. 27–28.
71. J. Q. Wilson, op. cit., pp. 85–89.
72. Jerome H. Skolnick, *Justice Without Trial* (New York: John Wiley and Sons, 1975), pp. 90–91.
73. Bayley and Mendelsohn, op. cit., p. 109.
74. Ibid., p. 114.
75. Ibid., p. 194.
76. U.S. Department of Justice, Law Enforcement Assistance Administration, National Criminal Justice Information and Statistics Service, *Crime in Eight American Cities—National Crime Panel Surveys of Atlanta, Baltimore, Cleveland, Dallas, Denver, Newark, Portland, and St. Louis* (Washington, D.C., July 1974), p. 4.
77. U.S. Department of Justice, Law Enforcement Assistance Administration, National Criminal Justice Information and Statistics Service, *Crime in the Nation's Five Largest Cities—National Crime Panel Surveys of Chicago, Detroit, Los Angeles, New York, and Philadelphia* (Washington, D.C., April 1974), p. 11.
78. National Advisory Commission on Criminal Justice Standards and Goals, *A National Strategy to Reduce Crime* (Washington, D.C., 1973), pp. 109–111.
79. Nicholas Alex, *Black in Blue* (New York: Appleton-Century-Crofts, 1969), Chap. 7.
80. Stephen C. Halpern, "Police Employee Organizations and Accountability Procedures in Three Cities: Some Reflections on Policy-Making," *Law and Society,* 8 (Summer 1974), 562–65.
81. Ibid., 569; Bopp and Schultz, op. cit., pp. 146–47.
82. See Fogelson, op. cit., pp. 298–99; Skolnick, 1975 ed., op. cit., p. 250.
83. Bopp and Schultz, ibid., p. 147.
84. Ibid., p. 149.
85. John F. Heaphy, "Recent Developments in Policing," *The Municipal Yearbook, 1979* (Washington, D.C.: International City Management Association, 1979), p. 256.
86. Jacob, op. cit., p. 25. In 1969, Jacob found a correlation of 0.98 between

the number of policemen and city size. Also, cities with populations of 250,000 or more people have consistently higher crime rates than do smaller jurisdictions. See Advisory Commission on Intergovernmental Relations, op. cit., p. 2.

87. ACIR, op. cit., p. 3.
88. *Crime in the United States*, op. cit., p. 6.
89. Ibid., p. 4.
90. Morton Grodzins, *The American System* (New York: Rand McNally, 1966), p. 93. Quoted ibid., p. 5.
91. The general apportionment of criminal justice responsibilities is: municipalities, police; counties, lower courts and prosecution; states, higher courts and corrections. Ibid., p. 6.
92. Peter B. Bloch and David Specht, *Neighborhood Team Policing*, U.S. Department of Justice, Law Enforcement Assistance Administration, National Institute of Law Enforcement and Criminal Justice (Washington, D.C., 1973).
93. Heaphy, op. cit., p. 257.
94. Elmer D. Groper, *American Police Administration* (New York: Macmillan, 1921), pp. 67–68.
95. The President's Commission on Law Enforcement and the Administration of Justice, *Task Force Report: The Police*, op. cit., pp. 6–7.
96. Public Law 90-351, June 19, 1968.
97. LEAA may waive the 40 percent pass-through requirement in the event that it is deemed inappropriate in view of the respective law enforcement planning responsibilities exercised by the state and its units of general local government and that adherence to the requirement would not contribute to the efficient development of the state plan.
98. U.S. Congress, House, Committee on Government Operations, *Block Grant Programs of the Law Enforcement Assistance Administration, Twelfth Report*, 92nd Cong., 2nd Sess., House Report No. 92–1072, May 1972, p. 7.
99. Ibid., p. 17.
100. U.S. Congress, Conference Report, 93rd Cong., 1st Sess., House Report No. 93–401, July 1973, p. 1. The administrative structure of LEAA was altered by this law too.
101. Fred A. Meyer, Jr., "The Impact of Federalism on Police Professionalism: The Role of State Planning Agencies," paper presented to the American Political Science Association Convention (Washington, D.C., September 1, 1979), pp. 7–8. (Mimeographed.)
102. Herman Goldstein, *Policing in a Free Society* (Cambridge, Mass.: Ballinger Publishing Co., 1977), p. 322.
103. Peter W. Greenwood and Joan Petersilia, *The Criminal Investigative Process: Summary and Policy Implications, Vol. 1* (Santa Monica, Calif.: The Rand Corporation, 1975).
104. Twentieth Century Fund, *Law Enforcement: The Federal Role, Report of the Task Force on the Law Enforcement Assistance Administration* (New York: McGraw-Hill, 1976), pp. 36–37.
105. *Statistical Abstract*, 1977, op. cit., Table 309.
106. Ibid.
107. However, in 1974 in its decision in *United States v. Calandra* (414 U.S. 338), the Court held that a witness may not refuse to answer grand jury questions on the grounds that they are based on evidence obtained in an illegal search and seizure.

PART THREE

Housing and health policies are interesting examples of basically private sector activities organized on a local basis that are now increasingly coming under public scrutiny and public controls. Housing has historically been developed by private entrepreneurs with public involvement generally limited to enforcement of a local code to maintain minimum standards. Health practitioners traditionally have practiced their trade in the private sector, too, and public intervention in the delivery of their services has remained very limited.

In both health and housing, however, there have been some significant public incursions into essentially private sector operations. The next two chapters present the background of private activity within the urban arena and trace the gradual development of local public sector activities and the more recent evolution of essentially post–New Deal national-urban policy linkages. In both these chapters, it is suggested that only through greater federal funding and administrative oversight and control can housing and health care services be distributed more equitably and provided more adequately to urban Americans.

7

Housing Policy:
A Case of a Weak Link

INTRODUCTION

In Chapters 4, 5, and 6, we discussed the national-urban policy linkages in education, public welfare, and police services; all are essentially public sector activities. In this chapter, we will be looking at housing in urban America. Unlike education, welfare, and police services, the housing market is operated and controlled largely by private sector interests. Local government has been involved in housing through building and sanitation codes and zoning, and more recently the federal government has been involved through mortgage guarantees and public and subsidized housing, but the intergovernmental linkages to improve urban housing conditions have been weak. Consequently, though we will look at national urban housing policies, it will be clear that with few exceptions, direct national-urban policy linkages for housing have not really evolved.

The quality and scope of our housing resources have improved since 1950. Between 1950 and 1976, the percentage of housing units lacking some indoor plumbing declined from 34 percent of all housing units to about 2.6 percent; overcrowded households with over 1.5 persons per room declined from 6.2 percent of the housing stock to under 1 percent.[1] In spite of this improvement, in 1976, 5.8 million residences were considered in need of rehabilitation.[2]

If one looks at just a few urban states, the problem of inadequate housing, which particularly affects the urban poor, becomes readily apparent. For example, according to Connecticut's Department of Community Affairs, in 1975 Connecticut had 25,000 substandard housing units —dilapidated, badly deteriorated, or lacking in basic plumbing. Connecticut had 141,000 low income families either living in overcrowded dwellings or spending more than one-quarter of their income for rent, while fewer than 5,000 units geared primarily to less than middle income groups were produced annually in Connecticut under state and federal programs. In New York State, the State Division of Housing and Community Renewal estimated that 64,000 new or largely rehabilitated units were needed in 1975 to replace substandard housing, primarily in its major cities. In 1974, in New York State, new starts under government-aided programs totaled 12,000, many of which were for upper middle income families. In New Jersey, the State Department of Community Affairs estimated that Newark had 40,000 substandard units that needed replacement or upgrading in 1975; in the entire state, 340,000 units needed replacement or upgrading. Only 6,000 low income and moderate income units were started in New Jersey under governmental programs in 1974 and 1,000 units were rehabilitated in 1974.[3]

A related problem is the affordability of housing.[4] In 1976, 78 percent of very poor households (with yearly incomes below $3,000) paid over 35 percent of their income for rental payments.[5] Over 28 percent of family units earning from $7,000 to $9,999 lacked affordable housing. In 1979, a U. S. General Accounting Office study expressed concern about the lack of available adequate rental housing for 15 million renters with annual incomes of $10,000 and the 11.9 million renters who spend 25 percent or more of their income on rent.

These figures clearly show that there are insufficient adequate and affordable housing resources in the United States, especially for the urban poor. Many aspects of housing in urban America could be examined. For example, we could examine how the middle class is being priced out of the new home market. However, since our purpose in this book is to examine the effects of connections or lack of connections between urban units and the national government on the development and implementation of urban policy, we will limit our discussion in this chapter to the effects of federal-urban linkages on the development of housing policy in urban areas. Throughout this discussion, however, it is important to remember that housing development has been primarily private in the United States and that the public sector role traditionally has been limited.

A review of the history of public sector housing programs from the nineteenth century to the present shows that policy and programming were initially local. Although the federal role in housing has increased in the past several years, a major role has been retained by local housing authorities and by private developers. But federal policy has not been aimed only at alleviating poor housing conditions for the poverty stricken. Policy has been two-pronged and at least partially contradictory. On the one hand, federal programs have been developed to renew our cities and rehabilitate the decaying urban centers. On the other hand, Federal Housing Administration and Veterans Administration mortgage guarantees have facilitated the exodus from the older cities of the middle class and more recently the working class, thus contributing to the decay of many of these older urban centers.

In the following pages, we will examine housing policy from the nineteenth-century tenement laws to the present. In so doing, we will analyze the way the housing problem has changed with the growth of suburbia and the growth of central city poverty. We will see that housing policies and programs, though they have become more national in both their initiation and implementation in the post–New Deal era, remain largely local programs involving local housing authorities and private developers with only modest congressional stipulations and federal executive oversight. Consequently, the national housing program has had relatively little overall program direction and program integration beyond these federal stipulations, nor has an effective national-urban policy linkage been developed.

Historical Perspective

The provision of housing has historically been a private sector activity in the United States. Public sector involvement traditionally has been regulatory in nature—though since the New Deal, public housing and loan guarantees have been available. The regulatory process when it has evolved has most often been local in scope. It has been the local jurisdictions that have established the primary constraints on the private housing market. One notable exception to this statement must be made. Because builders often require bank loans for their development enterprises, they are affected by national money and banking policy. Thus, when money is "cheap," that is, when interest rates are low, money is more available for loans for building than when money becomes "expensive" to borrow. The Federal Reserve Board has a major input into interest rate decisions since it regulates the flow of money and is responsible for establishing the national rediscount rate from which commercial banks set their own private interest rate for lending.

Early History

In his 1904 classic, *How the Other Half Lives,* Jacob A. Riis dramatically noted that the tenements of New York were "the hot-beds of epidemics that carry death to rich and poor alike . . . , that turned out in the last eight years a round half million beggars to prey upon our charities." [6] The view presented by Riis was shared by many other observers of the urban scene. In fact, a social concern about the provision of housing became widespread among nineteenth- and early twentieth-century urban social reformers. The housing ordinances that emerged in American cities in the nineteenth century were based on concerns with the social costs of slum housing and the need for control of such housing by the development of building codes. In addition to the moral cost of the slums, concern with cholera and fear of fire eventually led to some nineteenth-century housing reforms. Cholera epidemics had broken out in 1832 and 1849, and in New York City "the Great Fire" of December 16, 1835, destroyed 530 buildings at a loss of $15,000,000; the fire of September 6, 1839, destroyed forty-six buildings at a loss of $1,000,000. [7]

In response to the danger of cholera, a Boston Committee on the Expediency of Providing Better Tenements to the Poor was set up in June 1846. In the report of this committee, a Boston physician practicing in slum areas commented: "[T]he fatal effects of the sick being confined in apartments which did not admit of ventilation have been, with me, matters of frequent observation." [8] Such slum conditions, which in Boston particularly affected the Irish working class, led to an epidemic of cholera in . . . 1869. Structures lacked proper drainage and ventilation. In the buildings of the Fort Hill area of Boston, air and light were lacking, ventilation shafts were not larger than two square feet, and overcrowding often existed. [9] Although by 1868 a tenement law existed for the City of Boston, its requirements that "[e]very house shall have a fire escape"; water-closets need approval of the Board of Health; basements may not be occupied without a Board of Health permit; and all houses shall "have suitable conveniences for garbage"; were not seriously enforced. [10]

In 1865, the Council of Hygiene and Public Health of the Citizens Association of New York issued a report correlating the incidence of poor housing with disease. The report stated in part:

Typhus fever and consumption are found in the overcrowded tenant-houses, and in dark and noisome quarters excluded from sunlight and fresh air. Cholera infantum, dysentery, diarrhoeal diseases, and various typhoid maladies are found in badly drained and neglected streets and alleys, and in cellars, or in damp and filthy domiciles surrounded by nuisances and poisonous effluvia. In such localities, it has also been observed that scrofulous, rheumatic, and eruptive diseases prevail, and that the average or constant sickness rate in the families and houses so situated is very high, the proportionate number of persons sick, or the total days of sickness, being three, five, or even ten times the ratio of sickness in the localities where better sanitary care prevails.

The report went on to recommend that "effective measures be immediately undertaken to procure the introduction of needed improvements in the ventilation, lighting, and cleanliness of the tenant-houses of the city." [11]

Similarly, the real threat of epidemics led to tenement house reform in Illinois, aimed at Chicago. In 1867, the Commissioner of the Chicago Board of Health observed that Chicago tenements "without the energetic and vigilant attention of the Sanitary Authority" could become "nurseries of every form of contagious disease, and of perpetual epidemics." He went on to note that the tenements remained "a great menace to the public safety and health." [12] In 1881, the Illinois State Legislature passed a tenement law requiring cities of 50,000 residents or more to have building plans submitted to the City Health Department regarding arrangements for ventilation, light, and plumbing. Under this legislation, the Chicago Department of Health developed regulations regarding ventilation of water closets, and the placing and construction of drainage fixtures in dwellings that were to be erected.[13]

By 1867, largely as a response to the effect of cholera epidemics, New York City had developed a housing code establishing minimum standards for tenements. Tenements were defined as

every house, building, or portion thereof which is rented, leased, let or hired out to be occupied, or is occupied as the home or residence of more than three families living independently of one another and doing their cooking upon the premises, or by more than two families upon a floor, so living and cooking, but having a common right in the halls, stairways, yards, water closets, or privies.[14]

The statute provided that such residential units needed ventilators, fire escapes, good privies and water closets, and proper receptacles for garbage. The law also prohibited the housing of retail establishments in tenements. Further legislation regarding housing codes in New York City was urged by Lawrence Veiller, representing the Tenement House Committee of New York's Charity Organization Society. His efforts were largely responsible for the New York Tenement House Law of 1901. This law provided, by its precise requirements, sharply limited administrative discretion in enforcing housing codes. For example, the 1901 law provided for a "total window area of a water closet [of] . . . not . . . less than three square feet." [15] It also provided for a system of building permits and a registry of all tenements. The New York Tenement House Law of 1901 was to serve as a model for other housing code legislation. Other early housing codes that incorporated Lawrence Veiller's ideas were the Michigan Housing Act of 1917, the Minnesota Housing Act of 1917 (applying only to Minneapolis), the Iowa Housing Act of 1919, and the Milwaukee (Wisconsin) Housing Code of 1919. [16] Local jurisdictions still maintain housing codes as a means of eliminating slums, but they have not been very successful in enforcing them.

Limited Dividend Housing and the Evolution of Public Housing

These early housing policy reforms did not make any provision for public housing, nor were the legal standards and sanctions against violators of the law very stringent. However, the private sector's housing reform during the latter part of the nineteenth century provided an early model for public involvement in the provision of housing. Some social reformers and foundations attempted to establish model tenements. Support of model tenements was often based on the principle of *limited dividends*. The benefactor of such housing might establish a trust that operated on the basis of a limited return on investment. The initial limited dividend housing was established in England when the Peabody Donation Fund, established in 1862 in London, operated upon a dividend limited to 3 percent. This concept was adopted in New York City in 1882, when the Improved Dwellings Association established a block of thirteen tenement houses on the corner of East Seventy-Second Street and First Avenue in New York City. The terms of the stock issue limited the dividend to 5 percent. A similar enterprise, the Tenement-House Building Company, opened a block of houses on Cherry Street in New York City in December 1887. Dividends to stockholders in these dwellings were limited to 4 percent. Similarly in Boston, the Boston Cooperative Building Company, incorporated in 1871, built tenements with dividends to stockholders limited to 6 percent. The tenement homes established by Philadelphia developer Theodore Starr also were homes for working people and provided limited dividends on profit.

Limited dividend housing allowed "excessive" profits to be used for the management and maintenance of model tenements. This provision prevented the deterioration of such developments, and it also was compatible with private enterprise. As architect Theodore T. White observed: "[Such model tenements provided] a fair return on ... investment. ... [T]o make the example accomplish any great good, it must be shown that it is to the interest of capitalists to follow it." [17]

The movement from voluntary limited-dividend housing to city-supported and then state-supported limited dividend housing was highlighted by the establishment of the New York State Board of Housing in 1926. The Board was empowered to promote construction of buildings by limited dividend corporations. The 1926 statute provided that in buildings built under the provisions of that law, rents per month per room in the County of New York could not exceed $12.50 and average rents per month per room in the Counties of the Bronx and Kings

(Brooklyn) could not exceed $11.[18] Prior to 1942, fourteen limited dividend housing projects, valued at $31 million, had been completed in the New York City area; in 1942 two small limited dividend housing projects were approved elsewhere in the State of New York.[19]

Gradually the role of the federal government in the area of housing increased as it was granted loan-making authority and the ability to tie such loans to specified interest rates. Under President Herbert Hoover, a Federal Home Loan Bank Board was developed; under President Franklin D. Roosevelt, the Home Owner's Loan Corporation and the Federal Housing Administration were organized. These agencies established federal preeminence over determination of credit terms and interest rates regarding private development based on the utilization of federal sources of credit.[20]

The New Deal and Post–New Deal Period

In the years prior to the New Deal, only the states and local jurisdictions had methods, however insufficient, to cope with the problems of inadequate housing. Federal involvement dates from the 1930s, when the United States Housing Act of 1937 and the National Housing Act of 1934 were enacted. The 1937 act established a linkage between municipal, state, and federal authority in public housing, and the 1934 act involved the federal government in private home ownership.

• THE HOUSING ACT OF 1937

The key federal legislation to meet the problem of insufficient shelter is the United States Housing Act of 1937 and the many amendments and revisions enacted since its initial passage. At the outset, the law provided for loans to assist localities in *slum clearance* and the building of *low rental housing*. Federal contributions were to be made to localities on a yearly basis to cover acquisition and development cost. The emphasis of the program was to serve the working poor. Rental payments were to be set at a level that would meet current expense. The law's sponsor, Senator Robert F. Wagner of New York, observed: "[T]here are some people whom we cannot possibly reach; I mean those who have no means to pay the rent." [21]

The United States Housing Act of 1937 established the basic principle that local communities would decide for themselves whether or not to develop a public housing program. The federal government would support municipal public housing programs that met federal stipulations after a state had enacted enabling legislation. Thus, the public housing program represented a linking of municipal, state, and federal authority.

• FEDERAL HOUSING ADMINISTRATION AND VETERANS
ADMINISTRATION MORTGAGES

Federal programs to increase private sector single-home purchases have directly affected the urban poor. Because they enable the middle class and the working class to leave the central cities, they have encouraged the suburbanization that has, in turn, contributed to the decay of cities.

One such program is administered through the Federal Housing Administration (FHA). Established under the National Housing Act of 1934, the FHA insures lenders against loss should borrowers default on home mortgage payments. Mortgages can cover up to 97 percent of appraised value on new and existing houses; for veterans, mortgages can cover 100 percent of appraised value. Under this program, the largest number of FHA loans have been issued on moderately priced houses. In 1977, the median sales price of FHA-insured housing was $37,700. Ninety-two percent of home mortgages insured under FHA programs in 1977 were located within metropolitan areas.[22]

Armed services veterans and members of the armed forces are entitled to loans protected by Veterans Administration (VA) guarantees. The major share of such VA benefits accrues to middle income households—in fiscal 1976, to those households with net incomes averaging $22,240.[23] The VA, in contrast to the FHA (which charges one-half of 1 percent of the mortgage amount for insurance), charges little or nothing for its loan guarantees.[24] In fiscal 1977, VA guaranteed loans averaged $33,472 and these loans financed homes with an average purchase price of $34,485. With respect to newly constructed homes, the average guaranteed loan was $38,730 and the average price of such homes was $40,597. The VA also provides a direct loan program to veterans for home purchasing. During fiscal 1977, the VA loan guarantee and direct loan programs assisted more than 382,479 veterans in becoming home owners.[25] From the prices of VA- and FHA-supported home purchases and their emphasis on home ownership and family ownership, one can conclude that these programs have provided the impetus for suburbanization. By enabling middle class and working class families to purchase homes, often in the suburbs, these programs have aided the flight of the middle class and working class from the central cities to the suburbs. In a very real way, then, they have provided a federal-urban linkage that has served as a national policy to suburbanize America.

The Distribution of Housing Resources

In the late 1960s, an effort was made to look at the relationship of urban poverty to housing. In viewing Standard Metropolitan Statistical Areas of over 250,000 population—that is, the major SMSAs—several observations were made in a 1968 report for the National Commission on Urban Problems (the Manvel Report). The Commission found that in 1960, these SMSAs contained 31.2 million housing units, or 53.5 percent of the national housing supply. Three million of these units were substandard; they were either generally deteriorated or dilapidated in that they lacked hot water, running water, or a private toilet or bath. Over 2.9 million of these occupied units were overcrowded—that is, such units averaged more than one resident per room.

The poverty areas of the major SMSAs included 3,653,000 families in central city poverty areas (29.7 percent of all central city families) and 1,142,000 families in outlying portions of major SMSAs (9.3 percent of all families residing there). *Substandard units* comprised 25.1 percent of the total housing units in poverty areas as opposed to 5.2 percent elsewhere in the SMSAs. Of occupied units in poverty areas of major SMSAs, 16.3 percent were overcrowded compared to a rate of 7.4 percent overcrowding elsewhere in major SMSAs. In 1960, the defined poverty areas in major SMSAs had

> 58 percent of all substandard units; 39 percent of all the overcrowded units; 31 percent of all housing units in structures over 20 years old; 35 percent of the units in multi-unit structures; and 35 percent of all renter-occupied units; but only 13 percent of all the owner-occupied units. . . . [These] poverty areas accounted for 74 percent of all housing units in the major SMSAs that were occupied by nonwhites.[26]

The 1970 census did not carry descriptions relating to dilapidated or deteriorated housing. However, the 1970 census indicated that 3,511,000 units (5.5 percent of all units) lacked plumbing facilities.

The 1970 census indicated that 4,512,000 renter households paid 35 percent or more of their income for housing, and 2,521,000 renter households paid between 25 and 34 percent of family income on housing,[27] while it is estimated that a family or individual should spend approximately 25 percent of gross income on decent housing. These problems led to various housing programs in the late 1960s and the early 1970s, and fragmentary data issued since the appearance of the Manvel Report in 1968 show that the problems of adequate and affordable housing, especially for the urban poor, still exist. Throughout the 1960s, the poor became more heavily concentrated in central cities as FHA and VA mortgage programs helped middle class and working class families to buy homes in the suburbs.

By the late 1970s, a movement back to the cities by the upper middle class and young professionals had served to uproot some of the inner city poor.[28] An account of such displacement of the poor and lower income groups in Seattle, Washington, described the subsequent *gentrification* of a Seattle neighborhood in the following terms:

> Capital Hill, once a sedate economically and racially mixed neighborhood near downtown, is rapidly being taken over by the single, childless and the well-off. Along Broadway, the district's main street, neighborhood stores are being pushed out by shops selling Cuisanart food processors or Marimeko fabrics and restaurants decorated with hanging ferns. . . . With little cheap housing to absorb the displaced, the rental vacancy is under 1 percent; the influx of young professionals meant that property values and rents rose 14 percent [during 1978].[29]

Such movement back into the cities also has been encouraged by urban homesteading programs. These programs take abandoned homes and provide special terms of mortgage and rehabilitation financing to city residents willing to rehabilitate the homes. Such financing may be provided by local banks or by municipal or state housing authorities. In many cities, such as Wilmington, Delaware; Philadelphia, Pennsylvania; and Baltimore, Maryland, no preference is given to those of lower socioeconomic status. The national New Communities Act of 1974 provides that homes federally owned due to mortgage foreclosure may be awarded to cities for purposes of homesteading—in those instances where rehabilitation is economically feasible.[30] In 1976, the U.S. Department of Housing and Urban Development (HUD) conducted an Urban Homesteading Demonstration that involved twenty-two participating cities. HUD supplied the equivalent of $5 million in structurally sound homes and $5 million in rehabilitation loans. This was balanced by city commitments of $50 million for neighborhood improvement, homesteader support, and rehabilitation financing, as well as over $12 million in private financing for the rehabilitation of housing. Participating cities included Atlanta, Georgia; Baltimore, Maryland; Jersey City, New Jersey; Kansas City, Missouri; Boston, Massachusetts; Chicago, Illinois; Cincinnati, Ohio; Dallas, Texas; Decatur, Georgia; Gary, Indiana; Indianapolis, Indiana; Islip, Suffolk County, New York; Milwaukee, Wisconsin; Minneapolis, Minnesota; New York City, New York; Oakland, California; Philadelphia, Pennsylvania; Rockford, Illinois; South Bend, Indiana; Tacoma, Washington; and Wilmington, Delaware.[31]

Attempts to improve substantially the housing supply for lower income groups have not been the concern of private builders, the traditional providers of shelter for Americans. The response of government to the housing requirements of those people who cannot afford to buy and/or rehabilitate or rent decent private sector facilities also has been insufficient.

National-Urban Policy Linkages and the Siting of Housing for the Poor

Since most housing in this country is private and ownership (or rental) is handled through the private market, public controls are limited and public provision of housing is limited, too. The housing problem in America is not unrelated to the convergence of poverty and race; historically, and especially in contemporary urban experience, the poor have also been disproportionately nonwhite. Also, de jure residential discrimination historically abounded in American cities. For example, formal residential segregation was maintained in San Francisco by a municipal statute enacted in 1890 that required Chinese residents to live in one section of that city. In the early twentieth century, many Southern cities adopted similar statutes for black residents. Municipal statutes that maintained residential segregation, however, were declared unconstitutional by the Supreme Court in 1917. Subsequently, residential segregation was maintained by local practice as well as by restrictive covenants in property deeds prohibiting sales of property to "undesirables." Covenants might be aimed at blacks, Mexicans, Orientals, Southern Europeans, Armenians, Syrians, Jews, and Hindus. In 1948, in its decision in *Shelley* v. *Kraemer* (334 U.S. 1), the U.S. Supreme Court held that the courts could not enforce such discriminatory covenants.

The Court's decisions have not deterred jurisdictions from maintaining patterns of residential segregation; the Supreme Court has not been effective in providing national urban policy leadership for housing policy. Although restrictive covenants are unconstitutional, other methods have developed to screen out unwanted groups. Site selection and zoning are two mechanisms used to screen out poor and often black residents from various areas and to maintain racial and class segregation. Conflicts regarding site selection in public housing were particularly acute in the 1950s and 1960s. Meyerson and Banfield documented this conflict in Chicago in the 1950s.[32] Similar conflicts leading to segregated patterns of public housing occurred in Toledo, Ohio, and Philadelphia, Pennsylvania, in the 1960s,[33] and such conflicts continued into the 1970s. Zoning regulations requiring large lots of land per family and forbidding multistory dwellings have prevented the location of moderate cost housing in middle class neighborhoods and have screened out poor, often black, residents from many middle income areas, particularly in the suburbs. (Such regulations are a perversion of the zoning movement of the 1910s and 1920s which sought to improve the housing and environmental conditions of all urban dwellers.) In addition, real estate developers have in the past evaluated residents to screen out, in part or totally, certain racial or ethnic groups. In 1960, the Grosse Pointe Brokers Association and the Grosse Pointe Property Owners Association collaborated in the development of an assessment system regarding purchases of homes in Grosse Pointe, Michigan, a wealthy Detroit suburb. The U.S. Civil Rights Commission in 1961 described this process as follows:

> A private detective agency investigated prospective purchasers of Grosse Pointe homes. A committee of three brokers then graded the information to determine whether to admit the person to the area. Fifty points was passing. However, persons "of Polish descent had to score 55 points; southern Europeans, including those of Italian, Greek, Spanish, or Lebanese origin, had to score 65 points; and those of the Jewish faith had to score 85 points. Negroes and orientals were excluded entirely." [34]

Such policies extend beyond the fear of low income minorities and are clearly based on racial and ethnic exclusion. In 1979, the actions of real estate brokers in directing prospective buyers to particular sections on a racial basis were in fact declared unconstitutional by the U.S. Supreme Court. In the case of *Gladstone Realtors* v. *Village of Belwood*, the Court held that such steering was discriminatory in that it deprived residents of this Illinois community of the "social and professional benefits of living in an integrated community" and also that such practices adversely affected the value of homes in Belwood.[35]

Attempts have been made to use publicly supported housing, both public housing and publicly subsidized private developments, as a means of eliminating residential segregation. Such policies have received sanction from the 1976 Supreme Court decision in *Hills* v. *Gautreaux*. In this case, black tenants in Chicago public housing and black applicants for such housing claimed that federal housing funds were used to set up public housing projects in black areas that served to reinforce patterns of racial segregation. The Supreme Court held that the Department of Housing and Urban Development and the Chicago Housing Authority should provide some public housing units outside of racially concentrated black areas.[36]

During the late 1960s, HUD sought to encourage scattered sites for public housing by encouraging the building of low income housing for poor blacks in middle income, white communities. This led to the New York City Housing Authority's attempt to plan low-income housing in Forest Hills, a middle income, white, Queens neighborhood. HUD had stipulated that failure by the City of New York to place 7,500 units of low-income housing in middle class neighborhoods might result in the loss of all federal housing funds.[37] Considerable community protest was generated in the early 1970s by the announcement of plans to build public housing units in this area, and eventually the City of New York scaled down the scope of this Forest Hills public housing at an increased cost to the City of New York of $2,411,550 and the loss of millions of dollars in federal housing funds.[38]

Perhaps one of the results of this incident was to highlight the complexity of issues: class composition of neighborhoods, racial attitudes, and issues regarding provision of social services, education, and safety services all surround the provision of housing for low income groups. In any event, strong federal initiatives regarding such heavy concentrations of low income families in middle class areas have ceased, and the siting of publicly supported housing currently is determined by local political and social factors, rather than by national initiatives. This particular attempt by HUD to maintain a national-urban policy linkage was aborted.

Public Housing

Public housing is operated and owned by local housing authorities that operate within a municipality, a county, or a multicity or multicounty district. Federal assistance by the Department of Housing and Urban Development to local units has included direct loans for development, acquisition, and administration, and an annual contribution covering interest and amortization of long-term bonds issued by public housing authorities. Furthermore, local housing authorities, which are supported with federal funds, are exempt from federal income taxes. Additional subsidies by HUD are made on behalf of the aged, the disabled, the handicapped, and families displaced due to urban renewal, especially large and poor families. Also, Congress has stipulated that public housing rents should not exceed 25 percent of a tenant's gross allowable income.[39] In 1973, federal contributions to public housing totaled $1.1 billion. In 1974, the Housing and Community Development Act temporarily ended federally subsidized new construction starts of public housing. Consequently, any federally funded public housing starts begun in 1975 were initiated with money already in the program pipeline. In 1976, authorization for federal subsidization of new construction starts for federally funded public housing was renewed, and in fiscal 1976, federal spending for low-rent public housing totaled $1.44 billion.

Local authorities play a key role in determining public housing policy. Most significantly, they determine where facilities will be located and who will live in them, although the authorities must abide by some federal guidelines and restrictions. For example, the Housing and Community Development Act of 1974 stipulated that the minimum rent in public housing—regardless of jurisdiction—must now be at least 15 percent of gross allowable family income or the housing allowance allotment of a welfare assistance payment, whichever is greater.[40] As we noted earlier, a maximum rent payment of 25 percent of gross allowable income has also been set by law. Generally, local housing authorities determine admissions policies for poor families who cannot pay full maintenance charges as well as for the working class families who can afford rents that cover maintenance charges. The 1974 statute provides that "at least 20 percent of the units in new public housing must be rented to families (whose incomes) do not exceed 50 percent of the median income in the areas." Within these limits, housing authorities set criteria for determining the number of tenants in various income brackets who will be accepted in public housing. Mixed income housing is encouraged by this law.[41]

Mixed income level occupancy is often supported by groups that do not want public housing projects to turn into lower class ghettos. However, in some cases, the fear of racial (nonwhite) concentration in public housing adds social strain to the fear of the incursion of low income housing. An example of this phenomenon, cited earlier, arose in the early 1970s in the predominantly white middle class area of Forest Hills when New York City announced plans to build 840 low income units in the area. The community objected to the movement into the area of large concentrations of poor persons *with children* who would, it was felt, tax the services of the community and expose it to the social problems that oppress the slum dweller. In terms of New York City's economic and racial composition, the project poor would have been predominantly black. As Mario M. Cuomo, who negotiated a compromise with community representatives and city officials regarding the scope of the eventual Forest Hills public housing project, noted: "[T]he principal problem . . .[was] the concern of many in the community that the placing of 840 low-income units in their midst would bring as its concomitant increasing crime, vandalism, exodus and deterioration." [42] Eventually the project was scaled down to 432 low income housing units. Of these, 180 were to be set aside for the elderly poor, a less-threatening poverty group to the vast majority of people in the area. Given the terms of federal requirements, the scaling down of the project resulted in a need for a city equity contribution, whereas with the larger number of dwelling units, no city equity requirement would have been needed. [43] In this instance, although all dwelling units went to very low income families, the community perception of a social problem potential was scaled down by the smaller size of the project and by inclusion of the generally "harmless poor," the aged. In addition, by rejecting federal funds and absorbing substantial additional costs, the City of New York retained the flexibility of developing a smaller-scale project.

The Population of Low Income Public Housing

As of October, 1978, over 3.4 million people were housed in 1.1 million federally funded public housing units. Approximately 14 percent of the poor were housed in public housing facilities. [44] In 1977, 56 percent of the benefits of public housing accrued to households with incomes under $4,000 per year and 78 percent to households with incomes under $6,000 per year (see Table 1). The median yearly income of families living in public housing was $3,691.

In terms of providing shelter for low income people and permitting urban and suburban localities to play a major role in low income housing decisions, the public housing program has been very successful. Despite concern often expressed with segregated housing patterns, public housing provides adequate shelter for some low income residents. As Henry Aaron points out:

> Nearly half of all public housing is in large projects in Chicago or New York or small projects in small or medium-sized southern cities or towns. . . . Housing authorities in large cities have concentrated housing in densely populated projects because land is costly and large parcels are difficult to amass. Reasonably priced land is available in the suburbs, but suburbanites have successfully resisted the influx of large clusters of the poor who are often black. [45]

More specifically, as of December 31, 1977, although 26 percent of public housing units were situated in communities with populations of less than 25,000, most public housing units were located in more urban settings. Ten percent of public housing units were in communities with

Table 1 / LOW INCOME HOUSING: TOTAL ANNUAL FAMILY INCOME
OF ALL FAMILIES REEXAMINED FOR CONTINUED OCCUPANCY
DURING THE TWELVE MONTHS ENDING SEPTEMBER 30, 1977

(total number of families: 611,110)

Total Family Income	Percentage
Under $1,000	1
$1,000 – 1,499	2
1,500 – 1,999	5
2,000 – 2,499	16
2,500 – 2,999	12
3,000 – 3,499	11
3,500 – 3,999	9
4,000 – 4,999	13
5,000 – 5,999	9
6,000 – 6,999	6
7,000 – 7,999	4
8,000 – 8,999	3
9,000 and over	9
Median income	$3,691
Mean income	$4,692

Source: U.S. Department of Housing and Urban Development, 1977, *HUD Statistical Yearbook, 1977* (Washington, D.C.: U.S. Government Printing Office, 1978), p. 249.

populations between 25,000 and 100,000; 13 percent of such units were located in communities with populations between 100,000 and 250,000; and 28 percent were found in communities with populations of 500,000 or more.[46]

Public housing has followed a number of patterns depending on the dynamics of the community in which it is situated. In Dade County, Florida, public housing units are scattered at 100 sites throughout the city; in New York City, high-rise apartments remain a predominant form of public housing; in cities of over 500,000, such high-rise structures provide for 28 percent of public housing family occupancy.[47]

The use of public housing by big cities has increasingly provided shelter for low income populations. Robert C. Embry, Jr., when he was Commissioner of the City of Baltimore's Department of Housing and Community Development, observed:

We have a 50 percent black population. Over the last 20 years, the percentage of black families has risen from less than half to 90 percent of the tenants in our 13,000 units of public housing. The percentage of welfare tenants is now over 70 percent, whereas just 20 years ago, it was under

40 percent. . . . So, the trend is clearly that the families, now, are more broken families, more welfare families, more minority families, more aged families in public housing in Baltimore and this trend is repeated in cities throughout the United States.[48]

Indeed, in 1975, 79 percent of residents in the Boston Housing Authority's conventional public housing had no income earner in the family.[49]

In the fiscal year ending September 30, 1977, 139,667 families had moved into public housing projects. Their monthly rents averaged $61.91. In terms of the racial composition of these tenant families, black and white families each accounted for 44 percent of occupant families; Spanish-American families accounted for 10 percent; the remaining 2 percent included American Indians, Orientals, and other minorities. About one-third of these families in public housing projects were elderly.[50] Elderly families were poorer. Their average annual income was $2,971 and their average rent was $54.21 monthly. As a variety of programs (which will be discussed later in this chapter) have siphoned off self-supporting tenants, public housing throughout the nation has increasingly become the bailiwick of various types of "problem" families. Thus not only are there disproportionate numbers of the elderly poor in these housing units, but also 24 percent of occupant units housed female-headed households (often receiving public assistance) and 59 percent of the public housing population was under twenty-one years of age.[51]

Pruitt-Igoe: A Case Study of Deterioration in Public Housing

A classic case of a public housing project that had deteriorated was St. Louis's Pruitt-Igoe public housing project. These apartments were occupied in 1954 and had been demolished by 1974. The development contained 2,762 apartments in 33 eleven-story buildings near downtown St. Louis. In 1966, the median annual income of households in Pruitt-Igoe was $2,454. Thirty percent of the households with children included husband, wife, and children; 57 percent of the households included a female head of household and children. The median education of household heads was nine years; over half of the heads of household held unskilled jobs. The resident population was black and predominantly from southern and border state areas.[52] Deterioration occurred, in part, because of the attitudes of an oppressed, low income group. As one resident noted:

> People move in here with a chip on their shoulder against the white man and against anybody who has any kind of authority, so they try to take it out on everybody and everything. That's the reason why the project is all torn up and in the bad shape it's in.[53]

Studies of projects with predominantly very low income population groups have led to a belief that such homogeneous low income groupings are undesirable. Not only are such projects associated with deterioration of public housing structures, they also raise fears among middle income dwellers regarding the siting of public housing in middle income areas.

Some Alternatives to Public Housing: Housing Assistance and Rental Assistance

In 1965, Congress enacted a federal rent supplement program. The program provided that families with incomes below public housing income limits would be eligible for rent subsidies if they paid 25 percent of their income for rent and, at a minimum, 30 percent of fair market rents. After HUD agreed to make rent supplement payments, the housing developer would begin construction. The rent supplement payments would begin after the housing units were complete and occupied. One aim of the program was dispersing low income residents outside ghetto areas. This encouragement of residential integration led to white middle class opposition, and consequently by 1970, less than 46,000 family and individual units were receiving this aid.[54] Thus, an attempt to establish federal policy with respect to desegregating the housing of low income, often nonwhite, residents met with very limited initial success.

In 1968, the rental assistance approach was modified (this is known as the Section 236 Program). Renters would still pay one-fourth of adjusted income as rent. HUD would pay the difference between that sum and fair market rent or the difference between amortization of the mortgage at market rates and amortization at 1 percent. This continued subsidization of private and nonprofit organizations engaged in construction and rehabilitation of low and moderate income housing moderately increased the housing stock for poorer families.[55]

In the late 1970s, the rental assistance approach for assisting households of limited incomes expanded in scope. In fiscal 1978, about 2.3 million low and moderate income households were receiving rental assistance under a variety of programs and sufficient funds had been committed for fiscal 1979 to aid a total of 3.5 million households. This rental assistance involved tenant subsidy of existing housing as well as tenant subsidy in newly constructed or substantially rehabilitated housing. In newly constructed and rehabilitated housing, tenant subsidy sometimes was combined with direct support to the builders in the form of direct federal loans for construction of housing for the elderly and the handicapped or in some cases with federally insured mortgages. The Presidential budget for 1980 requested outlays of $5 billion which would allow extension of rental assistance to include an additional 300,-000 low income households.[56] By 1980, the principal rental assistance program was the Section 8 Program authorized by the Housing and Community Development Act of 1974,[57] and the 236 program was being phased out.

In 1968, an attempt (the Section 235 Program) also was made to assist families generally within the $4,000 to $8,000 income range to purchase homes (as the FHA and the VA assist higher income families). Under this program, participants were required to pay 20 percent of their adjusted income for amortization of their mortgage; 5 percent of gross income could be deducted from the calculation of income in the case of social security income and $300 could be deducted for each minor child.[58] If the homeowner's payment was under the level required for amortization, HUD would pay the lender the difference with the stipulation that the sum not exceed the difference between amortization over thirty years at the market rate and amortization at 1 percent. By 1970, the purchase of 131,000 housing units had been facilitated by this program.[59]

Unfortunately, the federal program to insure home mortgages for low income families, most often in older declining urban areas, did not work too well during much of the 1970s. Numerous foreclosures left HUD with thousands of foreclosed properties all over the country. The cost to the federal government of maintaining these unoccupied dwellings was staggering. In December 1975, it was estimated that HUD had spent $410,970 a day on 57,000 houses just to keep them empty. (In addition, in 1976 HUD had more than 277,000 federally-insured apartment units worth $3.4 billion in various stages of default and foreclosure.)

Not only were the direct financial costs of these foreclosures extremely high to HUD, but also the cost to the affected communities has been staggering. In Detroit, the city with the largest number of these properties, entire neighborhoods had deteriorated in the wake of HUD takeover of homes. Homes were boarded-up and abandoned after foreclosure, providing an environment conducive to vandalism and arson. Often properties were burned out before HUD could sell them. "We call it 'Hurricane HUD,'" Carl Levin, formerly President of the Detroit City Council, and now a Michigan Senator, said, "It's a plague." Some residents of Detroit refer to certain neighborhoods as "war zones." John Mogk, a law professor at Wayne State University in Detroit, has noted that once a home was abandoned, other homes in the area were also abandoned because the market value became depressed. Five hundred homes a month came into HUD possession in Detroit. By 1976, 13 percent (25,000) of all homes in Detroit had been taken over by HUD upon owner default on this federally insured mortgage program.

In 1976, federal regulations regarding Section 235 were revised.[60] The revised regulations restricted HUD-subsidized mortgages to new construction and substantially rehabilitated dwellings. Moreover, these regulations provided that HUD must directly approve a project before a commitment to insure a mortgage can be considered. These regulations have eliminated the high foreclosure rate problem.

As of 1980, mortgages under the revised Section 235 Program cannot ordinarily exceed $32,000 or, in high cost areas, $38,000. Since it is unusual to find housing at such prices in the urban real estate market and as the resident financial obligation of 20 percent of adjusted income on high cost mortgages would exceed the financial capacity of low income residents, *the program is of limited utility to such poor residents.* Indeed from January 1978 through August 1979, no revised Section 235 Program insured mortgages were endorsed by HUD's regional offices in Chicago, Illinois, and Washington, D.C. During this same period of time, HUD-endorsed insured revised Section 235 mortgages in the Detroit, Michigan area numbered 79 and in the New York City area, 596.[61]

Both the home assistance and rent subsidy programs sought to integrate lower income residents into multiclass suburban and central city areas. This integration approach has become in fact a predominant strategy under the Housing and Community Development Act of 1974 and its amendments.

A National-Urban Linkage: The Housing and Community Development Act of 1974 and Amendments

In 1974, Congress enacted the Housing Community Development Act[62] as an amendment to the U.S. Housing Act of 1937. This 1974 legislation provides the contemporary framework for national-urban housing policy. Upon enactment of the law, federal funds were to be appropriated for community development programs that would include the building and renovation of private housing. All previous private housing subsidies for low income families ceased to be operative with the enactment of this law except that institutions and individuals benefiting from the earlier support programs continue to be aided. FHA and VA mortgage guarantee programs were not affected by this law. The portion of this law that most particularly affects housing for the poor in urban areas is Section 8 (Lower-Income Housing Assistance).

The 1974 legislation, as it affects the provision of housing to the poor, differs from earlier federal housing laws in several significant ways. It temporarily took the federal government out of the construction phase of publicly assisted housing. In fact, no money was authorized by this act for building public housing facilities, though Title 9 of the law provided for an annual contribution to maintain existing public housing. In simple terms, the 1974 law provided a system of rent supplements to those eligible for participation. This aspect of the law was not too different from the 1960s rent supplement programs. Just as the programs of the 1960s used local housing authorities to establish annual contributions contracts, so too did the 1974 law authorize contracting with local housing authorities. If there is no operative housing authority in an area, HUD can contract directly with private operators. However, the local housing authorities are required to provide oversight in the construction of privately owned subsidized housing units. Builders—private developers as well as local housing authorities—may borrow money for construction from private lending institutions at the going market rate; they can use the promise of government rent subsidies as collateral. But to borrow money, potential builders must find willing lenders. The recession that followed the passage of this law did not provide economic conditions in which financial institutions were anxious to lend money to the housing industry. The risk was considered too great. As a result, very few new units were approved in the year following congressional enactment.[63]

The 1974 act, in modifying the earlier rent subsidy programs, provided more flexibility of income eligibility and broader rental limits for federally subsidized units. Maximum rents in subsidized units are generally not to exceed by more than 10 percent the fair market rent for private units. However, they may exceed the fair market rent by more than 20 percent where the Secretary of Housing and Urban Development determines that "special circumstances" warrant higher rentals. The act defines lower income families as families whose incomes generally do not exceed 80 percent of the median income of an area as determined by the Secretary of HUD, with adjustments for family size and variations due to "prevailing levels of construction costs" taken into account. The 1974 act also established a very low income category for families whose incomes do not exceed 50 percent of the median income for the area. At least 30 percent of families in Section 8–assisted housing at the time of initial renting are to be families in this category. This provision takes into account criticism raised that much federally assisted housing had not helped very poor families. On the other hand, the broad definition of low income permits new "higher" income families to be included in the program. Section 8 housing has served the purpose of dispersing low income housing units both within communities and between central cities and suburban communities. A HUD-financed study indicated that in fiscal years 1975 and 1976, the majority of Section 8 new units and rehabilitation units were located in census tracts where less than 20 percent of the population was nonwhite. Also, the majority of such units were approved in census tracts that previously had no low income housing with over twenty units.[64]

Section 8 has been criticized as benefiting too few people at too high a cost. Over 40 percent of the total population has an adjusted income that is less than 80 percent of their area's unadjusted median income. As Martin Mayer has observed: "Assuming everyone who is eligible for a Section 8 subsidy got it, and the average subsidy was $150 a month, the annual cost would be $55 billion."[65] In actual fact, only about 10 to 15 percent of those persons eligible receive Section 8 subsidies. Also, Section 8 fair market rents are set at different levels for different locations within the same metropolitan area. A two-bedroom apartment unit might have a fair market rent of $500 per month in a Chicago suburb or $175 per month in a less affluent area in Chicago.[86] But the 1974 act did recognize the housing needs of urban areas. It provided that 80 percent of the money appropriated for neighborhood rehabilitation and the financing of public facilities go to metropolitan areas and that the remaining 20 percent go to nonmetropolitan areas.

The 1976 Housing Act Amendments extended Section 236 rental assistance, revived Section 235 home purchase financing, and revived the public housing program including subsidy of capital construction. The Housing and Community Development Act of 1977 modified the Section 8 Program by authorizing HUD to provide payments to owners of Section 8 unoccupied projects that would be equal to mortgage payments required for occupied units. By assuring owners that vacant units would receive financial support under Section 8, encouragement was provided for owners to build and rehabilitate housing units.[67]

The Housing and Community Development Act Amendments of 1978 emphasized federal funding in the form of grants and other assistance for rehabilitation of housing in moderate and low income neighborhoods. The amendments (Public Law 95-557) stipulated that such projects "will directly benefit the residents of low or moderate income neighborhoods." Such activities are to be undertaken "in partnership with local government and other public and private entities." This provision clearly illustrates the linkage between public and private sectors which is a prominent characteristic of housing policy. More recently, the Housing and Community Development Amendments of 1979 authorized $675 million for Urban Development Action Grants. In addition, it reauthorized the rehabilitation loan program at a $140 million funding level and the community development block grant program at a $3.8 billion funding level. Also, $50 million was provided by this act in order to modernize and rehabilitate existing public housing.

Thus recent housing policy involves a mix of activities involving local government officials, private builders, and private financial institutions and has been supported by federal financial efforts and the establishment of national guidelines. Implementation of housing policies varies as the perception of the nature of the housing problem and the interplay of local public and private interests varies from jurisdiction to jurisdiction.

Urban Renewal

The Housing Act of 1949 set the stage for the federal government's involvement in urban renewal. Though urban renewal policy is not a housing policy per se, quite clearly it is directly related to the provision of housing to low income residents of older urban areas. An urban renewal project is based on the interdependence of the national government, the local government, and private enterprise. Local government, represented by its Local Public Authority (LPA), chooses a site and declares that it is blighted. It then utilizes its power of eminent domain to buy the land. The LPA then clears it for reuse and tries to attract private developers. In this process, many low income residents as well as small businesses are often displaced. The residents must find new homes in other areas. Sometimes they have to pay higher rents; often their relocation leads to overcrowding in other already deteriorating areas.

The federal government will underwrite two-thirds of the urban renewal program cost. This figure represents the difference between what the LPA received for the land from the private developer and the costs that the agency incurred for its purchase and then clearance. Put in somewhat different terms, the government power of eminent domain is used to assemble the land and then government resources are used to clear the land. Upon completion of this process, the private sector moves in and uses the site for redevelopment. Since private interests are concerned with making a profit, the displaced, usually low income, residents cannot afford to move back into their old neighborhoods. Also, sometimes the redevelopment is not primarily residential. Timothy Barnekov and Daniel Rich have observed that "[u]rban renewal is a modern manifestation of the mixture of private enterprise and public authority that, throughout our history, has been a principal ingredient in the provision of services at the local level." [68] The result of this mixture is often not beneficial to the poor and the powerless.

There have been many examples of the efforts of local redevelopment agencies to bulldoze existing neighborhoods and rebuild these areas into economically profitable enterprises. The primary economic motives of urban renewal became so apparent in the decades of the 1950s and 1960s that urban renewal in some cities became known as "Negro Removal," in reference to the dislocation of heavy concentrations of poor blacks in the older sections of many American urban areas.

San Francisco's Yerba Buena Center is one example of an urban renewal project that failed when local community interests organized to block the bulldozer.[69] Though in this case development was effectively blocked, in many more cases opposition was not successful. Pittsburgh, Baltimore, Wilmington (Delaware), St. Louis, and San Diego are just a few of the cities with large redeveloped areas. However, such local "success" of urban renewal may not result in improved national well-being.

Many urban renewal projects have been successful in uprooting low income groups to make way for commercial renewal. A 1979 report on Stamford, Connecticut, notes that while urban renewal has increased the commercial success of this city, a significant social price was paid. Clearance involved the eviction of 1,200 families—mostly poor—and the elimination of 400 small businesses from the downtown site. While the city's unemployment rate was reduced to less than 4 percent, the often nonwhite poor were "urban removed" to neighboring Norwalk and other communities.[70] Another instance of neglect of social concerns involving local implementation was the activity of Robert Moses as Construction Coordinator in New York City. His biographer, commenting on his urban renewal administrative activities, observed: "He selected the routes for a dozen expressways, had thousands of families evicted ... and demolished their residences." This activity involved steering expenditures "away from service *functions* and toward public works *construction*." [71]

Clearly urban renewal has stimulated commerce and enhanced the attractiveness of downtown areas such as San Francisco's Embarcadero Center, Pittsburgh's Golden Triangle, Denver's Mile High Center, and Baltimore's Civic Center. However, it has often resulted in large rental increases for the low income people who have been displaced. Moreover, the problem of urban renewal is its negative impact on low income housing stock. As Charles Hartman has observed:

> Redevelopment projects are leaving ... displacees in substandard conditions while destroying substantial numbers of decent low rent units. Overcrowding is being only marginally relieved, and in some cases exacerbated. General neighborhood conditions have deteriorated or become less satisfactory.... Further, once the overall stock of low-rent housing—decent or otherwise—diminishes, landlords tend to allow their properties to deteriorate and municipal services tend to decline. What may be rated as standard housing at the time the displacee moves in may be seriously substandard within a matter of two to three years.[72]

This lack of social concern for low income groups has been a characteristic of both private builders and commercial interests as well as local public officials. National officials have not exercised sufficient influence to ameliorate this situation significantly.

Community Development Block Grants Program

Under the 1974 Housing Act, Community Development Block Grants to communities were authorized essentially for capital development in subareas of cities that had been neglected. Since this chapter specifically deals with shelter or the impact of related programs on shelter, rather than area renewal, it will not deal with the Model Cities Act of 1965 and only a brief mention of the 1974 Community Development Block Grant (CDBG) Program will be made. The CDBG program has largely consisted of grants for physical improvements and public facilities development. It also has included some funds for housing rehabilitation. In fiscal 1977, 13 percent of the CDBG budget was allocated to rehabilitation loans and grants for housing. One impact of the CDBG program providing discretionary funds to urban communities is that the "[l]ocal priorities ... articulated under the block grant program represent a pattern of divestment of federal resources from some of the most impoverished, low income areas of the city toward a favoring of investment in the less seriously declining moderate-income areas." [73]

While Community Development Block Grants may help the residents of poor communities through social services, business renewal, and public works projects, their housing impact on low income groups has been small. In fiscal 1977, slightly over 16 percent of Community Development Block Grant funds (approximately $66 million) went to projects limiting benefits to low and moderate income persons.[74] In the face of criticism such as that raised by the Southern Regional Council that in surveyed cities "the bulk of CD allocations [were not] on projects that were of greatest possible benefit to the largest numbers of low- and moderate-income citizens," HUD in 1978 issued federal regulations indicating that the block grant program should principally benefit such persons.[75]

CONCLUSION

Though there have been some public initiatives in housing, the level of public sector participation has been restrained. Locally, some controls have been exercised over private home builders. Building codes and zoning laws regulate construction in most local communities. Local housing authorities also have some real control over public housing. Within federal guidelines, they can choose sites for public housing and select residents for it. Some federal funding is available to provide housing assistance to the needy, though the federal government's record is less than outstanding in this area as can be evidenced by the numbers of poor Americans who live in inadequate and unaffordable housing.

The national-urban housing policy linkages that do exist often tend to operate to the detriment of the urban poor and the working class, as well as to the detriment of the central city and the older urbanized suburbs. The cost of private housing is determined almost totally by private market pressures, which affect supply and demand. The major federal control on housing starts and ultimately the price level for the urban (as well as nonurban) market is tied to the money and banking decisions made by the Federal Reserve System rather than to the need for housing per se. Thus the major federal-urban linkage affecting housing starts is determined by monetary policy rather than social needs.

In the absence of adequate public sector involvement, many Americans have been priced out of the home ownership market; to buy houses, they would have to spend considerably more than the 25 percent of their gross incomes considered the maximum one should spend for housing. Renters, too, are hurt by insufficient public sector involvement. Housing of adequate quality and affordable price is not available to the needy and the near-needy who cluster in urban areas. Existing public housing is not enough to meet the demand for adequate housing by low income groups. The private market, which to date has not been able or willing to house the poor and near-poor in adequate and affordable dwellings, is now charged with the major responsibility to do so if they so choose. If it is more lucrative to continue to build houses in the suburbs for the middle class and the rich, then private builders may continue to do so. Local public housing authorities may build facilities for the needy, but they too now often depend on the private money market for capital. Our national urban housing policy provides that the private market is to be supported by public money.

FHA and VA insured mortgages provide the basis for another major national-urban housing policy linkage that has had a direct negative impact on many urban areas. FHA and VA mortgages led to the suburbanization of urban areas. It was the replacement of middle class populations by the poor and the needy and the concurrent loss of industry and tax revenues to the central cities that aided in the decay of many such cities. More recently, the availability of these guaranteed loans has led to the speed-up of urbanization of the suburbs and the spread of city problems to many of the older suburbs. Our national consciousness has not yet been raised to the point where we as a nation understand that this government-encouraged deterioration of the cities is costly to the whole nation in the form of higher taxes to provide housing, income, compensatory education, and other services to the remaining city dwellers. Also, while urban renewal may have renewed some downtown commercial areas, it also has contributed to the development of central city slums.

Overall, linkages between the federal government and local government have begun to alleviate some of the urban housing needs of lower income groups. Similarly, the linkages between the national government and the private sector have only begun to "make a dent" in meeting the urban housing needs of lower income Americans. Such policies have not yet solved the urban housing problems of low and moderate income Americans.

REFERENCES

1. Rochelle L. Stanfeld, "Searching for Solutions to Low-Income Housing Woes," *National Journal*, 10 (May 20, 1978), 798.
2. U.S. Department of Housing and Urban Development, *Annual Housing Survey, 1976* (Washington, D.C., 1978).
3. *The New York Times*, May 11, 1975, p. E8.
4. Affordable housing is considered housing that leases for one-fourth of income or housing that costs twice family income.
5. Stanfield, op. cit., 798.
6. Jacob A. Riis, *How the Other Half Lives* (New York: Charles Scribner's Sons, 1904), p. 3.
7. James Ford, Katherine Morrow, and George N. Thompson, *Slums and Housing* (Cambridge, Mass.: Harvard University Press, 1936), p. 92.
8. Ibid., p. 118.
9. Oscar Handlin, *Boston's Immigrants: 1790–1865* (Cambridge, Mass.: Harvard University Press, 1941), p. 116.
10. Edward E. Hale, *Workingmen's Homes* (Boston: James R. Osgood and Co., 1874), pp. 173–74.

11. Ford et al., op. cit., pp. 148–49.
12. Sophonisba P. Breckinridge, "Tenement House Legislation in Chicago," in Edith Abbott, *The Tenements of Chicago, 1908–1935* (Chicago: University of Chicago Press, 1936), p. 46.
13. Ibid., pp. 47–48.
14. Lawrence M. Friedman, *Government and Slum Housing* (Chicago, Ill.: Rand McNally, 1968), p. 26.
15. Ibid., p. 7.
16. Edith Elmer Wood, "The Development of Legislation," in *Public Housing in America*, ed. by M. B. Schnapper (New York: H. W. Wilson Co., 1939), pp. 71–72.
17. This section relies heavily on Marcus T. Reynolds, *The Housing of the Poor in American Cities* (College Park, Md.: McGrath Publishing Co., 1969, original publication, 1893), pp. 81–107. The quotation from White is on ibid., p. 107.
18. Ford et al., op. cit., p. 234.
19. State-supported programs of limited-dividend housing failed to develop in any other state in the 1930s and 1940s. See Dorothy Schaffter, *State Housing Agencies* (New York: Columbia University Press, 1942), pp. 366, 372–73.
20. Ford, op. cit., p. 240.
21. Friedman, op. cit., p. 109.
22. Robert E. Ryan, "Lines and Numbers," *HUD Challenge*, 10 (March 1979), 29.
23. U.S. Administrator of Veterans Affairs, *Annual Report, 1977* (Washington, D.C.: U.S. Government Printing Office, 1977), p. 76.
24. U.S. Administrator of Veterans Affairs, *Annual Report, 1971* (Washington, D.C.: Government Printing Office, 1972), p. 42.
25. U.S. Administrator of Veterans Affairs, *Annual Report, 1977*, op. cit., p. 76.
26. The extracted material appears in Allen D. Manvel, *Housing Conditions in Urban Poverty Areas: A Report Prepared for the National Commission on Urban Problems*, Research Report No. 9 (Washington, D.C.: National Commission on Urban Problems, 1968), pp. 1, 5. The quotation is on ibid., p. 5.
27. U.S. Bureau of the Census, *1970 Census of Housing*, "General Housing Characteristics," Advance Report HC (VI)-1 (Washington, D.C.: U.S. Government Printing Office, 1970), p. 1.
28. Blake Fleetwood, "The New Elite and the Urban Renaissance," *The New York Times Magazine*, January 14, 1979, pp. 17–19.
29. Robert Reinhold, "Reversal of Middle-Class Tide Sets Poor Adrift in Some Cities," *The New York Times*, February 18, 1979, p. E15.
30. James W. Hughes and Kenneth D. Bleakly, Jr., *Urban Homesteading* (New Brunswick, New Jersey: Rutgers University Center for Urban Policy Research, 1975), pp. 111, 246–47.
31. Barbara Haug, "Homesteading the Urban Frontier," *HUD Challenge*, 7 (January 1976), 27.
32. Martin Meyerson and Edward C. Banfield, *Politics, Planning and the Public Interest: The Case of Public Housing in Chicago* (Glencoe, Ill.: Free Press, 1955).
33. Robert E. Forman, *Black Ghettos, White Ghettos and Slums* (Englewood Cliffs, N.J.: Prentice-Hall, 1971), pp. 75–78.
34. U.S. Commission on Civil Rights, *Housing* (Washington, D.C.: U.S. Government Printing Office, 1961), p. 126.

35. *Gladstone Realtors* v. *Village of Belwood,* 441 S. Ct. 91 (April 17, 1979).
36. *Hills* v. *Gautreaux,* 96 S. Ct. 1538 (April 10, 1976).
37. Mario M. Cuomo, *Forest Hills Diary* (New York: Random House, 1974), p. 6.
38. Ibid., p. 201.
39. Henry J. Aaron, *Shelter and Subsidies: Who Benefits from Federal Housing Policies* (Washington, D.C.: The Brookings Institution, 1972), p. 113; see also U.S. Department of Housing and Urban Development, "Housing and Community Development Act of 1974," August 24, 1974, memorandum.
40. Under the Housing and Community Development Act of 1974, the definition of family income is revised to eliminate charity deductions for independents, and deductions for heads of households and their spouses; it does allow for deductions for foster care payments.
41. U.S. Congress, House, *Housing and Community Development Act of 1974, Conference Report,* H.R. 93–1279, 93rd Cong., 2nd Sess., August 1974, p. 135. For a more detailed discussion of this law, see pp. 174–76.
42. Cuomo, op. cit., p. 184.
43. Ibid., p. 201.
44. U.S. Congressional Budget Office, *The Long-Term Cost of Lower Income Housing Assistance Programs* (Washington, D.C., March, 1979), p. 27.
45. Aaron, op. cit., p. 121.
46. U.S. Department of Housing and Urban Development, *HUD Statistical Yearbook, 1977* (Washington, D.C.: U.S. Government Printing Office, 1978), p. 227.
47. "Myths/Realities of Public Housing," *Journal of Housing,* 30 (April 1973), 181–82.
48. Ibid., 184.
49. Martin Mayer, *The Builders* (New York: W. W. Norton and Co., 1978), p. 190.
50. Robert Ryan, "Lines and Numbers," *HUD Challenge,* 9 (May 1978), 29.
51. Louise R. White, "The Community Service Program: Meeting Tenant Needs," *HUD Challenge,* 8 (May 1977), 3.
52. This account relies on a description given in Lee Rainwater, *Behind Ghetto Walls: Black Families in a Federal Slum* (Chicago: Aldine, 1970), pp. 13–14.
53. Ibid., p. 20.
54. Aaron, op. cit., p. 134.
55. Stanfield, op. cit., 799.
56. U.S. Congressional Budget Office, op. cit., p. 1.
57. Ibid., p. 3.
58. Aaron, op cit., p. 136.
59. Ibid., p. 187.
60. U.S. Department of Housing and Urban Development, "HUD's Homeownership Subsidy Program," *HUD Fact Sheet* (Washington, D.C., January 1976).
61. Personal telephone communication, U.S. Department of Housing and Urban Development, Washington, D.C., September 26, 1979.
62. Public Law 93-383.
63. *The New York Times,* Nov. 2, 1975, pp. 1, 44.
64. U.S. Department of Housing and Urban Development, Community Development and Planning, *Community Development Block Grant Program, Third Annual Report* (Washington, D.C.: 1978), p. 164.
65. Mayer, op. cit., p. 224.
66. Ibid., p. 225.

67. M. Carter McFarlan, *Federal Government and Urban Problems* (Boulder, Colorado: Westview Press, 1978), p. 129.
68. Timothy K. Barnekov and Daniel Rich, *Privatism and Public Policy,* unpublished manuscript, p. 57.
69. Ibid.
70. Robert E. Tomasson, "The Ups and Downs of Urban Renewal," *New York Times,* February 4, 1979, p. 6E.
71. Robert A. Caro, *The Powerbroker: Robert Moses and the Fall of New York* (New York: Vintage Books, 1975), pp. 796–97.
72. Charles Hartman, "The Politics of Housing Displaced Persons," *Society,* 9 (July–August 1972), 61. Published by permission of Transaction, Inc. from *Society,* Vol. 9, No. 9. Copyright © 1972 by Transaction, Inc.
73. Victor Bach, "Prepared Statement," presented to U.S. Congress, House, Committee on Banking, Finance, and Urban Affairs, *Housing and Community Development Act of 1977, Hearings* before the Subcommittee on Housing and Urban Development, 95th Congress, 1st sess. (March 1, 1977), p. 630.
74. U.S. Department of Housing and Urban Development, Community Planning and Development, *Community Development Block Grant Program, Third Annual Report* (Washington, D.C.: March 1978), pp. 59, 62.
75. Ibid., pp. 53–54. See also 43 Fed. Reg. 8450–8451 (1978).

Program Fragmentation
and
the Health Care System

INTRODUCTION

A large part of the health sector in the United States operates through a private or nongovernmental market. The corner drugstore and the fee-for-service practitioner are within the private sector as are private, profit-making insurance companies such as Prudential and Aetna, and pharmaceutical companies such as Charles Pfizer, Parke-Davis, and Smith, Kline and French. In addition to the role of entrepreneurial insurance companies in the health care area, a substantial role is played by voluntary or nonprofit insurance companies such as Blue Cross (hospitalization insurance)–Blue Shield (medical/surgical insurance), and other independent voluntary insurance companies such as Kaiser Permanente and the Health Insurance Plan of Greater New York. Moreover, a substantial portion of our hospital system is made up of voluntary, substantially autonomous units. Also, seventy-seven percent of the nursing home facilities in this country, accounting for 67 percent of the beds, are proprietary profit-making ventures.[1]

There is some public sector activity in the area of health care. The federal government is involved in the direct operation of services through Veterans Administration hospital services as well as in the delivery of maternal and child health services through city and county health departments. More often, however, the localities, the states, and the federal government contract and subsidize the private sector through the use of public funds for Medicare and Medicaid payments to hospitals, physicians, and nursing homes. Another instance of government contracting with private enterprise involves the use of private insurance companies (often Blue Cross and Blue Shield) as intermediaries of the national government in processing claims under Medicare.

Such government pumping of funds into a private (both profit and nonprofit) system, operating in conjunction with substantial consumer demand has contributed to large-scale inflation in the health care delivery system. The effects of this situation can be observed by looking at the Consumer Price Index. Between 1965 and 1972, physician charges had increased cumulatively by 44.8 percent while hospital charges had cumulatively increased by 83.4 percent. In that seven-year period, the cumulative percentage increases in the overall Consumer Price Index were 29.5 percent.[2] Following the removal of price controls under the Economic Stabilization Program in the April 1974 to February 1976 period, the Consumer Price Index for physician fees increased by 12.8 percent, hospital service charges increased by 15.5 percent, while the Consumer Price Index for all items increased by 8.5 percent.[3] The American Hospital Association estimated that in 1977, the average national cost for a day of hospital care was almost $200.[4] Costs in urban areas were even higher. In the Washington, D.C. SMSA, for example, the average cost for a day of hospital care by the fall of 1978 had reached $284.[5]

In 1978, private insurance paid for 35.2 percent of hospital care and 39.1 percent of physician services, while 9.9 percent of hospital care services and 34.1 percent of physician services were paid for by individuals out of pocket. Individuals paid for 83.9 percent of drugs and drug-related items and 76.8 percent of dental payments out of pocket. The public sector expenditure for health care services, financed by all levels of government, is substantial, though uncoordinated and fragmented, as we will see. In 1977, the public sector provided over $65 billion, while the private sector health service bill was about $103 billion. This latter figure included payments made both by private consumers and by private insurers on their behalf.[6]

In this chapter we will examine some major health policies and programs that operate in urban America. It is important to keep in mind the heterogeneity and the public/private mix of services that affect urban health service and indeed the cost and uneven quality of overall American health services. Anne Somers, a noted health economist, has suggested: "Whatever the merits . . . to increase investments in health care substantially without altering the framework in which services are delivered will only exacerbate the inefficiencies and absurdities of the current organization of medical care in America." [7] The current organization and thus distribution of health service delivery cannot be altered separately through hundreds of local jurisdictions; such change must be superimposed on the health care delivery system by the national government. With this perspective in mind, we will proceed to look at the evolution of public sector health service delivery, as it has affected urban Americans, paying special attention to two sets of linkages: the public and private sector connection and the national and local connection. Although programs in other areas can be presented as interrelated or interdependent policy sectors, health care policy in the United States has developed essentially as a private sector entrepreneurial activity and therefore tends to be more like a "shot-silk robe" than a neat "patchwork quilt." [8]

Some Early Developments in Health Care

A variety of perspectives must be examined in the history of the health care delivery system in urban America. In particular, it is necessary to understand the role of the doctor as independent business person, the evolution of the hospital system, and finally the evolution of public sector activity in a system that has been essentially characterized by private sector activity. Until recently, the national-urban linkage has not been relevant to understanding the delivery of health care. Instead, the important linkage has been the relationship (or lack of one) between the private and the public sector and the preeminence of the private service deliverers. Especially important are the doctors and their professional organization, the American Medical Association (AMA), the physician-dominated voluntary hospitals represented by the American Hospital Association (AHA), as well as the private insurance companies, which together have been able substantially to monopolize and thus control health care service delivery in America.

Medical Training

The major component of any health care system is its trained personnel. Thus, the role of the doctor in health care is central. Though we now have a medical profession that controls both training and access to the profession, this was not always the case. In fact, these controls were not implemented by doctors until the early twentieth century. Other professional health personnel—including nurses, laboratory technicians, hospital administrators, and paramedical personnel—are also controlled regarding training and access. At this point, however, let us consider the development of training for doctors, since they are absolutely central to the organization of American health care.

During the nineteenth century, the quality of medical training was uneven; during the second half of the nineteenth century, the training of physicians was accomplished through the use of an apprenticeship system. Gradually, a few physicians joined together to form medical schools, though many of these early medical schools failed to maintain a high quality of training. After 1875, the quality of some of these training programs was severely criticized by the faculties of a few high-quality medical schools affiliated with private and state universities, including Harvard, Johns Hopkins, and the University of Michigan.[9]

The Private Practitioner, Laissez-Faire Ideology, and Fee for Service

In these early years of medical organization, physicians were able to earn an adequate income through fees derived from private patients. Surgeons received fees from private patients, though often they gave free care to charity patients in return for appointments to hospital staffs. The hospitals in the United States were organized initially on a voluntary basis and were designed to serve everyone. They were expected to be essentially self-supporting through charges to private patients. Because they were nonprofit institutions and received tax-exempt status, voluntary hospitals were expected to serve charity patients. In addition to the fee they received from their paying patients, hospitals received funds from local government jurisdictions for their care of the poor. Also, by the late nineteenth century, large donations were received by some hospitals from private philanthropists such as John D. Rockefeller, Edward S. Harkness, and Johns Hopkins. Such hospitals were usually established in America's major cities—in the cases mentioned, New York City and Baltimore. There was a parallel development to the voluntary hospital system: public hospitals were created in the cities to serve the poor. Many public hospitals including New York's Bellevue, Philadelphia's General Hospital, and Baltimore's City Hospitals evolved in the late nineteenth century from earlier almshouses for the poor.

The American medical system of the nineteenth century relied to a greater extent on the *fee-for-service* system of medical practice and the voluntary hospital than did European nations such as Britain, Holland, and Sweden, which had greater experience with both publicly supported hospitals and prepaid practice.[10] A laissez-faire ideology and a variety of medical practice systems led to the development of an extremely independent, unregulated medical system during the nineteenth century. Odin Anderson notes:

Before the turn of the [twentieth] century . . . [a]ll a physician had to do was to hang out his shingle after having served a time with a practicing physician who determined when the novice was ready. Both the American Medical Association, founded in 1847, and the new Association of American Medical Colleges began to move in the direction of raising the standards of medical education, hence in time the standards of practice. By 1909 they had succeeded in convincing state legislators to license only physicians who were graduates of medical schools certified by them, and in short order, within a decade, the number of medical schools dropped from 135 to 66.[11]

By 1920, American health services were clearly organized around the voluntary hospital system and the fee-for-service physician who often maintained a hospital affiliation. This basic system was supplemented by a tax-based municipal hospital system containing both hospital-based and hospital-affiliated physicians. State-supported hospitals connected to state university medical schools also maintained hospital-based and hospital-affiliated physicians. Within this system, the fee-paying patient was the main consumer of services. Care for the poor was a residual function and often ineffective.

Since 1945, the issue of universal and effective availability of health services at reasonable cost has been a key concern among both political and professional leaders.[12] In 1952, the President's Commission on the Health Needs of the Nation expressed this concern as follows:

Access to the means for the attainment and preservation of health is a basic human right. We set as a goal for this nation a situation in which adequate health personnel, facilities and organization make comprehensive health services available to all with a method of financing to make this care universally accessible.[13]

While a publicly supported health sector has always been a part of the American health service delivery system, this sector has not yet evolved into a system that is universally available and adequate to meet consumer/patient needs. In large measure, this failure is due to the success of the AMA, the private insurance companies, and other interested parties in forestalling any radical change in the role of the public sector in the delivery of health services.

The Development of the Public Sector

The initial concern and involvement with public sector health care in the United States was among local jurisdictions. State and federal involvement in public medicine existed in the nineteenth and early twentieth centuries, but it was quite limited. The states often provided a coordinative role; the federal government, through what was to become the U.S. Public Health Service, provided some disease control services. It was not until the twentieth century that state and more recently federal funding and oversight added significant new levels and dimensions to public health care service delivery.

The very earliest public health activity in the United States was the development between 1790 and 1830 of local health boards to administer quarantines in port cities. This, however, proved insufficient to meet the public health needs of an urbanizing and industrializing society. Along with the industrial and commercial developments in urban centers came a variety of public health problems. Urban mortality rates rose and eventually led to the development of more comprehensive local health boards that were granted administrative authority as well as advisory functions to operate quarantines and manage basic sanitation functions. Some assistance was provided to local health boards by the U.S. Marine Hospital Service (the precursor of the U.S. Public Health Service), primarily in administering quarantines.[14] The persistence of urban ill health during the nineteenth century can be seen by looking at vital statistics for New York City. In 1810, New York had an annual mortality rate of one death for every 46.5 persons in the population. By 1857 this rate had increased to one in 27.[15] Furthermore, between 1790 and 1875, yellow fever epidemics had struck Philadelphia, Norfolk, Savannah, and New Orleans.[16] As a result of these urban conditions, most large American cities had developed health boards with full-time salaried medical officers by 1870. The functions of these local boards of health between the 1850s and the 1870s included the development of urban sanitary codes, as well as pure food and drug regulations. Cities involved in such board of health developments included Philadelphia, New York, Baltimore, and Savannah. Until the 1870s, few states had departments of health to oversee such local activities.[17] However, by 1872, enough individuals were involved in public health activities to form the American Public Health Association.

In the latter part of the nineteenth century, public health expanded its focus as the work of Louis Pasteur, Robert Koch, and others emphasized the bacterial origin of many diseases. Their work showed that hygiene and sanitation could prevent the spread of disease and that vaccines and serums could produce new cures for disease. Thus, the scope of public health began to expand beyond sanitation to concerns with hygiene and immunization. By the 1870s, principal American cities were developing health offices that had as one of their functions the prevention of disease and which played a role in the investigation, diagnosis, and cure of diseases.

Early Federal Initiatives in Public Sector Medicine

Throughout American history, some limited national responsibility for public health services has been recognized. A federal public health service, for example, provided some public services in the nineteenth and twentieth centuries. Before 1935 and the passage of the Social Security Act, however, national responsibility was restricted to a very limited role in the delivery of health care. Even the landmark enactments in the field of public health at the federal level had a very narrow scope. For example, in 1798, health care services were initiated for merchant seamen.[18] In 1912, the U.S. Children's Bureau was established to encourage the creation of state programs to ensure nutritional adequacy and clinical treatment of mothers and their infants. The Sheppard-Towner Act (1921) also provided for federal Children's Bureau grants to the states for use in financing maternal and child health programs. Following World War I and World War II, the Veterans Bureau (now the Veterans Administration) expanded its national health facilities and responsibilities.

A landmark legislative enactment was the passage of the Social Security Act of 1935. The act provided for public health services to special risk populations (such as children) on the basis of federal-state matching grants. These grants were to be administered by the Children's Bureau and the Public Health Service. (In 1969, the health service functions of the Children's Bureau were transferred to the U.S. Public Health Service's Health Services Administration. Currently, they are administratively within the Division of Maternal and Child Health of the Bureau of Community Health Services.) In 1965, Titles XVIII and XIX of the Social Security Act—Medicare and Medicaid—were passed (over the opposition of the AMA, the AHA, the private insurance carriers, and other business interests). Medicare provided for national medical and hospital insurance for elderly beneficiaries and Medicaid provided federal funding on the basis of grants-in-aid for state-supported public assistance medical care for the medically indigent. Other federal initiatives included the Office of Economic Opportunity (OEO) Neighborhood Health Center Programs (now administered by the U.S. Public Health Service) and the federal heart-stroke-cancer legislation that led to the creation of a Regional Medical Program to encourage regional cooperation in the diagnosis and the treatment of these diseases. While the regional concept would have served well to aid central cities and suburbs organized into regional programs, the federal initiative was too unclear to provide impetus for such central city–suburban cooperation. In the next sections we will consider public sector health-related programs and the impact of such programs on urban health service delivery.

The U.S. Public Health Service

Local health service activities have often been directed and financially stimulated by activities of the U.S. Public Health Service. A short review of the history of this organization is useful since this federal involvement in the health sector was the first recognition of interdependence of jurisdictions in the field of health care. Early in our development as a nation, it was recognized that disease could spread beyond city and state boundaries and therefore some overarching jurisdiction was needed to facilitate some basic public health measures; for example, quarantines were used to control contagious diseases. The role of the federal government was limited at the outset, but as the nineteenth century turned into the twentieth century, the U.S. Public Health Service, though not the primary public health jurisdiction in the nation—major functions resided with local boards of health—was becoming an increasingly important partner in fighting the spread of disease.

The precursor of the Public Health Service was the Marine Hospital Service, initially within the U.S. Treasury Department, which was authorized by Congress in 1798 to serve sick American seamen arriving from foreign ports to American port cities. Seamen's wages were taxed to provide revenue for such services. Between 1798 and 1804, Marine hospitals served the ports of Norfolk, Virginia; Boston, Massachusetts; Newport, Rhode Island; and Charleston, South Carolina.[19] Eventually the service expanded to ports such as New Orleans and San Francisco. Over time other hospital functions were absorbed by what was then called the Marine Hospital Service. Later in the nineteenth century, Marine Service Hospitals were opened in Mobile, Alabama (1841); Portland, Maine (1859); and Chicago, Illinois (1873). Later specialized hospitals were built to serve special populations such as leprosy patients (Carville, Louisiana, 1935), tuberculosis patients (Fort Stanton, New Mexico, 1936; and Brooklyn, New York, 1942), drug addicts and other neuropsychiatric patients (Lexington, Kentucky, 1933; and Fort Worth, Texas, 1936).

In 1902, the name of the Marine Hospital Service was changed to the Public Health and Marine Hospital Service in recognition of the importance of the public health service in immunization and quarantine programs. Finally, in 1912, the predominance of public health activities by the Service resulted in a change of name to the U.S. Public Health Service.

Throughout the nineteenth century and the early twentieth century, the Marine Hospital Service and its successors helped control the diseases that were particularly prevalent in port cities and other poor and crowded urban areas of the United States. As a result, a national link was established that helped meet urban health needs.

One public health area in which the role of the national government gradually expanded was the establishment of quarantines. Although in the 1790s, states and cities had the authority to issue quarantine orders, federal officials had helped facilitate such quarantines. A relationship between the federal government and local jurisdictions in the area of public health was drawn as early as 1796 when Congress authorized the President to direct federal revenue officers as well as officers in charge of forts and revenue cutters to assist states in administering their health laws. In the face of cholera epidemics in the 1830s, the federal role in quarantines was expanded. In 1832, with traffic on the Mississippi serving as a source of the spread of cholera into the interior of the United States, Congress gave federal revenue cutters temporary authority to enforce state quarantine laws. By 1877, following severe yellow fever epidemics in the Mississippi Valley, Congress had temporarily established a National Board of Health with power to establish quarantines at ports of entry and to cooperate with state and municipal boards of health to prevent the introduction and spread of disease. With the passage of the Quarantine Act of 1878, national quarantine and other public health programs became the responsibility of the Marine Hospital Service.

In the late nineteenth century, the Marine Hospital Service established a number of federal quarantine stations. In the early twentieth century, the federal government took over state quarantine stations in Mobile, Alabama; New Orleans, Louisiana; Galveston, Texas; Boston, Massachusetts; and Baltimore, Maryland. The last state quarantine station federally acquired was at the port of New York in March 1921. These actions provided a federally supported health service in many urban areas. Such state, and later, federal quarantine systems were directed against the spread of major epidemics that attacked our nineteenth-century cities— particularly smallpox, yellow fever, and cholera. Between 1900 and 1914, the Service also sought to isolate cases of plague that occurred in cities such as San Francisco, Seattle, and New Orleans. In addition to the quarantine program, the U.S. Public Health Service in the 1920s and 1930s assisted states and cities in establishing milk sanitation programs, which particularly helped combat typhoid fever. In 1938, Congress gave the Service authority to administer grants-in-aid to the states for syphilis and gonorrhea control. In administering such funds, the U.S. Public Health Service helped states and local health departments develop treatment and prevention programs. Also the U.S. Public Health Service more recently has cooperated, through the development and distribution of vaccines, with state and local departments of health in immunization programs against infectious diseases including smallpox, diphtheria, and poliomyelitis. These U.S. Public Health Service programs provide for a linkage between federal health service activities and some specified urban health needs. Federal authority to emphasize such disease prevention and control functions and to provide general assistance to states in developing local health programs was strengthened by the Public Health Services Act of 1944. This act also gave the U.S. Public Health Service responsibility to cooperate with State Departments of Health in developing local tuberculosis and cancer detection and prevention programs. Such authority further established some, albeit limited, federal-state-local linkages for the delivery of health services.

Health Services Today

In 1976, comparative vital statistics published by the United Nations showed that American health care was not as adequate in meeting the needs of the general public as the health care systems of many other developed nations of the world. More specifically, on the basis of infant mortality and life expectancy, two widely used indicators of the adequacy of health services, the United States made a poor showing. Our national infant mortality rate of 15.2 per thousand live births was higher than that of fourteen other nations. Sweden, a country with a comparable standard of living, had an infant mortality rate of 8.3 per thousand live births. American males had a life expectancy at birth of sixty-nine years; this figure is lower than the comparable life expectancy of males in countries such as the Netherlands, Denmark, Japan, and Israel.[20] If the figures for the United States are disaggregated and race and poverty status are drawn out for further analysis, it becomes clear that our health system is particularly inadequate for the poor. Furthermore, since race and poverty often converge in this country, our health system is particularly inequitable for the nonwhite poor, who often cluster in our cities. In 1976, the infant mortality rate of nonwhite American children was 23.5 per thousand live births, a rate almost double that for white American children (13.3). Maternal mortality of nonwhite American mothers in childbirth was 26.5 (per 100,000 live births), a figure almost three times that of white American mothers.[21] Moreover, nonwhite Americans, in 1976, had a life expectancy over five years less than white Americans, 73.5 years of age for whites and 68.3 years of age for nonwhites.[22]

Another indicator of the difference in the quantity and/or quality of health care delivery can be seen by examining the national anemia rate. Because the poor are numerically heavily clustered in inner-city areas and urban suburbs, it is significant to note that the presence of anemia is often directly related to low income. Based on a 1973 analysis published in 1977 by the U.S. Public Health Service, the prevalence of anemia nationally was greatest for those with family incomes of less than $5,000 a year (17.1 per thousand persons) and substantial for those within the $5,000 to $9,999 range (10.8 per thousand persons). For families with incomes of $10,000 or more, the prevalence of anemia was 7.8 per thousand persons.[23] Among nonwhites the anemia rate was disproportionately high. Nonwhites had a prevalence of anemia of 14.3 per thousand population, while whites had a prevalence of anemia of 9.6 per thousand population.[24] Moreover, there was also an inverse correlation between low educational level of the head of the family and high incidence of anemia. Low income individuals also suffer a disproportionate share of heart conditions, mental and nervous conditions, arthritis and rheumatism, high blood pressure, orthopedic impairments, and visual impairments.[25] A Department of Health, Education, and Welfare White Paper noted:

On nearly every index we have, the poor and the racial minorities fare worse than their opposites. Their lives are shorter; they have more chronic and debilitating illnesses; their infant and maternal death rates are higher; their protection, through immunization, against infectious disease is far lower. They also have far less access to health services—and this is particularly true of poor and non-white children, millions of whom receive little or no dental or pediatric care.[26]

Expenditures for Health Care

For fiscal year 1978, national expenditures for health care were $192.4 billion or 9.1 percent of the gross national product.[27] Of this amount, federal, state, and local government programs amounted to approximately 41 percent of total national health expenditures.[28] Federal health programs accounted for approximately 30 percent of these 1978 expenditures for health care.[29] Although these figures seem to indicate a major government role in health care delivery, a substantial portion of the public funds allocated for health care are used to provide private sector services. Substantial portions of these funds are not, therefore, being used to provide public sector services, though some of the money is used for public health facilities and medical research. Since physicians' fees are often paid by the federal government, the public sector is reinforcing the market mechanism. In 1976, there were 425,000 physicians in the United States or 197 per 100,000 in the population.[30] Approximately 80 percent of these physicians operated on a fee-for-service basis.

Third parties, such as government, private insurance, philanthropy, and industry, financed about 67 percent of personal health care costs, 90 percent of hospital expenses, and 66 percent of physician charges in fiscal 1978. About one-third of total health care expenses were paid out of pocket by individuals.[31] (For those persons covered by Medicare, estimates are that only about 40 percent of a patient's hospital and medical bill is covered by governmental payment.[32]) Out-of-pocket payments limit or discourage individuals, particularly the less affluent, from seeking health care. Such less affluent individuals are disproportionately present in the central cities of our urban areas.

The Distribution of Health Resources

The distribution of health resources and the ability of the health service delivery system to meet urban needs depend on an array of characteristics of the primary private sector health delivery system itself. Such factors include the distribution of physicians and other health care practitioners, the location of hospitals and other institutional providers of health services, as well as the quality of their services and the availability of health services offered by prepaid group practice plans and neighborhood health service facilities.

America's health resources are poorly distributed. Because American health service is largely a private sector activity, the allocation of resources is largely related to private decisions rather than to need. Individual doctors decide where they will open their offices and practice regardless of the paucity of care in some areas. For example, some wealthy suburban areas have 200 physicians per 100,000 population, whereas the inner-city areas of the same metropolitan area may have 25 physicians per 100,000 population.[33] According to the Department of Health, Education, and Welfare (since May 1980, the Department of Health and Human Services), there were 1,100 areas with a total population of about 16 million persons that had a "critical shortage" of primary care physicians in 1978. Such areas had about 25 physicians per 100,000 population. Seventy-five percent of these areas were rural and 25 percent were urban. However, 50 percent of the population in these areas were rural and 50 percent were urban (and generally low income). In fact, urban low income areas increasingly suffer from a lack of private doctors. For example, the City of Chicago lost a third of its private doctors between 1950 and 1979, while its suburban areas gained almost the same number of new physicians. Also, primary care practice is increasingly less accessible to the general population. Whereas in 1931, 80 percent of practicing physicians were in general practice, by 1978 less than 15 percent of practicing physicians were involved in such practice.[34]

The U.S. National Health Service Corps as of March 1979 had assigned to medically underserved areas 701 MDs, 54 osteopaths, 205 nurse practitioners, 106 physician assistants, 47 social workers, and 242 dentists. Of physicians assigned to such areas, 183 were involved in family practice, 118 were specialized in internal medicine, 116 in pediatrics, and 12 in obstetrics and gynecology. Clearly such federally stimulated assistance is not sufficient to affect the medical and health care needs of these areas substantially.

Moreover, municipal hospitals and private hospitals serving inner-city areas increasingly have been closed, partly dismantled, or consolidated due to bankruptcy, low occupancy, and outmoded facilities. More than 200 such hospitals were closed between 1975 and 1977. In 1979, inner-city hospitals serving poor areas were closed in St. Louis, New Orleans, and Philadelphia, and consolidations reducing hospital beds in inner-city areas occurred in St. Louis and New Orleans. Other hospital closings were planned in New York, Chicago, San Antonio, and Wilmington, Delaware.[35] Thus, a system characterized by the dominance of fee-for-service medicine poorly allocates available physician services and hospital resources for the urban poor.

The Federal Role in Local Health Services

Prior to the enactment of the Social Security Act in 1935, there was little public involvement in the delivery of health care. Although this act did not provide for a national health service, it did provide financial assistance to states for the provision of health services to mothers and children. Since then other programs have been added, but health care remains largely a private sector activity, and the public programs that do exist do not provide comprehensive care. Dr. James A. Shannon, former director of the National Institutes of Health, has characterized present programs as balkanized, "broadly decentralized," and a "highly fragmented" set of "patchwork" activities that make it "difficult to consider broad issues in a coherent manner." [36] Moreover, these programs have often been implemented at great cost without ensuring equitable distribution of health care. In this section, we will discuss the contemporary role of the public sector in health care services, bearing in mind Dr. Shannon's caution about the programs to date. In particular, those aspects of federal legislation that especially have fostered policy linkages between the federal government and local jurisdictions will be examined.

Maternal and Child Health

At the present time, the U.S. Public Health Service's Bureau of Community Health Services has the authority to administer federal matching grants to states for the operation of maternal and child health programs with the funds going directly to local health departments. Often these funds provide that early childhood immunization and diagnostic services are maintained in urban areas; also provided by these funds is basic health care in urban areas for poor and working class women preceding and following maternity.[37] The exact nature of the services depends in significant measure on the particular problems, interests, and resources of city and county health departments. For the central city poor and working class residents, these public health programs often provide a basic source of health care service. States provide some funding and consultation services to local jurisdictions, but the exact nature of programming regarding public health activities may differ from locality to locality even within each separate state. Other public health programs carried out under provisions of the Social Security Act usually are implemented by the states and not the local jurisdictions. Thus, programs such as crippled children's programs, the cleft-palate program, and services that provide prosthetic devices for amputees, orthopedic care, and plastic surgery are administered by state units. In fiscal 1977, the total funds spent for maternal and child care services by federal, state, and local sources was $637 million. The federal expenditure amounted to $322 million, with states and localities spending $315 million.

In addition to maternal and child health, other public health services are provided at a local level. They are often locally funded, though some state and federal funding may be available from a variety of programs. Among these programs are communicable disease control programs (which include venereal disease control, a problem particularly affecting very poor areas); public health laboratories that provide chemical and bacteriological testing, relevant to air and water pollution as well as viral epidemics; and environmental sanitation dealing with water supply, waste disposal, control of insects and rodents, and food sanitation. While the programs addressed to solving these health problems are available to suburbs and rural areas, as well as to cities, the problems are often more critical in the central cities of the United States. These other public health activities amounted to over $3.729 billion in total governmental expenditure for fiscal year 1977. Of this amount, $1.289 billion represented federal expenditures, while $2.44 billion represented state and local expenditures.[38] The public health needs of urban areas are met in part by national, state, and local spending, with national revenues representing a significant source of revenue. It should, however, be noted that since localities are responsible for much of the publicly supported direct care services available for the poor and working class under the Public Health Service, quantity as well as quality of services varies from local jurisdiction to local jurisdiction. Also, many people who are neither poor nor working class do not have access to many of these direct care services. Given the high cost of health care services, often the middle income individual cannot afford adequate health care either.

Medicaid

The 1965 amendments to the Social Security Act established provisions for medical insurance for the aged (Title XVIII of the Social Security Act), known as *Medicare,* and medical assistance for the medically indigent (Title XIX of the Social Security Act), known as *Medicaid.* Although Medicaid was not presented as the major component of the law, in the years since its enactment it has taken on a significance beyond the expectations of many observers of the 1965 congressional scene. Medicare is a nationally administered medical insurance program that currently provides benefits for eligible aged and (under the 1972 amendments to the Social Security Act) disabled beneficiaries, as well as for persons in kidney dialysis treatment programs and those requiring kidney transplants; Medicaid programs are state programs for which national grants-in-aid are provided. Since poor residents of urban areas are often eligible for Medicaid, many poor people now are able to purchase medical care from private fee-for-service practitioners and hospitals that, prior to the implementation of Medicaid (1966), they had often been unable to use. (A number of hospitals routinely had provided charity care for the indigent patients prior to Medicaid.) Though Medicaid is limited to the poor—as determined by a state-administered means test criterion—and poor areas are understaffed by private fee-for-service practitioners, it does provide some improved health care services for poverty populations via a national health care policy linkage affecting urban areas. Medicaid programs are state programs and thus program options and eligibility standards vary from state to state as does the jurisdiction charged with program administration. Some states grant local jurisdictions a measure of control over their Medicaid programs and require local funds to be used for Medicaid services. The state and local programs operate with federal oversight maintained by the U.S. Health Care Financing Administration.

Medicaid programs in urban areas and within "urban states" may involve substantial state and local input.[39] Thus in 1980 the state and local share of Medicaid expenditures was 50 percent in California and New York. In other urban states the state and local share ranged between 40 and 50 percent.[40]

Depending on state policy, services may be more or less comprehensive in scope. A wide range of health care services, the quantity and quality of which are state determined with some federal restrictions, are available in some states for persons eligible for federal aided public assistance categories as well as those deemed medically indigent because of limited income and/or high medical costs. Very comprehensive Medicaid programs are found in Illinois, Michigan, Minnesota, California, Washington, and Massachusetts. These states provide services as diverse as coverage for prescribed drugs, prosthetic devices, eyeglasses, skilled and intermediate nursing home care, podiatry services, family planning services, and emergency hospital services.[41] A state can choose not to participate in this program, as indeed Arizona has chosen.

Though Medicaid provides benefits throughout the participating states to 22.8 million people (in 1978), it particularly benefits the disproportionate numbers of poor persons living in the inner-city ghettos who frequently use their Medicaid benefits in hospital outpatient clinics. In most cases, the predominant federal-state sharing of Medicaid expenses relieves such central cities of substantial financial burdens, though the state share may still be a burden for the state. For example, health services cost Massachusetts $818 million in 1975. Of this, $570 million was for Medicaid. The extent of this participation comes into clearer focus when this figure is compared to the $605 million in public welfare cash payments made by that state to the poor during the same year.[42] Where a substantial tax burden for Medicaid is carried by central cities or urban county jurisdictions, as is the case in New York City, this places a substantial stress on the revenue producing capabilities of local jurisdictions.

Medicaid benefits are disproportionately distributed to the more progressive states. While such distribution may help some heavily urban states, this policy may result in underservicing of other needy urban areas. For instance, in fiscal 1977, five states—New York, California, Pennsylvania, Michigan, and Illinois—received almost 44 percent of total federal Medicaid benefits.[43] Thus, in terms of distribution of benefits, the Medicaid program has resulted in distribution of benefits highly favorable to more affluent, socially concerned states.[44]

In conclusion, Medicaid has become a major source of the funding of medical services for the poor. However, even though all states that have Medicaid programs must provide inpatient and outpatient hospital services, other laboratory and X-ray services, skilled nursing facilities and home health services for those twenty-one and older, early periodic screening, diagnosis and treatment for individuals under twenty-one and family planning and physician services for patients receiving federally supported financial assistance, poor areas tend to be understaffed by private practitioners. Thus, many residents eligible for Medicaid benefits for fee-for-service care may not have these services *readily* available to them. In fiscal 1978, federal, state, and local authorities spent over $19 billion for Medicaid. This represented an almost fourfold increase in Medicaid from $4.9 billion in 1970. The federal share of this expenditure was over 56 percent. Regarding the distribution of Medicaid payments, over 39 percent of the payments go to nursing homes, 37 percent of the payments go to hospitals, and 11 percent of the payments are made to physicians.[45]

Mental Health Services

In 1963, President John F. Kennedy, in a special message to Congress, proposed a new federal thrust in mental health legislation. This approach was incorporated into the Community Mental Health Centers Act of 1963 (Public Law 81-164). More specifically, a system was established to provide treatment of the mentally ill in their own communities and to foster the development of community mental health centers. It provided for treatment within a specified geographic area, for comprehensive coverage, and continuity of care. Incorporated into this legislation was a recognition that local problems might be best solved locally; if a jurisdiction could not afford to maintain a mental health facility, the needy individual might move to another jurisdiction—where he might not be as well off physically or mentally—and become a burden on a new home jurisdiction. In addition, there was some hope that these centers could provide a wide range of social services to the neighborhood populations they were established to serve and thus assist in the general improvement of social conditions in the area. With the subsequent 1965 amendments, federal construction grants authorized under the 1963 act were supplemented by staffing grants. Amendments in 1968 (Public Law 90-51) and 1970 (Public Law 91-211) provided for extended periods of federal funding, and higher levels of support for local centers in the special areas of services to children, drug addicts, and alcoholics. These programs, which recognized to some limited extent that local jurisdictions need federal assistance to maintain adequate mental health facilities, still called for declining levels of federal participation, as well as state planning and local community participation.

In the years immediately following President Kennedy's policy initiatives, some increases in funding of mental health programs were made by federal, state, and local governments.[46] During the Nixon and Ford administrations, however, federal funding was reduced, especially for community mental health services. In fiscal 1974, general community mental health center federal grants for construction were $1.313 million and federal staffing grants for community mental health center personnel were at the $102.135 million level.[47] In 1975, the goal of deinstitutionalization of the mentally ill was emphasized by the Health Revenue Sharing and Health Services Act (Public Law 94-63).[48] This legislation provided that state and local public health services require the development and implementation of mental health plans designed for elimination of inappropriate placement of persons with mental health problems, and which ensured the availability of appropriate services for such persons. Also, the 1975 act strengthened federal program requirements with the addition of new required services. These services were: screening of patients who were under consideration for referral to a state hospital; transitional half-way house services for those who have been discharged from a mental health facility; and specialized service for the children and the elderly. Furthermore, centers were to provide services for those abusing drugs or alcohol if the community needed such services.

Ordinarily, federal financing for operating costs of community mental health services is made on the basis of eight consecutive one-year grants (excluding consultation and education costs). The maximum percentage of a center's operating costs that may be covered by a federal revenue grant under the Community Mental Health Centers Act is set as indicated in Table 1. There is, as demonstrated in Table 1, some increased federal funding preference given to poverty areas (predominantly in urban locations) by the Community Mental Health Centers Act. However, overall funding levels were reduced during the Carter administration. Some of the authorized appropriation levels for community mental health centers in fiscal 1980 are shown in Table 2.

Finally, community mental health centers are required by Congress to be a part of a comprehensive state plan covering all mental health services within the state. Such a state plan must be integrated in an overall health plan as required under the National Health Planning and Resources Development Act. Community mental health centers have been established more in the infrastructure of urban rather than rural health services. Since the beginning of the program, federal funding has assisted in the establishment of 675 centers making clinical care, preventive services, and social services available to 95 million people or 44 percent of the total population. Over 592 of these centers are fully

Table 1 / PERCENTAGE OF OPERATING REVENUE THAT MAY BE COVERED BY FEDERAL ASSISTANCE UNDER THE COMMUNITY MENTAL HEALTH CENTERS ACT

	Year of Operation						
	1	2	3	4	5	6	7
Catchment area							
Nonpoverty area	80	65	50	35	30	25	25
Poverty area	90	90	80	70	60	40	30

Source: *Highlights of the Community Mental Health Centers Act as Amended Through 1978* (Arlington, Virginia, 1979). Published by the National Mental Health Association.

Table 2 / FEDERAL FUNDING FOR COMMUNITY MENTAL
HEALTH CENTERS (FY 1980)

Category FY 1980	(in $ millions)
Planning	1.0
Operating	
Initial operations	35.0
Continuation	*
Consultation and education	3.0
Conversion to meeting	
service requirements	25.0

Source: *Highlights of the Community Mental Health Centers Act as Amended Through 1978* (Arlington, Virginia, 1979). Published by the National Mental Health Association.
* Congress did not authorize a specific amount but authorized "such sums as may be necessary."

operational in that they offer between a minimum of ten and a maximum of twelve statutorily specified mental health services. In 1977, these centers provided direct services to over 2 million people. In spite of the federal initiatives noted, funding for urban community–based mental health services has not been commensurate with the increased number of institutional patients transferred back into urban communities. In addition, uncertainty relating to the continuation of federal support has resulted in the inability or unwillingness of many communities to fully participate in the program.

Investment in the community mental health center movement in the 1960s and 1970s reinforced the ability of our institutions to treat mental illness in the community, rather than to rely as heavily as formerly on institutionalization. Increasingly, the role of mental hospitals has been changed from that of custodial institutions to "intensive treatment and rehabilitative centers." [49] As noted before, the initial hope was expressed that the community mental health centers would meet the social service needs as well as the clinical (psychological) needs of those individuals undergoing stress. These services would have particularly aided low income urban areas where the need for social services is especially apparent. The West Philadelphia Community Mental Health Consortium (a consortium made up of six Philadelphia hospitals, the Philadelphia Child Guidance Clinic, and the University of Pennsylvania) is an example of a community mental health center program seeking to combine these functions. It provided consultation services to police, schools, clergy, and non-Consortium service agencies, in addition to maintaining a network of neighborhood centers to deal with a variety of problems. It also provided clinical treatment and therapy, where needed.[50] In other words, the health center program tried to relate to the West Philadelphia community's needs. Increasingly, however, during the 1970s, community mental health center programs became traditionally individualistic clinically oriented psychiatric services. As a result, community mental health centers tend to be dominated by the perceptions of the traditional health service deliverer. Federal allocations of community mental health center funds tended through the 1970s to favor traditionally organized, direct clinical services, often at variance with local community perception of need.[51] This clinical orientation is illustrated by a psychiatrist's description of the function of "neighborhood psychiatry" in a Boston community mental health center.[52] The description of neighborhood psychiatric treatment involved the presentation of four cases presenting psychiatric treatment as involving direct patient clinical treatment rather than improvement of neighborhood social services and societal conditions.

Neighborhood Health Centers

As we have noted earlier, private medical practice in the United States has been organized on the basis of an individualistically oriented fee-for-service system. Thus, until recently there have been very few public sector programs to deal with the special needs of the urban poor, other than the provision of basic public health services. Though the policy linkages between local and national jurisdictions have been very weak, it is important to reiterate that the policy linkage between the public and the private sectors has traditionally been very weak in the health sector, too.

The early twentieth century saw the embryonic development of a movement to provide health care services to residents of poor areas by neighborhood health centers, often without charge. The neighborhood health center movement developed in the early 1900s, at a time when the urban population had increased to approximately 45 percent of the national population.[53] This movement sought to provide services to the immigrant poor who had moved into the urban slums of the United States in the late nineteenth and the early twentieth centuries. Some of this activity was provided by private sector voluntary agencies and in some cases local jurisdictions became involved in the development of the centers. Early health care programs aimed at preventing disease and helping the sick were developed in New York City's Henry Street Settlement House in 1893. In the same year, a public dispensary was developed in Chicago's Hull House.[54] A neighborhood health center emphasizing maternal and child care and neighborhood participation was organized by Wilbur C. Phillips in the Polish district of Milwaukee in 1911. Unlike the New York and Chicago programs, this program was carried out by the municipality. A child health station was established to serve 33 city blocks with a population of 16,000 persons and between 350 to 400 mothers and infants. Physicians serving the program would be paid a $2.00 fee for each session at the clinic. A similar health center was developed by Phillips in the Mohawk-Brighton district of Cincinnati in 1917. Within this district, councils representing 31 "blocks" of about

500 people each were elected by all neighborhood residents over the age of eighteen. These councils in turn elected a block worker to serve on the Citizen's Council of the Mohawk-Brighton district.[55] Both of these experiments represented early developments in the provision of neighborhood health center care and community participation. Both experiments were aborted ultimately by medical society opposition and the withdrawal of municipal support. In the Cincinnati case, the center was accused of constituting a "Red Plot." Nevertheless, various health centers did develop during the early twentieth century. A 1920 Red Cross report indicated that as of January 1, 1920, seventy-two community health centers existed in forty-nine communities. The report noted that seven cities had more than one center. Thirty-three of the centers were administered entirely by public authorities; twenty-seven were administered by private sources; and sixteen had combined public and private administrative control.[56]

The modern impetus for development of neighborhood health centers came from the Office of Economic Opportunity (OEO) Healthright Program, which was designed specifically to provide health services for the poor. (Such health centers are now operated with the participation and financial support of the U.S. Health Services Administration.) The OEO Comprehensive Health Services Program received a broad mandate from Congress. The program was

> to assure that services are made readily accessible to residents of [poverty] areas, are furnished in a manner most responsive to their needs and with their participation, and whenever possible are combined with . . . arrangements for providing employment, education, social or other assistance needed by families and individuals served.[57]

Two concepts derived from this legislation were (1) community involvement in planning and conducting the programs, and (2) the training of community residents as health workers and change agents.[58] By September 1974, there were 130 Comprehensive Neighborhood Health Service Programs funded by the Health Services Administration. Of these programs, 48 were functioning in 7 urbanized states: New York (15), California (12), Pennsylvania (7), Ohio (6) and Massachusetts, Missouri, and Texas (6 each).[59] These centers emphasized preventive care and early diagnosis. Services included medical and dental services, X-ray and pharmacy services, and other support services required for comprehensive care.

In 1978, Congress authorized continuing financial support for health centers, particularly emphasizing hospital-based primary care centers or health maintenance organization (HMO) ambulatory care service centers in medically underserved areas. For fiscal 1979, the national government had authorized $362 million which partially supported 864 community health centers in medically underserved areas.[60] These community health centers served over 3 million people.[61] Within the U.S. Health Services Administration (HSA), the Bureau of Community Health Services (BCHS) has the primary federal responsibility for maintaining the capacity for delivering primary care in medically underserved areas. The Community Health Centers Program of BCHS helps fund comprehensive health service projects for ambulatory patients.

An example of the type of neighborhood health program that has developed in some low income areas is the Uptown People's Health Center in Chicago, Illinois, which opened in August 1978. Within the target area of the Uptown People's Health Center, 30 percent of residents were unemployed, and 55 percent of the families were below the poverty level. Infant mortality within this community was one-third higher than the average of the City of Chicago; alcoholism was prevalent and deaths due to tuberculosis were twice the city average.[62] Residents of the area come from a number of racial and cultural backgrounds. They include blacks, Chinese, Japanese, Filipinos, Cubans, Koreans, Puerto Ricans, Mexicans, Asian Indians, American Indians, southern Appalachian whites, and white ethnics of Polish, Croatian, and German backgrounds.[63]

Most of the governmental funding for the Uptown People's Health Center is sent through the Cook County Health and Hospital's Governing Commission. Facilities provided by the center include sixteen examining rooms, a dental laboratory, a pharmacy and an X-ray room, two rooms for black lung testing (for those of coal-mining backgrounds from southern Appalachia), and a room for proctoscopy, as well as three waiting areas. The center is open six days a week for a total of forty hours. Patients are scheduled by appointments and generally see the same physician on each visit. Charges are based on patient ability to pay. The long-term goal of the clinic is to eventually have 50 percent of patients able to pay in full for services received. The clinic staff consists of thirty persons including four physicians.[64] The clinic treats a high incidence of cardiac and pulmonary problems, as well as urinary tract infections. Other ailments treated frequently include black lung, tuberculosis, and asthma. Also among Spanish-speaking patients, there is a high prevalence of diabetes. Cases of depression and hypertension, often related to conditions of unemployment and low income, are also frequent.[65]

Unfortunately, despite initial successes of neighborhood health centers in the provision of health services to poor populations, adequate funding has not been mandated. Thus, when there is a "sudden increase in attendance in . . . existing clinics as well as the high utilization in new clinics caused by a sudden increase in the demand for drugs, supplies, instruments and equipment that [are] not forthcoming," [66] the centers cannot provide all the necessary services. Barring a strong national health program with adequate funding, it is not likely that neighborhood health centers can have more than limited success. Though the federal government does finance a great deal of all the health care offered in poor areas, it has not been sufficient to eliminate the health care disabilities that affect many poor residents of urban areas. It should be noted that many federal agencies provide funds for local health care. For example, it was

Table 3 / AGENCIES INVOLVED IN DEVELOPING FUNDS FOR A
PREPAID GROUP PRACTICE PLAN IN EAST BALTIMORE

Federal
  National Medicaid Office
  Medicare (Social Security Administration)
  National Institute of Mental Health
  Office of Economic Opportunity
  Community Health Services
  Children's Bureau
  Model Cities (Housing and Urban Development)
  Federal Housing Authority
State
  Maryland Medicaid Program
  Hill Burton Agency
City
  City Department of Health
  City Welfare Department
  Model Cities Agency

Source: Robert J. Blendon, "The Age of Discontinuity: The Financing of Innovative Health Care Programs in Poverty Areas," *John Hopkins Medical Journal,* 128 (January 1970), 28.

estimated that a prepaid group practice plan, the East Baltimore Medical Plan in Baltimore, Maryland, received funding from eight federal agencies (see Table 3). In addition, state and local agencies also contributed, with two state agencies and three city agencies involved in funding for this group.

The introduction of neighborhood health centers, supported by federal funds, has increased the availability of health care services to poor urban areas, although an adequate health care system has not been developed. Also introduced has been the concept of neighborhood participation in the program and the planning of such neighborhood programs. To date, studies indicate that professional medical personnel have, however, retained fairly strong control over such programs. A somewhat greater community role would very likely encourage greater neighborhood trust and participation in neighborhood health center programs. Jeoffry Gordon suggests that to achieve the goal of community involvement, medical professionals must change their traditional approach to dealing with local communities. He notes that

> members of the medical professions ... involved in ... [the community political] process have tended to deny the political dimensions of health care. ... [T]his has limited their ability to deal with the situation and has hindered the development of the program.[67]

Health Planning

In 1966, Congress passed the Comprehensive Health Planning and Public Health Services Amendments (Public Law 89-749).[68] These amendments called for "the marshalling of all health resources—federal, state, and local—to assure comprehensive health services of high quality for every person." To be eligible for federal funds for planning and services, states were required to establish a health planning agency at the state level, a state plan, and an advisory council on which a majority of the members were consumer representatives. By August 1970, 55 of the 56 states and territories had established comprehensive health planning agencies; 127 federal grants had been authorized to finance such programs, which required broad community participation. Under the act, project grants were authorized for areawide health planning at the regional, metropolitan, and local levels, and federal grants were made available to state public health and mental health authorities who maintained programs in these respective areas. There was, at least in the conception of this program, some recognition of the need for interjurisdictional cooperation and an acknowledgment of the necessity for encouraging planned policy linkages between and within local jurisdictions. Furthermore, the federal government, by encouraging this intraregional cooperation, had established a principle of assistance to local governments for health planning. The results of this attempt to strengthen local planning have, however, been disappointing.

The Joint Center for Political Studies found that under the 1966 act, local comprehensive planning agencies failed to coordinate existing and planned health services, facilities, and personnel effectively. The Joint Center concluded:

> [T]hese agencies had failed to do their jobs effectively. The main problem was they lacked teeth. State agencies were generally tucked away inside state health departments or general planning offices, with no independent authority and only indirect contact with governors' offices. Local agencies could offer advice on whether money should be spent on a particular project, but had no power to actually stop a project if the local health department or medical establishment wanted to go ahead.[69]

Former Representative William R. Roy (Democrat, Kansas), when discussing health planning in his hometown of Topeka, Kansas, noted that "[W]hile we sat and talked about creating a health planning agency, one new hospital was built and another extended 40 percent—and they were 400 yards apart."[70] Moreover, these hospitals duplicated costly technology and were operating at much less than capacity. These factors led to an increase in hospital charge rates. Baltimore also experienced a failure in health planning, though the results of their failure were more closely tied to political entanglements within the health planning process than was the case in Topeka. In the Baltimore area, the Citizen's Health Council (CHC), consisting of sixteen consumer and twelve health service provider representatives, served as the areawide comprehensive health planning group. Their recommendations, however, were only advisory to the Baltimore Regional Planning Council (RPC), which in turn made recommendations to the State of Maryland Comprehensive Health Planning

Agency. In 1972, the CHC recommended that a Baltimore City hospital construct a general hospital in suburban Howard County. The decision to build a general hospital in Howard County was overruled by the RPC in favor of having a different Baltimore City hospital build the Howard County hospital. Faced with the issue of which hospital would build the Howard County general hospital, both Baltimore City hospitals pressured the Maryland Comprehensive Health Planning Agency. In 1974, it handed down a compromise decision. One Baltimore City hospital was allowed to build a "health park" including an extended care facility, a surgical center, a doctors' office building, a diagnostic wing, and an apartment house development for the elderly in Howard County. The other Baltimore City hospital was permitted to build a general hospital in Howard County. Given this sequence of events, it is reasonably clear that the health planning process was subordinated to the competing political appeals of the two hospitals in what turned out to be a protracted struggle lasting three and one-half years.[71]

In 1974, in a further attempt to strengthen local health planning, Congress passed the Health Planning and Resources Development Act. This legislation empowered local agencies, called Health Systems Agencies (HSAs), to block federal expenditures for health facilities that do not fit a local plan. Consumers of health care service, health care professionals, and local public officials are represented on the HSAs. The HSAs approve or disapprove applications for federal contracts under the Public Health Service Act, Community Mental Health Centers Act, and the Comprehensive Alcohol Abuse and Alcoholism Prevention Act. In addition, a State Health Planning and Development Agency (SHPDA) must approve or disapprove requests for funds originating from local HSAs. Finally, a Statewide Health Coordinating Council (SHC) must approve or disapprove state plans requesting federal formula grants for health programs. The law, which is administered by the U.S. Public Health Service was intended to encourage more rigorous local planning.

In spite of the passage of the 1974 act, the federal regulatory process affecting the health care delivery system has had some setbacks. Representative Paul G. Rogers (Democrat, Florida), chairman of the House Interstate and Foreign Commerce Subcommittee on Health and the Environment, in a 1976 address, noted the failure of the health planning process to regulate adequately the Computerized Axial Tomography (CAT) scanner, a very expensive medical machine that provides diagnostic information about organs formerly only available through surgery. After observing that such machines cost between $300,000 to $600,000 to purchase and install, Rogers observed:

[T]he Society of Neuroradiologists ... has estimated that there ought to be six or seven scanners in the Washington [D.C.] area.... We already have three and a dozen more on order right here in the nation's capital. This cost will run from about $4–7 million.[72]

Also, physicians in Dade County, Florida, which includes Miami, Florida, circumvented the local planning agency, the Health Systems Agency of South Florida, with respect to the installation of CAT scanners. The Health Systems Agency of South Florida determined that the Dade County health system had need for three such scanners for diagnostic testing of the brain. By 1977, seven such scanners had been installed in Dade County. Two of the scanners were placed in an ambulatory care facility and a physician's office. Such facilities did not fall under the regulatory provisions of the 1974 National Health Planning and Resources Development Act.[73] More recently the Health Planning and Resources Development Act of 1979 placed such technology, when it is located in an ambulatory care facility or a physician's office, and when it is used to service hospital inpatients, under its regulatory provisions.

Several Blue Cross and Blue Shield Plans have urged such noninstitutional providers—that is, those providing medical care in ambulatory care centers and physicians' offices—to seek voluntarily approval of such activities through local Health Systems Agencies.[74] Blue Shield Plans decide on reasonable rates of physician reimbursement in their role as voluntary health insurance plans. This role may allow such plans to exercise some influence upon physicians not to ignore the local health planning process with respect to the installation of CAT scanners and perhaps other expensive, complicated medical technology.

Between 1974 and 1978, a great deal of negotiation and discussion took place relating to the establishment of federal guidelines for local health systems agencies for use in planning hospital and other health services in local areas. Established were specific guidelines providing a ratio of community beds per population and specified average occupancy rates for hospitals. Other guidelines provided occupancy rates for obstetrical care and prenatal intensive and intermediate care. Utilization rates for adult open heart surgery were set at at least 350 open heart surgery cases per year; megavoltage radiotherapy would serve a population of at least 150,000 persons and would serve a minimum of 300 cancer patients per year; and computerized tomagraphic scanners would provide at least 2,500 indicated patient procedures per year.[75] While in the case of unique circumstances such guidelines were subject to modification at state and local levels, they represented a more prominent and active stance by the national government in activities of local Health System Agency activities and State Health Planning and Development Agencies. Indeed, in 1979, in reaction to this more active federal stance, Congress deleted a requirement that regional health plans have to conform to national planning guidelines. Instead, the 1979 Health Planning and Resources Development Act only requires HSAs to *report* and *explain* any inconsistencies between their plans and national guidelines to state planning agencies and the Secretary of Health, Education, and Welfare (now the Secretary of Health and Human Services).

What should be noted particularly at this point is that in spite of the

1979 modification in the law just noted, an interjurisdictional policy linkage has been initiated by the federal government, recognizing the need for and encouraging greater local planning efforts. The federal government has also provided guidelines that serve to support and give some leverage to local planning entities facing the institutional power of the local health system. In the context of an increasingly urban nation, this means that more attention is being paid to urban health planning.

Prepaid Group Practice

One attempt to improve the efficiency of delivery of medical care services has been the advent of the prepaid group practice model. The principles of prepaid group practice include:

1. *Prepayment,* which spreads the cost of health care over the covered population and provides adequate and stable revenue for organizing appropriate health care services.
2. *Group practice* by an autonomous full-time medical group, paid by capitation or other budget method and not on a fee-for-service basis.
3. *The practice of medicine* in a medical center by a hospital-based medical group; an organized central system with integrated facilities including satellite clinics to serve outlying neighborhoods.
4. *Voluntary enrollment,* such that no member of the program belongs unless he or she has chosen to participate in a dual choice situation.[76]
5. *Comprehensive service benefits* insured, including preventive medical care.[77]
6. *Its auspices* should be nonprofit and separate from that of its clinical practitioners.

Since prepaid care eliminates payment per visit, this type of system encourages *preventive medicine.*

Until the 1970s, this form of health care, though essentially an urban form, was oriented primarily to the working class and the middle class. For example, the Kaiser Permanente Program in San Francisco and the Group Health Cooperative in Seattle have particularly served the longshoremen's union. While serving a broader constituency, the Health Insurance Plan of Greater New York primarily serves employees of New York City. Similarly, Community Health Association of Washington, D.C., provides medical care for federal employees.[78] As of December 1970, twelve American prepaid group practice plans had memberships of over 25,000. These groups were located in the following urban areas: Oakland, California; Los Angeles, California; New York, New York; Portland, Oregon; Honolulu, Hawaii; Detroit, Michigan; Washington, D.C.; St. Paul, Minnesota; Cleveland, Ohio; Tacoma, Washington; and Seattle, Washington. Such programs increased their constituencies in the 1970s;

in 1979, about 7 million Americans received comprehensive health care service under prepaid group practice arrangements. However, these plans have not sufficiently filled the gap in providing for broad reform of the health care system.

Some prepaid group practice centers, including the Medical Foundation of Bellaire, Ohio, and the Kaiser Plan of Portland, Oregon, were funded in part by the Neighborhood Health Centers Program. This mechanism enabled the two systems to integrate the poor into general medical care delivery systems.[79] More recently, prepaid group practice has received legislative support from such diverse sources as the Nixon, Ford, and Carter administrations and Senator Edward F. Kennedy (Democrat, Massachusetts). Prepaid group practice organizations, known as Health Maintenance Organizations (HMOs), are provided some federal funding as a result of provisions initially included in the Health Maintenance Organization Act of 1973, and later modified by further HMO Amendments in 1976 and in 1978.[80] The 1973 act provided $325 million for the formation of new HMOs by 1980. The federal law allows federal certification of HMOs to override any state restrictions on their establishment. Furthermore, employers of twenty-five or more persons who offer health insurance as a fringe benefit must offer their employees the option of joining a federally certified HMO, if such a plan exists in the employee's area of access and if an area HMO is seeking inclusion in the employer's health benefits plan. To be federally certified, an HMO must meet much stricter requirements than conventional health insurance plans.[81]

HMOs have not expanded nearly as rapidly as many enthusiasts had hoped they would when President Nixon first announced a plan in 1971 to increase these centers to cover at least 20 percent of the nation's population. In part, the slowness of the development of new HMOs can be tied to the opposition of organized medicine. It can also be related to the provisions of the 1973 act and the 1976 amendments, which set the level of service an HMO must provide its subscribers far above those covered by the more traditional providers of health services. Thus HMOs have not been economically competitive with traditional health insurance plans. While currently HMOs have not increased as providers of service, commitment by the Carter Administration to the potential of HMOs runs high. The administration supported increased funding for HMO ambulatory care facilities in medically underserved areas as part of the HMO amendments of 1978. Moreover, in 1979, Undersecretary of Health, Education, and Welfare, Hale Champion, predicted that by 1989, HMOs would serve 20 million subscribers and provide cost "savings of between $20 billion and $24 billion while providing and fostering superior health care."[82] If more funding is made available for HMOs to be developed and maintained for urban poverty populations, this might lead to new forms of public involvement in the private delivery of services. It might also provide a federal-urban policy linkage that would improve central city health services by improving both the distribution and quality of services.

CONCLUSION

If legislative pressure at the national level is strong enough to foster the integration of the HMO concept with neighborhood health center functions for the poor, urban Americans might be provided with a more rational and more widely available health care delivery service. HMO reform could change the pattern of delivery of urban health care for both the poor and the nonpoor. Such community reform would certainly be encouraged by the federally mandated national health insurance programs currently being proposed. Moreover, the federal government already has played a role in changing the pattern of health care available to low income urban areas through the funding of neighborhood health centers and the encouragement of areawide health planning.

What remains to be done regarding the delivery of health services in urban areas will require federal support of a system directed to an equitable distribution of comprehensive and high quality health care delivery for all groups in American society. To facilitate the creation of such a system, two sets of well-articulated policy linkages will be required: It will be necessary for the public sector to exert more control over the public funds going to the private sector; it also will be necessary to provide local jurisdictions with federal funds and the regulatory mechanisms to develop and control the delivery of local health care services. Finally, the perspective expressed in 1971 by Dr. Ralph Millikan, then president of the Los Angeles Medical Society, must be altered. Dr. Millikan was quoted by the Citizens Board of Inquiry into Health Services for Americans as observing that: "Each is entitled to what he can get. The public is entitled to expect that good medical care will be available on the marketplace like a Cadillac or anything else." [83] Health care costs are now more analogous to Cadillacs than Fords. The inequities in health care service, which have been maintained by this condition, can best be ameliorated by more clearly articulated policy linkages based on greater federal participation in funding and the establishment of standards for local health service provision. Such linkages would go far to meeting the health needs of urban areas and especially the needs of their lower income ghettos.

REFERENCES

1. U.S. Congress, Senate, *Nursing Home Care in the United States: Failure in Public Policy, Introductory Report* for the Subcommittee on Long-Term Care of the Select Committee on Aging, 93rd Cong., 2nd Sess., November 1974, p. 22.

2. Howard A. Palley and Marian Lief Palley, "The Determination of Pricing Policy in the Health Care Delivery System," *American Behavioral Scientist,* 19 (September–October 1975), 108.
3. Jules H. Berman, "Medical Care in the United States," *Washington Social Legislation Bulletin,* 24 (January 24, 1977), 5. Such price control ended April 30, 1974.
4. U.S. Department of Health, Education, and Welfare, Public Health Service, *Health: United States, 1978* (Washington, D.C., 1978), p. 415.
5. *The Washington Post,* December 30, 1978, p. A1.
6. Robert M. Gibson, "National Health Expenditures, 1978," *Health Care Financing Review,* 1 (Summer 1979), 26–27.
7. Anne R. Somers, *Hospital Regulation: The Dilemma of Public Policy* (Princeton, N.J.: Princeton University Industrial Relations Section, 1969), p. 101.
8. These terms were used in another context by Arnold J. Toynbee, *The World and the West* (New York: Oxford University Press, 1953), p. 73.
9. Richard H. Shryock, *Medicine in America* (Baltimore, Md.: The Johns Hopkins Press, 1966), pp. 29–30.
10. Odin W. Anderson, *Health Care: Can There be Equity?* (New York: John Wiley, 1972), pp. 39–49. Anderson comments on the Swedish and British systems.
11. Ibid., p. 52.
12. See Eveline M. Burns, "Some Major Policy Decisions Facing the United States in the Financing and Organization of Health Care," *Bulletin of the New York Academy of Medicine,* 42 (December 1966), 1072; also see Richard M. Nixon, "Message from the President of the United States Relative to Building a National Health Strategy," 92nd Cong., 1st Sess., House Document No. 92–49, February 18, 1971, p. 2.
13. President's Commission on the Health Needs of the Nation, *Building America's Health: Findings and Recommendations,* Vol. 1 (Washington, D.C.: U.S. Government Printing Office, 1952), p. 3.
14. See pp. 217–19 for a discussion of the U.S. Public Health Service.
15. Richard H. Shryock, "The Origins and Significance of the Public Health Movement in the United States," *Annals of Medical History,* 1 (November 1929), 657.
16. Ibid., p. 658.
17. With the exception of Louisiana (1855) and Massachusetts (1869), state development of health departments did not commence until the 1870s. George Rosen, *A History of Public Health* (New York: M.D. Publications, 1958), p. 248.
18. This development was the precursor of the U.S. Public Health Service.
19. This section relies heavily on Ralph Chester Williams, *The United States Public Health Service 1798–1950* (Bethesda, Md.: Commissioned Officers Association of the United States Public Health Service, 1951), pp. 38–172. Boston's Marine Hospital was located at Charlestown, Massachusetts.
20. United Nations, *Demographic Yearbook, 1977* (New York: United Nations Publishing Service, 1978); U.S. Bureau of the Census, *Statistical Abstract of the United States* 99th edition (Washington, D.C., 1978), pp. 69, 74.
21. U.S. Bureau of the Census, ibid., p. 74. Most of the published health data is not presented with a separate Hispanic category. Therefore, Hispanics are included as either whites or nonwhites.

22. Ibid., p. 69.
23. U.S. Department of Health, Education, and Welfare, Public Health Service, Health Resources Administration, *Prevalence of Chronic Conditions of the Genitourinary, Nervous, Endocrine, Metabolic, and Blood and Blood-Forming Systems and of Other Selected Chronic Conditions, United States—1973,* Series 10, No. 109 (Rockville, Maryland, March 1977), p. 31.
24. Ibid.
25. U.S. Department of Health, Education, and Welfare, *Towards a Comprehensive Health Policy for the 1970s* (Washington, D.C., May 1971), p. 6.
26. Ibid., p. 2.
27. Gibson, op. cit., 10.
28. Ibid.
29. Ibid., 25, 29.
30. U.S. Comptroller General, *Report to the Congress of the United States* (Washington, D.C., May 1978), p. 35.
31. Gibson, op. cit., 26.
32. *The New York Times,* November 25, 1973.
33. AMA Center for Health Services Research and Development, *Distribution of Physicians in the U.S., 1971, Regional, State, Country, Metropolitan Areas* (Chicago, Ill.: American Medical Association, 1972).
34. Elizabeth Wehr, "Carter, Congress Seek Ways to Improve U.S. Health Care," *Congressional Quarterly* (May 12, 1979), 891; Roger M. Battistella and Thomas G. Rundall, "The Future of Primary Health Services," in *Health Care Policy in a Changing Environment,* ed. by Battistella and Rundall (Berkeley, California: McCutchan Publishing Corporation, 1978), p. 297.
35. Sheila Rule, "Inner City Hospitals Vanishing in the Wake of Sharply Rising Costs," *The New York Times,* September 2, 1979, pp. 1 and 32.
36. Quoted in Robert R. Alford, *Health Care Politics* (Chicago, Ill.: University of Chicago Press, 1975), p. 228.
37. This care is provided for nonurban jurisdictions, too.
38. Robert M. Gibson and Charles R. Fisher, "National Health Expenditures, Fiscal Year 1977," *Social Security Bulletin,* 41 (July 1978), 11.
39. *The New York Times,* July 17, 1974, p. 9.
40. U.S. Department of Health, Education, and Welfare, Health Care Financing Administration, *Data on Medicaid Program: Eligibility, Services, Expenditures* (Baltimore, Maryland, 1979), p. 38.
41. U.S. Department of Health, Education, and Welfare, Health Care Financing Administration, "Medical Services, State by State, December 1, 1977."
42. Neal R. Peirce, "Social Services: Can State Budgets Survive," *The Washington Post,* October 27, 1975, p. A27.
43. *Data on Medicaid Program . . . ,* op. cit., p. 40.
44. Bruce C. Stewart, *The Impact of Medicaid on Interstate Income Differentials* (East Lansing, Mich.: Michigan Department of Social Services, 1971), p. 19; Karen Davis and Cathy Schoen, *Health and the War on Poverty: A Ten Year Appraisal* (Washington, D.C.: The Brookings Institution, 1978), p. 67.
45. Gibson, op. cit., 26.
46. Ruth I. Knee and Warren C. Lamson, "Mental Health Services," in *Encyclopedia of Social Work, XVI,* Vol. I (New York: National Association of Social Workers, 1971), p. 809.
47. Executive Office of the President, Office of Management and Budgeting,

Budget of the United States for Fiscal Year 1976, Appendix (Washington, D.C.: U.S. Government Printing Office, 1975), p. 402. Also, federal grants for the staffing of facilities providing specialized treatment services for the children amounted to $11.794 million in fiscal year 1974.

48. Much of the accompanying discussion relies on material from: Mental Health Association, *Highlights of the Community Health Centers Act as Amended through 1978* (Arlington, Virginia, February 1979).

49. Imena A. Handy, "Judgments of Release Readiness as Related to Discharge from a Neuropsychiatric Hospital," *Community Mental Health Journal,* 10 (Summer 1974), 198.

50. Robert L. Leopold, "Urban Problems and the Community Mental Health Center: Multiple Mandates, Difficult Choices—Background and Current Status," *American Journal of Orthopsychiatry,* 41 (January 1971), 146–148.

51. Ibid., 145.

52. Stephen S. Shartstein, "Neighborhood Psychiatry: New Community Approach," *Community Mental Health Journal,* 10 (Spring 1974), 77–88.

53. In 1860, the U.S. population was estimated to have been only 19 percent urban. See U.S. Bureau of the Census, *Historical Statistics of the United States, Colonial Times to 1957* (Washington, D.C., 1960), p. 9.

54. George Rosen, "Public Health: Then and Now," *American Journal of Public Health,* 61 (August 1971), 1622–23.

55. Ibid., 1626.

56. Ibid., 1629, and James A. Tobey; "The Health Center Movement in the United States," *Modern Hospital,* 14 (1920), 212–14.

57. Economic Opportunity Act, as amended; 42 USC 2809 (1969).

58. Alan L. Sorkin, *Health Economics* (Lexington, Mass.: Lexington Books, 1975), p. 152.

59. U.S. Department of Health, Education, and Welfare, Public Health Service, Health Resources Administration, National Center for Health Statistics, *Health Resources Statistics, 1975* (Rockville, Maryland, 1976), p. 419.

60. U.S. Executive Office of the President, op. cit., p. 239.

61. George I. Lythcott, "The Health Services Administration: Improving the Access to Health Care of the Nation's Underserved," *Public Health Reports,* 93 (November–December, 1978), 638.

62. John Conroy, "The Uptown People's Health Center, Chicago, Illinois," *Public Health Reports,* 94 (July–August Supplement, 1979), 34.

63. Ibid., 35.

64. Ibid., 37.

65. Ibid., 37–38.

66. Geraldine B. Branch and Natalie Felix, "A Model Neighborhood Program at a Los Angeles Health Center," *HSMHA Reports,* 86 (August 1971), 690; also see Paul R. Torrens, "Administrative Problems of Neighborhood Health Centers," *Medical Care,* 9 (November–December 1971), 489.

67. See Jeoffry B. Gordon, "The Politics of Community Medicine Projects: A Conflict Analysis," *Medical Care* 7 (November–December 1969), 420.

68. For a discussion of the amendments, see Darwin Palmiere, "Health Services: Health and Hospital Planning Councils," in *Encyclopedia of Social Work, XVI,* op. cit., pp. 549–50.

69. "Health Planning on the Ground Floor," *Focus,* 3 (April 1975), 4.

70. Ibid.

71. Jonathan P. West, "Health Planning and Multi-Functional Regional Councils: Baltimore and Houston Experience," *Inquiry*, 12 (September 1975), 180–187.
72. John K. Iglehart, "The Cost and Regulation of Medical Technology: Future Policy Directions," *Health and Society*, 57 (Winter 1977), 32.
73. Ibid., pp. 32–33.
74. "Rhode Island Plans: Two Scanners are Enough," *The Blue Cross Consumer Exchange* (September 1977), p. 1; "Doctors Urged to Get Planning Approval for Office Scanners," *The Blue Cross and Blue Shield Consumer Exchange* (September 1978), p. 2.
75. 43 Fed. Reg. 13045–13050 (1978).
76. While voluntary enrollment is a principle of the Kaiser Permanente system, it is not a necessary component of all prepaid group practice systems.
77. Merwyn R. Greenlick, "The Impact of Prepaid Group Practice on American Medical Care: A Critical Evaluation," *The Annals of the American Academy of Political and Social Sciences*, 399 (January 1972), 103.
78. Ibid., 108.
79. George Goldstein, Jack Paradise, Merrit Neil, and James Wolfe, "Experiences in Providing Care to Poverty Populations," *Proceedings of the 19th Annual Group Health Institute* (Washington, D.C.: Group Health Association of America, 1969), p. 74.
80. U.S. Congress, Senate, Subcommittee on Health, Committee on Labor and Public Welfare, *Health Maintenance Organization Act of 1973, S. 14, Publ. L. 93–222*, 93rd Cong., 2nd Sess., 1974.
81. "HMOs: Are They the Answer to Your Medical Needs?" *Consumer Reports*, 39 (October 1974), 760.
82. "HMO's Expected to Triple," *The New York Times*, February 13, 1979, p. A16.
83. Quoted by Palley and Palley, op. cit., p. 109.

PART FOUR

The final two policy areas to be considered in this volume are transportation and the environment. Environmental concerns are very intense at the present time, and responses to demands for public control over private resource exploitation and private damage to the environment have been forthcoming from the national government. Transportation policy evolved initially at the local level, but there have been very significant national policy inputs since 1916. In both these policy areas, there has been public intervention in essentially private market systems. Thus, public roads support our automotive society; government railroad and bus subsidies have maintained private transit systems. Local jurisdictions, however, have increasingly moved into the area of public transit provision. In terms of environmental controls, resource use restrictions curtail private enterprise, too.

In the pages that follow, the evolution of transportation and environmental policy will be discussed. In both these policy areas, the national-urban policy linkages that have emerged in the 1970s will be considered to show the interjurisdictional dependencies and the resultant linkages that are evolving between units of government and between the public and private sectors.

Urban Transportation Linkages

INTRODUCTION

The specific problems of concern to students of urban transportation are fiscal costs, environmental pollution, congestion, and the poor quality and quantity of urban mass transit systems. These problems are difficult to resolve. Thus, inadequate mass transit systems have contributed to the deterioration of central cities and the increased use of private vehicles for travel. The increased use of private vehicles for travel has facilitated the demand for improved highway systems which in turn has encouraged the flight from the central cities to the suburban areas that has contributed to central city decay. The use of so many automobiles has led to the very high levels of environmental pollution that have recently led to our concern with the quality of the air. It has also contributed to the further deterioration of mass transit systems.

All these considerations are of recent vintage. From the turn of the century to the present, unequal emphasis has been placed on the three operative modes of urban transit—automobiles, commuter railroads, and public mass transit. That only the automobile, with its concomitant massive supporting highway system, dominates urban transit is a testament to both poor planning and the unwillingness of policy makers to accept the existing interdependence of government jurisdictions in their planning and development of facilities. Too often, planning for transportation has been concerned with physical factors and *not* with social impacts. We have been more concerned with moving goods and people than with the social effects of such movement. Also, an urban transit system must be related to a suburban ring as well as to a central city. In the words of Lewis Mumford, "Each great capital sits like a spider in the midst of its transportation web."[1] If urban mass transit stops arbitrarily at the city line, suburbanites will have to use other modes of transit to enter the central city. In addition, when mass transit systems end at municipal boundaries, central city residents who do not own private automobiles are hindered from finding reasonable transportation to availble jobs in suburban communities. The lack of transportation, then, adds to the unemployment and resultant increased poverty in central cities.

In today's world, the high costs of automobile travel—both personal costs for the vehicle and its maintenance, and the societal costs of traffic congestion, energy utilization, and environmental deterioration—make it increasingly apparent that a change in transportation policy is essential.

Transportation has been a concern of the federal government, state governments, and local jurisdictions for many years. The need for federal support was recognized as long ago as 1916 when the Federal Aid Highway Program was initiated. In fact, the federal role in transportation development has been substantial. In 1975, the United States Railway Association estimated that at least $450 billion—not including such limited support as loans to railroads—had been spent by the federal government for the development of transportation. By 1978, it was estimated by the Department of Transportation that the cost of the interstate highway system alone when it is completed in 1990 will be $100 billion.[2] Federal assistance has been largely auto-focused. Commuter rail and bus lines, until the post–World War II era, were private enterprises. Public mass transit has been under local sponsorship, and, until the passage of the 1974 National Mass Transportation Act, supported primarily by local revenues. The highway has dominated American transportation policy. Only now are we beginning to recognize that the lack of good social planning and the unwillingness to recognize the obvious linkages between government jurisdictions has impaired development of a rational transportation policy that addresses itself to transit modes other than cars and trucks.

In the sections that follow, we will first examine the scope of the existing urban transportation networks and then consider some of the resultant problems. A historical overview of national-urban transportation policies will be presented prior to a discussion of contemporary programs directed to solving the transportation problems of urban America.

Historical Development

Both interurban and intraurban transportation policy affect urban areas. During the nineteenth century, any transportation assistance provided by the federal government was directed toward movement between cities. The federal government's role was to facilitate railroad, canal, and harbor development. The modes of transportation made possible by federal subsidies for construction and maintenance activity were privately operated "coastal packets, steamships, and ferries, ... numerous toll roads, railroads and inter-urban transportation systems."[3] No federal-urban linkage existed for intraurban transportation until the 1960s.

Intercity Transportation and the Early Growth of American Cities

The growth of America's initial eastern cities was closely related to their development as ports. In the late eighteenth and early nineteenth centuries, the ports of Boston, Salem, New York City, Baltimore, and Charleston prospered from ocean-going commerce. Later, in the mid-nineteenth century, the clipper ships not only traversed the Atlantic Ocean, but also sailed west from San Francisco to China by way of the Pacific Ocean and then on to England.

Nineteenth-century urban growth also was related to the use of rivers, canals, and railroads for transport. In the early nineteenth century, Robert Livingston and Robert Fulton developed a steamboat company. Their most important success was the 1807 trip by their ship *The Clermont*, which steamed from New York to Albany up the Hudson River in thirty-two hours.[4] By 1830, the steamboat was a standard vehicle of transportation on eastern and western rivers. Mark Twain was to romanticize the steamboat as a center of social and commercial contact on the Mississippi River of the 1840s.[5] Canals also led to the development of inland cities. For example, the Erie Canal opened in 1824 and its operation led to the commercial growth of Buffalo, New York, as well as the upstate New York cities of Syracuse, Rochester, and Utica. Urban growth was stimulated by the opening of the Ohio and Erie Canal in 1832 between Portsmouth and Cleveland, Ohio. The completion in 1848 of the Illinois and Michigan Canal contributed to the urbanization of Chicago.[6]

Railroads, too, affected interurban development. By 1835, railroads connected Boston with Lowell and Worcester in Massachusetts, and Providence in Rhode Island. Similarly, railroad connections joined New York and Philadelphia, making stops en route at cities such as Amboy and

Camden, New Jersey. The Western Railroad pushed through the Massachusetts Berkshires to Albany, New York, in 1841. By 1853, the New York Central Railroad Company was formed. It went from New York City to Albany and Buffalo, New York. By 1858, the Pennsylvania Railroad connected Philadelphia and Pittsburgh by rail. The growth of the Illinois Central Railroad contributed to the doubling of the population of Illinois between 1850 and 1860. Before the Civil War, Chicago had become the terminus for twelve railroads. By 1860, the railroads of the East were connected to a number of western railroads such as the Lake Shore, the Michigan Southern, the Atlantic and Western, and the Pittsburgh, Fort Wayne, and Chicago.[7]

Despite the development of railroads and canal connections, in 1860 America's largest cities were still seaports. New York City had 813,000 residents, while neighboring Brooklyn had a population of 279,000. Philadelphia had a population of 565,000, Baltimore had 212,000, Boston had 177,000 and New Orleans had 168,000 residents. In the same year, the important canal and river ports and railroad terminals included smaller cities such as Cincinnati, Pittsburgh, St. Louis, Chicago, and Buffalo.

The Governmental Role in Highway Development

In 1816, when James Madison was President of the United States, he vetoed legislation that would have provided funds to make the Cumberland Road a national highway. In his veto message, he warned against interpreting the implied powers of the national government too liberally.[8] Not until one hundred years later when the Federal Aid Highway Act of 1916 was enacted, was federal aid provided to states for road construction (but not maintenance). Funding, when it was established, was based upon the area of the state, the population, and the mileage of rural mail routes. States usually had to provide an equal amount of their own money. To be eligible for the money, each state had to have a state highway department. By 1917, every state had such a department.[9]

At present, responsibility for highways is divided between counties, towns, cities, road districts, states, and the federal government. This division of responsibility for roads can be traced back to the colonial period. From this earliest period in American development until the waning years of the nineteenth century, maintenance and construction of highways was a local responsibility. Male inhabitants were required to provide several days' labor each year to build and maintain these roads (statute labor). Later, they were permitted to pay a flat sum in lieu of highway work. As late as 1889, statute labor was used in a majority of American states. During the second half of the nineteenth century, there were demands for better roads, and with these demands came changes in road administration and the type of labor utilized. The use of statute labor declined, and property taxes were enacted in many jurisdictions to raise revenues for roads. State highway departments were created, and local administrative units for supervising highway policies were enlarged. Building techniques improved, and trained personnel were employed.

In 1891, New Jersey instituted state aid to highways. This program evolved in recognition of the statewide benefits that would be accrued from good roads. By 1916, state financing of state highway systems had replaced state aid to localities as the major state funding mechanism and federal aid was made available to the states for highway building. By 1924, every state had a designated state highway system.[10] The organized pressure that emanated in part from these departments during the pre–World War II era served to support highways; similar support systems did not exist to demand public urban mass transit.

Some Twentieth Century Transportation Developments:
The Rise of the Automobile

Highway development in the United States in the early twentieth century permitted agrarian interests to gain access to urban markets. In the early 1900s, an alliance was formed between rural interests and the developing automobile industry aimed at securing federal aid to stimulate highway construction. This alliance led to federal involvement in highway development in 1916 with the passage of the Federal Aid Road Act; a similar partnership in support of highway construction has existed since that time. The original intent of the 1916 legislation was to ensure coordinated highway planning in states so that the roads would meet at state lines. Under this act, federally assisted transportation planning and highway construction was to be determined by the state highway agencies. Overall administration of the program with respect to uniform standards of organization and procedure was centered in the U.S. Bureau of Public Roads (BPR), which was located in the U.S. Department of Agriculture. The rural dominance exerted in this initial legislation is evidenced by the fact that ordinarily municipalities with populations of 2,500 or more were prohibited from receiving federal benefits under the 1916 act.[11] The one exception was in areas where houses in larger municipalities were on the average more than 200 feet apart—that is, in presumably rural sections of such municipalities.

Rural dominance of state highway departments was also assured by rural dominance of state legislatures (which lasted until the Supreme Court's 1962 reapportionment decision of *Baker* v. *Carr*).[12] In addition, early twentieth century urban interests did not press for federal aid for urban transportation. Levin and Abend note that during this period "city planners . . . failed to anticipate the true impact of the automobile either on traffic congestion or on land use." [13] Although some New Deal legislation[14] enacted in the 1930s permitted spending federal funds in urban areas for construction of highways and for the planning of urban highway development, federally aided highway construction during this period reflected the rural dominance pattern established by the 1916 Road Act. The Federal Bureau of Public Works continued to work closely with state highway departments more sensitive to rural than urban needs. The automobile industry continued to support these "highways only" efforts because of the obvious stimulus they provided for the purchase and use of automobiles.

Urban transportation needs within a "highways only" framework were not acknowledged until the enactment of the Federal Highways Act of 1944. This act provided for federal-state cooperation in developing a national infrastructure of interstate highways connecting the principal metropolitan areas of the nation. The act recognized urban needs by providing that 25 percent of federally aided highways should be located in urban areas with populations exceeding 5,000 persons. This latter provision stimulated suburbanization, which in turn has stimulated more highway construction. Twelve years later, the 1956 Federal-Aid Highway Act instituted a multibillion dollar program that provided 90 percent federal funding to states for interstate highway development. The 1956 act also established a Federal Highway Trust Fund maintained with the federal taxes collected from gasoline purchases. Accumulated funds have been set aside for building the interstate highway system. Because such financing was until recently restricted to highway building, it contributed to the priority given to highways.[15] Not until the late 1950s did representatives of larger cities begin to call for a more balanced multimodal urban transportation network.

Intraurban Transportation

Effects on Settlement Patterns

Urban transportation networks during the formative years of America's urbanization tended to concentrate urban populations on transit routes. If one worked in the central city, one's home could not be too far from a transportation route; thus the distance between the home and work was in effect controlled by transportation networks. This led to population concentration within a limited radius of the city. Transportation in a very real sense played a leading role in the congestion associated with cities. Since the earliest urban radius was limited by the area a person could cover on foot or by horse, cities usually had a radius of between two and three miles, and were limited to about twenty square miles.[16] Later in the nineteenth century, the development of intercity trolley lines, railroads, and rapid transit lines made it possible for the urban radius to be expanded further and for the production and employment of the central cities to serve larger areas. At this point, urban movement was expanded to about a five-mile radius; the urban areas were then limited to approximately seventy-nine square miles.[17] These systems were developed primarily to bring people and goods into the center city, where there was already a concentration of economic activity and too many people.

To some extent, the different population densities of contemporary cities can be related to transportation networks. The age of a city is an important element in establishing population density patterns since its age determines whether a city emerged as a major metropolitan area before or after the advent of the automobile. For example, Kansas City (Missouri), Seattle, and Houston are cities of the automobile age; Boston, Baltimore, San Francisco, and St. Louis all grew up before the auto appeared. The most important transit effect of this phenomenon is not which transit mode is favored, but rather how the population is dispersed. The auto-age cities are more spread out than the older pre-auto cities.[18]

While early transportation modes led to the concentration of people and economic activity in a limited radius around the downtown, transportation systems in more recent times have become agents of dispersal. Contemporary transit systems have eliminated the need for concentration and have promoted diffuse patterns of residential and industrial development. Thus, the development pattern of the contemporary urban area is often characterized by population growth on the fringes and decline in the center. For example, 1950 census data show that between 1910 and 1940, the density patterns in Chicago changed as transportation patterns changed; the residential population within two miles of the center of the city reached a peak in 1910 and declined sharply until 1940. In fact, during this period, population increased only outside the four-mile center zone with the maximum rate of growth occurring in areas eight miles and beyond. More recently, residential populations have moved out well beyond the eight-mile zone into areas that previously had not been included in the Chicago Metropolitan Area. Though the patterns associated with Chicago have not prevailed for all American cities, they are representative of a general tendency.[19]

The Development of Contemporary Intraurban Transit Modes

New York City's rapid transit system, the first American intracity mass rapid transit, "had its birth in the year 1864, when the armies of Grant and Lee were contending for the final mastery."[20] A rapid transit system began operation in 1871. James Blaine Walker, in his history of rapid transit, noted that the demand for such a system was derived "from the development of New York City and its growth northward, just as the demand for elevators came from the development of buildings and their growth skyward."[21] Thus, as it became more difficult to move about in an expanding and developing urban area, new transit modes evolved to help cope with movement of people. Elevated trains and subways were used in some cities, but by the turn of the twentieth century, the electric streetcar was the most popular system. In 1906, the electric streetcar, which ran on street rails, provided transportation from residential neighborhoods to the central business districts in America's larger cities. In that year, 90 percent of America's urban passengers used the electric streetcar. It routes were rigid, providing little more than the trip to and from the central business district. As George Hilton has noted:

> Cities as large as New Orleans and Washington, D.C., had but one cross-town car line each; every other line served the central business district. Only Chicago and Brooklyn developed comprehensive grids of street car lines.[22]

While some cities had rail rapid transit systems between residential areas and the central city, the heavy capital costs of such systems restricted them to the largest metropolitan areas such as New York, Chicago, Philadelphia, and Boston. Also, the building of such rapid transit lines by private firms generally ended with the financial panic of 1907. Major railroad commuter lines also served these same large cities (as well as San Francisco). Smaller-scale commuter railroad networks served other large cities in the United States.

The automobile has had a profound impact on the decline of commuter streetcar and railway service in urban transit because it has provided people the freedom of moving in different directions. This lateral mobility led to the decline of downtown shopping and many of the employment and recreational functions of many central cities. This observation is not true of New York City, which has continued to use rapid transit advantageously particularly at peak hours. Also, New York's commuter rail lines, the New Haven and the Long Island Railroads, continue to link New York City with Connecticut and Long Island suburbs, despite increased commuter reliance on the automobile. On the other hand, in Los Angeles, which lacked a clearly defined, commercially dominant, central business district, the streetcar system was replaced by primary reliance on the automobile. As such streetcar systems declined, the bus with its greater route flexibility became a secondary transportation source.[23] Older cities that have been able to retain a centralized focus have often continued to be served by rail transit. Such cities, as has been the case with New York City, often have had special characteristics. Some of these cities have been major financial centers. In other cities, natural barriers such as water have prevented residential spread. This latter phenomenon has been true of New York, Philadelphia, Boston, and Chicago. Cities with neither major financial centers nor natural barriers, such as Houston (an automobile-age city) and Indianapolis, have tended to be characterized by lower population densities and have relied entirely on buses and automobiles for intracity transportation.

The Contemporary Condition of Transportation

The automobile has been the dominant transportation mode for the majority of American citizens for so long that they do not appear to see any significant urban transportation problems beyond the technicalities of moving and parking automobiles.[24] By 1975, public transit accounted for only 6 percent of all work trips nationwide. The automobile carried the vast majority of the remaining passengers.[25] Since we have evolved into an automotive society, pressure for more highways at the expense of mass transit and commuter rail lines has often occurred. Our heavy reliance on the automobile has been responsible for many of the problems we associate with the contemporary crisis of urban America. The most notable problem is the population dispersion of the middle class and industry into outlying suburban areas and the perpetuation of poverty pockets in central cities and some older suburban communities. Some analysts of contemporary American urban politics argue that "[r]apid transit becomes a counterforce to the decentralization encouraged by highways."[26] Of course, any large-scale development of public transportation modes is very costly. In addition, rational planning of public urban transit requires cooperation from all levels of government; most particularly, it requires regional planning and cooperation. The demands for urban public transit are local, but local jurisdictions are the units of government least able to pay. Demands to the state often fall on deaf ears since the nonurban population does not see any direct benefits from supporting costly urban public transit systems.[27] As far as federal funding is concerned, there has been an increase in support of urban mass transit systems in recent years—though highways still receive more federal dollars than mass transit. In fiscal 1979, $7.9 billion was appropriated by the federal government for highways and $3.5 billion for mass transit.[28]

Some Social Effects of Transportation Network on Urban Populations

In 1968, a Department of Housing and Urban Development report noted:

> The form and quality of future cities is affected by many factors: Local administration, intergovernmental relations, municipal finance, private investment, water and sewer and other public facilities, and—basically—by urban transportation. The life of a city depends upon its transportation system. Inefficient transportation services increase the costs of local industry and commerce. They rob citizens of their time and comfort. They penalize especially the poor and the handicapped.[29]

Since the poor cannot afford automobiles, they are prevented from attaining the physical mobility associated with our contemporary society, and thus many of the benefits of urban society—primarily employment opportunities, but also participation in the variety of activities available to urban populations—are not available to them. Similarly, the handicapped have difficulty moving about, since private modes of transportation are not feasible for them. Other groups hampered by the inadequacy of our mass public transit systems are women and children. Often, the husband drives the family car to work while the wife remains at home.

Lack of transportation reduces her opportunities for involvement in community activities. She often requires someone to transport her if she wants to leave the neighborhood. This becomes less of a problem for more affluent families who tend to live in suburban areas where two cars are often the rule. In these families, the paucity of public transportation systems especially in the suburbs requires that someone—most often the mother—transport children to school and to after-school and weekend activities. Where a second car is not available, the opportunities for children to participate in activities outside their immediate neighborhood are almost totally eliminated. Thus, children who grow up in areas where public transportation is either inadequate or too expensive for many people to use on a regular basis find that all their relationships and activities must be within a limited geographic area. As a result, these children have little opportunity to experience the rest of the world.

Finally, the isolation resulting from inadequate transportation contributes to the ignorance that breeds distrust and ultimately fear and hatred. When populations are separated from each other, group isolation is bred. Such isolation encourages the maintenance of intergroup hostility and often contributes to the inability of separate groups to join together in order to improve the quality of urban life.

The Politics of the Automobiles

A recent federal report noted: "The transportation system was designed with little regard for its substantial undesirable side effects of all sorts, and its consumption of increasingly scarce resources, especially fuel." [30] Highways were developed in response to a variety of forces, including the successful lobbying efforts of the automobile industry and the road lobby. State highway departments and state legislatures responded favorably to their pressures. The rural dominance of state legislatures until the reapportionment decision of *Baker* v. *Carr* promoted highway development at the expense of urban transit, even though we were becoming a more urban society after 1920. Support in state legislatures for bigger and better highways was successful, and urban mass transit systems began to atrophy.

Since the existing public mass transit lines and private commuter rail lines were established in the first part of the twentieth century, it should not be surprising that transit hardware was deteriorating by the end of World War II. It needed expensive renovations and/or expensive new equipment. Funds for transportation were limited, and the decision was made at all levels of governmental jurisdiction to support private vehicular travel. This meant building more roads! Better roads and inferior mass transit led to a cycle in which people increasingly preferred cars and highways to mass transit. Since the public wanted highways, bigger and better road systems were built. Public mass transit was deteriorating. Ridership dropped on the existing lines; since ridership is one measure of acceptance of a transit mode, and ridership was down, investment in these lines declined. As investment in these lines declined, these modes further deteriorated, and usage fell further. Thus, more people took to the roads and the pattern continued. In 1929, 58 cents of every transportation dollar was spent on urban public transportation and 30 cents on automobiles. In 1966, 70 cents from every transportation dollar was spent on automobiles and only 15 cents was spent on urban public transit.[31] This change in spending priorities occurred at a time when user patterns were changing, too. It has been estimated that 23 billion rides on urban public transportation in 1945 had declined to 6.7 billion rides by 1975. This trend began to reverse itself in 1976, and by 1977, passenger rides had increased to a total of 7.6 billion (see Table 1). During this same period, however, automobile passenger miles in urban areas increased too. In fact, according to reports of the Department of Transportation, by the mid-1970s almost 92 percent of all urban passenger miles were by private automobile.[32]

Two current conditions must be considered if we are to more fully comprehend the role of the automobile as the primary transportation mode for Americans. *The costs of maintaining a public mass transit system are very high and the population of urban areas has been dispersing.* No commuter railroad in the United States is making a profit on commuter services. As population disperses, it is more difficult to find sufficient riders to maintain profitable commuter service. Some regional public authority bus lines are profitable, and in some places the state has assumed some fiscal responsibility for the commuter rail lines. For example, in the 1960s, Massachusetts and Connecticut began to subsidize

Table 1 / TREND OF TRANSIT PASSENGER TRIPS, 1940–77

(in millions)

Year	Light Rail	Heavy Rail	Total Rail	Trolley Coach	Motor Bus	Total Passenger Trips
1940	5,943	2,382	8,325	534	4,239	13,098
1945	9,426	2,698	12,124	1,244	9,886	23,254
1950	3,904	2,264	6,168	1,658	9,420	17,246
1955	1,207	1,870	3,077	1,202	7,250	11,529
1960	463	1,850	2,313	657	6,425	9,395
1965	276	1,858	2,134	305	5,814	8,253
1970	235	1,881	2,116	182	5,034	7,332
1975	124	1,673	1,810	78	5,084	6,972
1976	112	1,632	1,759	75	5,247	7,081
1977 (Preliminary)	103	2,123*	2,251	70	5,295	7,616

Source: American Public Transit Association (Washington, D.C., 1978).

* 1977 figures count a transfer from one subway line to another as two trips. Figures prior to 1977 counted transfers from one line to another as one trip.

commuter service on the New Haven Railroad, and Massachusetts began to aid the Boston and Maine line.[33]

Highways, however, are not affected by the problems that beset the other modes of transportation. Urban America has a very sophisticated series of highway networks. Given the dispersion of population, urban highway systems are metropolitan in scope, often generously financed by the federal government. In fact, in many areas, metropolitan planning agencies are active in highway planning. Thus, in the 1960s, area highway planning took place in cities as diverse as San Francisco, Seattle, and Los Angeles in the West; St. Louis and Kansas City in the Midwest; Houston in the Southwest; and Baltimore and Boston in the East. Sophisticated road systems also run through nonurban sections of the nation, a fact that should not be too surprising since one of the central participants in the transportation policy process is the state highway department. Lately, however, the most significant participant in highway development has been the federal government; it provides a major share of the funding for the development of transportation systems. It is perhaps the federal highway bureaucracy that deserves either the credit or the blame for the highway system and the cars that dominate American transportation today.

Mass Transit Systems

Despite the dominance of the automobile, mass transit systems are not becoming total vestiges of past civilizations. In fact, ever since the 1973 Arab oil embargo and the concomitant escalation of gasoline prices, there have been yearly increases in ridership. Thus, in the first ten months of 1978, the passenger load on heavy rail transit lines was up by 7.6 percent. Bus and light rail, that is, trolley lines, reported a 4 percent increase in ridership during this same ten-month time frame.[34] Perhaps it is ironic that during the height of the 1979 gasoline shortage, despite increases in rail ridership, the federal government approved cutbacks in rail service. In fact, Amtrak was permitted to eliminate six passenger routes totaling 5,000 miles.[35]

Mass transit systems are common in urban areas of the United States. Many of these systems are public, and most cannot make ends meet without public subsidies. Though systems exist, they are often inadequate and they are usually underutilized. Traditionally, mass transit lines were privately owned and were operated in many of our nation's urban complexes. These systems most often were bus lines. However, given the problems of low usage that have beset the systems, many have been purchased by urban jurisdictions. The changing character of urban mass transit can be seen by noting that between 1959 and 1971 the number of privately owned transit systems declined by 261. During this same time, public systems increased by 99. By 1971, there were 151 public mass transit systems in the United States, most of them operating in urban areas; in 1973, publicly owned systems accounted for 14 percent of our

1,063 mass transit systems; by 1977, virtually every major bus, trolley, and rail system was publicly owned.[36]

Though bus companies have been experiencing economic hardship, which has led to public takeover and public subsidies in many places, the federal government and many state and local jurisdictions have been trying to encourage the expanded utilization of buses. In some communities, bus experiments have been attempted. Mini buses, dial-a-bus plans, and limited-access express highway bus routes have all been attempted. In general, these programs have not led to greatly expanded use. According to the American Public Transit Association, total bus passengers numbered 6.425 billion in 1960; by 1970, this figure had declined to 5.034 billion. In 1973, the year of the first energy panic and a resultant sharp increase in gasoline prices, there was a slight revival of bus usage over the previous year from 4.495 billion passengers to 4.642 billion passengers,[37] and by 1977, this figure had increased to 5.295 billion (see Table 1).[38]

The Institute for Defense Analysis has determined that (1) improved service will attract riders, (2) increased fares will lead to a decline in ridership, (3) the chief users of mass transit are members of the work force, and (4) bus usage is lower in cities where the proportion of low-income households is higher.[39] These findings lead one to conclude that if service can be improved without increasing fares, then a mass transit system should be able to work in an area with a viable commuting work force. Improved service and facilities cost money, and in order to raise money, fares often have to be raised. If fares are raised, ridership will decline. If use declines, revenue will decline, thus making it impossible to raise the funds to improve the service. As a result of this problem, the participation of public jurisdictions in mass transit has increased. However, in many urban areas the cost of a public takeover or the cost of an adequate locally based public subsidy is not fiscally permissible. In such communities, even if the mass transit lines can survive, they provide insufficient and inadequate services, and people turn increasingly to private automobiles for travel.

Mass transit includes more than buses. It also includes rail rapid transit systems that use subways and elevated trains operating on exclusive rights-of-way. In 1980, twelve significant rail rapid transit systems operated in the United States. These systems are located in New York/New Jersey (three systems), Philadelphia/New Jersey (two systems), Cleveland/Shaker Heights (two systems), Chicago, Boston, San Francisco/Oakland, Washington, D.C., and Atlanta. The largest of these systems is in New York City and it is operated by the New York City Transit Authority, which is part of the New York Metropolitan Transit Authority. It accounts for about 75 percent of the revenue, revenue passengers, and passenger car miles of rail rapid transit lines in the major public systems. Chicago's system, which is operated by the Chicago Transit Authority, is approximately one-eighth the size of the New York City system.[40]

Rail transit is caught in the same fiscal squeeze that is hurting bus transit. According to the Institute of Defense Analysis, revenue passengers declined from 1.7 billion in 1960 to 1.6 billion in 1970. Even according to the somewhat higher estimates of the American Public Transit Association, total revenue passengers for rail transit had declined to about 1.858 billion by 1970.[41] However, by 1977, ridership had increased slightly to 2.123 billion. While the rail mass transit lines in the United States are operating at huge deficits, the lines that operate in Montreal and Toronto, Canada, have apparently been very successful. They have higher utilization and lower costs. The Institute for Defense Analysis has proposed that the successes of these two Canadian systems have resulted from (1) an emphasis on metropolitan planning and the interrelating of modes of transportation, (2) the use of high-density development within a context of a historic tradition of mass transit utilization, (3) a more efficient use of labor and technology, and (4) a different type of work force ridership.[42]

Commuter railroads, like bus lines and rapid transit, are faring poorly in the age of the automobile. Of the sixteen lines operating in the 1970s, all were losing money; their aggregate deficit was over $35 million.[43] All these lines have a tradition of private ownership, but more and more are becoming public. For example, in 1971, Congress bailed out the Northeast Corridor railroads with the development of the National Rail Passenger Corporation (AMTRAK), and in 1976, the Consolidated Rail Corporation (CONRAIL) was established in an additional federal move to assist the railroads.

One final point ought to be made at this juncture. Trolley cars seem to be making a comeback, perhaps because they cost less to build than railroad systems and are cheaper to operate than buses. By the second half of the 1970s, numerous cities were considering the use of light rail systems. Los Angeles, for example, which had its network of electric trolleys replaced by a freeway system in the 1940s and 1950s, was considering light rail. San Diego developed a light rail system and cities as diverse as Miami and Rochester, N.Y., were contemplating such systems, too. The traditional trolley lines of San Francisco and Boston are being upgraded, and San Francisco has been considering an expansion of its surface trolley network. Dayton, Ohio, with a population of 240,000 and a metropolitan area population of 850,000, officially embarked on a light rail building project. These forays into trolley development were explained in part by then Senator Robert Taft, Jr. (Republican, Ohio) when he observed that "[l]ight rail's ... advantage ... is that it resolves the dichotomy between the expenses of [heavy] rail and the undesirable service characteristics of buses."[44]

The Need to Plan

The Advisory Commission on Intergovernmental Relations has declared that planning for transportation facilities ranks along with water and air as fields most appropriate for areawide planning and coordination. This need for areawide planning has not been lost on local political leaders or on the federal Department of Transportation. The fiscal year 1973 *Annual Report* of the Department of Transportation noted:

> [It] became clear that burgeoning urban development was rapidly making local transportation systems obsolete, and that land use planning was therefore prerequisite to the design of transportation facilities.

The report went on to note that the Department of Transportation should develop:

> a clearer understanding of the relationship of transportation to community development patterns with special emphasis on the roles the federal and local governments should play in improving mobility within and access to urban centers.[45]

Regional authorities in many parts of the nation have been involved in the development of new and expanded mass transit systems and highways. Such authorities include the Southern California Association of Governments (6 counties and 152 cities in the Los Angeles area), the Atlanta Regional Commission, the Metropolitan Washington Council of Governments, and the Metropolitan Transportation Commission (San Francisco and eight other counties). At the state government level, the necessity for coordinated transportation planning has also been recognized. By 1975, thirty states had departments of transportation. Traditionally, however, departments dealing with transit policy have been fragmented; one unit coordinates roads and another mass transit systems. This fragmentation for transit development and planning is not entirely a phenomenon of the past. One participant at a meeting of the Council of State Governments and the U.S. Department of Transportation asked:

> [I]f we have a coordinated transportation plan and program we want to implement, or intermodal transportation problems that we want to solve, [why] can't we find a responsible multimodal office in the organizational structure of the U.S. DOT with multimodal responsibilities? [46]

The recognition of the need for regional multimodal transportation planning is, however, relatively recent. In fact, part of the reason for uncoordinated transportation policies dates back to the period prior to the more contemporary concerns for rational transportation planning. This historical lack of transportation planning is due in some measure to the private ownership of urban transportation modes until the post–World War II era. Highways were built with public funds. The program that was easiest to manage was the totally public program—the highway building program—whether local, state, or federal funds were being expended. (It can be argued that rational transportation planning might have led to more public mass transit than was developed in the first part of the twentieth century.) Earlier in this chapter, it was noted that state highway departments were usually more interested in building roads that would service rural populations than in building and then maintaining urban public transit facilities. Furthermore because the road builders and the state highway departments were organized for political action and there was no politically viable urban mass transit lobby in most places, the state legislatures were often supportive of the road builders and their allies in the state highway departments.

It was not until 1962 and the passage of the Highway Act of 1962 that urban areas of over 50,000 people had to develop a comprehensive transportation planning process to be eligible for federal highway aid. The federal government required that these planning processes be carried on in a cooperative manner by states and localities,[47] if funds were to be made available. It is perhaps unfortunate that the planning function did not dominate the development of transportation facilities. Though regional and state planning departments exist and increasingly state highway departments are being transformed into state departments of transportation, it need not follow that rational transportation policy has been generated. Thus Henry Maier, the Mayor of Milwaukee, has observed:

> We should stop this one-dimensional thinking which has deluded us too long, that freeways are a great thing for us in the central city. . . . All we have witnessed here in the main as far as the central city is concerned is the destruction of our assets, our industry, our middle class out along the highways, and the demolition along with that of some very necessary low-income housing.[48]

To take Maier's point one step further, though urban transportation should provide for the movement of people within an urban area it should not impede the efficiency and convenience of the urban area as a place to live and work. Movement both within a city and between urban jurisdictions should be planned so as to facilitate movement *but not at the expense of other urban functions.*[49]

Many of the strides that have been made toward better urban transportation planning have been necessitated by federal law or administrative regulations. Thus, the enhancement of further planning may require additional federal impetus. Certainly, this need has been recognized by most of the federal transportation legislation enacted since 1962. Also recognized by the post-1962 transportation legislation has been the obvious need to plan beyond single jurisdictions, to look to regions. Also, with the coming of the energy crisis and the environmental awareness of the 1970s, questions relating to the need for improved mass transit as a means of conserving energy and reducing environmental pollutants have been raised. To coordinate energy and conservation programs with transit policy, it is becoming apparent that federal guidelines and funds are necessary to implement policies. It is environmental-energy awareness that has led increasing numbers of decision makers to recognize the interdependence of government units and to realize that we can no longer afford to ignore obvious linkages between jurisdictions.

The National Response to the Urban Transit Condition: 1961 to the Present

As we noted earlier, the 1944 Federal-Aid Highway Act provided that 25 percent of funding for federally aided highways would be spent in urban areas. Also, although some people recognized urban mass transit needs, this act continued the long-standing highways-only national transportation policies. By the late 1950s, a crisis was apparent in the decline of urban mass transportation systems, particularly in the decline of intracity rail transit systems and commuter lines.[50]

In 1961, urban interests urged support of federal assistance to urban mass transportation. The coalition supporting an urban mass transportation policy included the mayors of major cities, city planners, urban renewal experts, and spokespersons of mass transit and commuter rail lines. In January 1961, Senator Harrison Willams of New Jersey (a state with a large suburban commuter population serviced by deteriorating railroad lines) introduced a bill that would have provided $325 million in federal assistance for mass transportation. The proposed legislation would have provided: (1) $250 million in a revolving fund for the purchase of new rail and bus equipment, rights of way, and terminals, (2) loans for state and local government or public authorities to be used in transportation programs but not for carrier operating expenses, (3) $50 million in matching grants to state or local governments for demonstration projects to show the feasibility of new transportation methods and systems, and (4) $25 million in matching grants for area and regional planning for mass transportation.[51]

As finally passed, the amount of fiscal relief provided urban mass transit was drastically scaled down. Instead of a revolving fund of $250 million for transit facilities and equipment, only $50 million was authorized; instead of $50 million in federal matching grants for demonstration projects, only $25 million was provided. However, the $25 million request in matching grants for area or regional planning funds, was *increased* to $75 million. Thus, the first national urban-focused mass transportation legislation provided some modest fiscal relief for urban mass transportation and showed an increased recognition of the need for regional planning of mass transportation systems.[52] Subsequently, the Federal Aid-Highway Act of 1962 also stimulated concern with urban multimodal transportation planning. While this act made no specific appropriation for urban transportation, it prohibited expenditures of federal funds after July 1, 1965, for highway construction in cities of over 50,000 population unless such jurisdictions included these construction activities in a comprehensive local plan providing for "various modes of transport."[53] Such plans were to be initiated by the state highway agencies, and federal funds for planning were made available to these agencies.

Beginning in 1962, pressure for extensive federal support for urban mass transportation began to be exerted in a more organized fashion. In 1962, representatives of major city governments, organized labor, the transit industry, and the railroads formed the Urban Passenger Transportation Association to support their concern for federal transit aid.[54] Two years later in a partial response to pressures from these groups, the Johnson administration's Urban Mass Transportation Act of 1964 was enacted, which provided some additional support for urban mass transit. This measure allocated $30 million for a demonstration grant program. More significantly, it initiated a capital grants program. Under this program, the federal government provided from general tax revenues up to two-thirds of the net cost [55] of local transportation projects; the local governments involved in such projects provided the remaining one-third.[56] To receive such grants (and federal loans), an urban transport plan was required.

Initially, federal responsibility for the urban mass transportation program was placed with the Department of Housing and Urban Development (HUD). However, the establishment of the Department of Transportation (DOT) in 1966 raised the question of which was the most appropriate federal agency to carry out the mass transit program. In February 1968, a joint departmental committee recommended the placement of administrative authority for mass transportation with DOT; five months later in July 1968, the federal Urban Mass Transportation Administration (UMTA) was established within DOT.

Despite the development of national concern for urban mass transit policy, inadequate federal funding of urban rapid transit led many urban planners to continue to prefer highway-oriented urban transportation systems. As John Robson, a former Undersecretary of Transportation, noted in 1969:

> Who can blame a mayor or county executive for choosing a highway-dominated urban transportation system when he is certain of getting from 50 percent to 90 percent Federal funding for it as opposed to a wait-in-line chance to share in the meagerly-funded mass transportation program. And who can blame urban planners for failing to plan public transportation facilities which are unlikely ever to be built.[57]

In recent years, urban mass transit has continued to receive limited federal funding support. The Urban Mass Transportation Act of 1970 established congressional authority to provide $3.1 billion in financial assistance to local mass transit over a five-year period. Within that general authority, Congress retained the right to make appropriations annually. Project planners were required to hold public hearings to assure local residents of an opportunity to indicate acceptability of local mass transportation plans.[58] As of 1974, federal funding under the 1970 act had been limited to demonstration grants, capital grants, or loans for investment in mass transit facilities. Prior to the passage of the National Mass Transportation Act of 1974, financing under UMTA had not been at a level high enough to provide an adequate mass transportation system. In fiscal 1971, federal expenditures for the UMTA program were

$600 million; and by 1974 the funding level had reached $1 billion. As of fiscal 1979, the funding level had reached $3.17 billion.[59] In 1975, the estimated cost of building just one urban mass transit system in Washington, D.C., was $4.5 billion.[60] Given the impact of ongoing inflation, in 1980 the cost of an urban transit system for a city the size of Washington could reach $7 billion. Local jurisdictions do not have available sufficient revenue to finance such systems solely from local sources. Only the federal government has the capacity to ensure successful financing of such development.

The 1973 Federal Aid–Highway Act

From the previous discussion of urban mass transit, it is clear that until 1961 the United States had a highways-only federal transit aid policy. It is clear, too, that the costs associated with both the capital construction and the maintenance of transportation networks far exceeds the fiscal capabilities of *all* urban jurisdictions. Only the federal government can afford to pay; only by way of intergovernmental cooperation can the obvious needs for transit interdependence be implemented. Prior to 1961, federal appropriations for transportation were influenced by an interplay of tradition, the often private character of mass transit, the slowness of the public's realization that mass transit was becoming increasingly a public need and that local jurisdictions could not cope with the costs, the opposition of a rurally dominated Congress to an urban program at the expense of rural highway development, the powerful lobbying role of the automotive industry, and the effective role of the Bureau of Public Roads in blocking urban mass transit legislation. The cities lacked technical and financial support and were underrepresented in the state and federal legislatures. In the face of such formidable obstacles, they saw little hope of changing the existing transportation program.[61]

The passage in 1973 of the Federal Aid–Highway Act provided for some far-reaching changes from earlier highways-only legislation. In particular, the 1973 legislation provided that Congress authorize more funds for highways to urbanized areas with populations over 200,000.[62] In addition, the 1973 act provided that a state can, upon the request of the responsible local official of an urbanized area, approve the use of urban-earmarked transit funds for rail or bus mass transit projects instead of highways, subject to the approval of the U.S. Secretary of Transportation. These funds can be diverted from the Highway Trust Fund as well as from general revenues. This represented a significant departure from previous policy on the use of Highway Trust Fund revenues. The traditional view was much like a fee-for-service philosophy: Highway Trust Fund money had to be spent for highways, since these funds had come from the gasoline tax which is akin to a user fee. The change in this view can be seen in the changing spending patterns. In fiscal 1974, federal transportation funds diverted from highway development to mass transit had come from general revenues. In fiscal 1975, similar diversion of funds was permitted and up to $200 million for bus purchases was allocated directly from the Highway Trust Fund;[63] in 1976, up to $800 million could be expended from the Highway Trust Fund rather than from general revenues for mass transit projects. Further, the 1976 funding provisions for the Urban Mass Transportation Act provided that states could reject completion of non-essential segments of interstate highway systems and that they could use the funds intended for these segments for mass transit.[64]

The determination to withdraw from an interstate highway segment and substitute a mass transit project under the act is made jointly by the governor and the local government of an urbanized area. Their request for withdrawal must be processed by the state highway department to determine whether the request is in accordance with the comprehensive urban transportation plan. If the transit proposal is found to be consistent with this plan, the request must then be submitted to the Secretary of Transportation for approval.[65] Funding for such an approved project must come from general federal revenues rather than the Highway Trust Fund. Finally, the 1973 act established a separate urban transportation fund. Under this provision, one-half of 1 percent of federal aid funds apportioned to states for federally aided transportation projects under the 1973 act is to be made available to metropolitan agencies responsible for comprehensive transportation planning in urban areas.

All these provisions underline the interrelationships between jurisdictions—with the federal government providing general guidelines and major funding, the local jurisdictions being responsible for the planning and implementation of transit plans, and the state governments overseeing the orderly development of multimodal transportation facilities. Thus, the 1973 law began to reinforce the obvious linkages between government units in the funding, planning, and implementation of urban transit systems.

The National Mass Transportation Act of 1974

The National Mass Transportation Act of 1974 showed additional recognition of the need for specific attention to urban transportation systems other than highway systems. Section 2 of the 1974 act stated:

> The Congress finds that . . . in recent years the maintenance of even minimal mass transportation service in urban areas has become so financially burdensome as to threaten the continuation of this essential public service; . . . the termination of such service or the continued increase in its cost to the user is undesirable, and may have a particularly serious adverse effect upon the welfare of a substantial number of low-income persons; . . . immediate Federal assistance is needed to enable many mass transportation systems to continue to provide vital service.[66]

Specifically, the 1974 law gave special recognition to the need for multimodal urban transportation planning by establishing a comprehensive planning and review procedure for urban areas to be eligible for federal aid for mass transit systems. Substitution of rapid transit projects for interstate highway segments, which was incorporated into the 1973 law, was continued in the 1974 legislation. The Secretary of Transportation was authorized to make almost $11 billion in grants and loans available for urban mass transit systems. This was the largest appropriation that had been made for such programs. The act represented a continued reorientation from the traditional rural-focused and highway-focused transportation policy that had persisted since 1916 when the first federal highway legislation was passed.

However, the development of the highway system is still a dominating force in national transportation policy, and the 1974 act provides that state departments of transportation will continue to play a pivotal role in the administration of transportation policy, particularly in the decision to substitute a rapid transit project for an urban extension of an interstate highway. Thus, although the federal authorization level is relatively high and although planning is required, the national-urban policy linkage is weakened somewhat by state transportation department intervention in the decision-making process.

1978 Surface Transportation Assistance Act

In November 1978, new legislation was enacted that extended the federal role in both highway development and maintenance and in the building of urban mass transit systems. The 1978 Surface Transportation Assistance Act authorized nearly $54 billion in federal aid for highways, highway safety, and mass transit for four years—fiscal year 1979 through fiscal year 1982. In addition, it provided for an extension of taxes for the Highway Trust Fund and set a 1990 deadline for the completion of the Interstate Highway System.

Though federal funding for mass transit systems is becoming more available, the United States, despite its looming concerns with gasoline shortages and pollution caused by automobile emissions, remains an automotive society. Thus, as cleared by Congress and signed into law by the President, Surface Transportation Assistance Act appropriations for fiscal 1979 provided $8.781 billion for highways and $3.85 billion for mass transit. Over a four-year period, $15.6 billion was authorized for mass transit, while most of the remainder of the $54 billion was authorized for highways or highway-related projects. In addition, the formula for distributing federal dollars for highways remains more attractive than the formula for disbursing federal funds for mass transit. Building interstate highways is still the best transportation funding deal for a state; the federal contribution remains $9 federal for every $1 provided by the state. Noninterstate highway projects now are eligible for 75 percent federal funding (prior to this legislation, the comparable figure had been 70 percent). Mass transit capital projects now are eligible for 80 percent federal funding and mass transit projects substituted by local authorities for interstate highway segments can now be eligible for 85 percent funding— though the interstate highway segment itself would receive 90 percent federal funds.[67] No further incursions were made into the Highway Trust Fund by this more recent legislation.[68]

Boston and the Development of Route 128 [69]

The effect of the federal highway aid thrust can be seen by examining the urban development that surrounds many of the nation's cities. One case of the influence of highway aid can be seen in the Boston metropolitan area.

In the months immediately following the end of World War II, the Massachusetts Department of Public Works initiated a study to develop a highway construction plan for the state. The result of this study was the *Master Highway Plan,* which was released in 1948. Among other suggestions, the plan called for the development of three circumferential highways around the city of Boston. Route 128 rims Boston approximately twelve miles from the center of the city; Route 495 follows the same course about twenty miles from the center of Boston. Route 295 was designed to circle the city one or two miles from the center, but except for one portion, it has not been built.

Route 128 was the first of these roads to be built. It was a unique undertaking since it was the first limited-access circumferential highway built around any major metropolitan area. Because it requires traffic to leave and enter only at designated interchanges and cross the highway only over bridges, the limited-access highway is efficient for private cars and trucks. For local bus transit, however, it is not efficient, since limited access makes it difficult for buses to take riders to the side streets where they live. Thus, Route 128's design "not only provided a positive means to turn the Boston suburban region over to the automobile, but it also created an effective barrier to the development of a circumferential local bus transit."

Since the road's opening in 1948, the utilization of Route 128 has continued to expand as a commuter and business road, and as an interstate by-pass around Boston. Also, housing and business developed in the metropolitan area outside of Boston in the 1950s and 1960s, further adding to the use of this roadway. Between 1940 and 1959, approximately 200,000 housing units were built in the Boston SMSA. Of these units, 64 percent (125,000) were built in areas with no major public transit routes into Boston. In the 1960s, 72 percent of the new housing was built outside the metropolitan area's major transit areas.

The construction of Route 128 certainly facilitated suburbanization and the movement of industrial and commercial activities into the suburbs. In addition, it has served as a natural terminus for roads and thus slowed highway construction within the metropolitan area. The outward portions of the Massachusetts Turnpike as well as Routes 1, 2, 24, and I-93 were completed as far as Route 128 during the 1950s and 1960s. Until 1959, only two major automobile roads were completed within the circumference of Route 128. Thus, movement into Boston was made difficult, perhaps further encouraging residential and business activity in the surburbs.

In 1948, an *antidiversion* provision was added to the Massachusetts state constitution. Such a provision earmarks all taxes generated by motor vehicle usage exclusively for highway-related uses. Thus, Route 128 and the other highways planned for the state highway system had state funds guaranteed. In 1956, when the National Highway Trust Fund was established, the federal gasoline tax was also covered by an antidiversion rule. This federal rule, as well as the general federal appropriations for 90 percent reimbursement for national limited-access roads (interstate highways) and 50 percent reimbursement to states for the construction of primary and secondary roads provided an impetus to build more highways. In fact, between 1958 and 1963, fifty miles of new highway was constructed in the Boston area. Because money was available for roads, roads were built. Homes were then built where there were roads, and industries moved into the highway-serviced communities, too.

Public transit did not receive the funding highways received. People moved out of areas served by public transit. The public transit system floundered badly. In January 1965, the Metropolitan Transit Authority (MTA) became the Massachusetts Bay Transportation Authority (MBTA) and began to serve outlying communities (the seventy-eight cities and towns that comprise the Boston SMSA) as well as the fourteen inner-core communities previously served by the MTA. Unfortunately this reorganization, though it did increase the tax base for public transportation, did not help too much. The transit problem was caused by ever-expanding automobile utilization and the resultant sprawl; reorganization could not stop the increasing transit deficits and general dependency on automobile transportation. In the 1960s, some attempt was made to increase highway routes into the city from Route 128 and to build the inner beltway. These plans ran into opposition from organized citizen groups whose members were slated for removal to make room for roads. The Irish, Italian, black, Chinese, Spanish, and nonethnic communities of Boston joined together and were able to block highway construction; they were successful except where contracts had already been signed.

The result of all of the conditions just described is that today the Boston area is an urban sprawl heavily dependent upon automobile transportation for the movement of people and goods. Highways and sprawl have begotten more highways and sprawl!

CONCLUSION

The National League of Cities, at its 1973 Annual Business Session, accepted the need for governmental interdependence in policy planning and implementation of transportation policy. They noted that "local systems of public transportation, serving urban and urbanized areas, should be considered by federal, state and local governments as an essential public service." They went on to suggest that "federal, state and local support for transportation planning must be coordinated and funds allocated to support comprehensive local planning efforts." [70]

It is certainly becoming clear to many observers of the urban scene that multimodal transportation systems are needed in urban areas to move both goods and people. Not all people are served by private transit; furthermore, in many places public mass transit would be cheaper in the long run than continued reliance on private automobiles. In addition, the environmental and energy costs of private transit via the highway network we have built in our nation are costs we can no longer support. The environmentalists' concerns, along with the costs for energy and the depletion of existing energy reserves, make transportation planning for multimodal development ever more important as we approach the twenty-first century.

It is clear that most private mass transit systems cannot absorb the costs of developing and maintaining transit systems. It is clear, too, that most local jurisdictions or regional transit authorities cannot cope with the attendant costs of mass transit system development and maintenance. Since World War II, the federal government has begun to act as a partner in highway development. With the development of an adequate federal-urban linkage that makes federal funds more available to urban areas, regional planning agencies may be able to stem the tide of private cars as the preferred transit mode of most Americans. Perhaps private automobiles are the preferred mode of transit only because mass transit systems have been limited in their routes, uncomfortable, and generally inadequate in the service provided. Perhaps recent federal legislation, by its greater encouragement of mass transit development, has begun to counter the automobile as the favorite transit mode and will lead to an urban society that can adequately maintain multimodal ground transportation systems.

REFERENCES

1. Lewis Mumford, *The Culture of Cities* (New York: Harcourt, Brace and World, 1938), p. 233.
2. *Congressional Quarterly Almanac, 1978* (Washington, D.C., 1979), p. 61.
3. Melvin R. Levin and Norman A. Abend, *Bureaucrats in Collision: Case Studies in Area Transportation Planning* (Cambridge, Mass.: The MIT Press, 1971), p. 28.
4. Nelson Manfred Blake, *A Short History of American Life* (New York: McGraw-Hill, 1952), p. 198.
5. Mark Twain, *Life on the Mississippi,* originally published 1875.
6. Blake, op. cit., p. 201.
7. Ibid., p. 204.

8. Edward A. Lutz, "Effect of New Federal Aid Highway Act on Federal-State Relations," in *Financing Highways* (Princeton, N.J.: Tax Institute, 1957), p. 57.
9. Frank G. Moore, "The State's Responsibility for State-Local Action," in *Financing Highways, ibid.,* p. 73.
10. This previous section on the historical development of state highway systems relies heavily upon ibid., pp. 71–73.
11. Levin and Abend, op. cit., p. 32.
12. For additional discussion of this point, see supra, p. 254.
13. Levin and Abend, op. cit., p. 32.
14. The National Industrial Recovery Act of 1933 and the Hayden-Cartwright Act of 1934.
15. George W. Hilton, *Federal Transit Subsidies* (Washington, D.C.: American Enterprise Institute for Public Policy Research, 1974), p. 10. A similar federal trust fund was established for airport construction in 1970.
16. Wilfred Owen, *The Metropolitan Transportation Problem* (Garden City, N.Y.: Anchor Books, 1966), p. 32.
17. Ibid.
18. Alan Lupo, Frank Colcard, and Edmund P. Fowler, *Rites of Way: The Politics of Transportation in Boston and the U.S. City* (Boston: Little, Brown, 1971), p. 174.
19. Owen, op. cit., pp. 16–18.
20. James Blaine Walker, *Fifty Years of Rapid Transit* (New York: The Law Printing Co., 1918), p. 2.
21. Ibid., p. 1.
22. George W. Hilton, "Rail Transit and the Pattern of Modern Cities," *Traffic Quarterly,* 21 (July 1967), 379.
23. Ibid., p. 383.
24. Frank J. Kendrick, "Urban Transportation Policy: Politics, Planning, and People," *Policy Studies Journal,* 3 (Summer 1975), 376.
25. U.S. Bureau of the Census, *Current Population Reports,* Series P-23, No. 99, "The Journey to Work in the U.S." (Washington, D.C.: U.S. Government Printing Office, 1975), p. 4.
26. Lupo et al., op. cit., p. 201.
27. Ibid., p. 177.
28. *Congressional Quarterly* (January 27, 1979), 150.
29. U.S. Department of Housing and Urban Development, Office of Metropolitan Development, Urban Transportation Administration, *Tomorrow's Transportation—New Systems for the Urban Future* (Washington, D.C., 1968), p. 5.
30. U.S. Department of Transportation, *Seventh Annual Report, F.Y. 1973* (Washington, D.C.: U.S. Government Printing Office, 1974), p. 3; for a discussion of the physical environmental effects of the automobile, see Chapter 10.
31. *Urban Mass Transportation in Perspective* (New York: Tax Foundation, 1968), p. 17, cited by Hilton, *Federal Transit Subsidies,* op. cit., p. 3.
32. U.S. Department of Transportation, *National Transportation Trends and Choices: To the Year 2,000* (Washington, D.C., 1977), p. 85.
33. Lupo et al., op. cit., p. 178.
34. *The New York Times,* December 19, 1978, p. D22.
35. *The New York Times,* August 30, 1979, p. A9.
36. *Urban America—Policies and Problems* (Washington, D.C.: Congressional Quarterly, 1978), p. 67.

37. *The Transit Fact Book, 1974–1975* (Washington, D.C.: American Public Transit Association, 1975), pp. 16–17.
38. *Urban America—Policies and Problems,* op. cit., p. 80.
39. U.S. Congress, House, Committee on Public Works, *Urban Transportation: Dilemmas at a Time of Decision, Staff Report,* of the Subcommittee on Investigations and Review, 93rd Cong., 1st Sess., April 1973, p. 4.
40. Ibid.
41. *Transit Fact Book, 1974–1975,* op. cit., p. 16.
42. U.S. Congress, House, *Urban Transportation,* op. cit., p. 5.
43. Ibid.; Office of Technology Assessment, *An Assessment of Planning for Mass Transit: Chicago Case Study* (Washington D.C., 1976), p. 8.
44. *The Washington Post,* June 30, 1975, p. A4.
45. U.S. Department of Transportation, *Seventh Annual Report,* op. cit. pp. 1–4.
46. Council of State Governments and U.S. Department of Transportation, *State Transportation Issues of the Seventies—Conference Summary* (Baltimore, Md., Sept. 28–29, 1972), p. 2.
47. Ibid., p. 26.
48: Ibid., p. 15.
49. Advisory Commission on Intergovernmental Relations, *Intergovernmental Responsibilities for Mass Transportation Facilities and Services in Metropolitan Areas* (Washington, D.C., April 1961), p. 5.
50. See the previous discussion on pp. 254–55.
51. *New York Times,* March 20, 1961, p. 24, cited in Levin and Abend, op. cit., p. 42.
52. Levin and Abend, ibid., pp. 44–45.
53. Public Law 87-866.
54. Hilton, op. cit., 6.
55. Net cost was considered to be the portion of project cost which could not be financed from transit operation revenues.
56. Public Law 88-365.
57. U.S. Congress, Senate, Committee on Banking and Currency, *Mass Transportation—1969, Hearings,* before the Subcommittee on Housing and Urban Affairs on S. 676, S. 1032, S. 2656, S. 2821, S. 3154, 91st Cong., 1st Sess., Oct. 1969, p. 358.
58. Public Law 91-453.
59. *1978 Congressional Quarterly Almanac* (Washington, D.C.: 1979), p. 541.
60. *The Washington Post,* June 30, 1975, p. A4.
61. Levin and Abend, op. cit., p. 35.
62. U.S. Department of Transportation, Federal Highway Administration, *The 1973 Federal Aid Highway Act, An Analysis* (Washington, D.C., n.d.), p. 4.
63. Ibid., pp. 4–5.
64. *Congressional Quarterly Almanac, 1978,* op. cit., p. 541.
65. Ibid., p. 3.
66. Public Law 93-503.
67. *1978 Congressional Quarterly Almanac,* op. cit., pp. 536–37.
68. Ibid., p. 541.
69. This section relies heavily upon the presentation of K. H. Schaeffer and Eliot Sclar, *Access for All* (Baltimore, Md.: Penguin Books, 1975), pp. 90–97.
70. "Transportation," in *National Municipal Policy* (Washington, D.C.: National League of Cities, 1973).

10

Environmental Interdependence and National-Urban Policy Linkages

INTRODUCTION

In order to understand the effects of pollutants on marine ecosystems, one needs to understand how pollutants are dispersed and concentrated. The dispersal of wastes depends on the materials involved. Most wastes, but far from them all, sink to the bottom. Others, such as solid waste, oil, and garbage, contain many floatable materials. Floating wastes can be transported great distances by current and wind. Early in 1970, the Heyerdahl expedition encountered wastes over large areas of water in mid-ocean, reporting that the ocean "was visibly polluted by human activity."[1]

It is evident from this observation that pollution generated by one area may have environmental impact upon other regions. This is just as true of air pollution as of water pollution. A jurisdiction cannot pollute its air without affecting the air of other jurisdictions. As a result of the obvious environmental interdependence of localities, local environmental planning cannot possibly respond to the impact of environmental forces on communities. Clearly, then, the need for linkages between levels of governmental jurisdictions is especially evident when we discuss the physical environment within the urban context.

But why is the environment being discussed in a book dealing with urban policy? Increasingly, the population, the production, and the affluence of our society is being channeled into urban areas. Some observers of environmental policy have argued that the interaction of these three factors causes the pollution that is destroying our environment.[2] It is also becoming more evident that both heavy production and heavy consumption are concentrating in urban America.[3] Growing affluence for many Americans has led to increased demand for goods and services and consequently to increased waste from production and consumption. The problem of waste is particularly serious in urban areas where a heavy concentration of waste producers has resulted in high levels of environmental pollution.[4] These conditions have led Lewis Moncrief to observe:

> With increasing population, increasing production, increasing urban concentrations, and increasing real median incomes for well over one hundred years, it is not surprising that our environment has taken a terrible beating in absorbing our filth and refuse.[5]

Although pollution as an urban problem is being stressed, to assume that all pollution and all resource depletion can be blamed on urban populations would be inaccurate. Water pollution, for example, is a rural as well as an urban problem. Conservation and purification must be both rural and urban concerns. However, the problem is most visible in urban areas where industrial wastes and municipal sewage are significant pollutants and the results affect numerous people.[6]

Thus far it has been implied that any rational policies for maintaining a healthy environment must be developed and enforced someplace other than in local jurisdictions, though implementation may ultimately be local. It has been noted also that urban areas tend to be impacted heavily by contemporary environmental pollution. As history provides perspective, we will discuss the evolution of contemporary American environmental concerns from the conservation movement of the late nineteenth century to the present. The conditions leading to our present concerns with air and water will be considered, along with the governmental responses to the environmental dilemmas of the last quarter of the twentieth century. This chapter will focus on national responses to the problems of environmental pollution as they relate to local and regional contamination of the environment. The reason for this focus is that the response from state and local governments as well as from the private sector to environmental policy development has been very limited, in contrast to the strong local traditions in such policy areas as public safety, education, welfare, and transportation and the dominance of the private sector in the housing and health policy areas. Also, contemporary awareness of the problems associated with the depletion of our environmental resources has occurred at a time in American history when national responses via legislation, funding, and administrative actions are more forthcoming than they were one hundred or even twenty-five years ago. Finally the problems associated with environmental pollution provide an excellent case study of national-urban policy *linkages* in an advanced technological society.

The Historical Perspective

At the turn of the twentieth century, conservationists addressed themselves to questions of environmental control largely in terms of quantity rather than quality of resources. They saw resources as both limited and precious and perceived that an unrestrained free market economy was not likely to preserve natural areas. They encouraged the government to protect public interests as well as strictly private interests. In addition, the conservationists sought to maintain natural resources through multiple use techniques.[7] In this latter sense, the conservationists must be distinguished from the preservationists of the same era who were more concerned with the aesthetic and religious qualities of natural resources than with their availability for many uses. Groups such as the Audubon Societies, the Sierra Club, and the Wilderness Society are part of the legacy of the conservation movement—along with the National Park Service, wildlife refuges, and state and local parks.[8]

During the second half of the twentieth century, some resurgence of environmentalism has been evident in American society. The contemporary environmentalists view the state of the environment as a "crisis" and have sought increased government intervention in pollution control. There has been a growing awareness during the past two decades that not only is resource development important, but so too is the quality of the environment. There are at least three reasons why the current concerns with the environment surfaced when they did: (1) Awareness of air pollution became more widespread since people could see it and they were breathing it; awareness of water pollution increased since people could taste it, and fishing was affected by it. (2) With the increased affluence of the second half of the twentieth century, more people have had more leisure time; they have the time to be concerned with the quality as well as the quantity of life. Leisure time also began to afford people the opportunity to consider (and utilize more fully) natural settings. (3) With the rapid urbanization of America and its concomitant population and industrial concentration the problem of pollution has become more severe.[9]

The Conservationists

Since the intellectual roots of the contemporary environmental movement can be traced to the conservation movement of the late nineteenth
and early twentieth centuries, it is interesting to gain some insight into
the perspectives of these early precursors of today's environmentalists.
An interesting statement on the emergence of the early environmental
movement was provided by John Rodman when he wrote:

> Infinite space had been crossed and was being settled; the Indians, the wild
> beasts, and the wilderness had been extirpated or caged up; the "develop-
> ment" of the new western lands was inhibited by lack of water; whole spe-
> cies such as the passenger pigeon, the buffalo, and the beaver were dead or
> thought to be dying; it was possible to envisage a day when the cornucopia
> of natural resources might run low. . . . The environmental movement . . .
> was born the way it is perenially born anew—out of anxiety produced by
> projecting certain trends, such as current rates of resource depletion and
> extermination of species, into the future.[10]

The conservation movement was not a grass-roots populist movement.
It was a scientific movement, with leadership stemming from professionals in scientific fields such as hydrology, forestry, agrostology, geol-
ogy, and anthropology. In fact, to understand the historic role of the
conservation movement, it is important to understand that the conservation movement was a national planning movement to promote the efficient development and use of natural resources. It was applied science
and not the principle of democratic protest that drew scientists from
their specific resource tasks to environmental concerns and from specific
programs to comprehensive concepts.[11] It must also not be overlooked
that the conservation movement of this early period was in reality part
of a policy trinity of "conservation, development, and use of natural
resources." [12]

The use of water, a subject to which the contemporary environmental
movement directs much of its attention, was a topic investigated by the
hydrographers of the late nineteenth-century U.S. Geological Survey. In
fact, the term *conservation* itself stemmed from the movement for multipurpose river development. The movement urged that reservoirs be constructed to conserve the spring flood waters for use during the dry sea-
son. The Geological Survey also focused its concern on the sediment
content and mineral quality of water as well as water power, irrigation,
and drainage use. Another aspect of the conservation movement was
represented by the movement to preserve national forest lands. Western
irrigators were predominant in urging a federal forestry program.
Throughout the 1890s, western irrigators petitioned, sometimes successfully, that the President establish national forests as watersheds.[13] They
argued that forests serve numerous interdependent functions. More specifically, forests absorb water, retard stream runoff, and increase the
ground water level. Also, because forests tend to slow down the spring

melting of snow, they help to prevent flooding and thus to save water for summer use. Finally, forests slow down soil erosion and silting in reservoirs and irrigation ditches. A balance between industrial and commercial use of federal reserves and conservation was established under the authority of the Forest Management Act of 1897 which gave the U.S. Secretary of the Interior authority "to regulate the occupancy and use" of federal reserves.[14] Such "balanced use" was the policy followed by Gifford Pinchot upon becoming Chief of the Division of Forestry in 1898 (and later of the Bureau of Forestry in 1900).

An early act of President Theodore Roosevelt, the American president most often associated with the conservation movement of this era, shared the environmentalist's concern with water usage. In 1907, Roosevelt appointed an Inland Waterways Commission that included Gifford Pinchot of the Forest Service, Frederick H. Newell of the Reclamation Service, Brigadier-General Alexander MacKenzie of the U.S. Corps of Engineers, and Lawrence O. Murray of the Department of Commerce and Labor, as well as congressional leaders and other federal administrative officials. The Commission's recommendations included environmental concerns and they advocated the multipurpose use of water. The Commission recommended that

> plans for the improvement of navigation on inland waterways . . . should take account of *the purification of the waters,* the development of power, the control of floods, the reclamation of lands by irrigation and drainage, and all other uses of the waters or benefits to be derived from their control.[15]

After the administration of Theodore Roosevelt, the momentum of the conservation movement in affecting public policy decisions diminished. Resource users ranging from Western cattlemen, mineral and oil developers, and foresters gained influence. Resource exploitation was no longer balanced by attempts to conserve resources. In fact, throughout the years of our nation's growth and development, the exploitation of resources had been accepted as a positive value not only by corporate leaders, but by a large cross-section of Americans. The significance of the conservation movement was, in the words of Samuel Hays, its thrust to transform

> a decentralized, non-technical, loosely organized society, where waste and inefficiency ran rampant, into a highly organized, technical, and centrally planned and directed social organization which could meet a complex world with efficiency and purpose.[16]

The antipollution concerns of contemporary environmentalists reflect a similar concern with social control via interjurisdictional linkages over the undesirable private and local municipal activities that result in high social costs for current and future generations of Americans.

The Contemporary Environmentalists

Although we tend to think of air and water pollution as contemporary problems related to the technology of the twentieth century, they existed long before that. Los Angeles, for example, had a smog problem as early as 1542. At that time Juan Rodriguez Cabrillo experienced a thermal inversion that trapped the smoke from the fires made by the Indians in the valley leading to the San Pedro Bay. Thus, even prior to the extensive industrialization of the Los Angeles area with its massive network of freeways and huge numbers of automobiles and trucks spewing forth their emissions, the area's clean air supply was limited by the mountains, the nature of the air currents, and the high quantity of ozone in the air.[17]

Contemporary pollution problems are, however, due in large measure to industrial society and the relative affluence of our increasing population. In the year before we entered World War II, R. Buckminster Fuller suggested that the total energy generated in the United States was equal to the muscular energy that would be generated if 153 slaves worked for every American. (A similar calculation for the present time would indicate the need for 500 slaves working for every American man, woman, and child.) We use massive quantities of energy, which in turn generate large quantities of waste products. As one observer has noted:

> If ten billion mere people, sans technological nimbus, inhabited the U.S., they could not create more congestion, blight and confusion. The three million high-technology U.S. farmers put more adverse pressure on their land and rivers than the hundred and fifty million low-productivity peasant families of China put upon their land and rivers.[18]

Since Americans as a people enjoy the affluence related to our technological advances, they must find some way to cope with its side effects. Voluntary actions by industrial pollutors[19] can only bring some relief to the environment. Encouraging industrial polluters to control their processes is necessary but not enough to protect our resources. Since the environment is a complicated interrelated system, a fragmented contemporary society with all its disparate functions and political jurisdictions is not sufficient to meet demands for maintaining environmental balance. Interdependence of various jurisdictions in policy formulation and implementation is necessary.

The impact of unplanned development, which is felt most intensely in densely populated urban areas, was aptly stated in 1963 by then Secretary of the Interior Stewart L. Udall:

> We can produce a wide range of goods and machines, but our manipulations have multiplied waste products that befoul the land, and have introduced frightening new forms of erosion that diminish the quality of indispensable resources and even imperil human health. The hazards appear on every hand; many new machines and processes corrupt the very air and water; ... an indiscriminate use of pesticides threatens both man and wildlife; and the omnipresent symbol of the age, the auto, in satisfying our incessant demand for greater mobility, has added to the congestion and unpleasantness of both cities and countrysides. .... At the same time that our requirements for fresh water were doubling, our national sloth more than doubled

our water pollution. We now are faced with the need to build 10,000 treatment plants and to spend $6,000,000,000 to conserve water supplies.[20]

Given the realities of resource depletion and pollution being generated by our modern industrial society, groups have developed in the past two decades to demand some changes. Organizations such as the Sierra Club, the Wilderness Society, the Audubon Societies, and Friends of the Earth first made Americans conscious of the problems of environmental deterioration. Over time other organizations have taken up the hue and cry for environmental protection. It might be noted that, when the environment first became a *major* issue in the early 1970s, many supporters of improved social welfare benefits for the poor claimed that the change in focus was an attempt to deflect interest away from the poor onto a *safe* issue; they claimed that air and water pollution abatement was a middle class issue. Some of this same concern was apparent nine years after the first Earth Day, an environmental movement "happening," in 1970. At a conference held in April 1979, cosponsored by the Sierra Club and the National Urban League, it was reported that some organizations representing city blacks made "heavy-handed demands" that they insisted the environmentalists accept as a condition for intergroup cooperation. In particular, they demanded the unstinting support by the environmentalists for the entire black-liberal-labor program of government reform including guaranteed jobs for all employment seekers. This precondition for coalition was presented despite the political infeasibility of its passage by Congress.[21]

The environmental movement of the 1970s brought environmental problems to the attention of many Americans who were previously not aware of resource depletion and environmental deterioration. Once concern was widespread, it was possible to pass more extensive environmental protection legislation than had existed to date.[22] Even before the environmental movement was in vogue, some environmental protection legislation was enacted by localities, states, and the national government, but this legislation was not adequate to deal with environmental problems. Such legislation developed no meaningful interjurisdictional connections to deal with environmental pollution and ultimate deterioration. In the urban context, we lacked the necessary national-urban policy linkages that would have reflected more closely some of the environmental interdependencies of our ecosystem.

The Extent of the Contemporary Problem

In early 1969, there was a massive oil spill in the harbor of Santa Barbara, California. This accident made the entire nation aware of how just such an accident could produce a temporary blight over a large area. Since then, environmental issues such as the blight of Lake Erie, Texas's polluted beaches, smog in mile-high Denver, lead in gasoline, and phosphates in detergents have made us realize that environmental problems are everywhere and that they affect everyone.[23]

Control Over Air and Water Pollution

Air and water are vital elements in the balance of nature. Poor quality air has been related to respiratory diseases and the corrosion of metal and textile fabrics. Poor quality water has been related to human diseases and to the death and contamination of fish and other sea life. Air and water pollution are related to the normal activities of modern urban areas. For instance, the steel industry, in areas such as Gary, Indiana; Pittsburgh, Pennsylvania; Baltimore, Maryland; and Birmingham, Alabama is a major water polluter. One study has observed:

> The steel industry [uses] upward of four trillion gallons of . . . [water] a year. Steel makers need water to cool and condense hot metal . . . and to "scrub" bases before using them for fuel. They also blast finished sheets of steel with a high-velocity water spray to knock off the waste scale clinging to the steel surface. The average steel plant produces one million ingot tons of steel each year. For each ingot a plant puts out, it also generates 125 pounds of suspended solids, 2.7 pounds of lubrication oils, 3.5 pounds of free acids (like sulfuric acid), 12.3 pounds of combined acids (like metal sulfates), eight ounces of emulsions, and between one and two ounces of such poisons as phenol, fluoride, ammonia and cyanide. Each ingot ton produced raises the temperature of the water used for cooling by $10°$.[24]

A report issued by the National Commission on Water Quality notes that, particularly in smaller cities where urban sewage runoff is not a severe pollutant, industrial wastes dominate pollution in terms of quality and toxic effect on the environment. The report suggests this generalization is true of water pollution in areas as geographically apart as the Kanawha River near Charleston, West Virginia, and the northern portions of Puget Sound in Washington.[25]

Water pollution may affect both the quantity and safety of the food supply available to meet the needs of an urban population. In August 1975, New York State officials warned that striped bass in the Hudson River and salmon from Lake Ontario were found to have unacceptable levels of polychlorinated biphenyl (PCB), a cancer-inducing chemical. An even more extreme example of the deleterious effects of pollution on the food supply was the closing of Lake Michigan as a commercial fishery due to the presence of PCB. Moreover, once such pollution occurs, it is not easily reversible. In August 1975, a spokesperson for the Wisconsin Department of Natural Resources observed: "We had hoped that the PCB would biodegrade but it has not yet happened." [26]

Air pollution also affects the liveability of urban areas. Air pollutants are discharged by automobiles and trucks, electrical generating plants, and industry. The sources of air pollution composition can be seen in

Table 1 / STATIONARY SOURCES OF VOLATILE ORGANIC COMPOUNDS, AUGUST 1978

(thousand metric tons per year)

Source category	Nationwide emissions*
Petroleum refinery fugitive emissions (leaks)	150
Surface coating of miscellaneous metal parts and products	200
Vegetable oil processing	70
Factory surface coating of flatwood paneling	50
Large appliance manufacture	35
Magnet wire insulation	10
Gasoline bulk plants	150
Metal furniture manufacture	100
Petroleum liquid storage, fixed roof tanks	700
Degreasing	700
Bulk gasoline terminals	250
Petroleum refinery vacuum systems, waste water separators and process unit turn-arounds	700
Cutback asphalt paving	700
Surface coating of automobiles, cans, metal coils, paper, and fabric products	900
Service stations, Stage I	400
Pharmaceutical manufacture	50
Rubber products manufacture	150
Graphic arts (printing)	400
Service stations, Stage II	500
Petroleum liquid storage, floating roof tanks	150
Organic chemical manufacture	
Process streams	450
Fugitive (leaks)	600
Dry cleaning	250
Architectural and miscellaneous coatings	300
Ship and barge transport of gasoline and crude oil	60
Wood furniture manufacture	200
Organic chemical manufacture	
Waste disposal	150
Storage and handling	300
Natural gas and crude oil production	200
Natural gas and natural gasoline plants	150
Adhesives	200
Other industrial surface coatings	300
Auto refinishing	150
Other solvent usage	3,000

Table 1 / *Continued*

Source category	Nationwide emissions*
Metals manufacture	
Other manufacturing	
Fuel combustion	4,000
Forest, agricultural, and other open burning	
Solid waste disposal	
Total stationary sources	16,700,000
Total transportation sources	10,600,000

Source: U.S. Environmental Protection Agency, Office of Air Quality Planning and Standards (Washington, D.C., 1979).

* Developed by EPA from national production and consumption information using average emission factors. The technique necessarily requires assumptions that cannot be confirmed in every case. EPA anticipates that the figures will change as better information is developed and generalized categories such as "other solvent usage" are more clearly defined.

Table 1. Urban air polluters include a wide variety of public and private producers and service deliverers. One of the major culprits is the electric power industry. For example, in the early 1970s, Chicago's Consolidated Edison plants emitted about 420,000 tons of sulfur oxide each year. In addition, automobile exhaust is responsible for billions of pounds of contaminants being poured into the atmosphere every year. Carbon monoxide emissions (mostly attributable to automobile exhausts) had reached a high of 81.3 million tons per year in 1973; they had dropped to 69.7 million tons in 1976[27]—a still not insubstantial quantity. Such automobile pollution is a major factor in the dangerously high smog levels found in Los Angeles, New York City, and other major urban centers. In fact, despite the marked overall decline reported in carbon monoxide emissions between 1973 and 1976, Los Angeles showed a small upward trend in the amount of carbon monoxide in its air.[28] Heavy industry also contributes heavily to air pollution. Air pollution is found around large cities generally; it is a particular characteristic of the urban centers of the Great Lakes Region. Leading industrial air polluters are petroleum refineries, as well as smelters, iron foundries, pulp and paper mills, and coal cleaning and refuse plants.

The Pollutant Standards Index (PSI) makes it possible to report pollution levels on a uniform basis all over the nation. This uniform reporting mechanism is required by the federal Clean Air Act Amendments of 1977. (See p. 288 for discussion of this law). The PSI is an indicator of daily maximum pollution levels. The figure will be over 100 when any of the five criteria pollutants (particulates, sulfur oxides, nitrogen oxides, hydrocarbons and carbon monoxide) reaches an unhealthy level (see Table 2). Thus in 1975 and 1976, Los Angeles, Denver, Cleveland, and St. Louis all had PSI values of over 100 for more than half of the year. The EPA re-

Table 2 / SUMMARY OF NATIONAL EMISSION ESTIMATES
(millions of tons a year)

Year	Particulates	Sulfur oxides	Nitrogen oxides	Hydrocarbons	Carbon monoxide
1970	26.8	34.2	22.7	33.9	113.7
1971	24.9	32.3	23.4	33.3	113.7
1972	23.4	36.7	24.6	34.1	115.8
1973	21.9	35.6	25.7	34.0	111.5
1974	20.3	34.1	25.0	32.9	103.3
1975	18.0	32.9	24.2	30.9	96.2

Source: Environmental Protection Agency, *Trends in the Quality of the Nation's Air* (Washington, D.C., March, 1977), p. 15.

ported the PSI for forty-three large cities for 1975 and found that all of these cities had unhealthful PSIs for at least twenty-seven days that year.[29]

Control of air and water pollution involves additional expense to manufacturers and consumers. Furthermore, it involves cooperation by industry and various levels of government. While urban pollution affects localities, an end to urban pollution requires federal policy intervention since open space is limited and our generation of solid waste, as well as our chemical poisoning of the environment and our depletion of resources is not geographically bounded. Our environmental problems are systemic; they are distributed throughout the whole national (and international) ecosystem as a result of population growth, technology, science, industry, and economic forces. The problems of halting environmental destruction cannot be left to private institutions. Not even regional areas acting alone can cope with environmental interactions and interdependencies. Thus, even the corporate leaders who view the federal government's intervention in environmental protection with mixed feelings accept the necessity and inevitability of government leadership and initiatives in environmental protection policy.[30]

Waste Disposal

Contemporary technological society is geared ultimately to the generation of garbage. Despite the levels of technology that have been developed in the United States, all we know about what to do with garbage is to throw it away. In a society based upon *growth*, the amount of garbage produced has multiplied immensely. Thus, the amount of waste products has increased substantially over the years. Our "throw away" society is running out of places to "throw it away." We are running out of places to hide our garbage, the end products of our technology.

Garbage disposal is primarily a local public function or a privately franchised function in the United States. There are five basic methods used to pick up garbage: (1) municipal collection and treatment and disposal;

(2) special district collection, treatment, and disposal; (3) regional collection, treatment, and disposal; (4) contracts with private industry for collection, treatment, and disposal; and (5) local collection and regional district treatment and disposal.[31] Garbage hauled away from homes and businesses is often burned—a process that then serves to pollute the atmosphere. Some wastes are treated and then hauled out to sea or into inland waterways which then pollutes the water and causes problems of sludge movement in tidal waters. Some treated waste has also been used as the basis for landfills. In all the methods just described, the wastes of our society remain within the environment—whether solid, liquid or gaseous—often acting as environmental pollutants.[32]

Municipal waste often takes the form of sewage sludge. Sewage sludge is the waste solid by-product of municipal waste-water treatment processes. Most sludge is incinerated or is used as sanitary landfill. Significant amounts are dumped at sea. New York dumps sludge; Los Angeles discharges sludge by pipelines into the sea. Since sludge is the residual product of waste-water treatment, it contains all the domestic and industrial contaminants that have entered the system.[33] In fact, the EPA estimates that by 1990 we will be dumping 10 million dry tons of sludge a year—15 percent of which will go into the sea.[34] This method of waste disposal is utilized despite the fact that burning such municipal wastes from larger American urban areas could generate energy equal to as much as 400,000 barrels of oil per day—about one-third of the Alaskan pipeline projected flow—"enough to provide lights for all of our nation's homes and commercial buildings." [35]

An alternative to the generation of waste products is the recycling of resources. Metal reused for tin cans and returnable glass bottles does not add to society's accumulating garbage. Neither does the process of turning organic waste material into fertilizer produce environmental damage. However, some modification of such a general statement about the benefits of recycling is in order. The EPA determined that PCBs have been found in Chicago's sludge. Also this sludge was found to have high levels of cadmium—a heavy metal that can cause kidney disease and possibly cancer. This might not have been too serious a problem were it not for the fact that the Metropolitan Sanitary District of Greater Chicago recycles most of its sludge.[36] In 1977, about 614 dry tons a day was distributed for reuse. This represented 71 percent of the total. Since sludge has high levels of valuable plant nutrients, such as nitrogen and phosphorus, it is often used as plant fertilizer. However, when such sludge is used to produce certain types of crops, its PCBs and cadmium can be taken in by parts of the plants and then passed along to humans when they eat the plants.

The mandatory deposit law enacted in 1972 by the Oregon State Legislature represents another attempt to recycle resources. This law was the first legislation of its kind in any state. The law requires a minimum refund of five cents on all cans and noncertified bottles for soft drinks and beer. (Certified containers are those that can be reused by more than one manufacturer and they require a minimum two cents deposit.) The bill also outlawed flip-top or pull-tab containers for beer and soft drinks. As of 1979, five other states also had bottle deposit laws. Vermont, Maine, Michigan, Iowa, and Connecticut all had such laws though the provisions varied from state to state.[37] These laws are significant since beverage containers represent approximately 19.7 percent of highway litter by item and 54 to 70 percent of highway litter by volume. Beverage containers comprise 21 percent of all packaging wastes, as well as 8 percent of the waste produced by households, institutions, and business and commercial establishments.[38] Other attempts to change from a "throw away" to a recycling society have been tried. For example, in El Cajon, California, the Environmental Protection Agency (EPA) and private industry cooperated in the development of a large-scale recycling plant that they expect will be able to profitably convert trash and garbage into fuel oil to help meet energy needs.[39]

Another kind of waste disposal problem has arisen in the past several decades as the extent of nuclear and other toxic wastes have become apparent. Thus in 1976 when Congress passed the Resource Conservation and Recovery Act,[40] a section of the bill was devoted to regulation of hazardous waste materials. What was not considered by the legislation was the residue of industrial wastes that had been disposed of previously, often in unplanned and haphazard fashion in a variety of sites throughout the United States. Several incidents involving toxic wastes have surfaced since the enactment of the 1976 legislation. Perhaps one of the most dramatic occurrences took place at the Love Canal in Niagara Falls, New York, in February 1979. Between 1942 and 1947, a partially excavated canal in Niagara Falls, New York, was used as a chemical dump by the Hooker Chemical Company. During a five-year period, they deposited 22,000 tons of toxic wastes in steel drums in the canal bed and covered them with clay. Some thirty years later—after housing subdivisions and a school had been built on an adjacent site—it was found that water mixed with chemical wastes had been seeping out of the canal and into the basements of nearby homes. Furthermore, it was determined that abnormally high rates of miscarriages, birth defects, and underweight children had been reported in the area.[41] Over 230 families were permanently evacuated from their homes and another 100 families were advised to leave their homes. Problems relating to nuclear fallout and waste also have become worrisome—especially since a potentially serious accident in 1979 at the Three Mile Island Nuclear Plant near Harrisburg, Pennsylvania.

The Development of a National Urban Environmental Protection Policy

Although there were some federal responses to the problems of resource depletion during Theodore Roosevelt's administration, they did not include the development of any pollution control program. In fact, the earliest—albeit limited—federal response to the problems associated with pollution came during the administration of William Howard Taft. In 1912, the Bureau of Mines developed an interest in smoke prevention. Though an Office of Air Pollution was developed in the Bureau of Mines, most efforts to identify and control sources of smoke were made by local jurisdictions. In fact, it was not until 1950 that the first national technical conference on air pollution was convened, at the request of President Harry S. Truman. The first national legislation dealing with environmental pollution was not enacted until 1955. This legislation remained the basic federal air pollution statute until the Clean Air Act was passed in 1963. The 1955 law declared that it is

> the policy of Congress to preserve and protect the primary responsibilities and rights of the States and local governments in controlling air pollution, to support and aid technical research, to devise and develop methods of abating such pollution, and to provide Federal technical services and financial aid to state and local government air pollution control agencies and other public or private agencies and institutions in the formulation and execution of their air pollution abatement research programs.[42]

The law also allocated $5 million a year for research, training, and demonstration projects as well as for grants-in-aid to state and local government agencies and other public and private air pollution agencies. It also provided for research to be done by the U.S. Public Health Service.

It is apparent from this legislative statement that urban areas with serious pollution problems had not yet started to solve the problems themselves; the purpose of the legislation was only to "nudge" the states and localities into developing air pollution abatement programs and to provide the federal government some limited means to encourage this effort.[43] The legislation was supported by many mayors and governors who found it difficult to develop stringent antipollution programs, given the exigencies of retaining their industrial tax base and the antipollution pressures of industry. (Thus the slogan of the industry-dominated Midwestern Air Pollution Control Association was "Air Pollution Control is a Local Concern.")[44]

Throughout the process leading to the ultimate passage of the bill, conflict centered on the appropriate role of the federal government in enforcing environmental protection legislation. The result of this concern was that the enacted legislation was couched in the language of state and local responsibility. Clearly, there was little acceptance of the need for interjurisdictional policy linkages or the use of coordinated funding and administrative effort to meet the interrelated problems causing pollution in the nation's thousands of separate political jurisdictions.

The 1963 Clean Air Act modified the state and local focus of the 1955 law and included an urban focus that was not part of the earlier legislation. As the law was finally approved, the federal government was granted greater enforcement powers than it had had under the 1955 law in the area of air pollution, but the standards it was to enforce were to be developed by state and local jurisdictions *not* the national government. There was, however, an increasing awareness that an enforcement mechanism at some governmental level was essential for the law to have any significant effect in curtailing air pollution.[45] To facilitate an environmental effort, a federal grant-in-aid program was established with a spending level of $95 million. Intrastate enforcement powers for the implementation of regional programs were granted the governors, but the governors had to request approval from the Secretary of Health, Education, and Welfare to take action, thus providing for some federal oversight.

Governmental actions to control the effects of pollutants on water were also largely local until the 1960s. Local jurisdictions that have unpalatable or unsafe water have traditionally installed local treatment plants to make water usable. But often the local jurisdictions that suffer from polluted water supplies are not themselves the offenders. Other communities further upstream and industries over whom the threatened community has no jurisdiction sometimes dump untreated or poorly treated waste into nearby waterways. It is to be expected, then, that citizens whose poor water is beyond their control will support the development of pollution control authority above the level of local government.[46] The earliest comprehensive congressional action to fight water pollution was the Water Pollution Control Act of 1948. The underlying assumption of this law was that the abatement of water pollution was a state responsibility. The federal government was provided authority for investigations, surveys, and research; it left primary responsibility for pollution control with the states. Though amendments to the 1948 law, enacted in 1956, advocated a state-federal partnership in attacking water pollution, they left the responsibility for the setting and enforcement of water pollution standards almost totally to the states. (Supervision of the law in the federal bureaucracy was given to the Public Health Service— a low-status agency connected to HEW with only indirect access to the Secretary of the Department.) There was no provision in the law for the federal government either to establish water pollution standards or to force the states to do so. The federal government did not have any power in most cases dealing with water pollution to initiate abatement action unless requested to do so by a governor or other state authority. The 1956 amendments did provide federal financial support for waste treatment plants, and by 1966 $3.4 billion was authorized for municipal sewage plants for the period from 1968 to 1971. The 1956 amendments provided also that there could be federal regulation of waste discharge through enforcement actions against individual dischargers.

By the early 1960s, it was clear to many observers of environmental politics that the states were not taking the necessary steps to help abate pollution and that federal enforcement procedures were, in fact, not at all adequate. After substantial maneuvering, Congress enacted a series of amendments to the 1956 law. These amendments are known collectively as the 1965 Water Quality Act. The major thrust of this bill was to encourage the states by providing $150 million annually for multicommunity and large construction programs and to pursue stronger measures against water pollution by granting the federal government new powers to hasten state activities. Administratively, it provided for the development of a federal Water Pollution Control Agency within HEW under the supervision of an assistant secretary. This gave water pollution control more status than it had had under the jurisdiction of the Public Health Service.[47] The major provisions of the law provided that (1) the states set water quality standards defining levels of permissible pollution for waterways within their jurisdictions, (2) the states provide implementation plans to go along with the standards, and (3) a federal enforcement procedure for violation of standards on interstate waterways occur within 180 days. A significant problem with this legislation was that it was applicable only to a small number of waterways. Of the 26,000 navigable waterways in this nation, only 4,000 are interstate and thus the federal government's 180-day enforcement procedure was restricted.[48]

The Clean Air Act of 1970 and the 1974 and 1977 Amendments

Until national emission standards were set for motor vehicles in 1965, the federal role in controlling the quality of the air was limited. Where states specifically requested help from the federal government, a federal role was possible. However, the responsibility for enforcing air pollution control standards belonged to the states. As the states and their subdivisions began to find it increasingly difficult to enforce their own air pollution standards, pressure was brought to bear on the federal government to intervene to the exclusion of the state governments.[49] The first federal preemption of state regulations occurred in 1965 when national emission standards were set for motor vehicles; they were defined as interstate pollution sources and thus the responsibility of the federal government. In 1967 and 1970, new federal laws that were enacted began to extend federal regulation beyond the concept of "mobile polluters." The 1967 Air Quality Act included the establishment of interstate air quality regions, thus recognizing that many of the air pollution problems do not stop at state boundaries and that air pollution abatement sometimes requires regional abatement plans. In 1975, there were 180 city-county or joint local air pollution agencies operating in the United States; by 1977, 57 percent of counties with populations of over 250,000 conducted air pollution control efforts.[50] In fact, joint local programs as well as multicounty programs had become increasingly popular in the 1970s.[51]

There were some regional attempts to control pollution even before the enactment of federal legislation. For example, the Los Angeles County Air Pollution Control District (LACAPCD) adopted a rule back in 1948 that any industry setting up equipment that emits air pollutants must first get authority from the LACAPCD to install the equipment and then must have a permit to operate the equipment. Seven thousand kinds of devices have been installed by industries in Los Angeles County to control air pollution. In 1957, the Los Angeles County Board of Supervisors banned the burning of fuel oils in industry for several months of the year. By 1975, a rule was in effect for that county requiring the burning of natural gas from April 15 to November 15 and at other times when the supplies of natural gas are available.[52] These observations on Los Angeles County should not be taken to mean that Los Angeles County has beaten the air pollution problem. Clearly it has not!

The Clean Air Act of 1970 was particularly significant since it led to an alteration in the focus of programming and regulation in the area of air pollution controls from the states to the national government. The Environmental Protection Agency (EPA), which was established in the summer of 1970 to oversee the administration and implementation of federal pollution legislation regarding water and air quality, solid waste disposal, radiation, and pesticide control, was charged with the federal administration of this law. In particular, whereas pre-1970 laws provided for the development of regional standards, the 1970 law produced some uniform national regulations including:

national ambient air quality standards; performance standards for new stationary sources; regulations for hazardous pollutants; emission standards for light motor vehicles, aircraft, and auto and aircraft fuels; and the requirement of Federal approval of State implementation deadlines.[53]

Except in the area of new motor vehicle controls—that is, fuel additives and hazardous pollutants—states were permitted to impose more stringent standards than those imposed by the federal government. (California was an exception to the stated limitation on states' rights since it had developed stricter motor vehicle controls than required by the federal government.) The 1974 Amendments to the Clean Air Act further restricted states' rights regarding pollution control. Thus, the 1974 amendments provide that the federal EPA and not the states will determine

when it is safe to burn coal; . . . will prescribe emission control measures to be taken to maintain primary ambient standards; will set up priorities in allocating continuous emission control equipment; [and] will review State implementation plans which must be amended to comply with the new regulations.[54]

A close examination of the 1974 law makes it apparent that the public role and especially the federal role in air quality control was growing and that there was greater federal financial support for programs to combat air pollution; federal funding levels for air pollution control were set at $500 million by fiscal 1977. The underlying philosophy of the Clean Air Act Amendments of 1974, as stated by the U.S. Environmental Protection Agency, provides a good statement of the changing focus (which was retained by the 1977 amendments) and a recognition of the obvious linkages that are necessary between government jurisdictions in order to have effective air pollution abatement:

1. The States are to be given the opportunity to design and implement the plan for achieving the environmental goals.
2. The federal government must take action when States do not adapt or carry out an adequate plan for achieving the goals.
3. Opportunity must be provided for public participation in the development of federal standards, State plans, and subsequent changes in such standards or plans. Furthermore, information must be made available to the public on State progress in carrying out the plan.[55]

Consistent with the EPA philosophy, the states were encouraged by EPA to submit regulations as replacements for EPA regulations. The EPA provided that states carry out their own control program, but it will take "corrective action" in cases where the states cannot or do not act to meet the standards of the Clean Air Act.[56]

In 1977, amendments to the 1970 law both modified and extended the Clean Air Act, though it did not "strike out on bold, new directions."[57] It delayed compliance for auto emission and city air quality standards and delayed the application of heavy fines for industrial polluters. The amendments also reduced discretionary authority and increased mandatory authority exercised by the EPA and the states in many air pollution control areas with respect to stationary source compliance.[58] Further, it provided for economic penalties to strengthen EPA's ability to enforce air pollution control standards.[59] More specifically, the 1977 amendments changed EPA policy in the following manner: (1) EPA and the states no longer can utilize primarily administrative order procedures to establish compliance schedules for major source violators, but they must to establish such schedules by judicial action (a procedure that limits EPA administrative discretion); (2) EPA was given new authority that enables it to seek civil penalties in civil actions as an incentive for compliance; and (3) EPA or a delegated state agency is now required to issue a notice of noncompliance to major polluters not in compliance with air pollution standards thirty days after a violation has been noted, and to establish a penalty if noncompliance continues.[60]

Even with the increased authority of national law, the states and the EPA have found it difficult to enforce compliance with clean air standards. The Comptroller General's Office has noted that of 19,973 major sources reported as being in full compliance with ambient air standards at the end of fiscal year 1977, 72 percent of these major sources were certified by the states on the basis of unverified information submitted by the sources.[61] The General Accounting Office further found that EPA's compliance monitoring classified many sources as in compliance that actually were in violation of state implementation plan requirements.[62] Furthermore, the small percentage of sources that are found not in compliance are often responsible for a major proportion of emissions of sulfur dioxide, hydrocarbons, and nitrogen oxides.[63]

The Water Pollution Act of 1972 and the Clean Water Act of 1977

The frustration of individuals charged with enforcing the state- and locally-focused Water Quality Act of 1965 made it apparent that some mechanism was needed to enforce water pollution regulations. During the search for such a policy vehicle, a forgotten piece of late-nineteenth-century legislation was rediscovered and revitalized. This legislation, the Refuse Act of 1899, established a thrust for a stronger federal role. It provided that: "It shall not be lawful to throw, discharge or deposit . . . any refuse matter of any kind or description whatever . . . into any navigable water of the United States" without obtaining a permit from the Army Corp of Engineers. Violators were subject to civil and criminal actions and furthermore could be sued by various governmental units or by private persons in the event that public agencies did not act.[64] By late 1972, a permit system that had been established by the Nixon Administration led 18,000 industrial units responsible for about 90 percent of the pollutants discharged into national waterways to apply for permits.[65] Also, during 1970 and 1971, a number of federal and private suits were initiated against industrial polluters. For example, a private suit in the state of Washington resulted in an agreement by a Rayonier pulp processing plant to construct a $22 million waste treatment facility.

• PROVISIONS OF THE LAW

During this same period, some members of Congress became convinced that comprehensive water pollution abatement legislation was necessary. In 1972, Congress passed the Water Pollution Control Act, and in 1977, they amended this law by passing the Clean Water Act of 1977. The 1972 act called for a fundamentally new approach to water pollution control that greatly increased federal authority regarding water pollution abatement. The legislation abandoned the ineffective "standards and enforcement method" of water pollution control. It called for an end to tolerance of limited pollution. Furthermore, it gave the federal government greater enforcement powers. The act established a federally delegated regulatory program under which categorical federal grants-in-aid were to be made to municipal dischargers so that they could comply with regulated discharge conditions. In addition, a National Pollution Discharge Elimination System (NPDES) was established. Under this system, certain limitations on discharges into the nation's waters were established: (1) A permit is required by any entity, governmental or nongovernmental, that discharges wastes into the nation's waters. (2) Discharge of any pollutant in violation of established allowances is forbidden. (3) Permit authority may be delegated by the Environmental Protection Agency to the states. Under the act, by July 1977, municipal facility point discharges were expected to meet a regulatory standard of subjection to secondary treatment technology and nonmunicipal facility point discharges were to meet a regulatory standard of subjection to the "best practicable control technology currently available." The effect of this provision is that municipal waste control is subject to somewhat stricter regulations than nonmunicipal water waste. Subsequently, the Clean Water Act of 1977 provided the EPA with authority to extend the July 1977 compliance deadline until April 1979 for those noncomplying dischargers that had made commitments to secure resources necessary to meet treatment requirements.[66]

In some instances, private industrial interests have been able to exert sufficient influence on the decision makers at the EPA to have the quality control standards relaxed for them. Such a case occurred in March 1976, when the EPA issued new regulations limiting the pollutants that the iron and steel industries can dump in lakes and rivers. It granted an exemption to these rules to eight plants situated along the Mahoning River in Ohio. The plants that were granted the exemption were owned by United States Steel Corporation, Republic Steel Corporation, and the Youngstown Sheet and Tube Company (which has since announced its plans to go out of business). All these companies are major American steel producers. An EPA statement explaining its decision noted that the plants were old and economically marginal and that the application of the national standards "might result in severe economic and employment disruptions." An EPA study further indicated that the affected plants, when operating at peak capacity, provide 24,500 jobs. This represents 20 percent of the total payroll, and 15 percent of the total employment of the Youngstown-Warren-Niles area. The companies told the EPA that if they were forced to comply with EPA pollution standards, they would either have to shut down their plants or sharply curtail their production to meet the costs of pollution control. Thus, EPA Administrator Russell Train decided to provide an exemption.[67]

The 1972 legislation involved intergovernmental activity of a complex nature. Treatment of waste in this country has long been considered primarily a municipal, county, or special district function. Under the provisions of this legislation, water pollution control activities were to shift from their traditional state and local base to a national regulatory base; such a shift conceptually allows for state-by-state application of a uniform waste control and treatment infrastructure. The federal government provided considerable incentive for compliance. A total of $18 billion was authorized for 1973–1975 (which President Nixon impounded and which was later made available) for the construction of waste treatment plants with the federal government providing 75 percent of the cost of new facilities.[68] While the EPA administrator has the power to withhold NPDES authority to states, ordinarily the act mandates delegation of such authority to the states upon gubernatorial request. (The exception to this rule can occur if the EPA administrator determines that there is insufficient state authority for adequate implementation of the requirements of the act.) As of January 1978, water pollution control authority had been issued to thirty states.[69] The states with no state programs or insufficient state programs become in effect operating subdivisions of EPA because the act provides that an assessment by EPA of inadequate performance can result in direct federal administration of water pollution control authority.

The Clean Water Act of 1977, amended the Water Pollution Act of 1972.[70] The 1977 amendments "were shaped in part by what might be described as 'institutional forces.'" In other words, the states, the localities, and the business community were influential in shaping this law. On the other hand, the 1972 law was more heavily influenced by public interest groups. The 1972 law had defined the federal role as broad and in some areas preeminent. Implementation of the 1972 law therefore led to some conflicting interpretations of the division of responsibilities and authority between the federal and state agencies. The 1977 amendments defined more precisely the roles of the different levels of government. These amendments require the states to set priorities for funding of treatment facilities, though EPA has the right to require the states to revise their priority lists. Also, the federal government provides 2 percent of the project costs for the resultant state administrative overhead. In addition, the financial authorizations for construction grants were extended by the 1977 legislation; they were set at $5 billion a year through fiscal year 1982. Moreover, the 1977 amendments addressed more fully than the 1972 law the problems of smaller jurisdictions and rural areas; the 1972 law had been very much a heavily urban-focused piece of legislation. The 1977 law provides that for innovative and alternative projects (which are usually low cost projects) the EPA will provide 85 percent of the costs rather than the usual 75 percent. These projects tend to be developed in rural areas. Furthermore, whereas EPA requires three-stage project development—planning, design and rationale as to how a project meets needs, and construction—the 1977 amendments provide that for rural areas the first two steps can be merged and thus a two-stage procedure is now available for these nonurban areas.

A major difficulty with the 1972 law was the failure of the EPA to secure compliance with the legislation. In some instances the federal government itself failed to comply with the law where it applied to governmental facilities. As the Chairman of the Subcommittee on Water Resources of the Senate Committee on Environment and Public Works noted, "in many areas the prime violator of the environmental laws has been the federal government itself." (In other instances, industrial and municipal noncompliance with the 1972 law could be attributed to delays in federal funding.) With the 1977 amendments, Congress sought to deal with this problem of noncompliance or inadequate compliance with the

1972 law. The 1977 amendments provided for a new classification of pollutant types with different requirements specified for each pollutant category. One result of this law is a much greater emphasis being placed on the control of toxic pollutants. Finally, the 1977 legislation reflected a strong congressional interest in the development and use of new waste treatment technology. Thus recycling and reuse of pollution control by-products, energy conservation, and multiple use of waters and lands that are components of wastewater treatment systems are promoted (with federal financial incentives) by the law.

It has been difficult to adequately implement water pollution abatement legislation. A 1979 General Accounting Office study found "widespread and frequent noncompliance with permit conditions and frequent failure to submit industrial self-monitoring reports which could conceal additional violations." [71] Among the violations noted by EPA sampling inspections were "a permittee [that had] discharged 715 pounds of phenols—more than seven times the permit limit . . . [Another] . . . permittee [that had] discharged 234 pounds of cyanide—more than eleven times the 20 pound permit limit." [72] Compliance monitoring was found to lack effectiveness due to "the lack of uniform EPA criteria, on how permittees should be classified, insufficient evidence on the cumulative effect of minor industrial permittees [violations], inadequate sampling inspection coverage, and effective permits taking too long to become enforceable due to lengthy adjudicatory hearings." [73] Also regarding state implementation, the General Accounting Office noted that in some cases states were not aggressively seeking enforcement action against permit violators. It observed that in its review of ten state enforcement orders issued to industrial violators, five did not result in compliance and in those five cases, state-pursued enforcement action occurred in only one case.[74]

• CASES OF REGIONAL ENFORCEMENT

In the enforcement of the 1972 and 1977 amendments, the local unit of water pollution control often is broader than that of the municipality or county. For example, regional jurisdiction has been established in the Central Valley–San Francisco Bay area. Central Valley is an agricultural area drained by the Sacramento and San Joaquin Rivers, which discharge into San Francisco Bay. The Central Valley area drains waste produced by irrigated agriculture into the rivers; the South (San Francisco) Bay area has coliform problems related to sewage discharge; the North (San Francisco) Bay has experienced fishkills that raise suspicions regarding industrial and municipal effluent. California has sought to develop water pollution controls through the establishment of a system of state boards organized on an areawide and comprehensive basis. In the Seattle area, a number of industries and municipalities discharge wastes into Puget Sound. The area around Puget Sound has a population of over 2 million. Control of water waste disposed in the Seattle region comes under the authority of the Municipality of Metropolitan Seattle (METRO), a regional sewage agency. This agency played an important role in cleaning up Seattle's Lake Washington. The Galveston Bay–Houston Ship Channel water route adjoins three major cities, Houston, Texas City, and Galveston. Houston is a center of chemical, metal, and pulp and paper industries that discharge waste into the channel and the bay. Permit enforcement regarding waste discharges is strictly enforced by a state agency, the Texas Water Quality Board. Thus, it should be evident that areawide agencies have been established in response to the inability of local units to police water pollution problems that have regional ecological impacts and that require regional control.[75] Indeed, where a drainage basin contains more than one state, water pollution control requires interstate cooperation. In fact, there are areas where interstate agencies that have water pollution control functions have been formed. Among the largest of these agencies are the Delaware River Basin Commission, the Ohio River Sanitation Commission, and the New England Interstate Water Pollution Control Commission. The three listed agencies all set water quality standards and are actively engaged in surveillance and monitoring activities.

The Safe Drinking Water Act

In December 1974, Congress passed the Safe Drinking Water Act. This legislation provides for regulation of water systems that commonly use ground water. The act sets requirements for states for controlling materials injected underground and for protecting "sole source aquifers" that are used for supplies of drinking water.[76] Soon after the passage of this law, the Environmental Protection Agency initiated an eighty-city survey to determine the presence in drinking water of organic chemicals suspected of being carcinogens or of causing genetic damage. Included in this study was an examination of trihalomethanes (THMs), which come into being when raw water supplies are chlorinated. This study indicated that when there are high levels of THM present in drinking water the incidence of cancer in the population increases. This initial study was followed by a second study that sought to determine how treatment methods affect the amount of organic chemicals found in the water supply.[77] To deal with the THM problem, the EPA proposed in February 1978 a maximum contaminant level of 100 parts per billion that would need to be met by all water systems serving populations of 75,000 or greater. Utilities were to be given eighteen months from the date of promulgation of the rules to comply with this maximum contaminant level. EPA also proposed regulations that would ordinarily require utilities serving populations of 75,000 or more to utilize expensive carbon filtration systems that would be "effective against a broad spectrum of chemicals of concern."[78] The regulations were opposed by municipal facilities on the grounds that they were not technically necessary in order to produce safe drinking water and that they were too costly.[79] The final EPA regulations of November 1979 provided that the maximum contaminant level of 100 parts per billion would need to be met for all communities with a population of 10,000 or more. Such regulations would be effective within two years for water systems serving populations of 75,000 or more and within four years for water systems serving populations of 10,000 or more. Final federal regulations regarding carbon filtration systems and/or other water treatment technology had not yet been decided upon as of July 1980.[80]

CONCLUSION

Waste is disposed of as gas into the atmosphere, as liquid into water, or as solid waste onto land, regardless of the source of the waste. Since industrial processes, automobiles, electricity generation, waste disposal, and space heating that produce pollution all tend to be concentrated in urban areas, it is no surprise that pollution has an urban source. Cities also have difficulty dispersing the wastes, due in part to wind velocity and inversion layers that block upward diffusion[81] and the depletion of "hiding places" for solid waste.

As concern for environmental controls has increased, more jurisdictions have begun to get into the environmental control act. The result has been a tendency to move toward the consolidation of pollution control agencies and to concentrate regulatory authority with the national government.

In reviewing environmental protection legislation it is apparent that policy formulation has greatly changed. There are grants-in-aid for states for program development and implementation, and there is collaboration between the federal government and state regulatory commissions. A federal role has evolved from informal review of state and local programs through the use of grants-in-aid, to active review in the 1965 Water Quality Act and the 1967 Air Quality Act, to the present laws that provide for a clearly delineated division of labor. It is the responsibility of the federal government to fund a considerable portion of necessary construction and to establish (at least minimum) standards; implementation, subject to some federal oversight, often has been designated as a state and local function. Within the urban context, the federal policy reflects a clear recognition of meaningful and rational national-urban policy linkages—at least in the realm of environmental controls.

REFERENCES

1. Council on Environmental Quality, *Ocean Dumping—A National Policy* (Washington, D.C.: U.S. Government Printing Office, 1970), p. 12.
2. See Barry Commoner's comments in "Dispute: The Closing Circle," *Environment*, 14 (April 1972), 25, 40–52.

3. Harvey Perloff, "A Framework for Dealing with the Urban Environment," in *Pollution and Public Policy*, ed. by David F. Paulsen and Robert B. Denhardt (New York: Dodd, Mead, 1973), p. 80.
4. Lewis W. Moncrief, "The Cultural Basis for our Environmental Crisis," *Science*, 170 (October 30, 1970), 310.
5. Ibid.
6. M. Kent Jennings, "Legislative Politics and Water Pollution Control," in Paulsen and Denhardt, op. cit., p. 243.
7. Paulsen and Denhardt, "Introduction," ibid., p. 5.
8. John Rodman, "Ecopolis: Prolegomena to the Development of a National Environmental Policy," *IDOC—International*, North American Edition, No. 47 (October 1972), 36.
9. Paulsen and Denhardt, op. cit., p. 6.
10. Rodman, op. cit., p. 36. Reprinted by permission.
11. Samuel P. Hays, *Conservation and the Gospel of Efficiency* (New York: Atheneum, 1969), p. 2. This discussion relies heavily on this source.
12. Perloff, op. cit., p. 81.
13. The General Land Revision Law of 1891 had granted the President authority to establish forest reserves by decree.
14. Hays, op. cit., pp. 22–23, 36.
15. Ibid., p. 108, our italics for emphasis.
16. Ibid., p. 265.
17. Earl Finbar Murphy, *Governing Nature* (Chicago, Ill.: Quadrangle Books, 1967), p. 114.
18. Max Ways, "How to Think About the Environment," *Fortune Magazine*, 81 (February 1970), 100–101.
19. It should be noted at this time that agriculture and mining also pollute the environment. Furthermore, when natural resources have been depleted, the nonurban populations that had been supported by these resources—through farming the land, or mining the resources—have no source of support. Thus, when resources are depleted and the environment polluted, these previously nonurban people often migrate to urban areas and become part of the twentieth century urban crisis.
20. Stewart L. Udall, *The Quiet Crisis* (New York: Avon, 1972), pp. 187–188.
21. Neal R. Peirce, "Can Diverse Coalition Find Common Ground for Action," *Today*, 1 (May 11, 1979), 6.
22. See pp. 286–294 for a discussion of legislation.
23. Council on Environmental Quality, *Environmental Quality, 1970* (Washington, D.C., 1970), p. 6.
24. David Zwick and Marcy Benstock, *Water Wasteland* (New York: Grossman Publishers, 1971), p. 44.
25. National Commission on Water Quality, *Regional Assessment* (Draft) (Washington, D.C., September 2, 1975), p. II-4.
26. *The New York Times*, August 8, 1975, p. 44.
27. *Environmental Quality, the Ninth Annual Report of the Council on Environmental Quality* (Washington, D.C., December, 1978), p. 14.
28. *Environmental Quality, 1978*, ibid., p. 14.
29. Ibid., pp. 3, 14.

30. Walter A. Rosenbaum, *The Politics of Environmental Concern*, 2nd ed. (New York: Praeger, 1977), p. 46.
31. John C. Bollens and Henry J. Schmandt, *The Metropolis*, 3rd ed. (New York: Harper & Row, 1975), p. 150.
32. Rosenbaum, op. cit., p. 42.
33. *Ocean Dumping—A National Policy*, op. cit., p. 5.
34. *EPA Journal Reprint* (October 1978), 6–7.
35. *EPA Journal Reprint* (February 1978), n.p.
36. *EPA Journal Reprint* (October 1978), op. cit., 7.
37. *Environmental Quality, 1978*, op. cit., p. 172.
38. Environmental Protection Division of the Congressional Research Service of the Library of Congress, *Environmental Protection Affairs of the Ninety-Third Congress*, U.S. Congress, Senate, Committee on Public Works, 94th Cong., 1st Sess., February 1975, pp. 154–155.
39. *The New York Times*, August 13, 1975, p. 25.
40. 90 Stat. 2795 (1976).
41. Dick Kirschten, "The New War on Pollution is Over the Land," *National Journal*, 11 (April 14, 1979), 605.
42. Randall B. Ripley, "Congress and Clean Air," in Paulsen and Denhardt, op. cit., pp. 176–80; quote cited on pp. 179–80.
43. Walter A. Rosenbaum, *The Politics of Environmental Concern* (New York: Praeger, 1973), p. 153.
44. Paul A. Sabatier, "State and Local Environmental Policy," *Policy Studies Journal*, 1 (Summer 1973), 220.
45. Rosenbaum, 1973, op. cit., p. 194.
46. Jennings, op. cit., p. 243.
47. Ibid., p. 250; Allen V. Keeze and Charles L. Schultze, *Pollution, Prices and Public Policy* (Washington, D.C.: The Brookings Institution, 1975), pp. 32–33.
48. Rosenbaum, 1973, op. cit., pp. 140–42.
49. *Environmental Protection Affairs of the Ninety-Third Congress*, op. cit., p. 29.
50. Bernard F. Hillenbrand, "The County Link," *EPA Journal*, 5 (May 1979), 33.
51. David R. Berman, *State and Local Politics* (Boston: Holbrook Press, 1975), p. 254.
52. Bernard L. Hyink, Seyom Brown, and Ernest W. Thacker, *Politics and Government in California*, 9th ed. (New York: Thomas Y. Crowell, 1975), pp. 262–64.
53. *Environmental Protection Affairs of the Ninety-Third Congress*, op. cit., p. 29.
54. Ibid., p. 30.
55. U.S. Environmental Protection Agency, *Air Program Policy Statement* (Washington, D.C., August 1974), p. 5.
56. Ibid., p. 9.
57. *Environmental Quality, 1977, the 8th Annual Report of the Council on Environmental Quality* (Washington, D.C., December 1977), p. 22.
58. U.S. General Accounting Office, *Improvements Needed in Controlling Air Pollution Sources, Report by the Comptroller General of the United States* (Washington, D.C., January 2, 1979), p. 3.
59. *Environmental Quality, 1977*, op. cit., p. 26.
60. *Improvements Needed in Controlling Air Pollution Sources*, op. cit., p. 3.
61. Ibid., p. 8.
62. Ibid., p. 9.

63. Ibid., p. 7.
64. 33 U.S.C. 407 which constitutes a section of the Rivers and Harbors Act of 1899.
65. Rosenbaum, 1973, op. cit., p. 144.
66. U.S. General Accounting Office, *More Effective Action by the Environmental Protection Agency Needed to Enforce Industrial Compliance with Water Pollution Discharge Permits, Report by the Comptroller General of the United States* (Washington, D.C., October 17, 1978), p. 2.
67. *The New York Times,* March 28, 1976, p. 50.
68. Sterling Brubaker, *In Command of Tomorrow* (Baltimore, Md.: Johns Hopkins University Press, 1975), p. 123. For a discussion of the court case that made the funds available, see *Train, Administrator, Environmental Protection Agency v. City of New York et al.,* 420 U.S. 35 (1975).
69. *Environmental Quality, 1978,* op. cit., p. 106.
70. This discussion of the 1977 amendments relies on Environmental Protection Agency, *A Guide to the Clean Water Act Amendment* (Washington, D.C.: November 1978), pp. 1–3.
71. *More Effective Action . . . ,* op. cit., p. 4.
72. Ibid., p. 6.
73. Ibid., p. 8.
74. Ibid., p. 27.
75. National Commission on Water Quality, *Regional Assessment* (Draft), op. cit., pp. I-1–II-14.
76. Public Law 93-523.
77. Dick Kirschten, "The Not-So-Clean Battle Over Cleaning the Nation's Drinking Water," *National Journal,* 10 (October 14, 1978), 1637.
78. Ibid., p. 1639.
79. Ibid.
80. 45 Fed. Reg. 68624 (1980).
81. Brubaker, op. cit., p. 111.

11

The New York City Fiscal Crisis: Its Implications for National-Urban Policy

INTRODUCTION

While considering the problems associated with urban America, one is continually forced to come back to the institutional framework established by the Founding Fathers. In particular, one must consider the federal structure. *Federalism* has led to the proliferation of state governments, which have in turn spawned a multiplicity of local governments. Through the years, these state and local jurisdictions have developed and maintained programs to improve the quality of life for their residents.[1] In addition, by virtue of the constitutional delegation of certain powers to the states—most notably, caring for "the general welfare" of the citizenry—local jurisdictions have, in fact, been responsible for developing programming options for many areas.

A clear example of governmental units not accepting the responsibilities of interdependence between jurisdictional units by developing adequate policy and program linkages is the 1975 New York City experience with fiscal crisis. To understand what happened in New York City, it is necessary "to identify and analyze those recurrent sequences of behavior that originate on one side of the boundary between the two types of systems and that become linked to phenomena on the other side in the process of unfolding." [2] Since the New York City fiscal crisis is a relatively clear case of the need for strong national urban policy linkages, it is worthwhile to examine the events leading up to the 1975 threats of default and some of the responses. Some recognition of the interdependence of jurisdictions could be seen in the demands made by many city and county executives as well as by some federal officials to the federal government for assistance to New York City. The need for strong national urban linkages is best illustrated through an examination of the development of the New York City fiscal crisis and the attempts by various levels of government to deal with this crisis. Thus in the pages that follow, the New York City fiscal crisis will be considered as a case study of the need to develop more adequate policy linkages.

As we have indicated elsewhere in this book, the potential for fiscal crisis exists in other urban areas too. While economic and fiscal difficulties in cities throughout the nation have not yet reached the crisis proportion that New York City has experienced, economic growth in cities such as Buffalo, St. Louis, Cleveland, Newark, and Pittsburgh lags significantly below the national average.[3] Also, a study conducted by the accounting and management firm of Touche Ross and Company and the First National Bank of Boston indicated that the cities of Stamford and Hartford (Connecticut), Boston, and Atlanta have maintained their tax, debt, and expense rates so as to foster fiscal stress.[4]

The interdependence of an urban jurisdiction with national and state jurisdictions and the resultant reality that urban problems constitute national problems can be well illustrated by examining the dynamics of the New York City fiscal crisis. In the pages that follow, the problems and processes affecting this financial debacle will be considered. Before examining the bond market factors that precipitated the financial crisis, it is important to review the social and economic factors that led to this economic crisis.[5]

The Social and Economic Background

The roots of New York City's fiscal crisis are representative of the same factors affecting other large central cities in the United States, especially the older central cities of the Northeast and North Central region. Particularly since World War II, these cities have been called upon to absorb rural-in-migrants from the South and Southwestern sections of the country and from Puerto Rico. In the East, this stream has been heavily Southern black and Puerto Rican. In the North Central cities, it has been Southern black and Mexican-American. Also, as a result of modern transportation systems, middle class families with school-age children have increasingly moved to the suburbs often leaving the aged—who are less able to cope with dependency on the automobile and home repairs on ranch and colonial style dwellings—in the central city.

In-migration of rural low-income populations—in New York City, Southern black and Puerto Rican—middle-class outmigration to the suburbs (as well as industrial migration to the suburbs), as well as the disproportionate number of aged persons in the central city has made New York City, as well as other central cities, a center for groups dependent on public human services. In New York City, between 1950 and 1970, the proportion of the city's population over the age of sixty-five had increased from 8 percent to 12.1 percent. During this same twenty-year period, the proportion of the city's families with incomes below the national median income level had risen from 36 percent to 49 percent. In addition, the Joint Economic Committee of the U.S. Congress found that New York City, unlike most other large cities, experienced almost no population decline between 1960 and 1973, though it lost a significant amount of private industry. Thus, the demand for city services remained constant in the early 1970s while its local revenue sources eroded. (However, preliminary 1980 U.S. census data indicates that New York City experienced a significant population decline over the *entire* decade of the 1970s.) Also, New York's poverty population did not decline as much during the prosperity of the 1960s as it did in most other large cities. The average decline in the size of the poverty population in the nation's twenty-four largest cities (as defined by the federal government) was over 25 percent; in New York the comparable figure was 10.16 percent.[6]

As industry and a considerable segment of the middle class left New York City between 1950 and 1970, New York City's tax base deteriorated. New York City lost industry and jobs because of industrial shifts out of the Northeast altogether, and within the Northeast into suburban areas. New York City experienced a decline in private sector jobs between 1960 and 1975, from 3.130 million in 1960 to almost 2.803 million in 1975.

Other economic factors also have affected New York City's fiscal circumstances. The onset of a national recession limited the revenue-collecting potential of New York City's sales and income taxes because such taxes tend to be most sensitive to economic activity. For instance, despite a 9.3 percent increase in consumer prices in New York City for the year ending June 30, 1975, the volume of taxable sales for that year rose only 1.7 percent. At the same time, high unemployment increased the number of families eligible for welfare programs as well as the demand on municipal services such as the city hospitals.

Because fiscal responsibility for health and welfare services falls significantly on local jurisdictions in New York State, such services require substantial outlays by New York City. In this respect, the outlays by New

York City are unique. New York State is one of twenty-one states that requires its local governments (usually counties) to contribute cash support to the Aid to Families with Dependent Children Program and to Medicaid payments. Of these twenty-one states, in fiscal 1974 only five states (New York, Minnesota, Wyoming, California, and Kansas) had local governments bearing more than 10 percent of the total AFDC cash assistance and Medicaid payments. The local share in New York State was approximately 23 percent (that represented about one-half of the nonfederal share and one-quarter of the total payments). In most places where local revenue is required for welfare expenditures, a county jurisdiction, which often includes some suburbs and thus has a broader tax base than the central city, is responsible for the raising of these revenues. New York City bears its local share alone. In 1975 New York City's welfare-related expenses amounted to $3.5 billion, or about one-third of its expenditures. Of this amount, one billion dollars had to be raised within New York City. Other high levels of municipal public expenditure for services relate to the city criminal justice system, the municipal hospital system, low and middle income housing programs, and the public transportation system.

The Nature of the Municipal Borrowing Problem

As we noted in Chapter 3, cities borrow money for a number of purposes. They borrow to finance capital projects, such as schools, public buildings, highways, and sewers. As taxes are collected only at stated periods and expenditures are made more frequently, cities—including New York City—borrow to match their flow of income to their necessary expenditures. Property taxes and state and federal grants are paid quarterly, semiannually, or annually. Payrolls and welfare payments must be met on a bimonthly or monthly basis. Short-term debt may be acquired to raise the necessary funds to meet these obligations while awaiting the anticipated revenue. New York's municipal borrowing ran into trouble in two respects. New York was engaged in deficit financing; also, it issued more short-term notes called *revenue anticipation notes,* than were covered by actual tax collections. In the ten years between 1965 and 1975, this practice resulted in an accumulated deficit of $2.6 billion. If the bond market is closed off to New York City, it cannot meet its obligation to pay off this debt and continue to provide essential public services. Until 1975 the city was able to conceal its deficit by placing operating expenses, which properly belong in the operating budget, in the capital budget (an area not as subject to immediate payment requirements). This gimmick was used by New York City in desperation so that it could claim a balanced operating budget.[7]

The Crisis

New York's financial crisis was not sudden, nor could one argue that it was totally unexpected. The conditions leading up to the fiscal crisis were present for a considerable period of time. The immediate cause of the crisis was New York City's inability to borrow money in the municipal bond market. This situation reflected a *loss in confidence* in New York City's fiscal management. Since New York's fiscal management depended on the bond market, this precipitated a significant financial problem for the city. Some stopgap measures were imposed to try to prevent New York from defaulting. The State of New York established the Municipal Assistance Corporation (MAC) to serve as an interim borrowing agency for the city, but MAC, too, had problems marketing its bonds. The city trimmed its budget, but large portions of its budget were nondiscretionary (salaries, welfare payments, and pensions). The payroll was cut; primary and secondary education as well as the city university budgets were reduced. Police, fire, and sanitation budgets were cut, too, and these agencies, along with other city agencies, had to lay off personnel. All city salaries were frozen, and thus the contracts the city had negotiated with the municipal unions were by mutual agreement not enforced. In September 1975, the State Legislature of New York enacted the Financial Emergency Act, which provided the city with a $2.3 billion package to meet its cash needs until early December: $750 million from the state and the remainder from pension funds and the financial community. This action was taken in the hope that the city would reenter the municipal bond market at that time. This legislation also established a Financial Emergency Control Board—dominated by state appointees—to administer the city's finances. The Board formalized a wage freeze, and required that the city pension funds be used to purchase MAC bonds.

In December 1975, Congress passed, and the President signed into law, provisions for loans up to $2.3 billion a year for 3 years to New York City. In 1978, a fifteen-year federal loan-guarantee program for New York City bonds equaling $1.65 billion was enacted. In exchange, the city (and the state) promised (implausibly) to achieve a balanced city budget by 1982. Also, the City and the State of New York pieced together a financial plan to meet the federal response. This program included the expansion of MAC borrowing authority as well as agreements with municipal unions regarding contract demands, and a pledge by the banking and insurance communities to buy $1 billion in unguaranteed long-term city bonds.[8] In addition, city services have been further curtailed in response to federal and state pressures. For example, libraries, health and hospital services, parks, and sanitation services have all been cut back to try to reduce New York City's expenditures. Also, some jobs have been eliminated through attrition. This had led to some concern by the affected communities that the curtailments are unreasonable and that they cause undue suffering in terms of loss of services and employment particularly to the black and Hispanic communities. Thus the local branches of the NAACP warned that if health and hospital services are reduced, there will be the possibility of "racial confrontation and disorder."[9] Also, the highest Puerto Rican city official, Deputy Mayor Herman Badillo, in leaving that office, issued a statement indicating that city cutbacks particularly affected the welfare of the black and Hispanic communities.

The Apparent Interdependencies

As we noted in Chapter 1, on September 23, 1975, Mayor William H. McNichols of Denver testified before the Joint Economic Committee concerning the New York City fiscal crisis. He noted the concern of other city officials with the predicament of New York City and urged the federal government to ease New York's fiscal plight.[10] Other cities, counties, and special districts are financially vulnerable, as are banks and other lending institutions. New York's fiscal dilemma can affect other local jurisdictions; it can cause serious dislocations in the credit industry since the banks hold a significant portion of New York's outstanding debt.[11] In addition, the cost to cities for borrowing money rose, partially in response to New York's financial trauma. Some cities have had difficulty in marketing their bonds. Yonkers and Buffalo, two large cities in New York State, have had this problem. Large cities all over the country have confronted unfavorably high interest rates in the "wake of the New York crisis." In July 1975, Philadelphia (a single-A rated city) sold bonds at a net interest cost of 8.8 percent; two days after this sale, Chelsea, Massachusetts (also a single-A rated city), sold bonds at a net interest cost of 6.7 percent. In August 1975, a Detroit city agency sold bonds (rated Baa) at a net interest cost of 9.9 percent; the next day Johnson County, Tennessee, had to accept a net interest cost of 7.3 percent on bonds (also rated Baa). While interest rates had recently risen in all these cities, in both these examples, the larger cities had to pay between 2 percent and 2.5 percent more than the smaller jurisdictions. City size was the only differentiating factor that seemed to affect the cost of borrowing in these four cases.[12]

While other cities have begun to experience problems that have brought them perilously close to bankruptcy, no city to date has had the economic and fiscal problems of New York City. The city that has received the most attention in the "post–New York City" period is Cleveland, Ohio.[13] However, whereas New York City's fiscal crisis was the result of economic forces interacting with fiscal and social forces, Cleveland's crisis was a political crisis that was made to resemble a fiscal crisis. In December 1978, Cleveland defaulted on $15.5 million in short-term notes, $14 million of which were held by local banks. However, a local budget official reported that there were mechanisms available that could have been utilized to have avoided the default. The City Council could have approved the Mayor's proposal (made a week earlier) to raise the local income tax from 1 to 1.5 percent (ultimately this tax was increased); the Council could have accepted the Mayor's plan to sell $6 million in unused city land; or, the Council and the banking community could have accepted the Mayor's proposal for a $90 million bond issue the previous March, and the banks could have refinanced the $14 million in notes. However, none of these alternatives were accepted because of a locking of political wills. The business and banking community and the City Council were intent on the City selling its municipal light plant to the big private utility company that provides the major portion of Cleveland's electricity—the Cleveland Electric Illuminating Company (CEI). Mayor Dennis J. Kucinich refused to budge in his opposition to the sale, and thus the Council and the banking community refused to help the Mayor out of a "tight political spot." This tight political spot resembled a fiscal crisis to the untrained eye, and to some people it looked quite similar to the New York City experience. It obviously was not a replay on a smaller scale of the New York City fiscal crisis. In fact, Cleveland officials learned quickly that they could not expect a similar response from the federal government. Whereas New York's fiscal fall was seen by federal officials as a potential national crisis—because of interdependencies—they viewed Cleveland as an isolated and very local case. Cleveland's crisis eventually was resolved by local retrenchment of services and a rise in the local tax rate.

More recently, Wayne County, Michigan (Detroit and environs), experienced a fiscal dilemma. Wayne County, the third largest county in the nation, could not meet its payroll in October 1979. As a result of this condition, several thousand county officials were threatened with job lay-offs through mid January 1980 (until the 1980 tax revenues came in). The state finally released funds to the county and services did not have to be curtailed. Other cities and counties face huge budget gaps, too, and though these other cities—such as Newark, New Jersey, and Pittsburgh, Pennsylvania—have not received the press attention that Cleveland received, their *fiscal* problems are quite real.[14]

Inasmuch as cities are creatures of the states in which they are located and thus New York City is a creature of the State of New York, it was reasonable to expect the state to come to the aid of the city. The State of New York accepted this responsibility by providing funds, establishing a state agency to float bonds, and by overseeing the city's budgetary process. But since the problem is so large, and it affects people and institutions in jurisdictions other than New York, the question becomes whether other jurisdictions—most especially the federal government— should assist New York City, and by extension, all cities as well. One of the major long-term causes for the fiscal crisis in New York has been the extent of the city's participation in the delivery of social welfare income payments and services and the delivery of health care services. This is a fiscal burden that could be assumed equitably by the national government.[15] The City of New York assumes approximately one-third of the cost for its welfare-related services. In fiscal 1975, these requirements necessitated that the City of New York raise $1 billion—not including state and federal contributions—to provide these services. If costs for the delivery of welfare-related income and services were totally nationalized, then New York and other local jurisdictions, mostly counties, would not have to foot the welfare bill. (Neither would states have to bear this fiscal burden.)

The argument can be made that dependent populations are not a single jurisdiction's problem. In fact, much of New York's dependent population does not have local origins; a considerable portion is one or two generations away from other states, most often in the South, or from Puerto Rico. Should not the whole population of the nation pay to maintain these people at minimal levels of decency? Why should New York City's population by itself pay to maintain the dependent populations that often come from other jurisdictions? In fact, since the origins of the welfare problem are national in scope, the costs should be spread more equitably across a national tax base. Such a change in policy would eliminate a major expenditure from New York City's budget. It would place the welfare function with the national government. This proposal would not only relieve New York City of its fiscal difficulties, it would also recognize the linkages between local and national jurisdictions.

Cities, with their limited and nonelastic tax bases, cannot themselves provide all of the essential services. Also, in many policy areas, to expect the cities to do so is to settle for inadequate and inappropriate public policy. It was such inappropriate expectations that led to New York's financial dilemma. New York is part of the whole. It cannot, in the words of Emma Lazarus, continue to accept and support "your tired, your poor, your huddled masses" and those who are often viewed by the sending jurisdiction as "wretched refuse" without external assistance. Without policy linkages recognizing the interdependencies of government units, the urban jurisdictions of this nation will face increasing fiscal deficiencies if they choose to provide adequate services. Mayor Romero Barcelo of San Juan, Puerto Rico, in discussing the fiscal dilemmas facing New York City, noted that if New York City does not meet its fiscal obligations, many people "will start looking back at the places they came from, and they will go back to their homes and cities." He further observed: "So the problem is not a New York problem, it is a problem of the nation."[16]

Though the federal government responded to the New York City fiscal crisis, its response to the crisis has been inadequate as illustrated by the fact that despite the City's promise to balance its budget in fiscal 1982, in 1979 there was a projected deficit of approximately $1 billion—not including new labor costs from 1980 labor-management settlements.[17]

The New York City fiscal crisis illustrates that the challenge of the 1980s is whether the nation will recognize the extent to which urban problems are national problems. A further challenge is the extent to which local, state, and national governments, as well as the private sector, will cooperate in seeking to create adequate public policies for urban America.

REFERENCES

1. Since the New Deal, many of these programs have had federal matching grants-in-aid available as program stimulants.

2. See Chapter 1, p. 4.
3. *The New York Times,* January 21, 1979, p. A33.
4. John Herbers, "Study Turns up Surprises on Fiscal Shape of Cities," *The New York Times,* March 21, 1979, p. D15.
5. The rest of this chapter relies heavily on Robert D. Reischauer, Peter K. Clark, and Peggy L. Cuciti, *New York City's Fiscal Problem: Its Origins, Potential Repercussions, and Some Alternative Policy Responses, Background Paper No. 1.* (Washington, D.C.: U.S. Congressional Budget Office, 1975).
6. *The New York Times,* November 2, 1975, p. 61.
7. See Steven R. Weisman, "How New York City Became a Fiscal Junkie," *The New York Times Magazine,* August 7, 1975, pp. 8–9, 71–72.
8. *1978 Congressional Quarterly Almanac* (Washington, D.C., 1979), pp. 258–64.
9. *The New York Times,* January 9, 1979, p. B1.
10. *The New York Times,* September 25, 1975, p. 1.
11. However, many bank deposits are insured by the Federal Deposit Insurance Corporation (FDIC) and the Federal Reserve Board agreed to prevent banks from defaulting.
12. U.S. Congress, Joint Economic Committee, "Opening Statement of Senator Hubert H. Humphrey," 94th Cong., 1st Sess., September 24, 1975.
13. The discussion about Cleveland, Ohio, was derived largely from *The Washington Post,* December 21, 1978, p. A10.
14. See Chapter 3 for a more detailed discussion of these fiscal problems.
15. Some commentators have suggested that even state assumption of these costs would be helpful. (It would have cost the State of New York $1.3 billion to pick up the local portion of welfare income and services.) This suggestion would not, however, recognize the national interdependencies and would not provide a national linkage.
16. *The New York Times,* October 20, 1975, p. 40.
17. George F. Will, "As New York Goes . . . ," *Newsweek,* 93 (January 8, 1979), 72.

Index

Abend, Norman A., 249
Abilene, Kan., 152
Abortion, 45
Academic Affiliates, 162
Adams, Charles F., 81
Advisory Commission in Intergovernmental
Relations, 10, 25, 58, 61, 64, 65, 79, 159,
163, 173, 258–259
Affirmative action guidelines, 100, 112
After-school care, 141
Aged, the: city population, 16–17, 20, 21,
36, 301; and health care, 16, 224, 226; and
housing, 195, 196, 198, 199; in poverty,
16–17, 21; and Social Security, 118, 136,
138; and welfare, 118, 124, 125, 130, 133,
134, 138, 141
Agency Academies, 162
Aid to the Blind (AB), 126, 134, 136, 138
Aid to Dependent Children (ADC), 126, 133
Aid to Families with Dependent Children
Program (AFDC), 16, 20, 25, 35, 45, 118,
119, 126–127, 128, 130, 131–132, 133,
134–135, 136, 137, 138, 139, 143, 302
Aid to the Permanently and Totally Disabled
(APTD), 133, 134, 135, 136, 139
Air Quality Act (1967), 286, 294
Akron, O., 44, 61
Alabama, 59, 130, 139
Alaska, 67, 79, 139, 169
Alcoholism, 140, 226, 227, 231
Almshouse. *See* Workhouse
American Assembly, Columbia University, 25
American Family Corporation, 51
American Hospital Association, 212, 213, 217
American Indians, 34, 102, 198
American Medical Association (AMA), 8,
213, 215, 217; Political Action Committee,
51

American Public Health Association, 216
American Public Transit Association, 257,
258
Americans for Democratic Action (ADA), 33
Anderson, Odin, 214–215
Antiabolitionists, 150, 151
Antirecession Fiscal Assistance (ARFA), 82
Arab oil embargo, 256
Arizona, 102, 139, 225
Arkansas, 79
Armenians: housing segregation, 193
Association of American Medical Colleges,
214
Atlanta, Ga., 19, 23, 25, 36, 76, 77, 161,
166, 192, 300
Audubon Societies, 273, 277
Automobile and Truck Dealers Election
Committee, 51
Automobiles: politics of, 254–256; and pol-
lution, 245–246, 278, 280, 286; as trans-
portation, 243, 245, 246, 249, 250, 251,
252–253, 256, 267, 301

Badillo, Herman, 41, 303–304
Baker v. *Carr*, 249, 254
Ball, Edward W., 50
Baltimore, Md., 15, 25, 35, 36, 44, 46, 60,
78, 121, 130, 131, 166, 192, 197–198,
204, 205, 214, 219, 233–234
Baltimore County, Md., 73
Baltimore Regional Planning Council (RCP),
233–234
Banfield, Edward B., 41, 193
Barcelo, Romero, 306
Barnekov, Timothy, 204
Baton Rouge, La., 76
Bayley, David H., 165
Bergen County, N.J., 61

309

Kennedy, Robert F., 167
Kennedy administration, 130–131
Kentucky, 43
"Key National Policy Issues for 1978: The Congressional Black Caucus Legislative Agenda," 38
King James, 150
Kings County, N.Y., 188
Koch, Robert, 216
Kreuger, Robert, 40
Kucinich, Dennis, 38, 305

Labor unions: automobile workers, 8; police, 155, 167; and political contributions, 51; teacher, 111–112
Laconia, Ill., 163
Lake Erie, 277
Lake Michigan, 278
Lake Ontario, 278
Land Grant College Act. See Morrill Act (1862)
Land-use planning, 77
Lanham Act (1940), 100
Law Enforcement Assistance Administration (LEAA), 162, 165–166, 169, 170–172, 173–174
Lazarus, Emma, 12, 306
Leach, Claude, 40
Legal aid, 140
Legal services, 130, 131
Levin, Carl, 41, 200
Levin, Melvin R., 249
Lexington, Ky., 218
Lexow Committee, 153
Liberalism, 47
Liberal Party, 42
Library Construction and Services Act (1964), 101
Lindsay, John V., 42, 167
Livingston, Robert, 247
Local Governments in Metropolitan Areas, 157
Local Public Authority (LPA), 203–204
Local Public Works (LPW), 82
Localism: in fund raising, 6; and police, 147–151, 154; in welfare, 117, 118, 119, 125, 140, 142
Localities: and criminal justice, 147–148, 174, 175; and education, 64; federal grants to, 23–24, 25; and health care, 212, 215–216, 217, 218, 221, 223–224, 225, 226–227, 228, 231–232, 234, 235–236, 238; and housing, 181, 185, 189, 195, 201, 202, 206; and police, 154, 158, 160, 171, 172; and pollution, 284; and proliferation of governments, 6, 68–70, 299; revenues of, 58, 59; and state aid, 59; and transportation, 243–244, 246, 254, 262–263, 264, 268; and waste disposal, 272–273, 281, 294; and welfare, 118, 120, 122, 126, 130, 140, 142, 302; and welfare funding, 118,

126, 129, 133, 140. See also Central cities; Cities; County; Municipalities; Special districts
Long, Clarence D., 33
Long, Huey, 125
Los Angeles, Calif.: crime rate, 166; federal aid to, 25; government, 73–74; and health care, 236; Hispanic population, 14; police, 169; pollution, 276, 282, 286–287; population, 36, 43; school busing, 109, 110; transportation, 252, 258, 276; waste disposal, 282
Los Angeles County, Calif., 127–128, 157
Los Angeles County Air Pollution Control District (LACAPCD), 286–287
Louisiana, 40
Louisville, Ky., 73, 109, 121
Love Canal, 283
Low income: defined, 17; and education, 97, 102; and health care, 220, 222, 228, 231; and housing, 184, 189, 192, 193–194, 195, 196–198, 199–200, 202, 205–206; and urban renewal, 203–204; and welfare, 131
Low-skilled jobs, 15

McGovern, George S., 46
MacIntyre, Duncan, 128
MacKenzie, Alexander, 275
McNichols, William H., 4, 304
Macomb County, Mich., 108
Madison, James, 248
Mahoning River, 290
Maine, 123, 138, 283
Maler, Henry, 260
Males: life expectancy, 220; and statute labor, 248
Manchester, Eng., 9
Manvel Report, 190, 191
Mapp v. Ohio, 174
Marijuana, 45, 47
Maryland, 60, 78, 92, 122, 130, 139
Massachusetts, 79, 92, 121, 123, 130, 138, 169, 225, 230, 255–256
Massachusetts Bay Transportation Authority (MBTA), 267
Massachusetts Department of Public Works, 266
Massachusetts General Court, 151
Mayer, Martin, 202
Mayors: black, 42, 77; election of, 38; and municipal government, 70–71, 73, 74; and police, 155
Meals on wheels, 133
Medicaid, 16, 60, 61, 129, 134, 212, 217, 224–226, 302
Medical Assistance to the Aged, 133, 139
Medical Foundation, Bellaire, O., 236
Medicare, 16, 47, 212, 217, 221
Megalopolis: administrative structure, 22–23, 26; defined, 11

Segregation: residential, 192–194; and school integration, 46, 47, 90, 107–110
Serviceman's Readjustment Act (1944), 100
Services: city, 49, 57–58, 63, 74, 302; funding, 16–17, 25–26, 34, 37, 81–82; and federal welfare programs, 118, 129–130, 132–133, 138–143; and interest groups, 8–9; legal, 130, 131; neighborhood centers, 130; New York City, 301, 302, 303–304, 305; private, 49–50; public, 48, 60–61; and public regarding middle class, 41–42; and revenue sharing, 81–82, 83; suburban, 48–49
Shannon, Dr. James A., 222–223
Shelley v. *Kramer*, 193
Sheppard-Towner Act (1921), 217
Sierra Club, 273, 277
Skolnick, Jerome, 160
Slaves, 150
Slovak-black coalition, 47
Slums, 128, 186, 188, 189, 207, 229
Smith-Hughes Act (1917), 100
Smog, 276, 277, 280
Social distance, 48
Social Security Act (1935), 45, 125, 132, 143, 216–217, 222–223. *See also* Aid to the Blind; Aid to Families with Dependent Children (AFDC); Old Age Assistance
Social Security Administration, 125, 137
Social Security Amendments: 1962, 139, 140; 1967, 139–140; 1972, 138–139; 1974, 141
Social Security Trust Fund, 134
Social Services and Child Support Amendments (Title XX), 24–25, 141–142
Social status: and education, 48
Somers, Anne, 213
South: central cities, 34, 35; and housing, 192; migrants from, 301; school desegregation, 90, 109; and slaves, 150; voting registration, 40
South Bend, Ind., 192
South Central Los Angeles, Calif., 127
South Dakota, 59
Southern California Association of Governments, 259
Southern Europeans: housing segregation, 193
Southwest Voter Registration Education Project, 41
Special act charters: defined, 70
Special districts: and fiscal allocation, 75; and proliferation of governments, 68–70, 72, 73; school, 59, 64; waste disposal, 282, 290
Sputnik I, 101
Stamford, Conn., 203–204, 300
Standard Metropolitan Statistical Areas (SMSAs), 10, 157–158, 190, 212, 266, 267, 268
Standard Oil Company of Indiana, 51
State Health Planning and Development Agency (SHPDA), 234, 235

State legislatures: and highways, 249, 254, 260; and police, 152; political alignments, 32, 35, 52; and urban crisis, 43, 48, 53
State and Local Fiscal Assistance Act (1972), 24, 81–83, 141. *See also* Revenue sharing
State Public Welfare Departments, 123
States: aid to cities, 64, 83–84; competitiveness of, 35, 79; and criminal justice, 147, 150, 171, 172; defined, 6; and education, 63, 92, 102, 112; and educational funding, 81, 82, 90, 91, 92–93, 95, 96, 98–99, 107, 112; and environmental protection, 272–273, 284–286, 286–289, 290–291; federal grants to, 23–24, 64, 124, 132; and fiscal allocation, 75, 78–79, 81–82; and health care, 16–17, 212, 215, 217, 219, 221, 222, 223–224, 225, 226–227, 230, 232–233; and highway construction, 63; and housing, 184, 189, 192; and law enforcement, 170, 171; lotteries, 64, 92; and Medicaid, 302; planning agencies, 171, 172; and police, 154, 155, 158–159, 160, 168, 169, 172; political alignments, 31, 35, 53; proliferation of governments, 299–300; revenues, 58–59; and transportation, 246, 248–249, 259–260, 264, 265; and welfare funding, 59, 63, 118, 125–126, 127, 128, 129–130, 132–133, 137–140, 143; welfare history, 122, 123–124; and welfare services, 139–142, 305
Statewide Health Coordinating Council (SHC), 234
Steamboats, 247
Steel industry, 278, 290
Stenvig, Frank, 38
Students: enrollments, 96; low-income, 102; riots, 109
Suburbs: composition of, 13–14; crime rate, 165; and education, 90, 95, 97; electorate, 36; flight to, 7, 17, 21, 26, 32, 33, 43, 53, 57–58, 61, 121, 253, 266–267, 301; government, 72; and health care, 220, 223–224; and housing, 191, 193, 196, 202; income level, 19; and police, 153, 159, 160; population, 10–11, 19, 21–22, 32–33; poverty in, 128, 253; and property taxes, 61; and school control, 94, 110–111; and school funding, 48–49, 94, 95; and services, 58, 74, 83; and transportation, 245, 246, 250, 253–254; unemployment rate, 35; and urban crisis, 4, 22–23; and welfare funding, 129, 131, 142, 143; white middle class, 21, 26, 108; white working class, 44
Supplemental Security Income Program (SSI), 16, 17, 20, 118, 119, 129, 132, 134, 137, 138–139, 143
Supreme Court of the U.S.: and education, 89–90, 95, 106–108; and law enforcement, 174–175; and reapportionment, 249, 254; and residential segregation, 192–194
Surface Transportation Assistance Act (1978), 265–266

1 2 3 4 5 6 7 8 9 0